core
SERVLETS and
JAVASERVER PAGES™

ISBN 0-13-089340-4

90000

9 780130 893406

core
SERVLETS and
JAVASERVER PAGES™

MARTY HALL

PH
PTR

Prentice Hall PTR, Upper Saddle River, NJ   07458
www.phptr.com

Sun Microsystems Press
A Prentice Hall Title

Editorial/Production Supervision: *Joanne Anzalone*
Acquisitions Editor: *Greg Doench*
Editorial Assistant: *Mary Treacy*
Marketing Manager: *Bryan Gambrel*
Manufacturing Manager: *Alexis R. Heydt*
Cover Design: *Anthony Gemmellaro*
Cover Design Direction: *Jerry Votta*
Art Director: *Gail Cocker-Bogusz*
Series Design: *Meg VanArsdale*

Sun Microsystems Press
Marketing Manager: *Michael LLwyd Alread*
Publisher: *Rachel Borden*

© 2000 Prentice Hall PTR
Prentice-Hall, Inc.
Upper Saddle River, NJ 07458

The products described in this manual may be protected by one or more U.S. patents, foreign patents, or pending patents.

All product names mentioned herein are the trademarks of their respective owners

Reprinted with corrections August, 2000

Printed in the United States of America

10 9 8 7 6 5 4

ISBN 0-13-08934904

Sun Microsystems Press
A Prentice Hall Title

Contents

CHAPTER 2

First Servlets   20

CHAPTER 3

Handling the Client Request: Form Data   64

CHAPTER 4

Handling the Client Request: HTTP Request Headers   92

CHAPTER 11

The JSP page Directive: Structuring Generated Servlets   246

CHAPTER 12

Including Files and Applets in JSP Documents   266

CHAPTER 15

Integrating Servlets and JSP   352

PART 3
Supporting Technologies   382

CHAPTER 16
Using HTML Forms   384

CHAPTER 17
Using Applets As Servlet Front Ends   432

CHAPTER 18

JDBC and Database Connection Pooling   460

APPENDIX

Acknowledgments

Many people have helped me out with this book. Without their assistance, I would still be on the third chapter. John Guthrie, Amy Karlson, Rich Slywczak, and Kim Topley provided valuable technical feedback on virtually every chapter. Others pointing out errors and providing useful suggestions include Don Aldridge, Camille Bell, Ben Benokraitis, Larry Brown, Carl Burnham, Andrew Burton, Rick Cannon, Kevin Cropper, Chip Downs, Frank Erickson, Payam Fard, Daniel Goldman, Rob Gordon, Andy Gravatt, Jeff Hall, Russell Holley, David Hopkins, Lis Immer, Herman Ip, Truong Le, Frank Lewis, Tanner Lovelace, Margaret Lyell, Paul McNamee, Mike Oliver, Barb Ridenour, Himanso Sahni, Bob Samson, Ron Tosh, Tsung-Wen Tsai, Peggy Sue Vickers, and Maureen Knox Yencha. Hopefully I learned from their advice. Mary Lou "Eagle Eye" Nohr spotted my errant commas, awkward sentences, typographical errors, and grammatical inconsistencies. She improved the result immensely. Joanne Anzalone produced the final version; she did a great job despite my many last-minute changes. Ralph Semmel provided a supportive work environment and a flexible schedule, not to mention interesting projects on which to put servlets and JSP to work. Greg Doench of Prentice Hall believed in the concept from the beginning and encouraged me to write the book. Rachel Borden got Sun Microsystems Press to believe in it also. Thanks to all.

Most of all, thanks to B.J., Lindsay, and Nathan for their patience with my funny schedule and my hogging the computer when they wanted to work or play on it. God has blessed me with a great family.

About the Author

Marty Hall is a Senior Computer Scientist in the Research and Technology Development Center at the Johns Hopkins University Applied Physics Lab, where he specializes in applications of Java and Web technology. He also teaches Java and Web programming in the Johns Hopkins part-time graduate program in Computer Science, where he directs the Distributed Computing and Web Technology concentration areas. When he gets a chance, he also teaches industry short courses on servlets, JavaServer Pages, and other Java technology areas. Marty's previous book is *Core Web Programming* (Prentice Hall, 1998). He can be reached at the following address:

Research and Technology Development Center
The Johns Hopkins University Applied Physics Laboratory
11100 Johns Hopkins Road
Laurel, MD 20723
hall@coreservlets.com

Introduction

In early 1996, I started using the Java programming language for the majority of my software development work. I did some CGI programming and even worked a little with the early servlet versions, but for the most part I did desktop and client-side applications. Over the last couple of years, however, there has been a growing emphasis on server-side applications, so I became more serious about servlets and JavaServer Pages. In the past year, there has been a virtual stampede toward the technology among developers, server vendors, and the authors of the Java platform specifications. So much so, in fact, that the technology is rapidly becoming the standard tool for building dynamic Web sites and connecting Web front ends to databases and applications on a server.

Unfortunately, however, it was extremely difficult to find good practical advice on servlet and JSP development. I found a number of servlet books, but only a handful of them covered recent versions of the specification, advanced techniques, or reflected real-world experience. The few that did, if they covered JSP at all, hadn't caught up to JSP 1.0, let alone JSP 1.1. Since JSP is a better fit than servlets for many situations, what good was a servlet book that didn't also cover JSP? In the last couple of months, some JSP books have started coming out. But the bulk of them don't cover servlets. What good is that? Since an integral part of JavaServer Pages is the use of scripting elements to create servlet code, you can't do effective JSP development without a thorough understanding of servlets. Besides, most real-world sites don't use just *one* of the two technologies; they combine them *both*. Finally, as I discovered when I started teaching servlet and JSP development to my students in the Johns Hopkins part-time graduate program (most of whom were professional software developers), few programmers were already comfortable with HTTP 1.1, HTML forms, and JDBC, three critical supporting technologies. Telling them to get a separate book for each of these areas was hardly reasonable: that brought to *five* the number of books programmers needed if they were going to do serious servlet/JSP development.

So, in mid-1999, I put together a short servlet and JSP tutorial with a few dozen examples, put it on the Web, and tried out the material in a couple of my courses. The response was overwhelming. After only a few months, I was getting several thousand visitors a day to the tutorial along with a myriad of requests to expand the coverage of the material. I eventually bowed to the inevitable and started writing. This book is the result. I hope you find it useful.

Real Code for Real Programmers

This book is aimed at serious software developers. This is not a book that touts the potential of e-commerce or pontificates about how Web-enabled applications will revolutionize your business. Instead, it is a hands-on book aimed at helping programmers who are already convinced of the need for dynamic Web sites get started building them right away. In showing how to build these sites, I try to illustrate the most important approaches and warn you of the most common pitfalls. Along the way, I include plenty of working code: more than a hundred documented Java classes, for instance. I try to give detailed examples of the most important and frequently used features, summarize the lesser-used ones, and refer you to the APIs (available on-line) for a few of the rarely used ones.

Nor is this a book that skims dozens of technologies at a high level. Although I don't claim that this is a definitive reference on every technology it touches on (e.g., there are a number of books this size just on JDBC), if the book covers a topic, it does so in enough detail for you to sit down and start writing real programs. The one exception to this rule is the Java programming language itself. Although I don't assume any familiarity with server-side programming, I do expect you to be familiar with the basics of Java language development. If you're not, you will need to pick up a good tutorial like *Core Java*, *Core Web Programming*, or *Thinking in Java*.

A word of caution, however. Nobody becomes a great developer just by reading. *You* have to write some real code, too. The more, the better. In each chapter, I suggest that you start by making a simple program or a small variation of one of the examples given, then strike off on your own with a more significant project. Skim the sections you don't plan on using right away, then come back when you are ready to try them out.

If you do this, you should quickly develop the confidence to handle the real-world problems that brought you here in the first place. You should be able to decide where servlets apply well, where JSP is better, and where a combination is best. You should not only know how to generate HTML content, but you should also understand building other media types like GIF images or Excel spreadsheets. You should understand HTTP 1.1 well enough to use its capabilities to enhance the effectiveness of your pages. You should have no qualms about developing Web interfaces to your corporate databases, using either HTML forms or applets as front ends. You should be able to spin off complex behaviors into JavaBeans components or custom JSP tag libraries, then decide when to use these components directly and when to start requests with servlets that set things up for separate presentation pages. You should have fun along the way. You should get a raise.

How This Book Is Organized

This book is divided into three parts: Servlets, JavaServer Pages, and Supporting Technologies.

Part I: Servlets

Part I covers servlet development with the 2.1 and 2.2 specifications. Although version 2.2 (along with JSP 1.1) is mandated by the Java 2 Platform, Enterprise Edition (J2EE), many commercial products are still at the earlier releases, so it is important to understand the differences. Also, although servlet code is portable across a huge variety of servers and operating systems, server setup and configuration details are not standardized. So, I include specific details for Apache Tomcat, Sun's JavaServer Web Development Kit (JSWDK), and the Java Web Server. Servlet topics include:

- When and why you would use servlets
- Obtaining and configuring the servlet and JSP software

- The basic structure of servlets
- The process of compiling, installing, and invoking servlets
- Generating HTML from servlets
- The servlet life cycle
- Page modification dates and browser caches
- Servlet debugging strategies
- Reading form data from servlets
- Handling both GET and POST requests with a single servlet
- An on-line resume posting service
- Reading HTTP request headers from servlets
- The purpose of each of the HTTP 1.1 request headers
- Reducing download times by compressing pages
- Restricting access with password-protected servlets
- The servlet equivalent of each standard CGI variable
- Using HTTP status codes
- The meaning of each of the HTTP 1.1 status code values
- A search engine front end
- Setting response headers from servlets
- The purpose of each of the HTTP 1.1 response headers
- Common MIME types
- A servlet that uses the Refresh header to repeatedly access ongoing computations
- Servlets that exploit persistent (keep-alive) HTTP connections
- Generating GIF images from servlets
- Cookie purposes and problems
- The Cookie API
- Some utilities that simplify cookie handling
- A customized search engine front end
- The purposes of session tracking
- The servlet session tracking API
- Using sessions to show per-client access counts
- An on-line store that uses session tracking, shopping carts, and pages automatically built from catalog entries

Part II: JavaServer Pages

JSP provides a convenient alternative to servlets for pages that mostly consist of fixed content. Part II covers the use of JavaServer Pages version 1.0 and 1.1. JSP topics include:

- When and why you would use JavaServer Pages
- How JSP pages are invoked
- Using JSP expressions, scriptlets, and declarations
- Predefined variables that can be used within expressions and scriptlets
- The page directive
- Designating which classes are imported
- Specifying the MIME type of the page
- Generating Excel spreadsheets
- Controlling threading behavior
- Participating in sessions
- Setting the size and behavior of the output buffer
- Designating pages to process JSP errors
- XML-compatible syntax for directives
- Including JSP files at the time the main page is translated into a servlet
- Including HTML or plain text files at the time the client requests the page
- Including applets that use the Java Plug-In
- Using JavaBeans with JSP
- Creating and accessing beans
- Setting bean properties explicitly
- Associating bean properties with input parameters
- Automatic conversion of bean property types
- Sharing beans among multiple JSP pages and servlets
- Creating JSP tag libraries
- Tag handler classes
- Tag library descriptor files
- The JSP taglib directive
- Simple tags
- Tags that use attributes
- Tags that use the body content between their start and end tags
- Tags that modify their body content
- Looping tags
- Nested tags

- Integrating servlets and JSP
- Forwarding requests from servlets to static and dynamic resources
- Using servlets to set up beans for use by JSP pages
- An on-line travel agency combining servlets and JSP
- Including JSP output in servlets
- Forwarding requests from JSP pages

Part III: Supporting Technologies

Part III covers three topics that are commonly used in conjunction with servlets and JSP: HTML forms, applets talking to servlets, and JDBC. Topics include:

- Sending data from forms
- Text controls
- Push buttons
- Check boxes and radio buttons
- Combo boxes and list boxes
- File upload controls
- Server-side image maps
- Hidden fields
- Grouping controls
- Tab ordering
- A Web server for debugging forms
- Sending GET data from an applet and having the browser display the results
- Having applets send GET data and process the results themselves (HTTP tunneling)
- Using object serialization to exchange high-level data structures between applets and servlets
- Having applets send POST data and process the results themselves
- Applets bypassing the HTTP server altogether

Conventions

Throughout the book, concrete programming constructs or program output are presented in a monospaced font. For example, when abstractly discussing server-side programs that use HTTP, I might refer to "HTTP servlets" or just "servlets," but when I say `HttpServlet` I am talking about a specific Java class.

User input is indicated in boldface, and command-line prompts are either generic (`Prompt>`) or indicate the operating system to which they apply (`DOS>`). For instance, the following indicates that "`Some Output`" is the result when "`java SomeProgram`" is executed on any platform.

```
Prompt> java SomeProgram
Some Output
```

Important standard techniques are indicated by specially marked entries, as in the following example.

Core Approach

Pay particular attention to items in "Core Approach" sections. They indicate techniques that should always or almost always be used.

Notes and warnings are called out in a similar manner.

About the Web Site

The book has a companion Web site at `http://www.coreservlets.com/`. This free site includes:

- Documented source code for all examples shown in the book; this code can be downloaded for unrestricted use
- On-line API (in Javadoc format) for all classes developed in the book
- Up-to-date download sites for servlet and JSP software
- Links to all URLs mentioned in the text of the book
- Information on book discounts
- Reports on servlet and JSP short courses
- Book additions, updates, and news

core
SERVLETS and
JAVASERVER PAGES™

Part 1

SERVLETS 2.1 AND 2.2

OVERVIEW OF SERVLETS AND JAVASERVER PAGES

Topics in This Chapter

- What servlets are
- When and why you would use servlets
- What JavaServer Pages are
- When and why you would use JSP
- Obtaining the servlet and JSP software
- Software installation and setup

Chapter 1

This chapter gives a quick overview of servlets and JavaServer Pages (JSP), outlining the major advantages of each. It then summarizes how to obtain and configure the software you need to write servlets and develop JSP documents.

1.1 Servlets

Servlets are Java technology's answer to Common Gateway Interface (CGI) programming. They are programs that run on a Web server, acting as a middle layer between a request coming from a Web browser or other HTTP client and databases or applications on the HTTP server. Their job is to:

1. **Read any data sent by the user.**
   This data is usually entered in a form on a Web page, but could also come from a Java applet or a custom HTTP client program.
2. **Look up any other information about the request that is embedded in the HTTP request.**
   This information includes details about browser capabilities, cookies, the host name of the requesting client, and so forth.

3. **Generate the results.**
   This process may require talking to a database, executing an RMI or CORBA call, invoking a legacy application, or computing the response directly.

4. **Format the results inside a document.**
   In most cases, this involves embedding the information inside an HTML page.

5. **Set the appropriate HTTP response parameters.**
   This means telling the browser what type of document is being returned (e.g., HTML), setting cookies and caching parameters, and other such tasks.

6. **Send the document back to the client.**
   This document may be sent in text format (HTML), binary format (GIF images), or even in a compressed format like gzip that is layered on top of some other underlying format.

Many client requests can be satisfied by returning pre-built documents, and these requests would be handled by the server without invoking servlets. In many cases, however, a static result is not sufficient, and a page needs to be generated for each request. There are a number of reasons why Web pages need to be built on-the-fly like this:

- **The Web page is based on data submitted by the user.**
  For instance, the results page from search engines and order-confirmation pages at on-line stores are specific to particular user requests.

- **The Web page is derived from data that changes frequently.**
  For example, a weather report or news headlines page might build the page dynamically, perhaps returning a previously built page if it is still up to date.

- **The Web page uses information from corporate databases or other server-side sources.**
  For example, an e-commerce site could use a servlet to build a Web page that lists the current price and availability of each item that is for sale.

In principle, servlets are not restricted to Web or application servers that handle HTTP requests, but can be used for other types of servers as well. For example, servlets could be embedded in mail or FTP servers to extend their functionality. In practice, however, this use of servlets has not caught on, and I'll only be discussing HTTP servlets.

1.2 The Advantages of Servlets Over "Traditional" CGI

Java servlets are more efficient, easier to use, more powerful, more portable, safer, and cheaper than traditional CGI and many alternative CGI-like technologies.

Efficient

With traditional CGI, a new process is started for each HTTP request. If the CGI program itself is relatively short, the overhead of starting the process can dominate the execution time. With servlets, the Java Virtual Machine stays running and handles each request using a lightweight Java thread, not a heavyweight operating system process. Similarly, in traditional CGI, if there are N simultaneous requests to the same CGI program, the code for the CGI program is loaded into memory N times. With servlets, however, there would be N threads but only a single copy of the servlet class. Finally, when a CGI program finishes handling a request, the program terminates. This makes it difficult to cache computations, keep database connections open, and perform other optimizations that rely on persistent data. Servlets, however, remain in memory even after they complete a response, so it is straightforward to store arbitrarily complex data between requests.

Convenient

Servlets have an extensive infrastructure for automatically parsing and decoding HTML form data, reading and setting HTTP headers, handling cookies, tracking sessions, and many other such high-level utilities. Besides, you already know the Java programming language. Why learn Perl too? You're already convinced that Java technology makes for more reliable and reusable code than does C++. Why go back to C++ for server-side programming?

Powerful

Servlets support several capabilities that are difficult or impossible to accomplish with regular CGI. Servlets can talk directly to the Web server, whereas regular CGI programs cannot, at least not without using a server-specific API. Communicating with the Web server makes it easier to translate relative URLs into concrete path names, for instance. Multiple servlets can also share data, making it easy to implement database connection pooling and similar resource-sharing optimizations. Servlets can also maintain information from request to request, simplifying techniques like session tracking and caching of previous computations.

Portable

Servlets are written in the Java programming language and follow a standard API. Consequently, servlets written for, say, I-Planet Enterprise Server can run virtually unchanged on Apache, Microsoft Internet Information Server (IIS), IBM WebSphere, or StarNine WebStar. For example, virtually all of the servlets and JSP pages in this book were executed on Sun's Java Web Server, Apache Tomcat and Sun's JavaServer Web Development Kit (JSWDK) with *no* changes whatsoever in the code. Many were tested on BEA WebLogic and IBM WebSphere as well. In fact, servlets are supported directly or by a plug-in on virtually *every* major Web server. They are now part of the Java 2 Platform, Enterprise Edition (J2EE; see http://java.sun.com/j2ee/), so industry support for servlets is becoming even more pervasive.

Secure

One of the main sources of vulnerabilities in traditional CGI programs stems from the fact that they are often executed by general-purpose operating system shells. So the CGI programmer has to be very careful to filter out characters such as backquotes and semicolons that are treated specially by the shell. This is harder than one might think, and weaknesses stemming from this problem are constantly being uncovered in widely used CGI libraries. A second source of problems is the fact that some CGI programs are processed by languages that do not automatically check array or string bounds. For example, in C and C++ it is perfectly legal to allocate a

100-element array then write into the 999th "element," which is really some random part of program memory. So programmers who forget to do this check themselves open their system up to deliberate or accidental buffer overflow attacks. Servlets suffer from neither of these problems. Even if a servlet executes a remote system call to invoke a program on the local operating system, it does not use a shell to do so. And of course array bounds checking and other memory protection features are a central part of the Java programming language.

Inexpensive

There are a number of free or very inexpensive Web servers available that are good for "personal" use or low-volume Web sites. However, with the major exception of Apache, which is free, most commercial-quality Web servers are relatively expensive. Nevertheless, once you have a Web server, no matter its cost, adding servlet support to it (if it doesn't come preconfigured to support servlets) costs very little extra. This is in contrast to many of the other CGI alternatives, which require a significant initial investment to purchase a proprietary package.

1.3 JavaServer Pages

JavaServer Pages (JSP) technology enables you to mix regular, static HTML with dynamically generated content from servlets. Many Web pages that are built by CGI programs are primarily static, with the parts that change limited to a few small locations. For example, the initial page at most on-line stores is the same for all visitors, except for a small welcome message giving the visitor's name if it is known. But most CGI variations, including servlets, make you generate the entire page via your program, even though most of it is always the same. JSP lets you create the two parts separately. Listing 1.1 gives an example. Most of the page consists of regular HTML, which is passed to the visitor unchanged. Parts that are generated dynamically are marked with special HTML-like tags and mixed right into the page.

Listing 1.1   A sample JSP page

```
<!DOCTYPE HTML PUBLIC "-//W3C//DTD HTML 4.0 Transitional//EN">
<HTML>
<HEAD><TITLE>Welcome to Our Store</TITLE></HEAD>
<BODY>
<H1>Welcome to Our Store</H1>
<SMALL>Welcome,
<!-- User name is "New User" for first-time visitors -->
<%= Utils.getUserNameFromCookie(request) %>
To access your account settings, click
<A HREF="Account-Settings.html">here.</A></SMALL>
<P>
Regular HTML for all the rest of the on-line store's Web page.
</BODY>
</HTML>
```

1.4 The Advantages of JSP

JSP has a number of advantages over many of its alternatives. Here are a few of them.

Versus Active Server Pages (ASP)

ASP is a competing technology from Microsoft. The advantages of JSP are twofold. First, the dynamic part is written in Java, not VBScript or another ASP-specific language, so it is more powerful and better suited to complex applications that require reusable components. Second, JSP is portable to other operating systems and Web servers; you aren't locked into Windows NT/2000 and IIS. You could make the same argument when comparing JSP to ColdFusion; with JSP you can use Java and are not tied to a particular server product.

Versus PHP

PHP is a free, open-source HTML-embedded scripting language that is somewhat similar to both ASP and JSP. The advantage of JSP is that the dynamic part is written in Java, which you probably already know, which already has an extensive API for networking, database access, distributed objects, and the like, whereas PHP requires learning an entirely new language.

Versus Pure Servlets

JSP doesn't provide any capabilities that couldn't in principle be accomplished with a servlet. In fact, JSP documents are automatically translated into servlets behind the scenes. But it is more convenient to write (and to modify!) regular HTML than to have a zillion `println` statements that generate the HTML. Plus, by separating the presentation from the content, you can put different people on different tasks: your Web page design experts can build the HTML using familiar tools and leave places for your servlet programmers to insert the dynamic content.

Versus Server-Side Includes (SSI)

SSI is a widely supported technology for inserting externally defined pieces into a static Web page. JSP is better because you have a richer set of tools for building that external piece and have more options regarding the stage of the HTTP response at which the piece actually gets inserted. Besides, SSI is really intended only for simple inclusions, not for "real" programs that use form data, make database connections, and the like.

Versus JavaScript

JavaScript, which is completely distinct from the Java programming language, is normally used to generate HTML dynamically on the *client*, building parts of the Web page as the browser loads the document. This is a useful capability but only handles situations where the dynamic information is based on the client's environment. With the exception of cookies, the HTTP request data is not available to client-side JavaScript routines. And, since JavaScript lacks routines for network programming, JavaScript code on the client cannot access server-side resources like databases, catalogs, pricing information, and the like. JavaScript can also be used on the server, most notably on Netscape servers and as a scripting language for IIS. Java is far more powerful, flexible, reliable, and portable.

Versus Static HTML

Regular HTML, of course, cannot contain dynamic information, so static HTML pages cannot be based upon user input or server-side data sources. JSP is so easy and convenient that it is quite reasonable to augment HTML pages that only benefit slightly by the insertion of dynamic data. Previously, the difficulty of using dynamic data precluded its use in all but the most valuable instances.

1.5 Installation and Setup

Before you can get started, you have to download the software you need and configure your system to take advantage of it. Here's an outline of the steps involved. Please note, however, that although your servlet code will follow a standard API, there is no standard for downloading and configuring Web or application servers. Thus, unlike most sections of this book, the methods described here vary significantly from server to server, and the examples in this section should be taken only as representative samples. Check your server's documentation for authoritative instructions.

Obtain Servlet and JSP Software

Your first step is to download software that implements the Java Servlet 2.1 or 2.2 and JavaServer Pages 1.0 or 1.1 specifications. If you are using an up-to-date Web or application server, there is a good chance that it already has everything you need. Check your server documentation or see the latest list of servers that support servlets at http://java.sun.com/products/servlet/industry.html. Although you'll eventually want to deploy in a commercial-quality server, when first learning it is useful to have a free system that you can install on your desktop machine for development and testing purposes. Here are some of the most popular options:

- **Apache Tomcat.**
  Tomcat is the official reference implementation of the servlet 2.2 and JSP 1.1 specifications. It can be used as a small stand-alone server for testing servlets and JSP pages, or can be integrated into the Apache Web server. However, many other servers have announced upcoming support, so these specifications will be

covered in detail throughout this book. Tomcat, like Apache itself, is free. However, also like Apache (which is very fast, highly reliable, but a bit hard to configure and install), Tomcat requires significantly more effort to set up than do the commercial servlet engines. For details, see `http://jakarta.apache.org/`.

- **JavaServer Web Development Kit (JSWDK).**
  The JSWDK is the official reference implementation of the servlet 2.1 and JSP 1.0 specifications. It is used as a small stand-alone server for testing servlets and JSP pages before they are deployed to a full Web server that supports these technologies. It is free and reliable, but takes quite a bit of effort to install and configure. For details, see
  `http://java.sun.com/products/servlet/download.html`.

- **Allaire JRun.**
  JRun is a servlet and JSP engine that can be plugged into Netscape Enterprise or FastTrack servers, IIS, Microsoft Personal Web Server, older versions of Apache, O'Reilly's WebSite, or StarNine WebSTAR. A limited version that supports up to five simultaneous connections is available for free; the commercial version removes this restriction and adds capabilities like a remote administration console. For details, see `http://www.allaire.com/products/jrun/`.

- **New Atlanta's ServletExec.** ServletExec is a servlet and JSP engine that can be plugged into most popular Web servers for Solaris, Windows, MacOS, HP-UX and Linux. You can download and use it for free, but many of the advanced features and administration utilities are disabled until you purchase a license. For details, see `http://newatlanta.com/`.

- **LiteWebServer (LWS) from Gefion Software.**
  LWS is a small free Web server derived from Tomcat that supports servlets version 2.2 and JSP 1.1. Gefion also has a free plug-in called WAICoolRunner that adds servlet 2.2 and JSP 1.1 support to Netscape FastTrack and Enterprise servers. For details, see http://www.gefionsoftware.com/.

- **Sun's Java Web Server.**
  This server is written entirely in Java and was one of the first Web servers to fully support the servlet 2.1 and JSP 1.0 specifications. Although it is no longer under active development because Sun is concentrating on the Netscape/I-Planet server, it is still a popular choice for learning

servlets and JSP. For a free trial version, see
`http://www.sun.com/software/jwebserver/try/`.Forafree
non-expiring version for teaching purposes at academic
institutions, see `http://freeware.thesphere.com/`.

Bookmark or Install the Servlet and JSP API Documentation

Just as no serious programmer should develop general-purpose Java applications without access to the JDK 1.1 or 1.2 API documentation, no serious programmer should develop servlets or JSP pages without access to the API for classes in the `javax.servlet` packages. Here is a summary of where to find the API:

- **`http://java.sun.com/products/jsp/download.html`**
  This site lets you download either the 2.1/1.0 API or the 2.2/1.1 API to your local system. You may have to download the entire reference implementation and then extract the documentation.
- **`http://java.sun.com/products/servlet/2.2/javadoc/`**
  This site lets you browse the servlet 2.2 API on-line.
- **`http://www.java.sun.com/j2ee/j2sdkee/techdocs/api/`**
  This address lets you browse the complete API for the Java 2 Platform, Enterprise Edition (J2EE), which includes the servlet 2.2 and JSP 1.1 packages.

If Sun or Apache place any new additions on-line (e.g., a place to browse the 2.1/1.0 API), they will be listed under Chapter 1 in the book source archive at `http://www.coreservlets.com/`.

Identify the Classes to the Java Compiler

Once you've obtained the necessary software, you need to tell the Java compiler (`javac`) where to find the servlet and JSP class files when it compiles your servlets. Check the documentation of your particular package for definitive details, but the necessary class files are usually in the `lib` subdirectory of the server's installation directory, with the servlet classes in `servlet.jar` and the JSP classes in `jsp.jar`, `jspengine.jar`, or `jasper.jar`. There are a couple of different ways to tell `javac` about these classes, the easiest of which is to put the JAR files in your CLASSPATH. If you've never dealt with the CLASSPATH before, it is the variable that specifies where `javac` looks for classes when compiling. If the variable is unspecified, javac looks in the current directory and the standard system libraries. If you set CLASSPATH yourself, be sure to include ".", signifying the current directory.

Following is a brief summary of how to set the environment variable on a couple of different platforms. Assume *dir* is the directory in which the servlet and JSP classes are found.

Unix (C Shell)

```
setenv CLASSPATH .:dir/servlet.jar:dir/jspengine.jar
```

Add :$CLASSPATH to the end of the setenv line if your CLASSPATH is already set and you want to add more to it, not replace it. Note that on Unix systems you use forward slashes to separate directories within an entry and colons to separate entries, whereas you use backward slashes and semicolons on Windows. To make this setting permanent, you would typically put this statement in your .cshrc file.

Windows

```
set CLASSPATH=.;dir\servlet.jar;dir\jspengine.jar
```

Add ;%CLASSPATH% to the end of the above line if your CLASSPATH is already set and you want to add more to it, not replace it. Note that on Windows you use backward slashes to separate directories within an entry and semicolons to separate entries, while you use forward slashes and colons on Unix. To make this setting permanent on Windows 95/98, you'd typically put this statement in your autoexec.bat file. On Windows NT or 2000, you would go to the Start menu, select Settings, select Control Panel, select System, select Environment, then enter the variable and value.

Package the Classes

As you'll see in the next chapter, you probably want to put your servlets into packages to avoid name conflicts with servlets other people write for the same Web or application server. In that case, you may find it convenient to add the top-level directory of your package hierarchy to the CLASSPATH as well. See Section 2.4 (Packaging Servlets) for details.

Configure the Server

Before you start the server, you may want to designate parameters like the port on which it listens, the directories in which it looks for HTML files, and so forth. This process is totally server-specific, and for commercial-quality Web servers should be clearly documented in the installation notes. However, with the small stand-alone servers that Apache and Sun provide as reference implementations of the servlet 2.2/JSP 1.1 specs (Apache Tomcat) or 2.1/1.0 specs (Sun JSWDK), there are a number of important but poorly documented settings that I'll describe here.

Port Number

Tomcat and the JSWDK both use a nonstandard port by default in order to avoid conflicts with existing Web servers. If you use one of these products for initial development and testing, and don't have another Web server running, you will probably find it convenient to switch to 80, the standard HTTP port number. With Tomcat 3.0, do so by editing *install_dir*/server.xml, changing 8080 to 80 in the line

```
<ContextManager port="8080" hostName="" inet="">
```

With the JSWDK 1.0.1, edit the *install_dir*/webserver.xml file and replace 8080 with 80 in the line

```
port NMTOKEN "8080"
```

The Java Web Server 2.0 also uses a non-standard port. To change it, use the remote administration interface, available by visiting http://*somehostname*:9090/, where *somehostname* is replaced by either the real name of the host running the server or by localhost if the server is running on the local machine.

JAVA_HOME Setting

If you use JDK 1.2 or 1.3 with Tomcat or the JSWDK, you must set the JAVA_HOME environment variable to refer to the JDK installation directory. This setting is unnecessary with JDK 1.1. The easiest way to specify this variable is to insert a line that sets it into the top of the startup (Tomcat) or startserver (JSWDK) script. For example, here's the top of the modified version of startup.bat and startserver.bat that I use:

```
rem Marty Hall: added JAVA_HOME setting below
set JAVA_HOME=C:\jdk1.2.2
```

DOS Memory Setting

If you start Tomcat or the JSWDK server from Windows 95 or 98, you probably have to modify the amount of memory DOS allocates for environment variables. To do this, start a fresh DOS window, click on the MS-DOS icon in the top-left corner of the window, and select `Properties`. From there, choose the `Memory` tab, go to the `Initial Environment` setting, and change the value from `Auto` to 2816. This configuration only needs to be done once.

Tomcat 3.0 CR/LF Settings

The first releases of Tomcat suffered from a serious problem: the text files were saved in Unix format (where the end of line is marked with a linefeed), not Windows format (where the end of the line is marked with a carriage return/linefeed pair). As a result, the startup and shutdown scripts failed on Windows. You can determine if your version suffers from this problem by opening `install_dir/startup.bat` in Notepad; if it appears normal you have a patched version. If the file appears to be one long jumbled line, then quit Notepad and open and immediately save the following files using Wordpad (*not* Notepad):

- *install_dir*/startup.bat
- *install_dir*/tomcat.bat
- *install_dir*/shutdown.bat
- *install_dir*/tomcatEnv.bat
- *install_dir*/webpages/WEB-INF/web.xml
- *install_dir*/examples/WEB-INF/web.xml

Start the Server

To start one of the "real" Web servers, check its documentation. In many cases, starting it involves executing a command called `httpd` either from the command line or by instructing the operating system to do so automatically when the system is first booted.

With Tomcat 3.0, you start the server by executing a script called `startup` in the main installation directory. With the JSWDK 1.0.1, you execute a similar script called `startserver`.

Compile and Install Your Servlets

Once you've properly set your CLASSPATH, as described earlier in this section, just use "javac ServletName.java" to compile a servlet. The resultant class file needs to go in a location that the server knows to check during execution. As you might expect, this location varies from server to server. Following is a quick summary of the locations used by the latest releases of Tomcat, the JSWDK, and the Java Web Server. In all three cases, assume install_dir is the server's main installation directory.

Tomcat

- **install_dir/webpages/WEB-INF/classes**
  Standard location for servlet classes.
- **install_dir/classes**
  Alternate location for servlet classes.
- **install_dir/lib**
  Location for JAR files containing classes.

Tomcat 3.1

Just before this book went to press, Apache released a beta version of Tomcat 3.1. If there is a final version of this version available when you go to download Tomcat, you should use it. Here is the new directory organization that Tomcat 3.1 uses:

- **install_dir/webapps/ROOT/WEB-INF/classes**
  Standard location for servlet classes.
- **install_dir/classes**
  Alternate location for servlet classes.
- **install_dir/lib**
  Location for JAR files containing classes.

The JSWDK

- **install_dir/webpages/WEB-INF/servlets**
  Standard location for servlet classes.
- **install_dir/classes**
  Alternate location for servlet classes.
- **install_dir/lib**
  Location for JAR files containing classes.

Java Web Server 2.0

- **install_dir/servlets**
  Location for frequently changing servlet classes. The server automatically detects when servlets in this directory change, and reloads them if necessary. This is in contrast to Tomcat and the JSWDK, where you have to restart the server when a servlet that is already in server memory changes. Most commercial servers have an option similar to this auto-reloading feature.
- **install_dir/classes**
  Location for infrequently changing servlet classes.
- **install_dir/lib**
  Location for JAR files containing classes.

I realize that this sounds a bit overwhelming. Don't worry, I'll walk you through the process with a couple of different servers when I introduce some real servlet code in the next chapter.

FIRST SERVLETS

Chapter 2

The previous chapter showed you how to install the software you need and how to set up your development environment. Now you want to really write a few servlets. Good. This chapter shows you how, outlining the structure that almost all servlets follow, walking you through the steps required to compile and execute a servlet, and giving details on how servlets are initialized and when the various methods are called. It also introduces a few general tools that you will find helpful in your servlet development.

2.1 Basic Servlet Structure

Listing 2.1 outlines a basic servlet that handles GET requests. GET requests, for those unfamiliar with HTTP, are the usual type of browser requests for Web pages. A browser generates this request when the user types a URL on the address line, follows a link from a Web page, or submits an HTML form that does not specify a METHOD. Servlets can also very easily handle POST requests, which are generated when someone submits an HTML form that specifies METHOD="POST". For details on using HTML forms, see Chapter 16.

To be a servlet, a class should extend HttpServlet and override doGet or doPost, depending on whether the data is being sent by GET or by POST. If you want the same servlet to handle both GET and POST and to take the same action for each, you can simply have doGet call doPost, or vice versa.

| Listing 2.1 | `ServletTemplate.java` |

```java
import java.io.*;
import javax.servlet.*;
import javax.servlet.http.*;

public class ServletTemplate extends HttpServlet {
  public void doGet(HttpServletRequest request,
                    HttpServletResponse response)
      throws ServletException, IOException {

    // Use "request" to read incoming HTTP headers
    // (e.g. cookies) and HTML form data (e.g. data the user
    // entered and submitted).

    // Use "response" to specify the HTTP response status
    // code and headers (e.g. the content type, cookies).

    PrintWriter out = response.getWriter();
    // Use "out" to send content to browser
  }
}
```

Both of these methods take two arguments: an `HttpServletRequest` and an `HttpServletResponse`. The `HttpServletRequest` has methods by which you can find out about incoming information such as form data, HTTP request headers, and the client's hostname. The `HttpServletResponse` lets you specify outgoing information such as HTTP status codes (200, 404, etc.), response headers (`Content-Type`, `Set-Cookie`, etc.), and, most importantly, lets you obtain a `PrintWriter` used to send the document content back to the client. For simple servlets, most of the effort is spent in `println` statements that generate the desired page. Form data, HTTP request headers, HTTP responses, and cookies will all be discussed in detail in the following chapters.

Since `doGet` and `doPost` throw two exceptions, you are required to include them in the declaration. Finally, you have to import classes in `java.io` (for `PrintWriter`, etc.), `javax.servlet` (for `HttpServlet`, etc.), and `javax.servlet.http` (for `HttpServletRequest` and `HttpServletResponse`).

Strictly speaking, `HttpServlet` is not the only starting point for servlets, since servlets could, in principle, extend mail, FTP, or other types of servers. Servlets for these environments would extend a custom class derived from `GenericServlet`, the parent class of `HttpServlet`. In practice, however, servlets are used almost exclusively for servers that communicate via HTTP (i.e., Web and application servers), and the discussion in this book will be limited to this usage.

2.2 A Simple Servlet Generating Plain Text

Listing 2.2 shows a simple servlet that just generates plain text, with the output shown in Figure 2–1. Section 2.3 (A Servlet That Generates HTML) shows the more usual case where HTML is generated. However, before moving on, it is worth spending some time going through the process of installing, compiling, and running this simple servlet. You'll find this a bit tedious the first time you try it. Be patient; since the process is the same each time, you'll quickly get used to it, especially if you partially automate the process by means of a script file such as that presented in the following section.

Listing 2.2 `HelloWorld.java`

```java
import java.io.*;
import javax.servlet.*;
import javax.servlet.http.*;

public class HelloWorld extends HttpServlet {
  public void doGet(HttpServletRequest request,
                    HttpServletResponse response)
      throws ServletException, IOException {
    PrintWriter out = response.getWriter();
    out.println("Hello World");
  }
}
```

Figure 2–1　Result of Listing 2.2 (`HelloWorld.java`).

Compiling and Installing the Servlet

The first thing you need to do is to make sure that your server is configured properly and that your CLASSPATH refers to the JAR files containing the standard servlet classes. Please refer to Section 1.5 (Installation and Setup) for an explanation of this process.

The next step is to decide where to put the servlet classes. This location varies from server to server, so refer to your Web server documentation for definitive directions. However, there are some moderately common conventions. Most servers have three distinct locations for servlet classes, as detailed below.

1. **A directory for frequently changing servlet classes.**
   Servlets in this directory are automatically reloaded when their class file changes, so you should use this directory during development. For example, this is normally *install_dir*/servlets with Sun's Java Web Server and IBM's WebSphere and *install_dir*/myserver/servlet-classes for BEA WebLogic, although most servers let the server administrator specify a different location. Neither Tomcat nor the JSWDK support automatic servlet reloading. Nevertheless, they still have a similar directory in which to place servlets; you just have to stop and restart the mini-server each time you change an existing servlet. With Tomcat 3.0, place servlets in *install_dir*/webpages/WEB-INF/classes. With the JSWDK 1.0.1, use *install_dir*/webpages/WEB-INF/servlets.

2. **A directory for infrequently changing servlet classes.**
   Servlets placed in this location are slightly more efficient since the server doesn't have to keep checking their modification dates. However, changes to class files in this directory require you to restart the server. This option (or Option 3 below) is the one to use for "production" servlets deployed to a high-volume site. This directory is usually something like *install_dir*/classes, which is the default name with Tomcat, the JSWDK, and the Java Web Server. Since Tomcat and the JSWDK do not support automatic servlet reloading, this directory works the same as the one described in Option 1, so most developers stick with that previous option.

3. **A directory for infrequently changing servlets in JAR files.**
   With the second option above, the class files are placed directly in the `classes` directory or in subdirectories corresponding to their package name. Here, the class files are packaged in a JAR file, and that file is then placed in the designated directory. With Tomcat, the JSWDK, the Java Web Server, and most other servers, this directory is *install_dir*/lib. You must restart the server whenever you change files in this directory.

Once you've configured your server, set your CLASSPATH, and placed the servlet in the proper directory, simply do "`javac HelloWorld.java`" to compile the servlet. In production environments, however, servlets are frequently placed into packages to avoid name conflicts with servlets written by other developers. Using packages involves a couple of extra steps that are covered in Section 2.4 (Packaging Servlets). Also, it is common to use HTML forms as front ends to servlets (see Chapter 16). To use them, you'll need to know where to place regular HTML files to make them accessible to the server. This location varies from server to server, but with the JSWDK and Tomcat, you place an HTML file in *install_dir*/webpages/path/file.html and then access it via `http://localhost/path/file.html` (replace `localhost` with the real hostname if running remotely). A JSP page can be installed anywhere that a normal HTML page can be.

Invoking the Servlet

With different servers, servlet classes can be placed in a variety of different locations, and there is little standardization among servers. To invoke servlets, however, there is a common convention: use a URL of the form `http://host/servlet/ServletName`. Note that the URL refers to `servlet`, singular, even if the real directory containing the servlet code is called `servlets`, plural, or has an unrelated name like `classes` or `lib`.

Figure 2–1, shown earlier in this section, gives an example with the Web server running directly on my PC ("localhost" means "the current machine").

Most servers also let you register names for servlets, so that a servlet can be invoked via `http://host/any-path/any-file`. The process for doing this is server-specific; check your server's documentation for details.

2.3 A Servlet That Generates HTML

Most servlets generate HTML, not plain text as in the previous example. To build HTML, you need two additional steps:

1. Tell the browser that you're sending back HTML, and
2. Modify the `println` statements to build a legal Web page.

You accomplish the first step by setting the HTTP `Content-Type` response header. In general, headers are set by the `setHeader` method of `Http-ServletResponse`, but setting the content type is such a common task that there is also a special `setContentType` method just for this purpose. The way to designate HTML is with a type of `text/html`, so the code would look like this:

```
response.setContentType("text/html");
```

Although HTML is the most common type of document servlets create, it is not unusual to create other document types. For example, Section 7.5 (Using Servlets to Generate GIF Images) shows how servlets can build and return custom images, specifying a content type of `image/gif`. As a second example, Section 11.2 (The contentType Attribute) shows how to generate and return Excel spreadsheets, using a content type of `application/vnd.ms-excel`.

Don't be concerned if you are not yet familiar with HTTP response headers; they are discussed in detail in Chapter 7. Note that you need to set response headers *before* actually returning any of the content via the `Print-Writer`. That's because an HTTP response consists of the status line, one or more headers, a blank line, and the actual document, *in that order*. The headers can appear in any order, and servlets buffer the headers and send them all at once, so it is legal to set the status code (part of the first line returned) even after setting headers. But servlets do not necessarily buffer the document itself, since users might want to see partial results for long pages. In version 2.1 of the servlet specification, the `PrintWriter` output is not buffered at all, so the first time you use the `PrintWriter`, it is too late to go back and set headers. In version 2.2, servlet engines are permitted to partially buffer the output, but the size of the buffer is left unspecified. You can use the `getBufferSize` method of `HttpServletResponse` to determine the size, or use `setBufferSize` to specify it. In version 2.2 with buffering enabled, you can set headers until the buffer fills up and is actually sent to the client. If you aren't sure if the buffer has been sent, you can use the `isCommitted` method to check.

Core Approach

Always set the content type **before** _transmitting the actual document._

The second step in writing a servlet that builds an HTML document is to have your `println` statements output HTML, not plain text. The structure of an HTML document is discussed more in Section 2.5 (Simple HTML-Building Utilities), but it should be familiar to most readers. Listing 2.3 gives an example servlet, with the result shown in Figure 2–2.

Listing 2.3 `HelloWWW.java`

```java
import java.io.*;
import javax.servlet.*;
import javax.servlet.http.*;

public class HelloWWW extends HttpServlet {
  public void doGet(HttpServletRequest request,
                    HttpServletResponse response)
      throws ServletException, IOException {
    response.setContentType("text/html");
    PrintWriter out = response.getWriter();
    String docType =
      "<!DOCTYPE HTML PUBLIC \"-//W3C//DTD HTML 4.0 " +
      "Transitional//EN\">\n";
    out.println(docType +
                "<HTML>\n" +
                "<HEAD><TITLE>Hello WWW</TITLE></HEAD>\n" +
                "<BODY>\n" +
                "<H1>Hello WWW</H1>\n" +
                "</BODY></HTML>");
  }
}
```

2.4 Packaging Servlets

In a production environment, multiple programmers may be developing servlets for the same server. So, placing all the servlets in the top-level servlet directory results in a massive hard-to-manage directory and risks name conflicts when two developers accidentally choose the same servlet name. Packages are the natural solution to this problem. Using packages results in changes in the way the servlets are created, the way that they are compiled,

Figure 2-2   Result of Listing 2.3 (`HelloWWW.java`).

and the way they're invoked. Let's take these areas one at a time in the following three subsections. The first two changes are exactly the same as with any other Java class that uses packages; there is nothing specific to servlets.

Creating Servlets in Packages

Two steps are needed to place servlets in packages:

1. **Move the files to a subdirectory that matches the intended package name.**
   For example, I'll use the `coreservlets` package for most of the rest of the servlets in this book. So, the class files need to go in a subdirectory called `coreservlets`.

2. **Insert a package statement in the class file.**
   For example, to place a class file in a package called `somePackage`, the *first* line of the file should read

   ```
   package somePackage;
   ```

For example, Listing 2.4 presents a variation of the `HelloWWW` servlet that is in the `coreservlets` package. The class file goes in *install_dir*/webpages/WEB-INF/classes/coreservlets for Tomcat 3.0, in *install_dir*/webpages/WEB-INF/servlets/coreservlets for the JSWDK 1.0.1, and in *install_dir*/servlets/coreservlets for the Java Web Server 2.0.

Listing 2.4   `HelloWWW2.java`

```java
package coreservlets;

import java.io.*;
import javax.servlet.*;
import javax.servlet.http.*;

public class HelloWWW2 extends HttpServlet {
  public void doGet(HttpServletRequest request,
                    HttpServletResponse response)
      throws ServletException, IOException {
    response.setContentType("text/html");
    PrintWriter out = response.getWriter();
    String docType =
      "<!DOCTYPE HTML PUBLIC \"-//W3C//DTD HTML 4.0 " +
      "Transitional//EN\">\n";
    out.println(docType +
                "<HTML>\n" +
                "<HEAD><TITLE>Hello WWW</TITLE></HEAD>\n" +
                "<BODY>\n" +
                "<H1>Hello WWW</H1>\n" +
                "</BODY></HTML>");
  }
}
```

Compiling Servlets in Packages

There are two main ways to compile classes that are in packages. The first
option is to place your package subdirectory right in the directory where the
Web server expects servlets to go. Then, you would set the CLASSPATH variable to point to the directory *above* the one actually containing your servlets,
that is, to the main servlet directory used by the Web server. You can then
compile normally from within the package-specific subdirectory. For example, if your base servlet directory is `C:\JavaWebServer2.0\servlets` and
your package name (and thus subdirectory name) is `coreservlets`, and you
are running Windows, you would do:

```
DOS>    set CLASSPATH=C:\JavaWebServer2.0\servlets;%CLASSPATH%
DOS>    cd C:\JavaWebServer2.0\servlets\coreservlets
DOS>    javac HelloWorld.java
```

The first part, setting the CLASSPATH, you probably want to do permanently,
rather than each time you start a new DOS window. On Windows 95/98 you
typically put the set CLASSPATH=... statement in your `autoexec.bat` file
somewhere *after* the line that sets the CLASSPATH to point to `servlet.jar` and

the JSP JAR file. On Windows NT or Windows 2000, you go to the Start menu, select Settings, select Control Panel, select System, select Environment, then enter the variable and value. On Unix (C shell), you set the CLASSPATH variable by

```
setenv CLASSPATH /install_dir/servlets:$CLASSPATH
```

Put this in your .cshrc file to make it permanent.

If your package were of the form name1.name2.name3 rather than simply name1 as here, the CLASSPATH should still point to the top-level servlet directory, that is, the directory containing name1.

A second way to compile classes that are in packages is to keep the source code in a location distinct from the class files. First, you put your package directories in any location you find convenient. The CLASSPATH refers to this location. Second, you use the -d option of javac to install the class files in the directory the Web server expects. An example follows. Again, you will probably want to set the CLASSPATH permanently rather than set it each time.

```
DOS> cd C:\MyServlets\coreservlets
DOS> set CLASSPATH=C:\MyServlets;%CLASSPATH%
DOS> javac -d C:\tomcat\webpages\WEB-INF\classes HelloWWW2.java
```

Keeping the source code separate from the class files is the approach I use for my own development. To complicate my life further, I have a number of different CLASSPATH settings that I use for different projects, and typically use JDK 1.2, not JDK 1.1 as the Java Web Server expects. So, on Windows I find it convenient to automate the servlet compilation process with a batch file servletc.bat, as shown in Listing 2.5 (line breaks in the set CLASSPATH line inserted only for readability). I put this batch file in C:\Windows\Command or somewhere else in the Windows PATH. After this, to compile the HelloWWW2 servlet and install it with the Java Web Server, I merely go to C:\MyServlets\coreservlets and do "servletc HelloWWW2.java". The source code archive at http://www.coreservlets.com/ contains variations of servletc.bat for the JSWDK and Tomcat. You can do something similar on Unix with a shell script.

Invoking Servlets in Packages

To invoke a servlet that is in a package, use the URL

```
http://host/servlet/packageName.ServletName
```

instead of

```
http://host/servlet/ServletName
```

Thus, if the Web server is running on the local system,

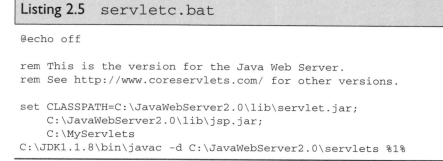

Listing 2.5 `servletc.bat`

```
@echo off

rem This is the version for the Java Web Server.
rem See http://www.coreservlets.com/ for other versions.

set CLASSPATH=C:\JavaWebServer2.0\lib\servlet.jar;
    C:\JavaWebServer2.0\lib\jsp.jar;
    C:\MyServlets
C:\JDK1.1.8\bin\javac -d C:\JavaWebServer2.0\servlets %1%
```

```
http://localhost/servlet/coreservlets.HelloWWW2
```

would invoke the `HelloWWW2` servlet, as illustrated in Figure 2–3.

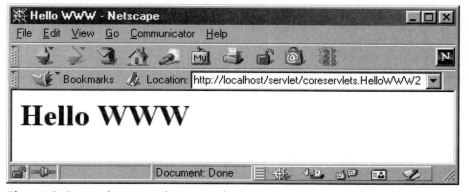

Figure 2–3   Invoking a servlet in a package via
`http://hostname/servlet/packagename.servletName`.

2.5 Simple HTML-Building Utilities

An HTML document is structured as follows:

```
<!DOCTYPE ...>
<HTML>
<HEAD><TITLE>...</TITLE>...</HEAD>
<BODY ...>
...
</BODY>
</HTML>
```

You might be tempted to omit part of this structure, especially the DOCTYPE line, noting that virtually all major browsers ignore it, even though the

HTML 3.2 and 4.0 specifications require it. I strongly discourage this practice. The advantage of the DOCTYPE line is that it tells HTML validators which version of HTML you are using, so they know which specification to check your document against. These validators are very valuable debugging services, helping you catch HTML syntax errors that your browser guesses well on, but that other browsers will have trouble displaying. The two most popular on-line validators are the ones from the World Wide Web Consortium (http://validator.w3.org/) and from the Web Design Group (http://www.htmlhelp.com/tools/validator/). They let you submit a URL, then they retrieve the page, check the syntax against the formal HTML specification, and report any errors to you. Since a servlet that generates HTML looks like a regular Web page to visitors, it can be validated in the normal manner unless it requires POST data to return its result. Remember that GET data is attached to the URL, so you can submit a URL that includes GET data to the validators.

Core Approach

Use an HTML validator to check the syntax of pages that your servlets generate.

Admittedly it is a bit cumbersome to generate HTML with println statements, especially long tedious lines like the DOCTYPE declaration. Some people address this problem by writing detailed HTML generation utilities in Java, then use them throughout their servlets. I'm skeptical of the utility of an extensive library for this. First and foremost, the inconvenience of generating HTML programmatically is one of the main problems addressed by JavaServer Pages (discussed in the second part of this book). JSP is a better solution, so don't waste effort building a complex HTML generation package. Second, HTML generation routines can be cumbersome and tend not to support the full range of HTML attributes (CLASS and ID for style sheets, JavaScript event handlers, table cell background colors, and so forth). Despite the questionable value of a full-blown HTML generation library, if you find you're repeating the same constructs many times, you might as well create a simple utility file that simplifies those constructs. For standard servlets, there are two parts of the Web page (DOCTYPE and HEAD) that are unlikely to change and thus could benefit from being incorporated into a simple utility file. These are shown in Listing

2.6, with Listing 2.7 showing a variation of HelloWWW2 that makes use of this utility. I'll add a few more utilities throughout the book.

Listing 2.6   ServletUtilities.java

```
package coreservlets;

import javax.servlet.*;
import javax.servlet.http.*;

public class ServletUtilities {
  public static final String DOCTYPE =
    "<!DOCTYPE HTML PUBLIC \"-//W3C//DTD HTML 4.0 " +
    "Transitional//EN\">";

  public static String headWithTitle(String title) {
    return(DOCTYPE + "\n" +
           "<HTML>\n" +
           "<HEAD><TITLE>" + title + "</TITLE></HEAD>\n");
  }
  ...
}
```

Listing 2.7   HelloWWW3.java

```
package coreservlets;

import java.io.*;
import javax.servlet.*;
import javax.servlet.http.*;

public class HelloWWW3 extends HttpServlet {
  public void doGet(HttpServletRequest request,
                    HttpServletResponse response)
      throws ServletException, IOException {
    response.setContentType("text/html");
    PrintWriter out = response.getWriter();
    out.println(ServletUtilities.headWithTitle("Hello WWW") +
                "<BODY>\n" +
                "<H1>Hello WWW</H1>\n" +
                "</BODY></HTML>");
  }
}
```

Figure 2–4   Result of the `HelloWWW3` servlet.

2.6 The Servlet Life Cycle

Earlier in this book, I vaguely referred to the fact that only a single instance of a servlet gets created, with each user request resulting in a new thread that is handed off to `doGet` or `doPost` as appropriate. I'll now be more specific about how servlets are created and destroyed, and how and when the various methods are invoked. I'll give a quick summary here, then elaborate in the following subsections.

When the servlet is first created, its `init` method is invoked, so that is where you put one-time setup code. After this, each user request results in a thread that calls the `service` method of the previously created instance. Multiple concurrent requests normally result in multiple threads calling `service` simultaneously, although your servlet can implement a special interface that stipulates that only a single thread is permitted to run at any one time. The `service` method then calls `doGet`, `doPost`, or another `doXxx` method, depending on the type of HTTP request it received. Finally, when the server decides to unload a servlet, it first calls the servlet's `destroy` method.

The init Method

The `init` method is called when the servlet is first created and is *not* called again for each user request. So, it is used for one-time initializations, just as with the `init` method of applets. The servlet can be created when a user first invokes a URL corresponding to the servlet or when the server is first started, depending on how you have registered the servlet with the Web server. It will be created for the first user request if it is not explicitly registered but is instead just placed in one of the standard server directories. See the discussion of Section 2.2 (A Simple Servlet Generating Plain Text) for details on these directories.

There are two versions of `init`: one that takes no arguments and one that takes a `ServletConfig` object as an argument. The first version is used when the servlet does not need to read any settings that vary from server to server. The method definition looks like this:

```
public void init() throws ServletException {
  // Initialization code...
}
```

For examples of this type of initialization, see Section 2.8 (An Example Using Servlet Initialization and Page Modification Dates) later in this chapter. Section 18.8 (Connection Pooling: A Case Study) in the chapter on JDBC gives a more advanced application where `init` is used to preallocate multiple database connections.

The second version of `init` is used when the servlet needs to read server-specific settings before it can complete the initialization. For example, the servlet might need to know about database settings, password files, server-specific performance parameters, hit count files, or serialized cookie data from previous requests. The second version of `init` looks like this:

```
public void init(ServletConfig config)
    throws ServletException {
  super.init(config);
  // Initialization code...
}
```

Notice two things about this code. First, the `init` method takes a `Servlet-Config` as an argument. `ServletConfig` has a `getInitParameter` method with which you can look up initialization parameters associated with the servlet. Just as with the `getParameter` method used in the `init` method of applets, both the input (the parameter name) and the output (the parameter value) are strings. For a simple example of the use of initialization parameters, see Section 2.7 (An Example Using Initialization Parameters); for a more complex example, see Section 4.5 (Restricting Access to Web Pages) where the location of a password file is given through the use of `getInitParameter`. Note that although you *look up* parameters in a portable manner, you *set* them in a server-specific way. For example, with Tomcat, you embed servlet properties in a file called `web.xml`, with the JSWDK you use `servlets.properties`, with the WebLogic application server you use `weblogic.properties`, and with the Java Web Server you set the properties interactively via the administration console. For examples of these settings, see Section 2.7 (An Example Using Initialization Parameters).

The second thing to note about the second version of init is that the first line of the method body is a call to super.init. This call is critical! The ServletConfig object is used elsewhere in the servlet, and the init method of the superclass registers it where the servlet can find it later. So, you can cause yourself huge headaches later if you omit the super.init call.

Core Approach

If you write an init *method that takes a* ServletConfig *as an argument,* **always** *call* super.init *on the first line.*

The service Method

Each time the server receives a request for a servlet, the server spawns a new thread and calls service. The service method checks the HTTP request type (GET, POST, PUT, DELETE, etc.) and calls doGet, doPost, doPut, doDelete, etc., as appropriate. Now, if you have a servlet that needs to handle both POST and GET requests identically, you may be tempted to override service directly as below, rather than implementing both doGet and doPost.

```
public void service(HttpServletRequest request,
                    HttpServletResponse response)
  throws ServletException, IOException {
// Servlet Code
}
```

This is not a good idea. Instead, just have doPost call doGet (or vice versa), as below.

```
public void doGet(HttpServletRequest request,
                  HttpServletResponse response)
  throws ServletException, IOException {
// Servlet Code
}

public void doPost(HttpServletRequest request,
                   HttpServletResponse response)
  throws ServletException, IOException {
doGet(request, response);
}
```

Although this approach takes a couple of extra lines of code, it has five advantages over directly overriding service:

1. You can add support for other services later by adding `doPut`, `doTrace`, etc., perhaps in a subclass. Overriding `service` directly precludes this possibility.

2. You can add support for modification dates by adding a `get-LastModified` method. If you use `doGet`, the standard `service` method uses the `getLastModified` method to set `Last-Modi-fied` headers and to respond properly to conditional `GET` requests (those containing an `If-Modified-Since` header). See Section 2.8 (An Example Using Servlet Initialization and Page Modification Dates) for an example.

3. You get automatic support for `HEAD` requests. The system just returns whatever headers and status codes `doGet` sets, but omits the page body. `HEAD` is a useful request method for custom HTTP clients. For example, link validators that check a page for dead hypertext links often use `HEAD` instead of `GET` in order to reduce server load.

4. You get automatic support for `OPTIONS` requests. If a `doGet` method exists, the standard `service` method answers `OPTIONS` requests by returning an `Allow` header indicating that `GET`, `HEAD`, `OPTIONS`, and `TRACE` are supported.

5. You get automatic support for `TRACE` requests. `TRACE` is a request method used for client debugging: it just returns the HTTP request headers back to the client.

Core Tip

If your servlet needs to handle both `GET` *and* `POST` *identically, have your* `doPost` *method call* `doGet`, *or vice versa. Don't override* `service` *directly.*

The doGet, doPost, and doXxx Methods

These methods contain the real meat of your servlet. Ninety-nine percent of the time, you only care about `GET` and/or `POST` requests, so you override `doGet` and/or `doPost`. However, if you want to, you can also override `doDelete` for `DELETE` requests, `doPut` for `PUT`, `doOptions` for `OPTIONS`, and `doTrace` for `TRACE`. Recall, however, that you have automatic support for `OPTIONS` and `TRACE`, as described in the previous section on the `service` method. Note that there is no `doHead` method. That's because the system automatically uses the status line and header settings of `doGet` to answer `HEAD` requests.

The Single ThreadModel Interface

Normally, the system makes a single instance of your servlet and then creates a new thread for each user request, with multiple simultaneous threads running if a new request comes in while a previous request is still executing. This means that your `doGet` and `doPost` methods must be careful to synchronize access to fields and other shared data, since multiple threads may be trying to access the data simultaneously. See Section 7.3 (Persistent Servlet State and Auto-Reloading Pages) for more discussion of this. If you want to prevent this multithreaded access, you can have your servlet implement the `SingleThreadModel` interface, as below.

```
public class YourServlet extends HttpServlet
                     implements SingleThreadModel {
   ...
}
```

If you implement this interface, the system guarantees that there is never more than one request thread accessing a single instance of your servlet. It does so either by queuing up all the requests and passing them one at a time to a single servlet instance, or by creating a pool of multiple instances, each of which handles one request at a time. This means that you don't have to worry about simultaneous access to regular fields (instance variables) of the servlet. You *do*, however, still have to synchronize access to class variables (`static` fields) or shared data stored outside the servlet.

Synchronous access to your servlets can significantly hurt performance (latency) if your servlet is accessed extremely frequently. So think twice before using the `SingleThreadModel` approach.

The destroy Method

The server may decide to remove a previously loaded servlet instance, perhaps because it is explicitly asked to do so by the server administrator, or perhaps because the servlet is idle for a long time. Before it does, however, it calls the servlet's `destroy` method. This method gives your servlet a chance to close database connections, halt background threads, write cookie lists or hit counts to disk, and perform other such cleanup activities. Be aware, however, that it is possible for the Web server to crash. After all, not all Web servers are written in reliable programming languages like Java; some are written in languages (such as ones named after letters of the alphabet) where it is easy to read or write off the ends of arrays, make illegal typecasts, or have dangling pointers due to memory reclamation errors. Besides, even Java technology won't prevent someone from tripping over the power cable running to the computer. So, don't count on `destroy` as the only mechanism for saving state to disk. Activities like hit counting or accumulating lists of cookie values that indicate special access should also proactively write their state to disk periodically.

2.7 An Example Using Initialization Parameters

Listing 2.8 shows a servlet that reads the `message` and `repeats` initialization parameters when initialized. Figure 2–5 shows the result when `message` is `Shibboleth`, `repeats` is `5`, and the servlet is registered under the name `ShowMsg`. Remember that, although servlets *read* init parameters in a standard way, developers *set* init parameters in a server-specific manner. Please refer to your server documentation for authoritative details. Listing 2.9 shows the configuration file used with Tomcat to obtain the result of Figure 2–5, Listing 2.10 shows the configuration file used with the JSWDK, and Figures 2–6 and 2–7 show how to set the parameters interactively with the Java Web Server. The result is identical to Figure 2–5 in all three cases.

Because the process of setting init parameters is server-specific, it is a good idea to minimize the number of separate initialization entries that have to be specified. This will limit the work you need to do when moving servlets that use init parameters from one server to another. If you need to read a large amount of data, I recommend that the init parameter itself merely give the location of a parameter file, and that the real data go in that file. An example of this approach is given in Section 4.5 (Restricting Access to Web Pages), where the initialization parameter specifies nothing more than the location of the password file.

Core Approach

For complex initializations, store the data in a separate file and use the init parameters to give the location of that file.

Listing 2.8   ShowMessage.java

```java
package coreservlets;

import java.io.*;
import javax.servlet.*;
import javax.servlet.http.*;

/** Example using servlet initialization. Here, the message
 *  to print and the number of times the message should be
 *  repeated is taken from the init parameters.
 */

public class ShowMessage extends HttpServlet {
  private String message;
  private String defaultMessage = "No message.";
  private int repeats = 1;

  public void init(ServletConfig config)
      throws ServletException {
    // Always call super.init
    super.init(config);
    message = config.getInitParameter("message");
    if (message == null) {
      message = defaultMessage;
    }
    try {
      String repeatString = config.getInitParameter("repeats");
      repeats = Integer.parseInt(repeatString);
    } catch(NumberFormatException nfe) {
      // NumberFormatException handles case where repeatString
      // is null *and* case where it is something in an
      // illegal format. Either way, do nothing in catch,
      // as the previous value (1) for the repeats field will
      // remain valid because the Integer.parseInt throws
      // the exception *before* the value gets assigned
      // to repeats.
    }
  }

  public void doGet(HttpServletRequest request,
                    HttpServletResponse response)
      throws ServletException, IOException {
    response.setContentType("text/html");
    PrintWriter out = response.getWriter();
    String title = "The ShowMessage Servlet";
    out.println(ServletUtilities.headWithTitle(title) +
                "<BODY BGCOLOR=\"#FDF5E6\">\n" +
                "<H1 ALIGN=CENTER>" + title + "</H1>");
```

Listing 2.8   ShowMessage.java (continued)

```
    for(int i=0; i<repeats; i++) {
      out.println(message + "<BR>");
    }
    out.println("</BODY></HTML>");
  }
}
```

Figure 2–5   The ShowMessage servlet with server-specific initialization parameters.

Listing 2.9 shows the setup file used to supply initialization parameters to servlets used with Tomcat 3.0. The idea is that you first associate a name with the servlet class file, then associate initialization parameters with that name (not with the actual class file). The setup file is located in *install_dir*/webpages/WEB-INF. Rather than recreating a similar version by hand, you might want to download this file from http://www.core-servlets.com/, modify it, and copy it to *install_dir*/webpages/WEB-INF.

Listing 2.10 shows the properties file used to supply initialization parameters to servlets in the JSWDK. As with Tomcat, you first associate a name with the servlet class, then associate the initialization parameters with the name. The properties file is located in *install_dir*/webpages/WEB-INF.

Listing 2.9   web.xml (for Tomcat)

```xml
<?xml version="1.0" encoding="ISO-8859-1"?>

<!DOCTYPE web-app
    PUBLIC "-//Sun Microsystems, Inc.//DTD Web Application 2.2//EN"
    "http://java.sun.com/j2ee/dtds/web-app_2.2.dtd">

<web-app>
  <servlet>
    <servlet-name>
      ShowMsg
    </servlet-name>

    <servlet-class>
      coreservlets.ShowMessage
    </servlet-class>

    <init-param>
      <param-name>
        message
      </param-name>
      <param-value>
        Shibboleth
      </param-value>
    </init-param>

    <init-param>
      <param-name>
        repeats
      </param-name>
      <param-value>
        5
      </param-value>
    </init-param>
  </servlet>
</web-app>
```

Listing 2.10 `servlets.properties`

```
# servlets.properties used with the JSWDK

# Register servlet via servletName.code=servletClassFile
# You access it via http://host/examples/servlet/servletName
ShowMsg.code=coreservlets.ShowMessage

# Set init params via
#    servletName.initparams=param1=val1,param2=val2,...
ShowMsg.initparams=message=Shibboleth,repeats=5

# Standard setting
jsp.code=com.sun.jsp.runtime.JspServlet

# Set this to keep servlet source code built from JSP
jsp.initparams=keepgenerated=true
```

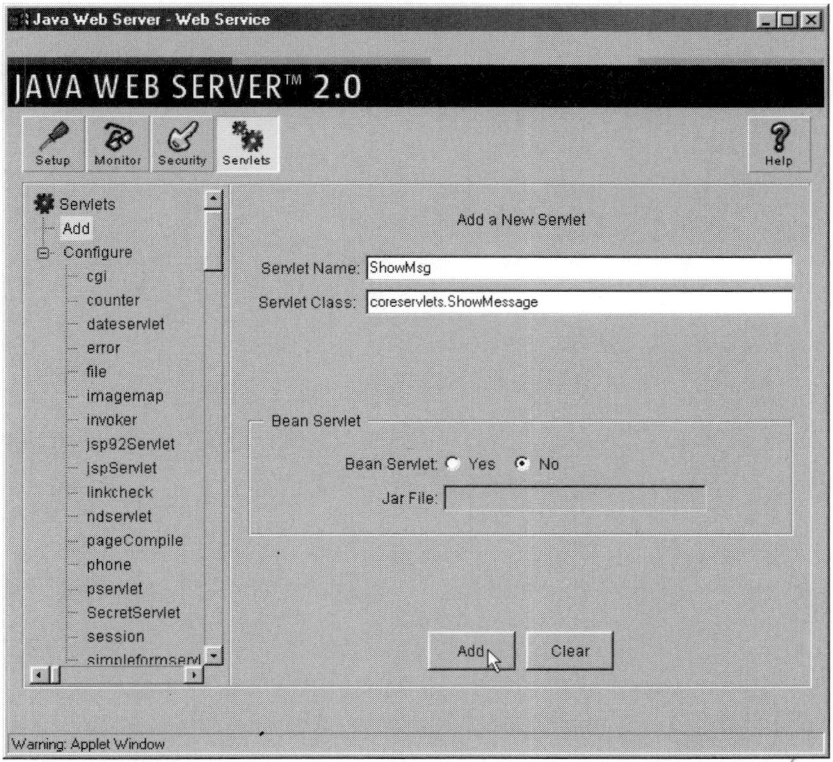

Figure 2-6 Registering a name for a servlet with the Java Web Server. Servlets that use initialization parameters must first be registered this way.

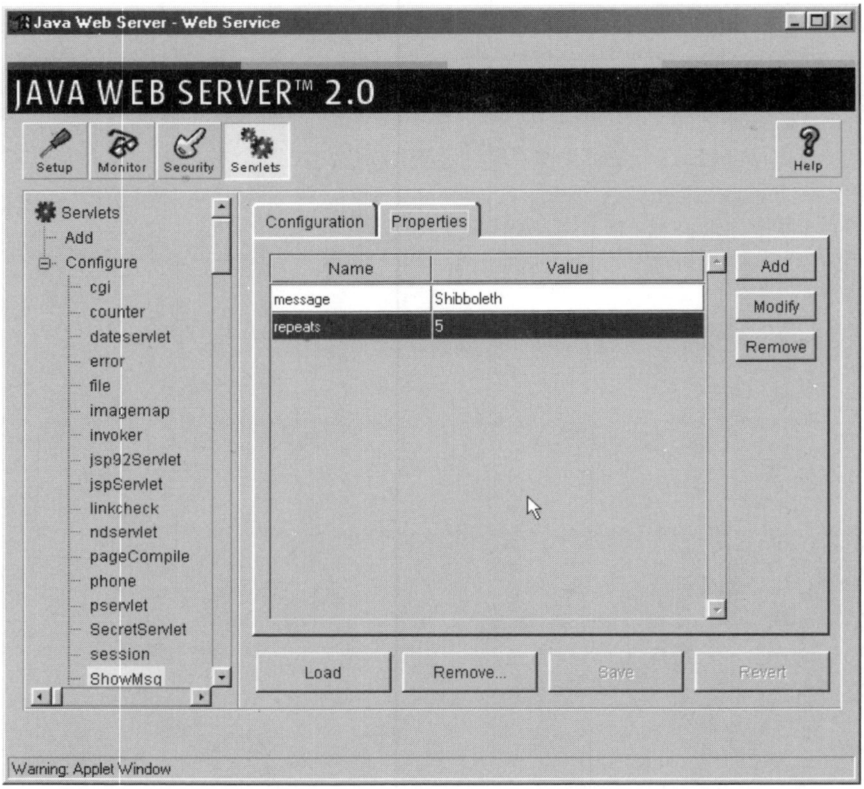

Figure 2–7   Specifying initialization parameters for a named servlet with the Java Web Server.

2.8   An Example Using Servlet Initialization and Page Modification Dates

Listing 2.11 shows a servlet that uses `init` to do two things. First, it builds an array of 10 integers. Since these numbers are based upon complex calculations, I don't want to repeat the computation for each request. So I have `doGet` look up the values that `init` computed instead of generating them each time. The results of this technique are shown in Figure 2–8.

However, since all users get the same result, `init` also stores a page modification date that is used by the `getLastModified` method. This method should return a modification time expressed in milliseconds since 1970, as is standard

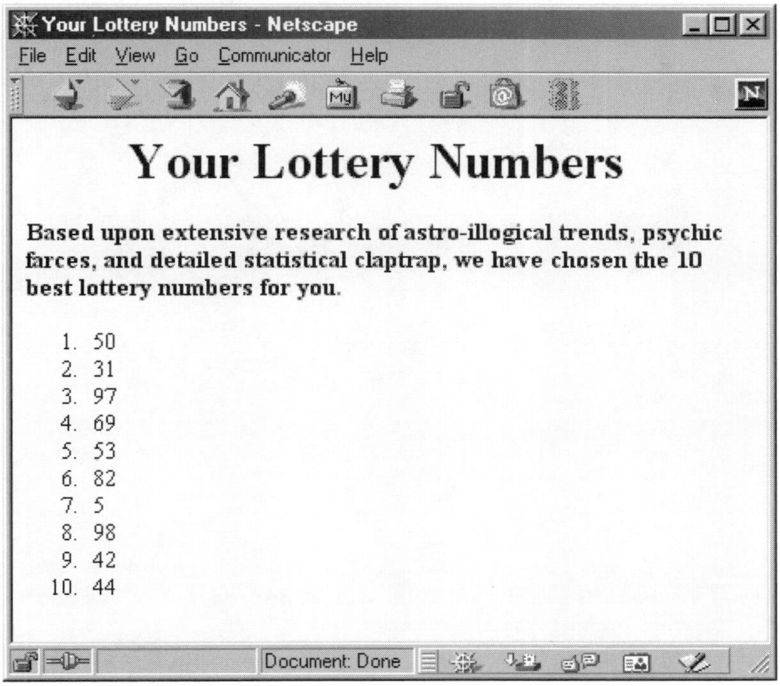

Figure 2-8   Output of `LotteryNumbers` servlet.

with Java dates. The time is automatically converted to a date in GMT appropriate for the `Last-Modified` header. More importantly, if the server receives a conditional GET request (one specifying that the client only wants pages marked `If-Modified-Since` a particular date), the system compares the specified date to that returned by `getLastModified`, only returning the page if it has been changed after the specified date. Browsers frequently make these conditional requests for pages stored in their caches, so supporting conditional requests helps your users as well as reducing server load. Since the `Last-Modified` and `If-Modified-Since` headers use only whole seconds, the `getLastModified` method should round times down to the nearest second.

Figures 2–9 and 2–10 show the result of requests for the same servlet with two slightly different `If-Modified-Since` dates. To set the request headers and see the response headers, I used `WebClient`, a Java application shown in Section 2.10 (WebClient: Talking to Web Servers Interactively) that lets you interactively set up HTTP requests, submit them, and see the results.

Listing 2.11 `LotteryNumbers.java`

```
package coreservlets;

import java.io.*;
import javax.servlet.*;
import javax.servlet.http.*;

/** Example using servlet initialization and the
 *  getLastModified method.
 */

public class LotteryNumbers extends HttpServlet {
  private long modTime;
  private int[] numbers = new int[10];

  /** The init method is called only when the servlet
   *  is first loaded, before the first request
   *  is processed.
   */

  public void init() throws ServletException {
    // Round to nearest second (ie 1000 milliseconds)
    modTime = System.currentTimeMillis()/1000*1000;
    for(int i=0; i<numbers.length; i++) {
      numbers[i] = randomNum();
    }
  }

  public void doGet(HttpServletRequest request,
                    HttpServletResponse response)
      throws ServletException, IOException {
    response.setContentType("text/html");
    PrintWriter out = response.getWriter();
    String title = "Your Lottery Numbers";
    out.println(ServletUtilities.headWithTitle(title) +
                "<BODY BGCOLOR=\"#FDF5E6\">\n" +
                "<H1 ALIGN=CENTER>" + title + "</H1>\n" +
```

Listing 2.11 `LotteryNumbers.java` (continued)

```
            "<B>Based upon extensive research of " +
            "astro-illogical trends, psychic farces, " +
            "and detailed statistical claptrap, " +
            "we have chosen the " + numbers.length +
            " best lottery numbers for you.</B>" +
            "<OL>");
  for(int i=0; i<numbers.length; i++) {
    out.println("  <LI>" + numbers[i]);
  }
  out.println("</OL>" +
            "</BODY></HTML>");
}

/** The standard service method compares this date
 *  against any date specified in the If-Modified-Since
 *  request header. If the getLastModified date is
 *  later, or if there is no If-Modified-Since header,
 *  the doGet method is called normally. But if the
 *  getLastModified date is the same or earlier,
 *  the service method sends back a 304 (Not Modified)
 *  response, and does <B>not</B> call doGet.
 *  The browser should use its cached version of
 *  the page in such a case.
 */

public long getLastModified(HttpServletRequest request) {
  return(modTime);
}

// A random int from 0 to 99.

private int randomNum() {
  return((int)(Math.random() * 100));
}
}
```

```
┌─ Web Client ─────────────────────────────────────── _ □ ✕ ┐
│                                                             │
│   Host:  localhost                                          │
│                                                             │
│   Port:  80                                                 │
│                                                             │
│   Request Line:  GET /servlet/coreservlets.LotteryNumbers HTTP/1.0  │
│                                                             │
│ Request Headers:                                            │
│ ┌─────────────────────────────────────────────────────┐ ▲ │
│ │ If-Modified-Since: Thu, 23 Dec 1999 15:56:05 GMT      │   │
│ │                                                       │   │
│ │                                                       │   │
│ │                                                       │ ▼ │
│ └─────────────────────────────────────────────────────┘   │
│  ◄                                                      ►   │
│                                                             │
│                    ┌─ Submit Request ─┐                     │
│                    └──────────────────┘                     │
│                                                             │
│                        Results                              │
│ ┌─────────────────────────────────────────────────────┐ ▲ │
│ │ HTTP/1.1 200 OK                                       │   │
│ │ Server: JavaWebServer/2.0                             │   │
│ │ Last-Modified: Thu, 23 Dec 1999 15:58:05 GMT          │   │
│ │ Content-Type: text/html                               │   │
│ │ Connection: close                                     │   │
│ │ Date: Thu, 23 Dec 1999 16:06:35 GMT                   │   │
│ │                                                       │   │
│ │ <!DOCTYPE HTML PUBLIC "-//W3C//DTD HTML 4.0 Transitional//EN"> │   │
│ │ <HTML>                                                │ ▼ │
│ └─────────────────────────────────────────────────────┘   │
│  ◄                                                      ►   │
│                  ┌─ Interrupt Download ─┐                   │
│                  └──────────────────────┘                   │
└─────────────────────────────────────────────────────────────┘
```

Figure 2–9 Accessing the `LotteryNumbers` servlet with an unconditional `GET` request or with a conditional request specifying a date before servlet initialization results in the normal Web page.

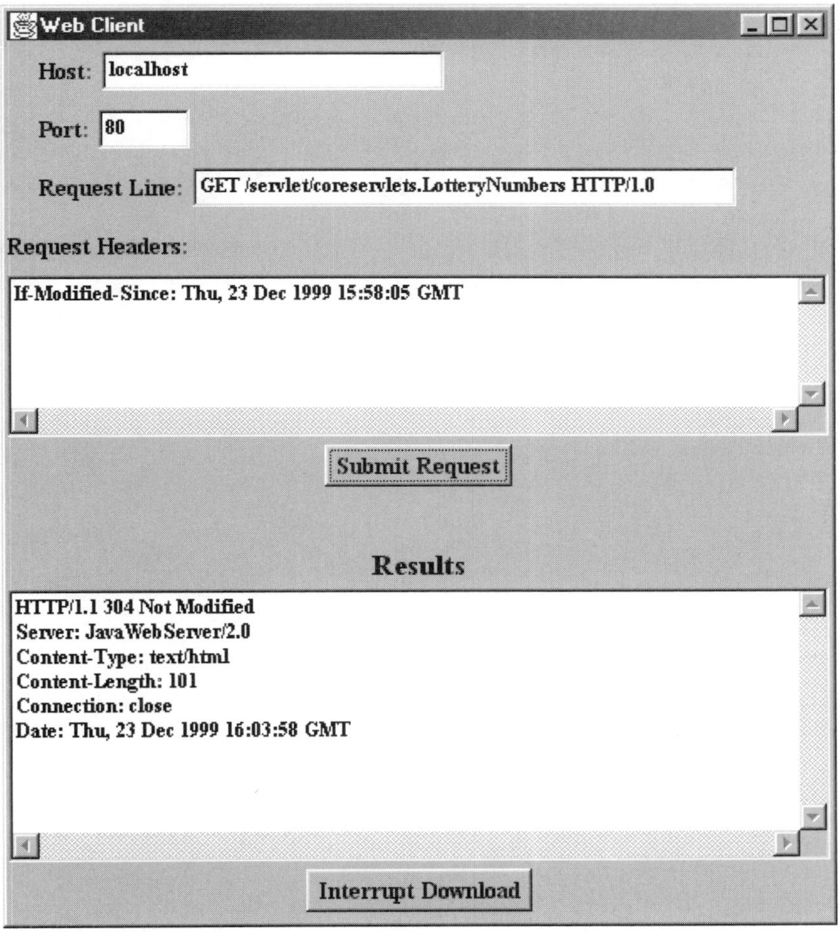

Figure 2–10 Accessing the LotteryNumbers servlet with a conditional GET request specifying a date at or after servlet initialization results in a 304 (Not Modified) response.

2.9 Debugging Servlets

Naturally, when *you* write servlets, you never make mistakes. However, some of your colleagues might make an occasional error, and you can pass this advice on to them. Seriously, though, debugging servlets can be tricky because you don't execute them directly. Instead, you trigger their execution by means of an HTTP request, and they are executed by the Web server. This remote execution makes it difficult to insert break points or to read debugging messages and stack traces. So, approaches to servlet debugging differ somewhat from those used in general development. Here are seven general strategies that can make your life easier.

1. **Look at the HTML source.**
   If the result you see in the browser looks funny, choose "View Source" from the browser's menu. Sometimes a small HTML error like <TABLE> instead of </TABLE> can prevent much of the page from being viewed. Even better, use a formal HTML validator on the servlet's output. See Section 2.5 (Simple HTML-Building Utilities) for a discussion of this approach.

2. **Return error pages to the client.**
   Sometimes certain classes of errors can be anticipated by the servlet. In these cases, the servlet should build descriptive information about the problem and return it to the client in a regular page or by means of the sendError method of HttpServletResponse. See Chapter 6 (Generating the Server Response: HTTP Status Codes) for details on sendError. For example, you should plan for cases when the client forgets some of the required form data and send an error page detailing what was missing. Error pages are not always possible, however. Sometimes something unexpected goes wrong with your servlet, and it simply crashes. The remaining approaches help you in those situations.

3. **Start the server from the command line.**
   Most Web servers execute from a background process, and this process is often automatically started when the system is booted. If you are having trouble with your servlet, you should consider shutting down the server and restarting it from the command line. After this, System.out.println or System.err.println calls can be easily read from the window in which the server was started. When something goes wrong with

your servlet, your first task is to discover *exactly* how far the servlet got before it failed and to gather some information about the key data structures during the time period just before it failed. Simple `println` statements are surprisingly effective for this purpose. If you are running your servlets on a server that you cannot easily halt and restart, then do your debugging with the JSWDK, Tomcat, or the Java Web Server on your personal machine, and save deployment to the real server for later.

4. **Use the log file.**
   The `HttpServlet` class has a method called `log` that lets you write information into a logging file on the server. Reading debugging messages from the log file is a bit less convenient than watching them directly from a window as with the previous approach, but using the log file does not require stopping and restarting the server. There are two variations of this method: one that takes a `String`, and the other that takes a `String` and a `Throwable` (an ancestor class of `Exception`). The exact location of the log file is server-specific, but it is generally clearly documented or can be found in subdirectories of the server installation directory.

5. **Look at the request data separately.**
   Servlets read data from the HTTP request, construct a response, and send it back to the client. If something in the process goes wrong, you want to discover if it is because the client is sending the wrong data or because the servlet is processing it incorrectly. The `EchoServer` class, shown in Section 16.12 (A Debugging Web Server), lets you submit HTML forms and get a result that shows you *exactly* how the data arrived at the server.

6. **Look at the response data separately.**
   Once you look at the request data separately, you'll want to do the same for the response data. The `WebClient` class, presented next in Section 2.10 (WebClient: Talking to Web Servers Interactively), permits you to connect to the server interactively, send custom HTTP request data, and see everything that comes back, HTTP response headers and all.

7. **Stop and restart the server.**
   Most full-blown Web servers that support servlets have a designated location for servlets that are under development. Servlets in this location (e.g., the `servlets` directory for the Java Web Server) are supposed to be automatically reloaded when their associated class file changes. At times, however, some servers can

get confused, especially when your only change is to a lower-level class, not to the top-level servlet class. So, if it appears that changes you make to your servlets are not reflected in the servlet's behavior, try restarting the server. With the JSWDK and Tomcat, you have to do this *every* time you make a change, since these mini-servers have no support for automatic servlet reloading.

2.10 WebClient: Talking to Web Servers Interactively

This section presents the source code for the WebClient program discussed in Section 2.9 (Debugging Servlets) and used in Section 2.8 (An Example Using Servlet Initialization and Page Modification Dates) and extensively throughout Chapter 16 (Using HTML Forms). As always, the source code can be downloaded from the on-line archive at http://www.coreservlets.com/, and there are no restrictions on its use.

WebClient

This class is the top-level program that you would use. Start it from the command line, then customize the HTTP request line and request headers, then press "Submit Request."

Listing 2.12 WebClient.java

```
import java.awt.*;
import java.awt.event.*;
import java.util.*;

/**
 *  A graphical client that lets you interactively connect to
 *  Web servers and send custom request lines and
 *  request headers.
 */

public class WebClient extends CloseableFrame
    implements Runnable, Interruptible, ActionListener {
  public static void main(String[] args) {
    new WebClient("Web Client");
  }
```

Listing 2.12 WebClient.java (continued)

```java
private LabeledTextField hostField, portField,
        requestLineField;
private TextArea requestHeadersArea, resultArea;
private String host, requestLine;
private int port;
private String[] requestHeaders = new String[30];
private Button submitButton, interruptButton;
private boolean isInterrupted = false;

public WebClient(String title) {
  super(title);
  setBackground(Color.lightGray);
  setLayout(new BorderLayout(5, 30));
  int fontSize = 14;
  Font labelFont =
    new Font("Serif", Font.BOLD, fontSize);
  Font headingFont =
    new Font("SansSerif", Font.BOLD, fontSize+4);
  Font textFont =
    new Font("Monospaced", Font.BOLD, fontSize-2);
  Panel inputPanel = new Panel();
  inputPanel.setLayout(new BorderLayout());
  Panel labelPanel = new Panel();
  labelPanel.setLayout(new GridLayout(4,1));
  hostField = new LabeledTextField("Host:", labelFont,
                                   30, textFont);
  portField = new LabeledTextField("Port:", labelFont,
                                   "80", 5, textFont);
  // Use HTTP 1.0 for compatibility with the most servers.
  // If you switch this to 1.1, you *must* supply a
  // Host: request header.
  requestLineField =
    new LabeledTextField("Request Line:", labelFont,
                         "GET / HTTP/1.0", 50, textFont);
  labelPanel.add(hostField);
  labelPanel.add(portField);
  labelPanel.add(requestLineField);
  Label requestHeadersLabel =
    new Label("Request Headers:");
  requestHeadersLabel.setFont(labelFont);
  labelPanel.add(requestHeadersLabel);
  inputPanel.add(labelPanel, BorderLayout.NORTH);
  requestHeadersArea = new TextArea(5, 80);
  requestHeadersArea.setFont(textFont);
  inputPanel.add(requestHeadersArea, BorderLayout.CENTER);
  Panel buttonPanel = new Panel();
  submitButton = new Button("Submit Request");
  submitButton.addActionListener(this);
  submitButton.setFont(labelFont);
  buttonPanel.add(submitButton);
```

Listing 2.12 `WebClient.java` (continued)

```
    inputPanel.add(buttonPanel, BorderLayout.SOUTH);
    add(inputPanel, BorderLayout.NORTH);
    Panel resultPanel = new Panel();
    resultPanel.setLayout(new BorderLayout());
    Label resultLabel =
      new Label("Results", Label.CENTER);
    resultLabel.setFont(headingFont);
    resultPanel.add(resultLabel, BorderLayout.NORTH);
    resultArea = new TextArea();
    resultArea.setFont(textFont);
    resultPanel.add(resultArea, BorderLayout.CENTER);
    Panel interruptPanel = new Panel();
    interruptButton = new Button("Interrupt Download");
    interruptButton.addActionListener(this);
    interruptButton.setFont(labelFont);
    interruptPanel.add(interruptButton);
    resultPanel.add(interruptPanel, BorderLayout.SOUTH);
    add(resultPanel, BorderLayout.CENTER);
    setSize(600, 700);
    setVisible(true);
  }

  public void actionPerformed(ActionEvent event) {
    if (event.getSource() == submitButton) {
      Thread downloader = new Thread(this);
      downloader.start();
    } else if (event.getSource() == interruptButton) {
      isInterrupted = true;
    }
  }

  public void run() {
    isInterrupted = false;
    if (hasLegalArgs())
      new HttpClient(host, port, requestLine,
              requestHeaders, resultArea, this);
  }

  public boolean isInterrupted() {
    return(isInterrupted);
  }

  private boolean hasLegalArgs() {
    host = hostField.getTextField().getText();
    if (host.length() == 0) {
      report("Missing hostname");
      return(false);
    }
```

Listing 2.12 `WebClient.java` (continued)

```
    String portString =
      portField.getTextField().getText();
    if (portString.length() == 0) {
      report("Missing port number");
      return(false);
    }
    try {
      port = Integer.parseInt(portString);
    } catch(NumberFormatException nfe) {
      report("Illegal port number: " + portString);
      return(false);
    }
    requestLine =
      requestLineField.getTextField().getText();
    if (requestLine.length() == 0) {
      report("Missing request line");
      return(false);
    }
    getRequestHeaders();
    return(true);
  }

  private void report(String s) {
    resultArea.setText(s);
  }

  private void getRequestHeaders() {
    for(int i=0; i<requestHeaders.length; i++)
      requestHeaders[i] = null;
    int headerNum = 0;
    String header =
      requestHeadersArea.getText();
    StringTokenizer tok =
      new StringTokenizer(header, "\r\n");
    while (tok.hasMoreTokens())
      requestHeaders[headerNum++] = tok.nextToken();
  }
}
```

HttpClient

The `HttpClient` class does the real network communication. It simply sends
the designated request line and request headers to the Web server, then
reads the lines that come back one at a time, placing them into a `TextArea`
until either the server closes the connection or the `HttpClient` is interrupted
by means of the `isInterrupted` flag.

Listing 2.13 `HttpClient.java`

```java
import java.awt.*;
import java.net.*;
import java.io.*;

/**
 *  The underlying network client used by WebClient.
 */

public class HttpClient extends NetworkClient {
  private String requestLine;
  private String[] requestHeaders;
  private TextArea outputArea;
  private Interruptible app;

  public HttpClient(String host, int port,
                    String requestLine, String[] requestHeaders,
                    TextArea outputArea, Interruptible app) {
    super(host, port);
    this.requestLine = requestLine;
    this.requestHeaders = requestHeaders;
    this.outputArea = outputArea;
    this.app = app;
    if (checkHost(host))
      connect();
  }

  protected void handleConnection(Socket uriSocket)
      throws IOException {
    try {
      PrintWriter out = SocketUtil.getWriter(uriSocket);
      BufferedReader in = SocketUtil.getReader(uriSocket);
      outputArea.setText("");
      out.println(requestLine);
      for(int i=0; i<requestHeaders.length; i++) {
        if (requestHeaders[i] == null)
          break;
        else
          out.println(requestHeaders[i]);
      }
      out.println();
      String line;
      while ((line = in.readLine()) != null &&
             !app.isInterrupted())
        outputArea.append(line + "\n");
      if (app.isInterrupted())
        outputArea.append("---- Download Interrupted ----");
    } catch(Exception e) {
      outputArea.setText("Error: " + e);
    }
  }
}
```

Listing 2.13 `HttpClient.java` **(continued)**

```
  private boolean checkHost(String host) {
    try {
      InetAddress.getByName(host);
      return(true);
    } catch(UnknownHostException uhe) {
      outputArea.setText("Bogus host: " + host);
      return(false);
    }
  }
}
```

NetworkClient

The `NetworkClient` class is a generic starting point for network clients and is extended by `HttpClient`.

Listing 2.14 `NetworkClient.java`

```
import java.net.*;
import java.io.*;

/** A starting point for network clients. You'll need to
 *  override handleConnection, but in many cases
 *  connect can remain unchanged. It uses
 *  SocketUtil to simplify the creation of the
 *  PrintWriter and BufferedReader.
 *
 *  @see SocketUtil
 */

public class NetworkClient {
  protected String host;
  protected int port;

  /** Register host and port. The connection won't
   *  actually be established until you call
   *  connect.
   *
   *  @see #connect
   */

  public NetworkClient(String host, int port) {
    this.host = host;
    this.port = port;
  }
```

Listing 2.14 `NetworkClient.java` (continued)

```java
/** Establishes the connection, then passes the socket
 *  to handleConnection.
 *
 *  @see #handleConnection
 */

public void connect() {
  try {
    Socket client = new Socket(host, port);
    handleConnection(client);
  } catch(UnknownHostException uhe) {
    System.out.println("Unknown host: " + host);
    uhe.printStackTrace();
  } catch(IOException ioe) {
    System.out.println("IOException: " + ioe);
    ioe.printStackTrace();
  }
}

/** This is the method you will override when
 *  making a network client for your task.
 *  The default version sends a single line
 *  ("Generic Network Client") to the server,
 *  reads one line of response, prints it, then exits.
 */

protected void handleConnection(Socket client)
    throws IOException {
  PrintWriter out =
    SocketUtil.getWriter(client);
  BufferedReader in =
    SocketUtil.getReader(client);
  out.println("Generic Network Client");
  System.out.println
    ("Generic Network Client:\n" +
     "Made connection to " + host +
     " and got '" + in.readLine() + "' in response");
  client.close();
}

/** The hostname of the server we're contacting. */

public String getHost() {
  return(host);
}

/** The port connection will be made on. */

public int getPort() {
  return(port);
}
}
```

SocketUtil

SocketUtil is a simple utility class that simplifies creating some of the streams used in network programming. It is used by NetworkClient and HttpClient.

Listing 2.15 SocketUtil.java

```java
import java.net.*;
import java.io.*;

/** A shorthand way to create BufferedReaders and
 *  PrintWriters associated with a Socket.
 */

public class SocketUtil {
  /** Make a BufferedReader to get incoming data. */

  public static BufferedReader getReader(Socket s)
      throws IOException {
    return(new BufferedReader(
          new InputStreamReader(s.getInputStream())));
  }

  /** Make a PrintWriter to send outgoing data.
   *  This PrintWriter will automatically flush stream
   *  when println is called.
   */

  public static PrintWriter getWriter(Socket s)
      throws IOException {
    // 2nd argument of true means autoflush
    return(new PrintWriter(s.getOutputStream(), true));
  }
}
```

CloseableFrame

CloseableFrame is an extension of the standard Frame class, with the addition that user requests to quit the frame are honored. This is the top-level window on which WebClient is built.

Listing 2.16 CloseableFrame.java

```java
import java.awt.*;
import java.awt.event.*;

/** A Frame that you can actually quit. Used as
 *  the starting point for most Java 1.1 graphical
 *  applications.
 */

public class CloseableFrame extends Frame {
  public CloseableFrame(String title) {
    super(title);
    enableEvents(AWTEvent.WINDOW_EVENT_MASK);
  }

  /** Since we are doing something permanent, we need
   *  to call super.processWindowEvent <B>first</B>.
   */

  public void processWindowEvent(WindowEvent event) {
    super.processWindowEvent(event); // Handle listeners
    if (event.getID() == WindowEvent.WINDOW_CLOSING)
      System.exit(0);
  }
}
```

LabeledTextField

The LabeledTextField class is a simple combination of a TextField and a Label and is used in WebClient.

Listing 2.17 LabeledTextField.java

```java
import java.awt.*;

/** A TextField with an associated Label.
 */

public class LabeledTextField extends Panel {
  private Label label;
  private TextField textField;

  public LabeledTextField(String labelString,
                          Font labelFont,
                          int textFieldSize,
                          Font textFont) {
    setLayout(new FlowLayout(FlowLayout.LEFT));
    label = new Label(labelString, Label.RIGHT);
    if (labelFont != null)
      label.setFont(labelFont);
    add(label);
    textField = new TextField(textFieldSize);
    if (textFont != null)
      textField.setFont(textFont);
    add(textField);
  }

  public LabeledTextField(String labelString,
                          String textFieldString) {
    this(labelString, null, textFieldString,
         textFieldString.length(), null);
  }

  public LabeledTextField(String labelString,
                          int textFieldSize) {
    this(labelString, null, textFieldSize, null);
  }

  public LabeledTextField(String labelString,
                          Font labelFont,
                          String textFieldString,
                          int textFieldSize,
                          Font textFont) {
    this(labelString, labelFont,
         textFieldSize, textFont);
    textField.setText(textFieldString);
  }
```

Listing 2.17 `LabeledTextField.java` (continued)

```
/** The Label at the left side of the LabeledTextField.
 *   To manipulate the Label, do:
 *   <PRE>
 *     LabeledTextField ltf = new LabeledTextField(...);
 *     ltf.getLabel().someLabelMethod(...);
 *   </PRE>
 *
 * @see #getTextField
 */

public Label getLabel() {
  return(label);
}

/** The TextField at the right side of the
 *   LabeledTextField.
 *
 * @see #getLabel
 */

public TextField getTextField() {
  return(textField);
}
}
```

Interruptible

Interruptible is a simple interface used to identify classes that have an isInterrupted method. It is used by HttpClient to poll WebClient to see if the user has interrupted it.

Listing 2.18 Interruptible.java

```
/**
 *  An interface for classes that can be polled to see
 *  if they've been interrupted. Used by HttpClient
 *  and WebClient to allow the user to interrupt a network
 *  download.
 */

public interface Interruptible {
  public boolean isInterrupted();
}
```

HANDLING THE CLIENT REQUEST: FORM DATA

Topics in This Chapter

- Using `getParameter` to read single values from prespecified parameters in the form data

- Using `getParameterValues` to read multiple values from prespecified parameters in the form data

- Using `getParameterNames` to discover what parameters are available

- Handling both GET and POST requests with a single servlet

- A servlet that makes a table of the input parameters

- An on-line resumé posting service

- Filtering HTML-specific characters

Chapter 3

One of the main motivations for building Web pages dynamically is so that the result can be based upon user input. This chapter shows you how to access that input.

3.1 The Role of Form Data

If you've ever used a search engine, visited an on-line bookstore, tracked stocks on the Web, or asked a Web-based site for quotes on plane tickets, you've probably seen funny-looking URLs like `http://host/path?user=Marty+Hall&origin=bwi&dest=lax`. The part after the question mark (i.e., `user=Marty+Hall&origin=bwi&dest=lax`) is known as *form data* (or *query data*) and is the most common way to get information from a Web page to a server-side program. Form data can be attached to the end of the URL after a question mark (as above), for GET requests, or sent to the server on a separate line, for POST requests. If you're not familiar with HTML forms, Chapter 16 (Using HTML Forms) gives details on how to build forms that collect and transmit data of this sort.

Extracting the needed information from this form data is traditionally one of the most tedious parts of CGI programming. First of all, you have to read the data one way for GET requests (in traditional CGI, this is usually through the QUERY_STRING environment variable) and a different way for POST requests (by reading the standard input in traditional CGI). Second, you have to chop the pairs at the ampersands, then separate the parameter names (left of the equal signs) from the parameter values (right of the equal signs). Third, you have to URL-decode the values. Alphanumeric characters are sent unchanged, but spaces are converted to plus signs and other characters are converted to %XX where XX is the ASCII (or ISO Latin-1) value of the character, in hex. Then, the server-side program has to reverse the process. For example, if someone enters a value of "~hall, ~gates, and ~mcnealy" into a textfield with the name users in an HTML form, the data is sent as "users=%7Ehall%2C+%7Egates%2C+and+%7Emcnealy", and the server-side program has to reconstitute the original string. Finally, the fourth reason that parsing form data is tedious is that values can be omitted (e.g., "param1=val1&**param2=**&param3=val3") or a parameter can have more than one value (e.g., "**param1=val1**&param2=val2&**param1=val3**"), so your parsing code needs special cases for these situations.

3.2 Reading Form Data from Servlets

One of the nice features of servlets is that all of this form parsing is handled automatically. You simply call the getParameter method of the HttpServletRequest, supplying the case-sensitive parameter name as an argument. You use getParameter exactly the same way when the data is sent by GET as you do when it is sent by POST. The servlet knows which request method was used and automatically does the right thing behind the scenes. The return value is a String corresponding to the URL-decoded value of the first occurrence of that parameter name. An empty String is returned if the parameter exists but has no value, and null is returned if there was no such parameter. If the parameter could potentially have more than one value, you should call getParameterValues (which returns an array of strings) instead of getParameter (which returns a single string). The return value of getParameterValues is null for nonexistent parameter names and is a one-element array when the parameter has only a single value.

Parameter names are case sensitive so, for example, request.getParameter("Param1") and request.getParameter("param1") are *not* interchangeable.

Core Warning

The values supplied to `getParameter` *and* `getParameterValues` *are case sensitive.*

Finally, although most real servlets look for a specific set of parameter names, for debugging purposes it is sometimes useful to get a full list. Use `getParameterNames` to get this list in the form of an `Enumeration`, each entry of which can be cast to a `String` and used in a `getParameter` or `getParameterValues` call. Just note that the `HttpServletRequest` API does not specify the order in which the names appear within that `Enumeration`.

Core Warning

Don't count on `getParameterNames` *returning the names in any particular order.*

3.3 Example: Reading Three Explicit Parameters

Listing 3.1 presents a simple servlet called `ThreeParams` that reads form data parameters named `param1`, `param2`, and `param3` and places their values in a bulleted list. Listing 3.2 shows an HTML form that collects user input and sends it to this servlet. By use of an ACTION of `/servlet/core-servlets.ThreeParams`, the form can be installed anywhere on the system running the servlet; there need not be any particular association between the directory containing the form and the servlet installation directory. Recall that the specific locations for installing HTML files vary from server to server. With the JSWDK 1.0.1 and Tomcat 3.0, HTML pages are placed somewhere in *install_dir*/webpages and are accessed via `http://host/path/file.html`. For example, if the form shown in Listing 3.2 is placed in *install_dir*/webpages/forms/ThreeParams-Form.html and the server is accessed from the same host that it is running on, the form would be accessed by a URL of `http://local-host/forms/ThreeParamsForm.html`.

Figures 3–1 and 3–2 show the result of the HTML front end and the servlet, respectively.

Listing 3.1   `ThreeParams.java`

```
package coreservlets;

import java.io.*;
import javax.servlet.*;
import javax.servlet.http.*;

public class ThreeParams extends HttpServlet {
  public void doGet(HttpServletRequest request,
                    HttpServletResponse response)
     throws ServletException, IOException {
    response.setContentType("text/html");
    PrintWriter out = response.getWriter();
    String title = "Reading Three Request Parameters";
    out.println(ServletUtilities.headWithTitle(title) +
               "<BODY BGCOLOR=\"#FDF5E6\">\n" +
               "<H1 ALIGN=CENTER>" + title + "</H1>\n" +
               "<UL>\n" +
               "  <LI><B>param1</B>: "
               + request.getParameter("param1") + "\n" +
               "  <LI><B>param2</B>: "
               + request.getParameter("param2") + "\n" +
               "  <LI><B>param3</B>: "
               + request.getParameter("param3") + "\n" +
               "</UL>\n" +
               "</BODY></HTML>");
  }
}
```

Although you are required to specify *response* settings (see Chapters 6 and 7) before beginning to generate the content, there is no requirement that you read the *request* parameters at any particular time.

If you're accustomed to the traditional CGI approach where you read POST data through the standard input, you should note that you can do the same thing with servlets by calling getReader or getInputStream on the HttpServletRequest and then using that stream to obtain the raw input. This is a bad idea for regular parameters since the input is neither parsed (separated into entries specific to each parameter) nor URL-decoded (translated so that plus signs become spaces and %XX gets replaced by the

ASCII or ISO Latin-1 character corresponding to the hex value *XX*). However, reading the raw input might be of use for uploaded files or POST data being sent by custom clients rather than by HTML forms. Note, however, that if you read the POST data in this manner, it might no longer be found by getParameter.

Listing 3.2   ThreeParamsForm.html

```
<!DOCTYPE HTML PUBLIC "-//W3C//DTD HTML 4.0 Transitional//EN">
<HTML>
<HEAD>
  <TITLE>Collecting Three Parameters</TITLE>
</HEAD>
<BODY BGCOLOR="#FDF5E6">
<H1 ALIGN="CENTER">Collecting Three Parameters</H1>

<FORM ACTION="/servlet/coreservlets.ThreeParams">
  First Parameter:  <INPUT TYPE="TEXT" NAME="param1"><BR>
  Second Parameter: <INPUT TYPE="TEXT" NAME="param2"><BR>
  Third Parameter:  <INPUT TYPE="TEXT" NAME="param3"><BR>
  <CENTER>
    <INPUT TYPE="SUBMIT">
  </CENTER>
</FORM>

</BODY>
</HTML>
```

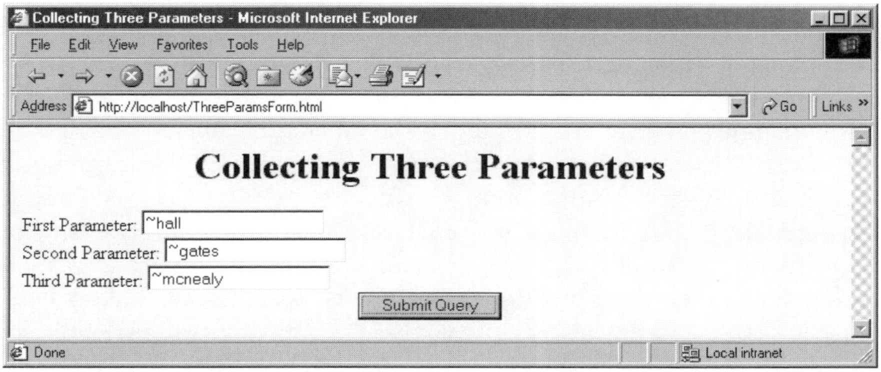

Figure 3–1   HTML front end resulting from ThreeParamsForm.html.

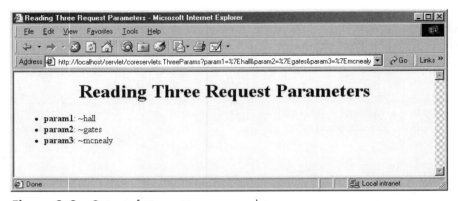

Figure 3–2   Output of `ThreeParams` servlet.

3.4 Example: Reading All Parameters

The previous example extracted parameter values from the form data based upon prespecified parameter names. It also assumed that each parameter had exactly one value. Here's an example that looks up *all* the parameter names that are sent and puts their values in a table. It highlights parameters that have missing values as well as ones that have multiple values.

First, the servlet looks up all the parameter names by the `getParameter-Names` method of `HttpServletRequest`. This method returns an `Enumeration` that contains the parameter names in an unspecified order. Next, the servlet loops down the `Enumeration` in the standard manner, using `has-MoreElements` to determine when to stop and using `nextElement` to get each entry. Since `nextElement` returns an `Object`, the servlet casts the result to a `String` and passes that to `getParameterValues`, yielding an array of strings. If that array is one entry long and contains only an empty string, then the parameter had no values and the servlet generates an italicized "No Value" entry. If the array is more than one entry long, then the parameter had multiple values and the values are displayed in a bulleted list. Otherwise, the one main value is placed into the table unmodified. The source code for the servlet is shown in Listing 3.3, while Listing 3.4 shows the HTML code for a front end that can be used to try the servlet out. Figures 3–3 and 3–4 show the result of the HTML front end and the servlet, respectively.

Notice that the servlet uses a doPost method that simply calls doGet. That's because I want it to be able to handle *both* GET and POST requests. This approach is a good standard practice if you want HTML interfaces to have some flexibility in how they send data to the servlet. See the discussion of the service method in Section 2.6 (The Servlet Life Cycle) for a discussion of why having doPost call doGet (or vice versa) is preferable to overriding service directly. The HTML form from Listing 3.4 uses POST, as should *all* forms that have password fields (if you don't know why, see Chapter 16). However, the ShowParameters servlet is not specific to that particular front end, so the source code archive site at www.coreserv-lets.com includes a similar HTML form that uses GET for you to experiment with.

Listing 3.3 ShowParameters.java

```
package coreservlets;

import java.io.*;
import javax.servlet.*;
import javax.servlet.http.*;
import java.util.*;

public class ShowParameters extends HttpServlet {
  public void doGet(HttpServletRequest request,
                    HttpServletResponse response)
      throws ServletException, IOException {
    response.setContentType("text/html");
    PrintWriter out = response.getWriter();
    String title = "Reading All Request Parameters";
    out.println(ServletUtilities.headWithTitle(title) +
                "<BODY BGCOLOR=\"#FDF5E6\">\n" +
                "<H1 ALIGN=CENTER>" + title + "</H1>\n" +
                "<TABLE BORDER=1 ALIGN=CENTER>\n" +
                "<TR BGCOLOR=\"#FFAD00\">\n" +
                "<TH>Parameter Name<TH>Parameter Value(s)");
    Enumeration paramNames = request.getParameterNames();
    while(paramNames.hasMoreElements()) {
      String paramName = (String)paramNames.nextElement();
      out.print("<TR><TD>" + paramName + "\n<TD>");
      String[] paramValues =
        request.getParameterValues(paramName);
      if (paramValues.length == 1) {
        String paramValue = paramValues[0];
        if (paramValue.length() == 0)
          out.println("<I>No Value</I>");
```

Listing 3.3   `ShowParameters.java` (continued)

```
      else
        out.println(paramValue);
    } else {
      out.println("<UL>");
      for(int i=0; i<paramValues.length; i++) {
        out.println("<LI>" + paramValues[i]);
      }
      out.println("</UL>");
    }
  }
  out.println("</TABLE>\n</BODY></HTML>");
}

public void doPost(HttpServletRequest request,
                   HttpServletResponse response)
    throws ServletException, IOException {
  doGet(request, response);
}
}
```

Listing 3.4   `ShowParametersPostForm.html`

```
<!DOCTYPE HTML PUBLIC "-//W3C//DTD HTML 4.0 Transitional//EN">
<HTML>
<HEAD>
  <TITLE>A Sample FORM using POST</TITLE>
</HEAD>
<BODY BGCOLOR="#FDF5E6">
<H1 ALIGN="CENTER">A Sample FORM using POST</H1>

<FORM ACTION="/servlet/coreservlets.ShowParameters"
      METHOD="POST">
  Item Number: <INPUT TYPE="TEXT" NAME="itemNum"><BR>
  Quantity: <INPUT TYPE="TEXT" NAME="quantity"><BR>
  Price Each: <INPUT TYPE="TEXT" NAME="price" VALUE="$"><BR>
  <HR>
  First Name: <INPUT TYPE="TEXT" NAME="firstName"><BR>
  Last Name: <INPUT TYPE="TEXT" NAME="lastName"><BR>
  Middle Initial: <INPUT TYPE="TEXT" NAME="initial"><BR>
  Shipping Address:
  <TEXTAREA NAME="address" ROWS=3 COLS=40></TEXTAREA><BR>
  Credit Card:<BR>
    <INPUT TYPE="RADIO" NAME="cardType"
                     VALUE="Visa">Visa<BR>
    <INPUT TYPE="RADIO" NAME="cardType"
                     VALUE="Master Card">Master Card<BR>
```

Listing 3.4 `ShowParametersPostForm.html` **(continued)**

```
  <INPUT TYPE="RADIO" NAME="cardType"
                   VALUE="Amex">American Express<BR>
  <INPUT TYPE="RADIO" NAME="cardType"
                   VALUE="Discover">Discover<BR>
  <INPUT TYPE="RADIO" NAME="cardType"
                   VALUE="Java SmartCard">Java SmartCard<BR>
Credit Card Number:
<INPUT TYPE="PASSWORD" NAME="cardNum"><BR>
Repeat Credit Card Number:
<INPUT TYPE="PASSWORD" NAME="cardNum"><BR><BR>
<CENTER>
  <INPUT TYPE="SUBMIT" VALUE="Submit Order">
</CENTER>
</FORM>

</BODY>
</HTML>
```

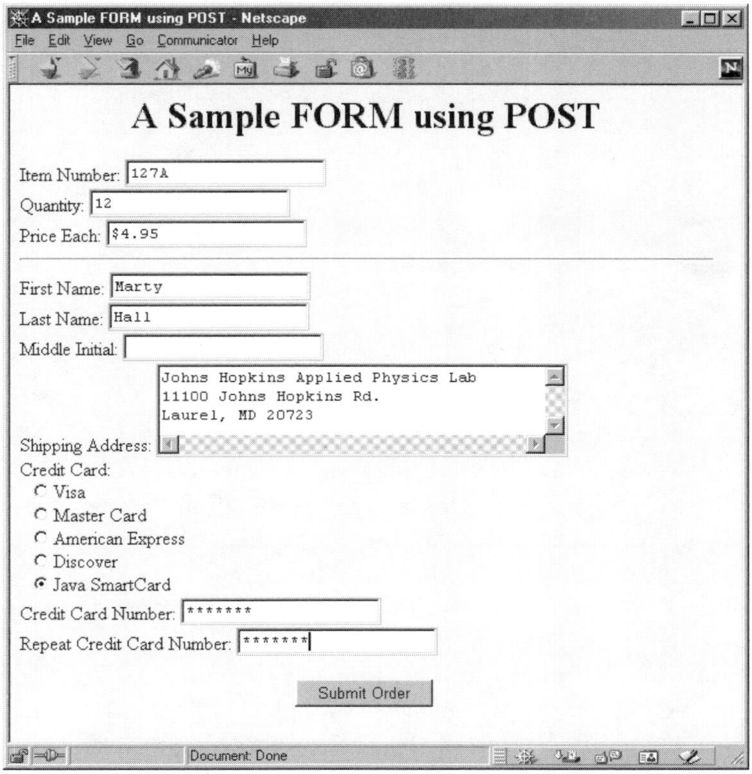

Figure 3-3 HTML front end that collects data for `ShowParameters` servlet.

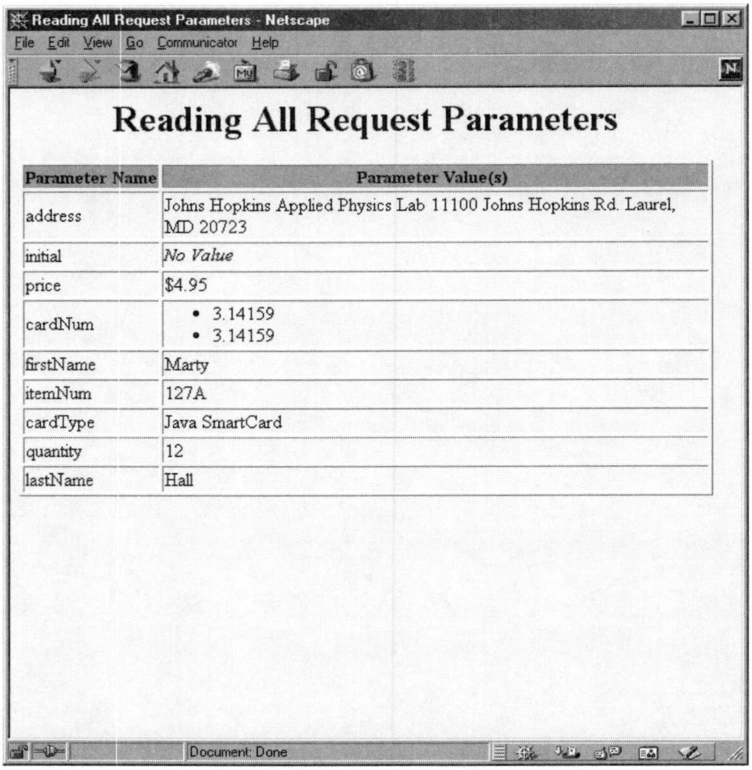

Figure 3–4   Output of `ShowParameters` servlet.

3.5 A Resumé Posting Service

On-line job services have become increasingly popular of late. A reputable site provides a useful service to job seekers by giving their skills wide exposure and provides a useful service to employers by giving them access to a large pool of prospective employees. This section presents a servlet that handles part of such a site: the submission of on-line resumés.

Listing 3.5 and Figure 3–5 show the HTML form that acts as the front end to the resumé-processing servlet. If you are not familiar with HTML forms, they are covered in detail in Chapter 16. The important thing to understand here is that the form uses POST to submit the data and that it gathers values for the following parameter names:

DILBERT reprinted by permission of United Syndicate, Inc.

- **headingFont**
  Headings will be displayed in this font. A value of "default" results in a sans-serif font such as Arial or Helvetica.

- **headingSize**
  The person's name will be displayed in this point size. Subheadings will be displayed in a slightly smaller size.

- **bodyFont**
  The main text (languages and skills) will be displayed in this font.

- **bodySize**
  The main text will be displayed in this point size.

- **fgColor**
  Text will be this color.

- **bgColor**
  The page background will be this color.

- **name**
  This parameter specifies the person's name. It will be centered at the top of the resumé in the font and point size previously specified.

- **title**
  This parameter specifies the person's job title. It will be centered under the name in a slightly smaller point size.

- **email**
  The job applicant's email address will be centered under the job title inside a `mailto` link.

- **languages**
  The programming languages listed will be placed in a bulleted list in the on-line resumé.

- **skills**
  Text from the skills text area will be displayed in the body font at the bottom of the resumé under a heading called "Skills and Experience."

Listing 3.6 shows the servlet that processes the data from the HTML form. When the "Preview" button is pressed, the servlet first reads the font and color parameters. Before using any of the parameters, it checks to see if the value is null (i.e., there is an error in the HTML form and thus the parameter is missing) or is an empty string (i.e., the user erased the default value but did not enter anything in its place). The servlet uses a default value appropriate to each parameter in such a case. Parameters that represent numeric values are passed to Integer.parseInt. To guard against the possibility of improperly formatted numbers supplied by the user, this Integer.parseInt call is placed inside a try/catch block that supplies a default value when the parsing fails. Although it may seem a bit tedious to handle these cases, it generally is not too much work if you make use of some utility methods such as replaceIfMissing and replaceIfMissingOrDefault in Listing 3.6. Tedious or not, users will sometimes overlook certain fields or misunderstand the required field format, so it is critical that your servlet handle malformed parameters gracefully and that you test it with both properly formatted and improperly formatted data.

Core Approach

Design your servlets to gracefully handle missing or improperly formatted parameters. Test them with malformed data as well as with data in the expected format.

Once the servlet has meaningful values for each of the font and color parameters, it builds a cascading style sheet out of them. If you are unfamiliar with style sheets, they are a standard way of specifying the font faces, font sizes, colors, indentation, and other formatting information in an HTML 4.0 Web page. Style sheets are usually placed in a separate file so that several Web pages at a site can share the same style sheet, but in this case it is more convenient to embed the style information directly in the page by using the STYLE element. For more information on style sheets, see http://www.w3.org/TR/REC-CSS1.

After creating the style sheet, the servlet places the job applicant's name, job title, and e-mail address centered under each other at the top of the page. The heading font is used for these lines, and the e-mail address is placed inside a mailto: hypertext link so that prospective employers can contact the applicant directly by clicking on the address. The programming languages specified in the languages parameter are parsed using StringTokenizer (assuming spaces and/or commas are used to separate the language names) and placed in a bulleted list beneath a "Programming Languages" heading. Finally, the text from the `skills` parameter is placed at the bottom of the page beneath a "Skills and Experience" heading.

Figures 3–6 through 3–8 show a couple of possible results. Listing 3.7 shows the underlying HTML of the first of these results.

Listing 3.5 `SubmitResume.html`

```
<!DOCTYPE HTML PUBLIC "-//W3C//DTD HTML 4.0 Transitional//EN">
<HTML>
<HEAD>
  <TITLE>Free Resume Posting</TITLE>
  <LINK REL=STYLESHEET
        HREF="jobs-site-styles.css"
        TYPE="text/css">
</HEAD>
<BODY>
<H1>hotcomputerjobs.com</H1>
<P CLASS="LARGER">
To use our <I>free</I> resume-posting service, simply fill
out the brief summary of your skills below. Use "Preview"
to check the results, then press "Submit" once it is
ready. Your mini resume will appear on-line within 24 hours.</P>
<HR>
<FORM ACTION="/servlet/coreservlets.SubmitResume"
      METHOD="POST">
<DL>
<DT><B>First, give some general information about the look of
your resume:</B>
<DD>Heading font:
    <INPUT TYPE="TEXT" NAME="headingFont" VALUE="default">
<DD>Heading text size:
    <INPUT TYPE="TEXT" NAME="headingSize" VALUE=32>
<DD>Body font:
    <INPUT TYPE="TEXT" NAME="bodyFont" VALUE="default">
<DD>Body text size:
    <INPUT TYPE="TEXT" NAME="bodySize" VALUE=18>
<DD>Foreground color:
    <INPUT TYPE="TEXT" NAME="fgColor" VALUE="BLACK">
<DD>Background color:
    <INPUT TYPE="TEXT" NAME="bgColor" VALUE="WHITE">

<DT><B>Next, give some general information about yourself:</B>
<DD>Name: <INPUT TYPE="TEXT" NAME="name">
<DD>Current or most recent title:
    <INPUT TYPE="TEXT" NAME="title">
<DD>Email address: <INPUT TYPE="TEXT" NAME="email">
<DD>Programming Languages:
    <INPUT TYPE="TEXT" NAME="languages">
```

Listing 3.5   `SubmitResume.html` (continued)

```
<DT><B>Finally, enter a brief summary of your skills and
    experience:</B> (use &lt;P&gt; to separate paragraphs.
    Other HTML markup is also permitted.)
<DD><TEXTAREA NAME="skills"
              ROWS=15 COLS=60 WRAP="SOFT"></TEXTAREA>
</DL>
  <CENTER>
    <INPUT TYPE="SUBMIT" NAME="previewButton" Value="Preview">
    <INPUT TYPE="SUBMIT" NAME="submitButton" Value="Submit">
  </CENTER>
</FORM>
<HR>
<P CLASS="TINY">See our privacy policy
<A HREF="we-will-spam-you.html">here</A>.</P>
</BODY>
</HTML>
```

Listing 3.6   `SubmitResume.java`

```java
package coreservlets;

import java.io.*;
import javax.servlet.*;
import javax.servlet.http.*;
import java.util.*;

/** Servlet that handles previewing and storing resumes
 *  submitted by job applicants.
 */

public class SubmitResume extends HttpServlet {
  public void doPost(HttpServletRequest request,
                     HttpServletResponse response)
      throws ServletException, IOException {
    response.setContentType("text/html");
    PrintWriter out = response.getWriter();
    if (request.getParameter("previewButton") != null) {
      showPreview(request, out);
    } else {
      storeResume(request);
      showConfirmation(request, out);
    }
  }
```

Listing 3.6   `SubmitResume.java` **(continued)**

```java
// Shows a preview of the submitted resume. Takes
// the font information and builds an HTML
// style sheet out of it, then takes the real
// resume information and presents it formatted with
// that style sheet.

private void showPreview(HttpServletRequest request,
                         PrintWriter out) {
  String headingFont = request.getParameter("headingFont");
  headingFont = replaceIfMissingOrDefault(headingFont, "");
  int headingSize =
    getSize(request.getParameter("headingSize"), 32);
  String bodyFont = request.getParameter("bodyFont");
  bodyFont = replaceIfMissingOrDefault(bodyFont, "");
  int bodySize =
    getSize(request.getParameter("bodySize"), 18);
  String fgColor = request.getParameter("fgColor");
  fgColor = replaceIfMissing(fgColor, "BLACK");
  String bgColor = request.getParameter("bgColor");
  bgColor = replaceIfMissing(bgColor, "WHITE");
  String name = request.getParameter("name");
  name = replaceIfMissing(name, "Lou Zer");
  String title = request.getParameter("title");
  title = replaceIfMissing(title, "Loser");
  String email = request.getParameter("email");
  email =
    replaceIfMissing(email, "contact@hotcomputerjobs.com");
  String languages = request.getParameter("languages");
  languages = replaceIfMissing(languages, "<I>None</I>");
  String languageList = makeList(languages);
  String skills = request.getParameter("skills");
  skills = replaceIfMissing(skills, "Not many, obviously.");
  out.println
    (ServletUtilities.DOCTYPE + "\n" +
     "<HTML>\n" +
     "<HEAD>\n" +
     "<TITLE>Resume for " + name + "</TITLE>\n" +
     makeStyleSheet(headingFont, headingSize,
                    bodyFont, bodySize,
                    fgColor, bgColor) + "\n" +
     "</HEAD>\n" +
     "<BODY>\n" +
     "<CENTER>\n"+
     "<SPAN CLASS=\"HEADING1\">" + name + "</SPAN><BR>\n" +
     "<SPAN CLASS=\"HEADING2\">" + title + "<BR>\n" +
     "<A HREF=\"mailto:" + email + "\">" + email +
        "</A></SPAN>\n" +
```

Listing 3.6   `SubmitResume.java` (continued)

```java
        "</CENTER><BR><BR>\n" +
        "<SPAN CLASS=\"HEADING3\">Programming Languages" +
        "</SPAN>\n" +
        makeList(languages) + "<BR><BR>\n" +
        "<SPAN CLASS=\"HEADING3\">Skills and Experience" +
        "</SPAN><BR><BR>\n" +
        skills + "\n" +
        "</BODY></HTML>");
}


// Builds a cascading style sheet with information
// on three levels of headings and overall
// foreground and background cover. Also tells
// Internet Explorer to change color of mailto link
// when mouse moves over it.

private String makeStyleSheet(String headingFont,
                              int heading1Size,
                              String bodyFont,
                              int bodySize,
                              String fgColor,
                              String bgColor) {
  int heading2Size = heading1Size*7/10;
  int heading3Size = heading1Size*6/10;
  String styleSheet =
    "<STYLE TYPE=\"text/css\">\n" +
    "<!--\n" +
    ".HEADING1 { font-size: " + heading1Size + "px;\n" +
    "            font-weight: bold;\n" +
    "            font-family: " + headingFont +
    "              Arial, Helvetica, sans-serif;\n" +
    "}\n" +
    ".HEADING2 { font-size: " + heading2Size + "px;\n" +
    "            font-weight: bold;\n" +
    "            font-family: " + headingFont +
    "              Arial, Helvetica, sans-serif;\n" +
    "}\n" +
    ".HEADING3 { font-size: " + heading3Size + "px;\n" +
    "            font-weight: bold;\n" +
    "            font-family: " + headingFont +
    "              Arial, Helvetica, sans-serif;\n" +
    "}\n" +
    "BODY { color: " + fgColor + ";\n" +
    "       background-color: " + bgColor + ";\n" +
    "       font-size: " + bodySize + "px;\n" +
    "       font-family: " + bodyFont +
    "         Times New Roman, Times, serif;\n" +
```

Listing 3.6   `SubmitResume.java` **(continued)**

```
    "}\n" +
    "A:hover { color: red; }\n" +
    "-->\n" +
    "</STYLE>";
  return(styleSheet);
}

// Replaces null strings (no such parameter name) or
// empty strings (e.g., if textfield was blank) with
// the replacement. Returns the original string otherwise.

private String replaceIfMissing(String orig,
                                String replacement) {
  if ((orig == null) || (orig.length() == 0)) {
    return(replacement);
  } else {
    return(orig);
  }
}

// Replaces null strings, empty strings, or the string
// "default" with the replacement.
// Returns the original string otherwise.

private String replaceIfMissingOrDefault(String orig,
                                         String replacement) {
  if ((orig == null) ||
      (orig.length() == 0) ||
      (orig.equals("default"))) {
    return(replacement);
  } else {
    return(orig + ", ");
  }
}

// Takes a string representing an integer and returns it
// as an int. Returns a default if the string is null
// or in an illegal format.

private int getSize(String sizeString, int defaultSize) {
  try {
    return(Integer.parseInt(sizeString));
  } catch(NumberFormatException nfe) {
    return(defaultSize);
  }
}
```

Listing 3.6   `SubmitResume.java` (continued)

```java
// Given "Java,C++,Lisp", "Java C++ Lisp" or
// "Java, C++, Lisp", returns
// "<UL>
//    <LI>Java
//    <LI>C++
//    <LI>Lisp
//  </UL>"

private String makeList(String listItems) {
  StringTokenizer tokenizer =
    new StringTokenizer(listItems, ", ");
  String list = "<UL>\n";
  while(tokenizer.hasMoreTokens()) {
    list = list + "  <LI>" + tokenizer.nextToken() + "\n";
  }
  list = list + "</UL>";
  return(list);
}

// Show a confirmation page when they press the
// "Submit" button.

private void showConfirmation(HttpServletRequest request,
                              PrintWriter out) {
  String title = "Submission Confirmed.";
  out.println(ServletUtilities.headWithTitle(title) +
              "<BODY>\n" +
              "<H1>" + title + "</H1>\n" +
              "Your resume should appear on-line within\n" +
              "24 hours. If it doesn't, try submitting\n" +
              "again with a different email address.\n" +
              "</BODY></HTML>");
}

// Why it is bad to give your email address to untrusted sites

private void storeResume(HttpServletRequest request) {
  String email = request.getParameter("email");
  putInSpamList(email);
}

private void putInSpamList(String emailAddress) {
  // Code removed to protect the guilty.
}
}
```

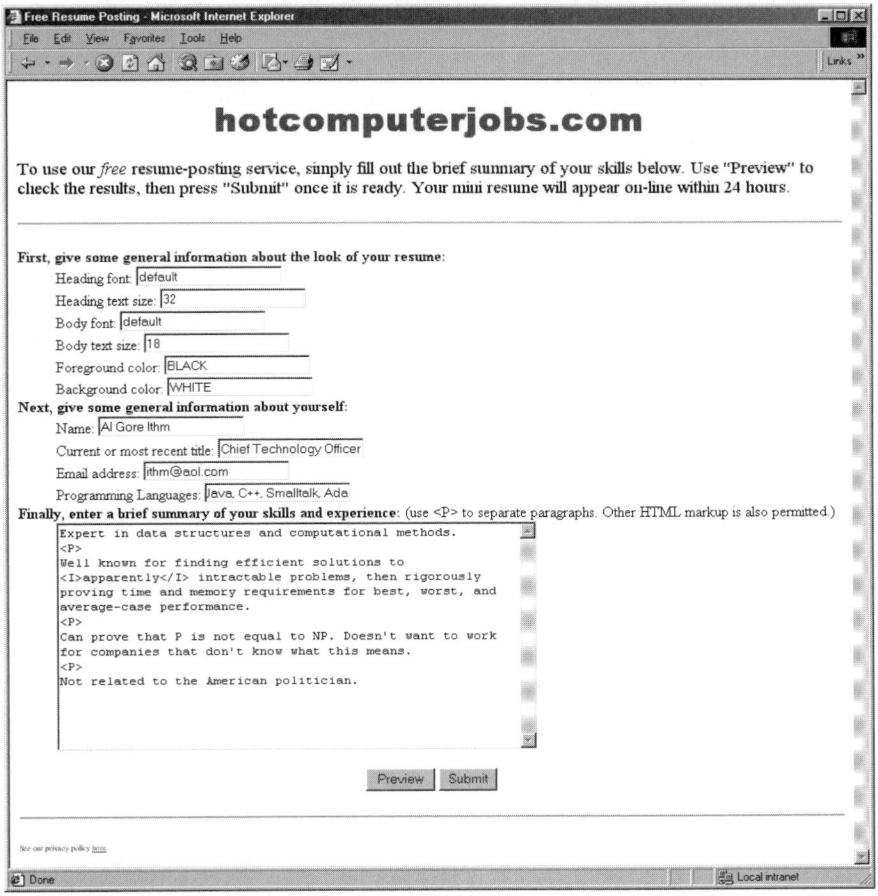

Figure 3–5 Front end to SubmitResume servlet.

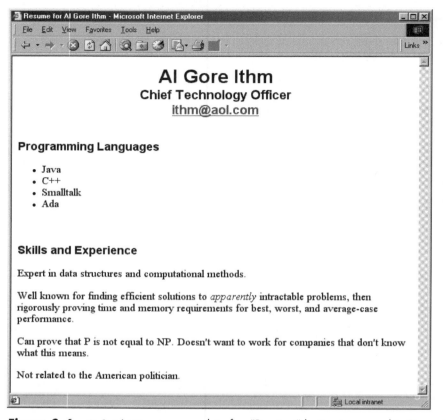

Figure 3–6   SubmitResume servlet after "Preview" button is pressed in Figure 3–5.

Listing 3.7   HTML source of SubmitResume **output shown in Figure 3–6.**

```
<!DOCTYPE HTML PUBLIC "-//W3C//DTD HTML 4.0 Transitional//EN">
<HTML>
<HEAD>
<TITLE>Resume for Al Gore Ithm</TITLE>
<STYLE TYPE="text/css">
<!--
.HEADING1 { font-size: 32px;
            font-weight: bold;
            font-family: Arial, Helvetica, sans-serif;
}
```

Listing 3.7   HTML source of `SubmitResume` output shown in
Figure 3–6. (continued)

```
.HEADING2 { font-size: 22px;
           font-weight: bold;
           font-family: Arial, Helvetica, sans-serif;
}

.HEADING3 { font-size: 19px;
           font-weight: bold;
           font-family: Arial, Helvetica, sans-serif;
}
BODY { color: BLACK;
       background-color: WHITE;
       font-size: 18px;
       font-family: Times New Roman, Times, serif;
}
A:hover { color: red; }
-->
</STYLE>
</HEAD>
<BODY>
<CENTER>
<SPAN CLASS="HEADING1">Al Gore Ithm</SPAN><BR>
<SPAN CLASS="HEADING2">Chief Technology Officer<BR>
<A HREF="mailto:ithm@aol.com">ithm@aol.com</A></SPAN>
</CENTER><BR><BR>
<SPAN CLASS="HEADING3">Programming Languages</SPAN>

<UL>
  <LI>Java
  <LI>C++
  <LI>Smalltalk
  <LI>Ada
</UL><BR><BR>
<SPAN CLASS="HEADING3">Skills and Experience</SPAN><BR><BR>
Expert in data structures and computational methods.
<P>

Well known for finding efficient solutions to
<I>apparently</I> intractable problems, then rigorously
proving time and memory requirements for best, worst, and
average-case performance.
<P>
Can prove that P is not equal to NP. Doesn't want to work
for companies that don't know what this means.
<P>
Not related to the American politician.
</BODY></HTML>
```

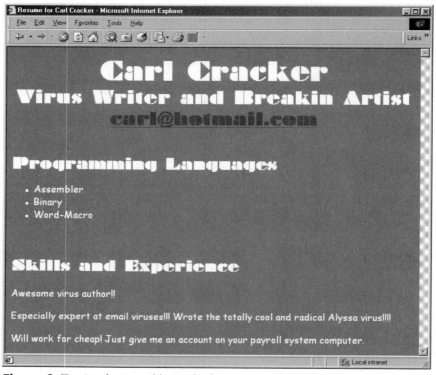

Figure 3-7   Another possible result of `SubmitResume` servlet.

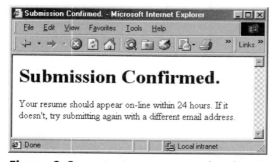

Figure 3-8   `SubmitResume` servlet when "Submit" button is pressed.

3.6 Filtering Strings for HTML-Specific Characters

Normally, when a servlet wants to generate HTML that will contain characters like < or >, it simply uses < or >, the standard HTML character entities. Similarly, if a servlet wants a double quote or an ampersand to appear inside an HTML attribute value, it uses " or &. Failing to make these substitutions results in malformed HTML code, since < or > will often get interpreted as part of an HTML markup tag, a double quote in an attribute value may be interpreted as the end of the value, and ampersands are just plain illegal in attribute values. In most cases, it is easy to note the special characters and use the standard HTML replacements. However, there are two cases when it is not so easy to make this substitution manually.

The first case where manual conversion is difficult occurs when the string is derived from a program excerpt or another source where it is already in some standard format. Going through manually and changing all the special characters can be tedious in such a case, but forgetting to convert even one special character can result in your Web page having missing or improperly formatted sections (see Figure 3–9 later in this section).

The second case where manual conversion fails is when the string is derived from HTML form data. Here, the conversion absolutely must be performed at runtime, since of course the query data is not known at compile time. Failing to do this for an internal Web page can also result in missing or improperly formatted sections of the servlet's output if the user ever sends these special characters. Failing to do this filtering for externally-accessible Web pages also lets your page become a vehicle for the *cross-site scripting attack*. Here, a malicious programmer embeds GET parameters in a URL that refers to one of your servlets. These GET parameters expand to HTML <SCRIPT> elements that exploit known browser bugs. However, by embedding the code in a URL that refers to your site and only distributing the URL, not the malicious Web page itself, the attacker can remain undiscovered more easily and can also exploit trusted relationships to make users think the scripts are coming from a trusted source (your servlet). For more details on this issue, see http://www.cert.org/advisories/CA-2000-02.html and http://www.microsoft.com/technet/security/crssite.asp.

Code for Filtering

Replacing <, >, ", and & in strings is a simple matter, and there are a number
of different approaches that would accomplish the task. However, it is important to remember that Java strings are immutable (i.e., can't be modified), so
string concatenation involves copying and then discarding many string seg-
ments. For example, consider the following two lines:

```
String s1 = "Hello";
String s2 = s1 + " World";
```

Since s1 cannot be modified, the second line makes a copy of s1 and appends
"World" to the copy, then the copy is discarded. To avoid the expense of generating these temporary objects (garbage), you should use a mutable data structure,
and StringBuffer is the natural choice. Listing 3.8 shows a static filter
method that uses a StringBuffer to efficiently copy characters from an input
string to a filtered version, replacing the four special characters along the way.

Listing 3.8   ServletUtilities.java

```
package coreservlets;

import javax.servlet.*;
import javax.servlet.http.*;

public class ServletUtilities {

  // Other methods in ServletUtilities shown elsewhere...

  /** Given a string, this method replaces all occurrences of
   *  '<' with '&lt;', all occurrences of '>' with
   *  '&gt;', and (to handle cases that occur inside attribute
   *  values), all occurrences of double quotes with
   *  '&quot;' and all occurrences of '&' with '&amp;'.
   *  Without such filtering, an arbitrary string
   *  could not safely be inserted in a Web page.
   */

  public static String filter(String input) {
    StringBuffer filtered = new StringBuffer(input.length());
    char c;
    for(int i=0; i<input.length(); i++) {
      c = input.charAt(i);
      if (c == '<') {
        filtered.append("&lt;");
      } else if (c == '>') {
        filtered.append("&gt;");
```

Listing 3.8 `ServletUtilities.java` (continued)

```
      } else if (c == '"') {
        filtered.append("&quot;");
      } else if (c == '&') {
        filtered.append("&amp;");
      } else {
        filtered.append(c);
      }
    }
    return(filtered.toString());
  }
}
```

Example

By means of illustration, consider a servlet that attempts to generate a Web page containing the following code listing:

```
if (a<b) {
  doThis();
} else {
  doThat();
}
```

If the code was inserted into the Web page verbatim, the <b would be interpreted as the beginning of an HTML tag, and all of the code up to the next > would likely be interpreted as malformed pieces of that tag. For example, Listing 3.9 shows a servlet that outputs this code fragment, and Figure 3–9 shows the poor result. Listing 3.10 presents a servlet that changes nothing except for filtering the string containing the code fragment, and, as Figure 3–10 illustrates, the result is fine.

Listing 3.9 `BadCodeServlet.java`

```
package coreservlets;

import java.io.*;
import javax.servlet.*;
import javax.servlet.http.*;

/** Servlet that displays a fragment of some Java code,
 *  but forgets to filter out the HTML-specific characters
 *  (the less-than sign in this case).
 */

public class BadCodeServlet extends HttpServlet {
  private String codeFragment =
```

Listing 3.9 `BadCodeServlet.java` **(continued)**

```java
"if (a<b) {\n" +
"  doThis();\n" +
"} else {\n" +
"  doThat();\n" +
"}\n";

public String getCodeFragment() {
  return(codeFragment);
}

public void doGet(HttpServletRequest request,
                  HttpServletResponse response)
    throws ServletException, IOException {
  response.setContentType("text/html");
  PrintWriter out = response.getWriter();
  String title = "The Java 'if' Statement";

  out.println(ServletUtilities.headWithTitle(title) +
              "<BODY>\n" +
              "<H1>" + title + "</H1>\n" +
              "<PRE>\n" +
              getCodeFragment() +
              "</PRE>\n" +
              "Note that you <I>must</I> use curly braces\n" +
              "when the 'if' or 'else' clauses contain\n" +
              "more than one expression.\n" +
              "</BODY></HTML>");
}
}
```

Listing 3.10 `FilteredCodeServlet.java`

```java
package coreservlets;

/** Subclass of BadCodeServlet that keeps the same doGet method
 *  but filters the code fragment for HTML-specific characters.
 *  You should filter strings that are likely to contain
 *  special characters (like program excerpts) or strings
 *  that are derived from user input.
 */

public class FilteredCodeServlet extends BadCodeServlet {
  public String getCodeFragment() {
    return(ServletUtilities.filter(super.getCodeFragment()));
  }
}
```

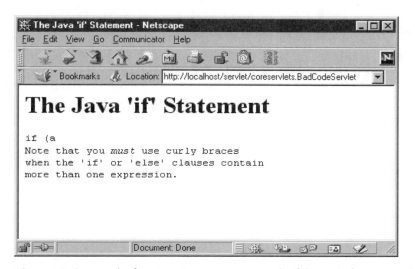

Figure 3–9   Result of `BadCodeServlet`: much of the code fragment is lost, and the text following the code fragment is incorrectly displayed in a monospaced font.

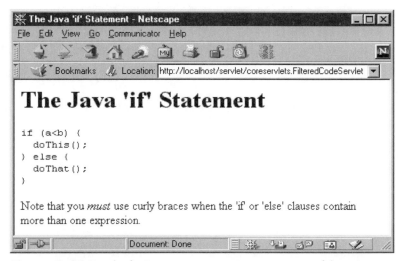

Figure 3–10   Result of `FilteredCodeServlet`: use of the `filter` method solves problems with strings containing special characters.

HANDLING THE CLIENT REQUEST: HTTP REQUEST HEADERS

Topics in This Chapter

- Reading HTTP request headers from servlets
- Building a table of all the request headers
- The purpose of each of the HTTP 1.1 request headers
- Reducing download times by compressing pages
- Restricting access with password-protected servlets

Chapter

One of the keys to creating effective servlets is understanding how to manipulate the HyperText Transfer Protocol (HTTP). Getting a thorough grasp of this protocol is not an esoteric, theoretical topic, but rather a practical issue that can have an immediate impact on the performance and usability of your servlets. This chapter discusses the HTTP information that is sent from the browser to the server in the form of request headers. It explains each of the HTTP 1.1 request headers, summarizing how and why they would be used in a servlet. The chapter also includes three detailed examples: listing all request headers sent by the browser, reducing download time by encoding the Web page with gzip when appropriate, and establishing password-based access control for servlets.

Note that HTTP request headers are distinct from the form data discussed in the previous chapter. Form data results directly from user input and is sent as part of the URL for GET requests and on a separate line for POST requests. Request headers, on the other hand, are indirectly set by the browser and are sent immediately following the initial GET or POST request line. For instance, the following example shows an HTTP request that might result from submitting a book-search request to a servlet at http://www.somebookstore.com/search. The request includes the headers Accept, Accept-Encoding, Connection, Cookie, Host, Referer, and User-Agent, all of which might be important to the operation of the servlet, but none of which can be derived from the form data or deduced automatically: the servlet needs to explicitly read the request headers to make use of this information.

```
GET /search?keywords=servlets+jsp HTTP/1.1
Accept: image/gif, image/jpg, */*
Accept-Encoding: gzip
Connection: Keep-Alive
Cookie: userID=id456578
Host: www.somebookstore.com
Referer: http://www.somebookstore.com/findbooks.html
User-Agent: Mozilla/4.7 [en] (Win98; U)
```

4.1 Reading Request Headers from Servlets

Reading headers is straightforward; just call the `getHeader` method of `HttpServletRequest`, which returns a `String` if the specified header was supplied on this request, `null` otherwise. Header names are not case sensitive. So, for example, `request.getHeader("Connection")` and `request.get-Header("connection")` are interchangeable.

Although `getHeader` is the general-purpose way to read incoming headers, there are a couple of headers that are so commonly used that they have special access methods in `HttpServletRequest`. I'll list them here, and remember that Appendix A (Servlet and JSP Quick Reference) gives a separate syntax summary.

- **getCookies**
  The `getCookies` method returns the contents of the `Cookie` header, parsed and stored in an array of `Cookie` objects. This method is discussed more in Chapter 8 (Handling Cookies).

- **getAuthType and getRemoteUser**
  The `getAuthType` and `getRemoteUser` methods break the `Authorization` header into its component pieces. Use of the `Authorization` header is illustrated in Section 4.5 (Restricting Access to Web Pages).

- **getContentLength**
  The `getContentLength` method returns the value of the `Content-Length` header (as an `int`).

- **getContentType**

  The getContentType method returns the value of the Content-Type header (as a String).

- **getDateHeader and getIntHeader**

  The getDateHeader and getIntHeader methods read the specified header and then convert them to Date and int values, respectively.

- **getHeaderNames**

  Rather than looking up one particular header, you can use the getHeaderNames method to get an Enumeration of all header names received on this particular request. This capability is illustrated in Section 4.2 (Printing All Headers).

- **getHeaders**

  In most cases, each header name appears only once in the request. Occasionally, however, a header can appear multiple times, with each occurrence listing a separate value. Accept-Language is one such example. If a header name is repeated in the request, version 2.1 servlets cannot access the later values without reading the raw input stream, since getHeader returns the value of the first occurrence of the header only. In version 2.2, however, getHeaders returns an Enumeration of the values of all occurrences of the header.

Finally, in addition to looking up the request headers, you can get information on the main request line itself, also by means of methods in Http-ServletRequest.

- **getMethod**

  The getMethod method returns the main request method (normally GET or POST, but things like HEAD, PUT, and DELETE are possible).

- **getRequestURI**

  The getRequestURI method returns the part of the URL that comes after the host and port but before the form data. For example, for a URL of

  http://randomhost.com/servlet/search.BookSearch,

  getRequestURI would return

  /servlet/search.BookSearch.

- **getProtocol**

  Lastly, the getProtocol method returns the third part of the request line, which is generally HTTP/1.0 or HTTP/1.1.

Servlets should usually check `getProtocol` before specifying *response* headers (Chapter 7) that are specific to HTTP 1.1.

4.2 Printing All Headers

Listing 4.1 shows a servlet that simply creates a table of all the headers it receives, along with their associated values. It also prints out the three components of the main request line (method, URI, and protocol). Figures 4–1 and 4–2 show typical results with Netscape and Internet Explorer.

Listing 4.1   ShowRequestHeaders.java

```java
package coreservlets;

import java.io.*;
import javax.servlet.*;
import javax.servlet.http.*;
import java.util.*;

/** Shows all the request headers sent on this
 *  particular request.
 */

public class ShowRequestHeaders extends HttpServlet {
  public void doGet(HttpServletRequest request,
                    HttpServletResponse response)
      throws ServletException, IOException {
    response.setContentType("text/html");
    PrintWriter out = response.getWriter();
    String title = "Servlet Example: Showing Request Headers";
    out.println(ServletUtilities.headWithTitle(title) +
                "<BODY BGCOLOR=\"#FDF5E6\">\n" +
                "<H1 ALIGN=CENTER>" + title + "</H1>\n" +
                "<B>Request Method: </B>" +
                request.getMethod() + "<BR>\n" +
                "<B>Request URI: </B>" +
                request.getRequestURI() + "<BR>\n" +
                "<B>Request Protocol: </B>" +
                request.getProtocol() + "<BR><BR>\n" +
```

Listing 4.1   `ShowRequestHeaders.java` (continued)

```
                 "<TABLE BORDER=1 ALIGN=CENTER>\n" +
                 "<TR BGCOLOR=\"#FFAD00\">\n" +
                 "<TH>Header Name<TH>Header Value");
    Enumeration headerNames = request.getHeaderNames();
    while(headerNames.hasMoreElements()) {
      String headerName = (String)headerNames.nextElement();
      out.println("<TR><TD>" + headerName);
      out.println("    <TD>" + request.getHeader(headerName));
    }
    out.println("</TABLE>\n</BODY></HTML>");
  }

  /** Let the same servlet handle both GET and POST. */

  public void doPost(HttpServletRequest request,
                     HttpServletResponse response)
      throws ServletException, IOException {
    doGet(request, response);
  }
}
```

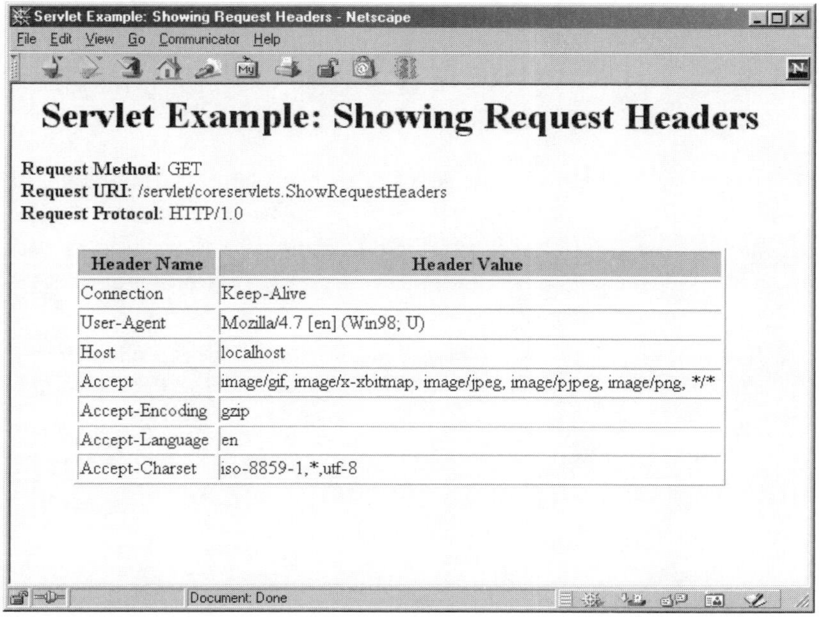

Figure 4–1   Request headers sent by Netscape 4.7 on Windows 98.

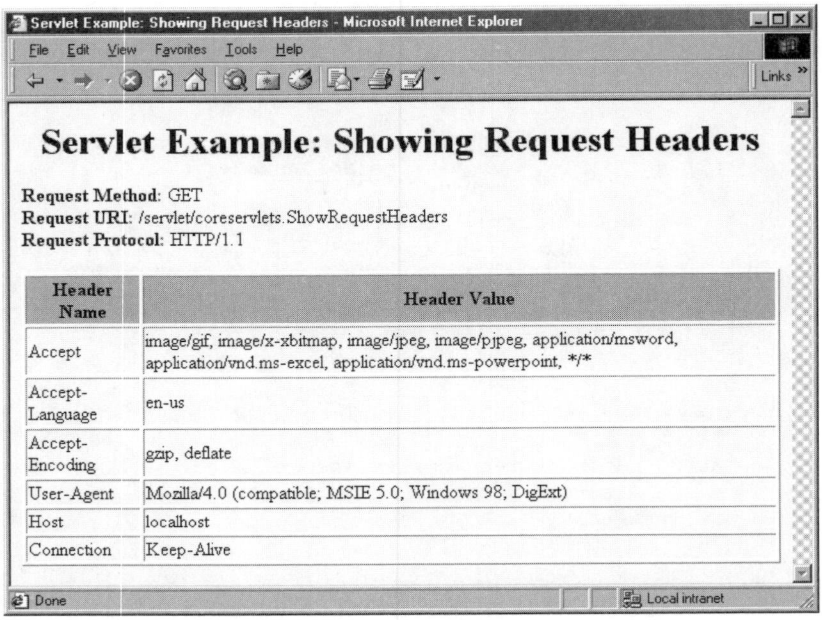

Figure 4–2   Request headers sent by Internet Explorer 5 on Windows 98.

4.3 HTTP 1.1 Request Headers

Access to the request headers permits servlets to perform a number of optimizations and to provide a number of features not otherwise possible. This section presents each of the possible HTTP 1.1 request headers along with a brief summary of how servlets can make use of them. The following sections give more detailed examples.

Note that HTTP 1.1 supports a superset of the headers permitted in HTTP 1.0. For additional details on these headers, see the HTTP 1.1 specification, given in RFC 2616. There are a number of places the official RFCs are archived on-line; your best bet is to start at http://www.rfc-editor.org/ to get a current list of the archive sites.

Accept

This header specifies the MIME types that the browser or other client can handle. A servlet that can return a resource in more than one format can examine the `Accept` header to decide which format to use. For example, images in PNG format have some compression advantages over those in GIF, but only a few browsers support PNG. If you had images in both formats, a servlet could call `request.getHeader("Accept")`, check for `image/png`, and if it finds it, use *xxx*`.png` filenames in all the `IMG` elements it generates. Otherwise it would just use *xxx*`.gif`.

See Table 7.1 in Section 7.2 (HTTP 1.1 Response Headers and Their Meaning) for the names and meanings of the common MIME types.

Accept-Charset

This header indicates the character sets (e.g., ISO-8859-1) the browser can use.

Accept-Encoding

This header designates the types of encodings that the client knows how to handle. If it receives this header, the server is free to encode the page by using the format specified (usually to reduce transmission time), sending the `Content-Encoding` response header to indicate that it has done so. This encoding type is completely distinct from the MIME type of the actual document (as specified in the `Content-Type` response header), since this encoding is reversed *before* the browser decides what to do with the content. On the other hand, using an encoding the browser doesn't understand results in totally incomprehensible pages. Consequently, it is critical that you explicitly check the `Accept-Encoding` header before using any type of content encoding. Values of `gzip` or `compress` are the two standard possibilities.

Compressing pages before returning them is a very valuable service because the decoding time is likely to be small compared to the savings in transmission time. See Section 4.4 (Sending Compressed Web Pages) for an example where compression reduces download times by a factor of 10.

Accept-Language

This header specifies the client's preferred languages, in case the servlet can produce results in more than one language. The value of the header should be one of the standard language codes such as `en`, `en-us`, `da`, etc. See RFC 1766 for details.

Authorization

This header is used by clients to identify themselves when accessing password-protected Web pages. See Section 4.5 (Restricting Access to Web Pages) for an example.

Cache-Control

This header can be used by the client to specify a number of options for how pages should be cached by proxy servers. The request header is usually ignored by servlets, but the Cache-Control *response* header can be valuable to indicate that a page is constantly changing and shouldn't be cached. See Chapter 7 (Generating the Server Response: HTTP Response Headers) for details.

Connection

This header tells whether or not the client can handle persistent HTTP connections. These let the client or other browser retrieve multiple files (e.g., an HTML file and several associated images) with a single socket connection, saving the overhead of negotiating several independent connections. With an HTTP 1.1 request, persistent connections are the default, and the client must specify a value of close for this header to use old-style connections. In HTTP 1.0, a value of keep-alive means that persistent connections should be used.

Each HTTP request results in a new invocation of a servlet, regardless of whether the request is a separate connection. That is, the server invokes the servlet only after the server has already read the HTTP request. This means that servlets need help from the server to handle persistent connections. Consequently, the servlet's job is just to make it *possible* for the server to use persistent connections, which is done by sending a Content-Length response header. Section 7.4 (Using Persistent HTTP Connections) has a detailed example.

Content-Length

This header is only applicable to POST requests and gives the size of the POST data in bytes. Rather than calling request.getIntHeader("Content-Length"), you can simply use request.getContentLength(). However, since servlets take care of reading the form data for you (see Chapter 3, "Handling the Client Request: Form Data"), you are unlikely to use this header explicitly.

Content-Type

Although this header is usually used in responses *from* the server, it can also be part of client requests when the client attaches a document as the POST data or when making PUT requests. You can access this header with the shorthand getContentType method of HttpServletRequest.

Cookie

This header is used to return cookies to servers that previously sent them to the browser. For details, see Chapter 8 (Handling Cookies). Technically, Cookie is not part of HTTP 1.1. It was originally a Netscape extension but is now very widely supported, including in both Netscape and Internet Explorer.

Expect

This rarely used header lets the client tell the server what kinds of behaviors it expects. The one standard value for this header, 100-continue, is sent by a browser that will be sending an attached document and wants to know if the server will accept it. The server should send a status code of either 100 (Continue) or 417 (Expectation Failed) in such a case. For more details on HTTP status codes, see Chapter 6 (Generating the Server Response: HTTP Status Codes).

From

This header gives the e-mail address of the person responsible for the HTTP request. Browsers do not send this header, but Web spiders (robots) often set it as a courtesy to help identify the source of server overloading or repeated improper requests.

Host

Browsers are required to specify this header, which indicates the host and port as given in the *original* URL. Due to request forwarding and machines that have multiple hostnames, it is quite possible that the server could not otherwise determine this information. This header is not new in HTTP 1.1, but in HTTP 1.0 it was optional, not required.

If-Match

This rarely used header applies primarily to PUT requests. The client can supply a list of entity tags as returned by the ETag response header, and the operation is performed only if one of them matches.

If-Modified-Since

This header indicates that the client wants the page only if it has been changed after the specified date. This option is very useful because it lets browsers cache documents and reload them over the network only when they've changed. However, servlets don't need to deal directly with this header. Instead, they should just implement the getLastModified method to have the system handle modification dates automatically. An illustration is given in Section 2.8 (An Example Using Servlet Initialization and Page Modification Dates).

If-None-Match

This header is like If-Match, except that the operation should be performed only if *no* entity tags match.

If-Range

This rarely used header lets a client that has a partial copy of a document ask for either the parts it is missing (if unchanged) or an entire new document (if it has changed since a specified date).

If-Unmodified-Since

This header is like If-Modified-Since in reverse, indicating that the operation should succeed only if the document is older than the specified date. Typically, If-Modified-Since is used for GET requests ("give me the document only if it is newer than my cached version"), whereas If-Unmodified-Since is used for PUT requests ("update this document only if nobody else has changed it since I generated it").

Pragma

A Pragma header with a value of no-cache indicates that a servlet that is acting as a proxy should forward the request even if it has a local copy. The *only* standard value for this header is no-cache.

Proxy-Authorization

This header lets clients identify themselves to proxies that require it. Servlets typically ignore this header, using `Authorization` instead.

Range

This rarely used header lets a client that has a partial copy of a document ask for only the parts it is missing.

Referer

This header indicates the URL of the referring Web page. For example, if you are at Web page 1 and click on a link to Web page 2, the URL of Web page 1 is included in the `Referer` header when the browser requests Web page 2. All major browsers set this header, so it is a useful way of tracking where requests came from. This capability is helpful for tracking advertisers who refer people to your site, for changing content slightly depending on the referring site, or simply for keeping track of where your traffic comes from. In the last case, most people simply rely on Web server log files, since the `Referer` is typically recorded there. Although it's useful, don't rely too heavily on the `Referer` header since it can be easily spoofed by a custom client. Finally, note that this header is `Referer`, not the expected `Referrer`, due to a spelling mistake by one of the original HTTP authors.

Upgrade

The `Upgrade` header lets the browser or other client specify a communication protocol it prefers over HTTP 1.1. If the server also supports that protocol, both the client and the server can switch protocols. This type of protocol negotiation is almost always performed before the servlet is invoked. Thus, servlets rarely care about this header.

User-Agent

This header identifies the browser or other client making the request and can be used to return different content to different types of browsers. Be wary of this usage, however; relying on a hard-coded list of browser versions and associated features can make for unreliable and hard-to-modify servlet code. Whenever possible, use something specific in the HTTP headers instead. For example, instead of trying to remember which browsers support gzip on which platforms, simply check the `Accept-Encoding` header. Admittedly, this is not always possible, but when it is not, you should ask yourself if the browser-specific feature you are using really adds enough value to be worth the maintenance cost.

Most Internet Explorer versions list a "Mozilla" (Netscape) version first in their `User-Agent` line, with the real browser version listed parenthetically. This is done for compatibility with JavaScript, where the `User-Agent` header is sometimes used to determine which JavaScript features are supported. Also note that this header can be easily spoofed, a fact that calls into question the reliability of sites that use this header to "show" market penetration of various browser versions. Hmm, millions of dollars in marketing money riding on statistics that could be skewed by a custom client written in less than an hour, and I should take those numbers as accurate ones?

Via
This header is set by gateways and proxies to show the intermediate sites the request passed through.

Warning
This rarely used catchall header lets clients warn about caching or content transformation errors.

4.4 Sending Compressed Web Pages

Several recent browsers know how to handle gzipped content, automatically uncompressing documents that are marked with the `Content-Encoding` header and then treating the result as though it were the original document. Sending such compressed content can be a real timesaver, since the time required to compress the document on the server and then uncompress it on the client is typically dwarfed by the savings in download time, especially when dialup connections are used.

Browsers that support content encoding include most versions of Netscape for Unix, most versions of Internet Explorer for Windows, and Netscape 4.7 and later for Windows. Earlier Netscape versions on Windows

DILBERT reprinted by permission of United Syndicate, Inc.

and Internet Explorer on non-Windows platforms generally do not support content encoding. Fortunately, browsers that support this feature indicate that they do so by setting the `Accept-Encoding` request header. Listing 4.2 shows a servlet that checks this header, sending a compressed Web page to clients that support gzip encoding and sending a regular Web page to those that don't. The result showed a *tenfold* speedup for the compressed page when a dialup connection was used. In repeated tests with Netscape 4.7 and Internet Explorer 5.0 on a 28.8K modem connection, the compressed page averaged less than 5 seconds to completely download, whereas the uncompressed page consistently took more than 50 seconds.

Core Tip

Gzip compression can dramatically reduce the download time of long text pages.

Implementing compression is straightforward since gzip format is built in to the Java programming languages via classes in `java.util.zip`. The servlet first checks the `Accept-Encoding` header to see if it contains an entry for gzip. If so, it uses a `GZIPOutputStream` to generate the page, specifying `gzip` as the value of the `Content-Encoding` header. You must explicitly call `close` when using a `GZIPOutputStream`. If gzip is not supported, the servlet uses the normal `PrintWriter` to send the page. To make it easy to create benchmarks with a single browser, I also added a feature whereby compression could be suppressed by including `?encoding=none` at the end of the URL.

Listing 4.2   `EncodedPage.java`

```java
package coreservlets;

import java.io.*;
import javax.servlet.*;
import javax.servlet.http.*;
import java.util.zip.*;

/** Example showing benefits of gzipping pages to browsers
 *  that can handle gzip.
 */

public class EncodedPage extends HttpServlet {
  public void doGet(HttpServletRequest request,
                    HttpServletResponse response)
      throws ServletException, IOException {
    response.setContentType("text/html");
    String encodings = request.getHeader("Accept-Encoding");
    String encodeFlag = request.getParameter("encoding");

    PrintWriter out;
    String title;
    if ((encodings != null) &&
        (encodings.indexOf("gzip") != -1) &&
        !"none".equals(encodeFlag)) {
      title = "Page Encoded with GZip";
      OutputStream out1 = response.getOutputStream();
      out = new PrintWriter(new GZIPOutputStream(out1), false);
      response.setHeader("Content-Encoding", "gzip");
    } else {
      title = "Unencoded Page";
      out = response.getWriter();
    }
    out.println(ServletUtilities.headWithTitle(title) +
                "<BODY BGCOLOR=\"#FDF5E6\">\n" +
                "<H1 ALIGN=CENTER>" + title + "</H1>\n");
    String line = "Blah, blah, blah, blah, blah. " +
                  "Yadda, yadda, yadda, yadda.";
    for(int i=0; i<10000; i++) {
      out.println(line);
    }
    out.println("</BODY></HTML>");
    out.close();
  }
}
```

Figure 4–3   Since the Windows version of Internet Explorer 5.0 supports gzip, this page was sent gzipped over the network and reconstituted by the browser, resulting in a large saving in download time.

4.5 Restricting Access to Web Pages

Many Web servers support standard mechanisms for limiting access to designated Web pages. These mechanisms can apply to static pages as well as those generated by servlets, so many authors use their server-specific mechanisms for restricting access to servlets. Furthermore, most users at e-commerce sites prefer to use regular HTML forms to provide authorization information since these forms are more familiar, can provide more explanatory information, and can ask for additional information beyond just a username and password. Once a servlet that uses form-based access grants initial access to a user, it would use session tracking to give the user access to other pages that require the same level of authorization. See Chapter 9 (Session Tracking) for more information.

Nevertheless, form-based access control requires more effort on the part of the servlet developer, and HTTP-based authorization is sufficient for many simple applications. Here's a summary of the steps involved for "basic" authorization. There is also a slightly better variation called "digest" authorization, but among the major browsers, only Internet Explorer supports it.

1. Check whether there is an `Authorization` header. If there is no
    such header, go to Step 2. If there is, skip over the word "basic"
    and reverse the base64 encoding of the remaining part. This
    results in a string of the form `username:password`. Check the
    username and password against some stored set. If it matches,
    return the page. If not, go to Step 2.

2. Return a 401 (`Unauthorized`) response code and a header of the
    following form:
    `WWW-Authenticate: BASIC realm="some-name"`
    This response instructs the browser to pop up a dialog box tell-
    ing the user to enter a name and password for `some-name`, then
    to reconnect with that username and password embedded in a
    single base64 string inside the `Authorization` header.

If you care about the details, base64 encoding is explained in RFC 1521
(remember, to retrieve RFCs, start at `http://www.rfc-editor.org/` to get a
current list of the RFC archive sites). However, there are probably only two
things you need to know about it. First, it is not intended to provide security, as the encoding can be easily reversed. So, it does not obviate the need
for SSL to thwart attackers who might be able to snoop on your network
connection (no easy task unless they are on your local subnet). SSL, or
Secure Sockets Layer, is a variation of HTTP where the entire stream is
encrypted. It is supported by many commercial servers and is generally
invoked by using `https` in the URL instead of `http`. Servlets can run on
SSL servers just as easily as on standard servers, and the encryption and
decryption is handled transparently before the servlets are invoked. The
second point you should know about base64 encoding is that Sun provides
the `sun.misc.BASE64Decoder` class, distributed with both JDK 1.1 and 1.2,
to decode strings that were encoded with base64. Just be aware that classes
in the `sun` package hierarchy are not part of the official language specification, and thus are not guaranteed to appear in all implementations. So, if

you use this decoder class, make sure that you explicitly include the class file when you distribute your application.

Listing 4.3 presents a password-protected servlet. It is explicitly registered with the Web server under the name SecretServlet. The process for registering servlets varies from server to server, but Section 2.7 (An Example Using Initialization Parameters) gives details on the process for Tomcat, the JSWDK and the Java Web Server. The reason the servlet is registered is so that initialization parameters can be associated with it, since most servers don't let you set initialization parameters for servlets that are available merely by virtue of being in the servlets (or equivalent) directory. The initialization parameter gives the location of a Java Properties file that stores user names and passwords. If the security of the page was very important, you'd want to encrypt the passwords so that access to the Properties file would not equate to knowledge of the passwords.

In addition to reading the incoming Authorization header, the servlet specifies a status code of 401 and sets the outgoing WWW-Authenticate header. Status codes are discussed in detail in Chapter 6 (Generating the Server Response: HTTP Status Codes), but for now, just note that they convey high-level information to the browser and generally need to be set whenever the response is something other than the document requested. The most common way to set status codes is through the use of the setStatus method of HttpServletResponse, and you typically supply a constant instead of an explicit integer in order to make your code clearer and to prevent typographic errors.

WWW-Authenticate and other HTTP response headers are discussed in Chapter 7 (Generating the Server Response: HTTP Response Headers), but for now note that they convey auxiliary information to support the response specified by the status code, and they are commonly set through use of the setHeader method of HttpServletResponse.

Figures 4–4, 4–5, and 4–6 show the result when a user first tries to access the page, after the user enters an unknown password, and after the user enters a known password. Listing 4.4 gives the program that built the simple password file.

Listing 4.3   `ProtectedPage.java`

```java
package coreservlets;

import java.io.*;
import javax.servlet.*;
import javax.servlet.http.*;
import java.util.Properties;
import sun.misc.BASE64Decoder;

/** Example of password-protected pages handled directly
 *  by servlets.
 */

public class ProtectedPage extends HttpServlet {
  private Properties passwords;
  private String passwordFile;

  /** Read the password file from the location specified
   *  by the passwordFile initialization parameter.
   */

  public void init(ServletConfig config)
      throws ServletException {
    super.init(config);
    try {
      passwordFile = config.getInitParameter("passwordFile");
      passwords = new Properties();
      passwords.load(new FileInputStream(passwordFile));
    } catch(IOException ioe) {}
  }

  public void doGet(HttpServletRequest request,
                    HttpServletResponse response)
      throws ServletException, IOException {
    response.setContentType("text/html");
    PrintWriter out = response.getWriter();
    String authorization = request.getHeader("Authorization");
    if (authorization == null) {
      askForPassword(response);
    } else {
      String userInfo = authorization.substring(6).trim();
```

Listing 4.3   `ProtectedPage.java` (continued)

```java
      BASE64Decoder decoder = new BASE64Decoder();
      String nameAndPassword =
        new String(decoder.decodeBuffer(userInfo));
      int index = nameAndPassword.indexOf(":");
      String user = nameAndPassword.substring(0, index);
      String password = nameAndPassword.substring(index+1);
      String realPassword = passwords.getProperty(user);
      if ((realPassword != null) &&
          (realPassword.equals(password))) {
        String title = "Welcome to the Protected Page";
        out.println(ServletUtilities.headWithTitle(title) +
                    "<BODY BGCOLOR=\"#FDF5E6\">\n" +
                    "<H1 ALIGN=CENTER>" + title + "</H1>\n" +
                    "Congratulations. You have accessed a\n" +
                    "highly proprietary company document.\n" +
                    "Shred or eat all hardcopies before\n" +
                    "going to bed tonight.\n" +
                    "</BODY></HTML>");
      } else {
        askForPassword(response);
      }
    }
  }

  // If no Authorization header was supplied in the request.

  private void askForPassword(HttpServletResponse response) {
    response.setStatus(response.SC_UNAUTHORIZED); // Ie 401
    response.setHeader("WWW-Authenticate",
                       "BASIC realm=\"privileged-few\"");
  }

  public void doPost(HttpServletRequest request,
                     HttpServletResponse response)
      throws ServletException, IOException {
    doGet(request, response);
  }
}
```

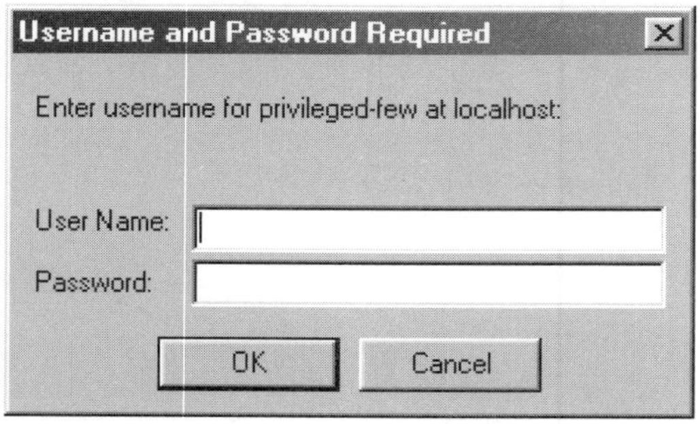

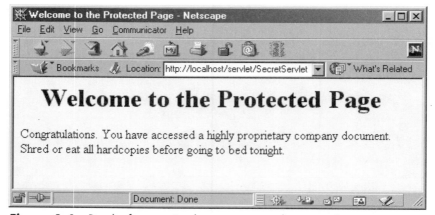

Figure 4–4   Initial result when accessing `SecretServlet` (the registered name for the `ProtectedPage` servlet).

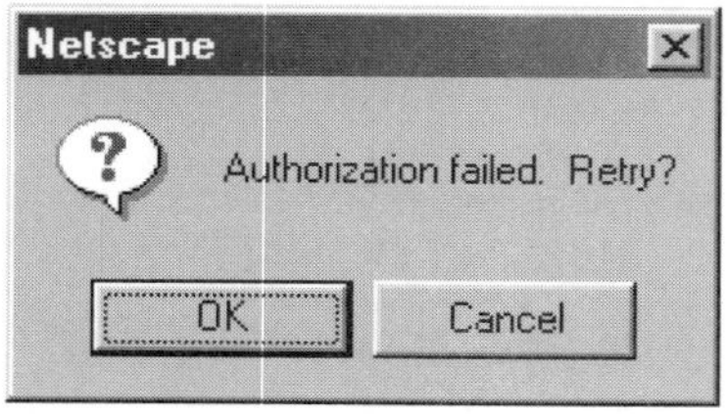

Figure 4–5   Result after entering incorrect name or password.

Figure 4–6   Result after entering known name and password.

Listing 4.4 `PasswordBuilder.java`

```java
import java.util.*;
import java.io.*;

/** Application that writes a simple Java properties file
 *  containing usernames and associated passwords.
 */

public class PasswordBuilder {
  public static void main(String[] args) throws Exception {
    Properties passwords = new Properties();
    passwords.put("marty", "martypw");
    passwords.put("bj", "bjpw");
    passwords.put("lindsay", "lindsaypw");
    passwords.put("nathan", "nathanpw");
    // This location should *not* be Web-accessible.
    String passwordFile =
      "C:\\JavaWebServer2.0\\data\\passwords.properties";
    FileOutputStream out = new FileOutputStream(passwordFile);
    // Using JDK 1.1 for portability among all servlet
    // engines. In JDK 1.2, use "store" instead of "save"
    // to avoid deprecation warnings.
    passwords.save(out, "Passwords");
  }
}
```

ACCESSING THE STANDARD CGI VARIABLES

Topics in This Chapter

- The idea of "CGI variables"
- The servlet equivalent of each standard CGI variable
- A servlet that shows the values of all CGI variables

Chapter

I f you come to servlets with a background in traditional Common Gateway Interface (CGI) programming, you are probably used to the idea of "CGI variables." These are a somewhat eclectic collection of information about the current request. Some are based on the HTTP request line and headers (e.g., form data), others are derived from the socket itself (e.g., the name and IP address of the requesting host), and still others are taken from server installation parameters (e.g., the mapping of URLs to actual paths).

Although it probably makes more sense to think of different sources of data (request data, server information, etc.) as distinct, experienced CGI programmers may find it useful to see the servlet equivalent of each of the CGI variables. If you don't have a background in traditional CGI, first, count your blessings; servlets are easier to use, more flexible and more efficient than standard CGI. Second, just skim this chapter, noting the parts not directly related to the incoming HTTP request. In particular, observe that you can use `getServletContext().getRealPath` to map a URI (the part of the URL that comes after the host and port) to an actual path and that you can use `request.getRemoteHost` and `request.getRemoteAddress` to get the name and IP address of the client.

5.1 Servlet Equivalent of CGI Variables

For each standard CGI variable, this section summarizes its purpose and the means of accessing it from a servlet. As usual, once you are familiar with this information, you may want to use Appendix A (Servlet and JSP Quick Reference) as a reminder. Assume `request` is the `HttpServletRequest` supplied to the `doGet` and `doPost` methods.

AUTH_TYPE

If an `Authorization` header was supplied, this variable gives the scheme specified (`basic` or `digest`). Access it with `request.getAuth-Type()`.

CONTENT_LENGTH

For POST requests only, this variable stores the number of bytes of data sent, as given by the `Content-Length` request header. Technically, since the `CONTENT_LENGTH` CGI variable is a string, the servlet equivalent is `String.valueOf(request.getContentLength())` or `request.getHeader("Content-Length")`. You'll probably want to just call `request.getContentLength()`, which returns an `int`.

CONTENT_TYPE

`CONTENT_TYPE` designates the MIME type of attached data, if specified. See Table 7.1 in Section 7.2 (HTTP 1.1 Response Headers and Their Meaning) for the names and meanings of the common MIME types. Access `CONTENT_TYPE` with `request.getContentType()`.

DOCUMENT_ROOT

The `DOCUMENT_ROOT` variable specifies the real directory corresponding to the URL `http://host/`. Access it with `getServletContext().get-RealPath("/")`. In older servlet specifications you accessed this variable with `request.getRealPath("/")`; the older access method is no longer supported. Also, you can use `getServletContext().getRealPath` to map an arbitrary URI (i.e., URL suffix that comes after the hostname and port) to an actual path on the local machine.

HTTP_XXX_YYY

Variables of the form `HTTP_HEADER_NAME` were how CGI programs obtained access to arbitrary HTTP request headers. The `Cookie` header became `HTTP_COOKIE`, `User-Agent` became `HTTP_USER_AGENT`, `Referer` became `HTTP_REFERER`, and so forth. Servlets should just use `request.getHeader` or one of the shortcut methods described in Chapter 4 (Handling the Client Request: HTTP Request Headers).

PATH_INFO

This variable supplies any path information attached to the URL after the address of the servlet but before the query data. For example, with `http://host/servlet/coreservlets.SomeSer-let/foo/bar?baz=quux`, the path information is `/foo/bar`. Since servlets, unlike standard CGI programs, can talk directly to the server, they don't need to treat path information specially. Path information could be sent as part of the regular form data and then translated by `get-ServletContext().getRealPath`. Access the value of `PATH_INFO` by using `request.getPathInfo()`.

PATH_TRANSLATED

`PATH_TRANSLATED` gives the path information mapped to a real path on the server. Again, with servlets there is no need to have a special case for path information, since a servlet can call `getServletCon-text().getRealPath` to translate partial URLs into real paths. This translation is not possible with standard CGI because the CGI program runs entirely separately from the server. Access this variable by means of `request.getPathTranslated()`.

QUERY_STRING

For `GET` requests, this variable gives the attached data as a single string with values still URL-encoded. You rarely want the raw data in servlets; instead, use `request.getParameter` to access individual parameters, as described in Chapter 3 (Handling the Client Request: Form Data). However, if you do want the raw data, you can get it via `request.getQueryString()`.

REMOTE_ADDR

This variable designates the IP address of the client that made the request, as a `String` (e.g., `"198.137.241.30"`). Access it by calling `request.getRemoteAddr()`.

REMOTE_HOST

REMOTE_HOST indicates the fully qualified domain name (e.g., white-house.gov) of the client that made the request. The IP address is returned if the domain name cannot be determined. You can access this variable with request.getRemoteHost().

REMOTE_USER

If an Authorization header was supplied and decoded by the server itself, the REMOTE_USER variable gives the user part, which is useful for session tracking in protected sites. Access it with request.get-RemoteUser(). For decoding Authorization information directly in servlets, see Section 4.5 (Restricting Access to Web Pages).

REQUEST_METHOD

This variable stipulates the HTTP request type, which is usually GET or POST but is occasionally HEAD, PUT, DELETE, OPTIONS, or TRACE. Servlets rarely need to look up REQUEST_METHOD explicitly, since each of the request types is typically handled by a different servlet method (doGet, doPost, etc.). An exception is HEAD, which is handled automatically by the service method returning whatever headers and status codes the doGet method would use. Access this variable by means of request.getMethod().

SCRIPT_NAME

This variable specifies the path to the servlet, relative to the server's root directory. It can be accessed through request.getServletPath().

SERVER_NAME

SERVER_NAME gives the host name of the server machine. It can be accessed by means of request.getServerName().

SERVER_PORT

This variable stores the port the server is listening on. Technically, the servlet equivalent is String.valueOf(request.getServerPort()), which returns a String. You'll usually just want request.getServer-Port(), which returns an int.

SERVER_PROTOCOL

The `SERVER_PROTOCOL` variable indicates the protocol name and version used in the request line (e.g., `HTTP/1.0` or `HTTP/1.1`). Access it by calling `request.getProtocol()`.

SERVER_SOFTWARE

This variable gives identifying information about the Web server. Access it by means of `getServletContext().getServerInfo()`.

5.2 A Servlet That Shows the CGI Variables

Listing 5.1 presents a servlet that creates a table showing the values of all the CGI variables other than `HTTP_XXX_YYY`, which are just the HTTP request headers described in Chapter 4. Figure 5–1 shows the result for a typical request.

Listing 5.1 `ShowCGIVariables.java`

```
package coreservlets;

import java.io.*;
import javax.servlet.*;
import javax.servlet.http.*;
import java.util.*;

/** Creates a table showing the current value of each
 *  of the standard CGI variables.
 */

public class ShowCGIVariables extends HttpServlet {
  public void doGet(HttpServletRequest request,
                    HttpServletResponse response)
      throws ServletException, IOException {
    response.setContentType("text/html");
    PrintWriter out = response.getWriter();
    String[][] variables =
      { { "AUTH_TYPE", request.getAuthType() },
        { "CONTENT_LENGTH",
          String.valueOf(request.getContentLength()) },
        { "CONTENT_TYPE", request.getContentType() },
```

| Listing 5.1 | `ShowCGIVariables.java` (continued) |

```java
      { "DOCUMENT_ROOT",
        getServletContext().getRealPath("/") },
      { "PATH_INFO", request.getPathInfo() },
      { "PATH_TRANSLATED", request.getPathTranslated() },
      { "QUERY_STRING", request.getQueryString() },
      { "REMOTE_ADDR", request.getRemoteAddr() },
      { "REMOTE_HOST", request.getRemoteHost() },
      { "REMOTE_USER", request.getRemoteUser() },
      { "REQUEST_METHOD", request.getMethod() },
      { "SCRIPT_NAME", request.getServletPath() },
      { "SERVER_NAME", request.getServerName() },
      { "SERVER_PORT",
        String.valueOf(request.getServerPort()) },
      { "SERVER_PROTOCOL", request.getProtocol() },
      { "SERVER_SOFTWARE",
        getServletContext().getServerInfo() }
    };
    String title = "Servlet Example: Showing CGI Variables";
    out.println(ServletUtilities.headWithTitle(title) +
                "<BODY BGCOLOR=\"#FDF5E6\">\n" +
                "<H1 ALIGN=CENTER>" + title + "</H1>\n" +
                "<TABLE BORDER=1 ALIGN=CENTER>\n" +
                "<TR BGCOLOR=\"#FFAD00\">\n" +
                "<TH>CGI Variable Name<TH>Value");
    for(int i=0; i<variables.length; i++) {
      String varName = variables[i][0];
      String varValue = variables[i][1];
      if (varValue == null)
        varValue = "<I>Not specified</I>";
      out.println("<TR><TD>" + varName + "<TD>" + varValue);
    }
    out.println("</TABLE></BODY></HTML>");
  }

  /** POST and GET requests handled identically. */

  public void doPost(HttpServletRequest request,
                     HttpServletResponse response)
      throws ServletException, IOException {
    doGet(request, response);
  }
}
```

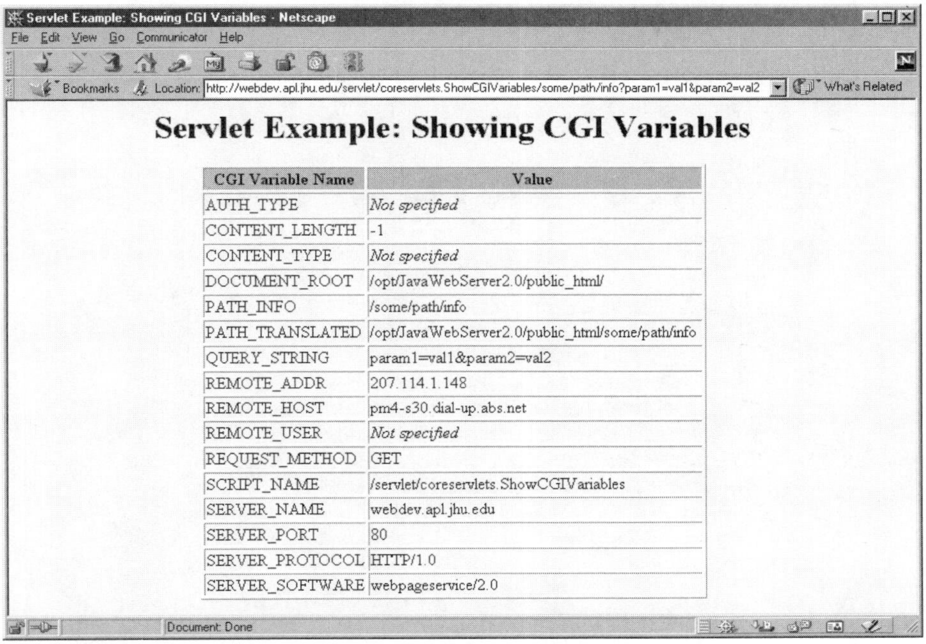
Servlet Example: Showing CGI Variables

CGI Variable Name	Value
AUTH_TYPE	*Not specified*
CONTENT_LENGTH	-1
CONTENT_TYPE	*Not specified*
DOCUMENT_ROOT	/opt/JavaWebServer2.0/public_html/
PATH_INFO	/some/path/info
PATH_TRANSLATED	/opt/JavaWebServer2.0/public_html/some/path/info
QUERY_STRING	param1=val1&param2=val2
REMOTE_ADDR	207.114.1.148
REMOTE_HOST	pm4-s30.dial-up.abs.net
REMOTE_USER	*Not specified*
REQUEST_METHOD	GET
SCRIPT_NAME	/servlet/coreservlets.ShowCGIVariables
SERVER_NAME	webdev.apl.jhu.edu
SERVER_PORT	80
SERVER_PROTOCOL	HTTP/1.0
SERVER_SOFTWARE	webpageservice/2.0

Figure 5–1 The standard CGI variables for a typical request.

GENERATING THE SERVER RESPONSE: HTTP STATUS CODES

Topics in This Chapter

- The purpose of HTTP status codes
- The way to specify status codes from servlets
- The meaning of each of the HTTP 1.1 status code values
- A servlet that uses status codes to redirect users to other sites and to report errors

Chapter 6

When a Web server responds to a request from a browser or other Web client, the response typically consists of a status line, some response headers, a blank line, and the document. Here is a minimal example:

```
HTTP/1.1 200 OK
Content-Type: text/plain

Hello World
```

The status line consists of the HTTP version (HTTP/1.1 in the example above), a status code (an integer; 200 in the above example), and a very short message corresponding to the status code (OK in the example). In most cases, all of the headers are optional except for Content-Type, which specifies the MIME type of the document that follows. Although most responses contain a document, some don't. For example, responses to HEAD requests should never include a document, and there are a variety of status codes that essentially indicate failure and either don't include a document or include only a short error message document.

Servlets can perform a variety of important tasks by manipulating the status line and the response headers. For example, they can forward the user to other sites; indicate that the attached document is an image, Adobe Acrobat file, or HTML file; tell the user that a password is required to access the document; and so forth. This chapter discusses the various status codes and what can be accomplished with them, and the following chapter discusses the response headers.

6.1 Specifying Status Codes

As just described, the HTTP response status line consists of an HTTP version, a status code, and an associated message. Since the message is directly associated with the status code and the HTTP version is determined by the server, all a servlet needs to do is to set the status code. The way to do this is by the `setStatus` method of `HttpServletResponse`. If your response includes a special status code *and* a document, be sure to call `setStatus` *before* actually returning any of the content via the `PrintWriter`. That's because an HTTP response consists of the status line, one or more headers, a blank line, and the actual document, *in that order*. The headers can appear in any order, and servlets buffer the headers and send them all at once, so it is legal to set the status code (part of the first line returned) even after setting headers. But servlets do not necessarily buffer the document itself, since users might want to see partial results for long pages. In version 2.1 of the servlet specification, the `PrintWriter` output is not buffered at all, so the first time you use the `PrintWriter`, it is too late to go back and set headers. In version 2.2, servlet engines are permitted to partially buffer the output, but the size of the buffer is left unspecified. You can use the `get-BufferSize` method of `HttpServletResponse` to determine the size, or use `setBufferSize` to specify it. In version 2.2 with buffering enabled, you can set status codes until the buffer fills up and is actually sent to the client. If you aren't sure if the buffer has been sent, you can use the `isCommitted` method to check.

Core Approach

*Be sure to set status codes **before** sending any document content to the client.*

The setStatus method takes an int (the status code) as an argument, but instead of using explicit numbers, it is clearer and more reliable to use the constants defined in HttpServletResponse. The name of each constant is derived from the standard HTTP 1.1 message for each constant, all uppercase with a prefix of SC (for *Status Code*) and spaces changed to underscores. Thus, since the message for 404 is "Not Found," the equivalent constant in HttpServletResponse is SC_NOT_FOUND. In version 2.1 of the servlet specification, there are three exceptions. The constant for code 302 is derived from the HTTP 1.0 message (Moved Temporarily), not the HTTP 1.1 message (Found), and the constants for codes 307 (Temporary Redirect) and 416 (Requested Range Not Satisfiable) are missing altogether. Version 2.2 added the constant for 416, but the inconsistencies for 307 and 302 remain.

Although the general method of setting status codes is simply to call response.setStatus(int), there are two common cases where a shortcut method in HttpServletResponse is provided. Just be aware that both of these methods throw IOException, whereas setStatus doesn't.

- **public void sendError(int code, String message)** *indicates that the requested resource is not available*
  The sendError method sends a status code (usually 404) along with a short message that is automatically formatted inside an HTML document and sent to the client.

- **public void sendRedirect(String url)**
  The sendRedirect method generates a 302 response along with *indicates that the resource has temporarily moved to another location, but that future references should still use the original URI to access the resource* a Location header giving the URL of the new document. With servlets version 2.1, this must be an absolute URL. In version 2.2, either an absolute or a relative URL is permitted and the system automatically translates relative URLs into absolute ones before putting them in the Location header.

Setting a status code does not necessarily mean that you don't need to return a document. For example, although most servers automatically generate a small "File Not Found" message for 404 responses, a servlet might want to customize this response. Remember that if you do send output, you have to call setStatus or sendError *first*.

6.2 HTTP 1.1 Status Codes and Their Purpose

The following sections describe each of the status codes available for use in servlets talking to HTTP 1.1 clients, along with the standard message associated with each code. A good understanding of these codes can dramatically increase the capabilities of your servlets, so you should at least skim the descriptions to see what options are at your disposal. You can come back to get details when you are ready to make use of some of the capabilities. Note that Appendix A (Servlet and JSP Quick Reference) presents a brief summary of these codes in tabular format.

The complete HTTP 1.1 specification is given in RFC 2616, which you can access on-line by going to http://www.rfc-editor.org/ and following the links to the latest RFC archive sites. Codes that are new in HTTP 1.1 are noted, since many browsers support only HTTP 1.0. You should only send the new codes to clients that support HTTP 1.1, as verified by checking request.getRequestProtocol.

The rest of this section describes the specific status codes available in HTTP 1.1. These codes fall into five general categories:

- **100-199**
  Codes in the 100s are informational, indicating that the client should respond with some other action.
- **200-299**
  Values in the 200s signify that the request was successful.
- **300-399**
  Values in the 300s are used for files that have moved and usually include a Location header indicating the new address.
- **400-499**
  Values in the 400s indicate an error by the client.
- **500-599**
  Codes in the 500s signify an error by the server.

The constants in HttpServletResponse that represent the various codes are derived from the standard messages associated with the codes. In servlets, you usually refer to status codes only by means of these constants. For example, you would use response.setStatus(response.SC_NO_CONTENT) rather than response.setStatus(204), since the latter is unclear to readers and is prone to typographical errors. However, you should note that servers are allowed to vary the messages slightly, and clients pay attention only to the numeric value. So, for example, you might see a server return a status line of HTTP/1.1 200 Document Follows instead of HTTP/1.1 200 OK.

100 (Continue)

If the server receives an Expect request header with a value of 100-continue, it means that the client is asking if it can send an attached document in a follow-up request. In such a case, the server should either respond with status 100 (SC_CONTINUE) to tell the client to go ahead or use 417 (Expectation Failed) to tell the browser it won't accept the document. This status code is new in HTTP 1.1.

101 (Switching Protocols)

A 101 (SC_SWITCHING_PROTOCOLS) status indicates that the server will comply with the Upgrade header and change to a different protocol. This status code is new in HTTP 1.1.

200 (OK)

A value of 200 (SC_OK) means that everything is fine. The document follows for GET and POST requests. This status is the default for servlets; if you don't use setStatus, you'll get 200.

201 (Created)

A status code of 201 (SC_CREATED) signifies that the server created a new document in response to the request; the Location header should give its URL.

202 (Accepted)

A value of 202 (SC_ACCEPTED) tells the client that the request is being acted upon, but processing is not yet complete.

203 (Non-Authoritative Information)

A 203 (SC_NON_AUTHORITATIVE_INFORMATION) status signifies that the document is being returned normally, but some of the response headers might be incorrect since a document copy is being used. This status code is new in HTTP 1.1.

204 (No Content)

A status code of 204 (SC_NO_CONTENT) stipulates that the browser should continue to display the previous document because no new document is available. This behavior is useful if the user periodically reloads a page by pressing the "Reload" button, and you can determine that the previous page is already up-to-date. For example, a servlet might do something like this:

```
int pageVersion =
  Integer.parseInt(request.getParameter("pageVersion"));
if (pageVersion >= currentVersion) {
  response.setStatus(response.SC_NO_CONTENT);
} else {
  // Create regular page
}
```

However, this approach does not work for pages that are automatically reloaded via the `Refresh` response header or the equivalent `<META HTTP-EQUIV="Refresh" ...>` HTML entry, since returning a 204 status code stops future reloading. JavaScript-based automatic reloading could still work in such a case, though. See the discussion of `Refresh` in Section 7.2 (HTTP 1.1 Response Headers and Their Meaning) for details.

205 (Reset Content)

A value of 205 (`SC_RESET_CONTENT`) means that there is no new document, but the browser should reset the document view. This status code is used to force browsers to clear form fields. It is new in HTTP 1.1.

206 (Partial Content)

A status code of 206 (`SC_PARTIAL_CONTENT`) is sent when the server fulfills a partial request that includes a `Range` header. This value is new in HTTP 1.1.

300 (Multiple Choices)

A value of 300 (`SC_MULTIPLE_CHOICES`) signifies that the requested document can be found several places, which will be listed in the returned document. If the server has a preferred choice, it should be listed in the `Location` response header.

301 (Moved Permanently)

The 301 (`SC_MOVED_PERMANENTLY`) status indicates that the requested document is elsewhere; the new URL for the document is given in the

`Location` response header. Browsers should automatically follow the link to the new URL.

302 (Found)

This value is similar to 301, except that the URL given by the `Location` header should be interpreted as a temporary replacement, not a permanent one. Note: in HTTP 1.0, the message was `Moved Temporarily` instead of `Found`, and the constant in `HttpServletResponse` is `SC_MOVED_TEMPORARILY`, not the expected `SC_FOUND`.

Core Note

The constant representing 302 is `SC_MOVED_TEMPORARILY`, *not* `SC_FOUND`.

Status code 302 is very useful because browsers automatically follow the reference to the new URL given in the `Location` response header. It is so useful, in fact, that there is a special method for it, `sendRedirect`. Using `response.sendRedirect(url)` has a couple of advantages over using `response.setStatus(response.SC_MOVED_TEMPORARILY)` and `response.setHeader("Location", url)`. First, it is shorter and easier. Second, with `sendRedirect`, the servlet automatically builds a page containing the link to show to older browsers that don't automatically follow redirects. Finally, with version 2.2 of servlets (the version in J2EE), `sendRedirect` can handle relative URLs, automatically translating them into absolute ones. You must use an absolute URL in version 2.1, however.

If you redirect the user to another page within your own site, you should pass the URL through the `encodeURL` method of `HttpServlet-Response`. Doing so is a simple precaution in case you ever use session tracking based on URL-rewriting. URL-rewriting is a way to track users who have cookies disabled while they are at your site. It is implemented by adding extra path information to the end of each URL, but the servlet session-tracking API takes care of the details automatically. Session tracking is discussed in Chapter 9, and it is a good idea to use `encodeURL` routinely so that you can add session tracking at a later time with minimal changes to the code.

Core Approach

If you redirect users to a page within your site, plan ahead for session tracking by using
`response.sendRedirect(response.encodeURL(url))`,
rather than just
`response.sendRedirect(url).`

This status code is sometimes used interchangeably with 301. For example, if you erroneously ask for `http://host/~user` (missing the trailing slash), some servers will reply with a 301 code while others will use 302.

Technically, browsers are only supposed to automatically follow the redirection if the original request was GET. For details, see the discussion of the 307 status code.

303 (See Other)

The 303 (`SC_SEE_OTHER`) status is similar to 301 and 302, except that if the original request was POST, the new document (given in the `Location` header) should be retrieved with GET. This code is new in HTTP 1.1.

304 (Not Modified)

When a client has a cached document, it can perform a conditional request by supplying an `If-Modified-Since` header to indicate that it only wants the document if it has been changed since the specified date. A value of 304 (`SC_NOT_MODIFIED`) means that the cached version is up-to-date and the client should use it. Otherwise, the server should return the requested document with the normal (200) status code. Servlets normally should not set this status code directly. Instead, they should implement the `getLastModified` method and let the default `service` method handle conditional requests based upon this modification date. An example of this approach is given in Section 2.8 (An Example Using Servlet Initialization and Page Modification Dates).

305 (Use Proxy)

A value of 305 (`SC_USE_PROXY`) signifies that the requested document should be retrieved via the proxy listed in the `Location` header. This status code is new in HTTP 1.1.

307 (Temporary Redirect)

The rules for how a browser should handle a 307 status are identical to those for 302. The 307 value was added to HTTP 1.1 since many browsers erroneously follow the redirection on a 302 response even if the original message is a POST. Browsers are supposed to follow the redirection of a POST request only when they receive a 303 response status. This new status is intended to be unambiguously clear: follow redirected GET *and* POST requests in the case of 303 responses; follow redirected GET but *not* POST requests in the case of 307 responses. Note: For some reason there is no constant in HttpServletResponse corresponding to this status code. This status code is new in HTTP 1.1.

Core Note

There is no SC_TEMPORARY_REDIRECT *constant in* HttpServletResponse, *so you have to use 307 explicitly.*

---

400 (Bad Request)

A 400 (SC_BAD_REQUEST) status indicates bad syntax in the client request.

401 (Unauthorized)

A value of 401 (SC_UNAUTHORIZED) signifies that the client tried to access a password-protected page without proper identifying information in the Authorization header. The response must include a WWW-Authenticate header. For an example, see Section 4.5, "Restricting Access to Web Pages."

403 (Forbidden)

A status code of 403 (SC_FORBIDDEN) means that the server refuses to supply the resource, regardless of authorization. This status is often the result of bad file or directory permissions on the server.

404 (Not Found)

The infamous 404 (SC_NOT_FOUND) status tells the client that no resource could be found at that address. This value is the standard "no such page" response. It is such a common and useful response that there is a special method for it in the HttpServletResponse class: sendError("message"). The advantage of sendError over setStatus is that, with sendError, the server automatically generates an error page showing the error message. Unfortunately, however, the default behavior of Internet Explorer 5 is to ignore the error page you send back and displays its own, even though doing so contradicts the HTTP specification. To turn off this setting, go to the Tools menu, select Internet Options, choose the Advanced tab, and make sure "Show friendly HTTP error messages" box is not checked. Unfortunately, however, few users are aware of this setting, so this "feature" prevents most users of Internet Explorer version 5 from seeing any informative messages you return. Other major browsers and version 4 of Internet Explorer properly display server-generated error pages. See Figures 6–3 and 6–4 for an example.

Core Warning

By default, Internet Explorer version 5 ignores server-generated error pages.

405 (Method Not Allowed)

A 405 (`SC_METHOD_NOT_ALLOWED`) value indicates that the request method (`GET`, `POST`, `HEAD`, `PUT`, `DELETE`, etc.) was not allowed for this particular resource. This status code is new in HTTP 1.1.

406 (Not Acceptable)

A value of 406 (`SC_NOT_ACCEPTABLE`) signifies that the requested resource has a MIME type incompatible with the types specified by the client in its `Accept` header. See Table 7.1 in Section 7.2 (HTTP 1.1 Response Headers and Their Meaning) for the names and meanings of the common MIME types. The 406 value is new in HTTP 1.1.

407 (Proxy Authentication Required)

The 407 (`SC_PROXY_AUTHENTICATION_REQUIRED`) value is similar to 401, but it is used by proxy servers. It indicates that the client must authenticate itself with the proxy server. The proxy server returns a `Proxy-Authenticate` response header to the client, which results in the browser reconnecting with a `Proxy-Authorization` request header. This status code is new in HTTP 1.1.

408 (Request Timeout)

The 408 (SC_REQUEST_TIMEOUT) code means that the client took too long to finish sending the request. It is new in HTTP 1.1.

409 (Conflict)

Usually associated with PUT requests, the 409 (SC_CONFLICT) status is used for situations such as an attempt to upload an incorrect version of a file. This status code is new in HTTP 1.1.

410 (Gone)

A value of 410 (SC_GONE) tells the client that the requested document is gone and no forwarding address is known. Status 410 differs from 404 in that the document is known to be permanently gone, not just unavailable for unknown reasons, as with 404. This status code is new in HTTP 1.1.

411 (Length Required)

A status of 411 (SC_LENGTH_REQUIRED) signifies that the server cannot process the request (assumedly a POST request with an attached document) unless the client sends a Content-Length header indicating the amount of data being sent to the server. This value is new in HTTP 1.1.

412 (Precondition Failed)

The 412 (SC_PRECONDITION_FAILED) status indicates that some precondition specified in the request headers was false. It is new in HTTP 1.1.

413 (Request Entity Too Large)

A status code of 413 (SC_REQUEST_ENTITY_TOO_LARGE) tells the client that the requested document is bigger than the server wants to handle now. If the server thinks it can handle it later, it should include a Retry-After response header. This value is new in HTTP 1.1.

414 (Request URI Too Long)

The 414 (SC_REQUEST_URI_TOO_LONG) status is used when the URI is too long. In this context, "URI" means the part of the URL that came after the host and port in the URL. For example, in http://www.y2k-disaster.com:8080/we/look/silly/now/,theURIis/we/look/silly/now/. This status code is new in HTTP 1.1.

415 (Unsupported Media Type)

A value of 415 (SC_UNSUPPORTED_MEDIA_TYPE) means that the request had an attached document of a type the server doesn't know how to handle. This status code is new in HTTP 1.1.

416 (Requested Range Not Satisfiable)

A status code of 416 signifies that the client included an unsatisfiable Range header in the request. This value is new in HTTP 1.1. Surprisingly, the constant that corresponds to this value was omitted from HttpServletResponse in version 2.1 of the servlet API.

Core Note

In version 2.1 of the servlet specification, there is no SC_REQUESTED_RANGE_NOT_SATISFIABLE constant in HttpServletResponse, so you have to use 416 explicitly. The constant is available in version 2.2 and later.

417 (Expectation Failed)

If the server receives an Expect request header with a value of 100-continue, it means that the client is asking if it can send an attached document in a follow-up request. In such a case, the server should either respond with this status (417) to tell the browser it won't accept the document or use 100 (SC_CONTINUE) to tell the client to go ahead. This status code is new in HTTP 1.1.

500 (Internal Server Error)

500 (SC_INTERNAL_SERVER_ERROR) is the generic "server is confused" status code. It often results from CGI programs or (heaven forbid!) servlets that crash or return improperly formatted headers.

501 (Not Implemented)

The 501 (SC_NOT_IMPLEMENTED) status notifies the client that the server doesn't support the functionality to fulfill the request. It is used, for example, when the client issues a command like PUT that the server doesn't support.

502 (Bad Gateway)

A value of 502 (SC_BAD_GATEWAY) is used by servers that act as proxies or gateways; it indicates that the initial server got a bad response from the remote server.

503 (Service Unavailable)

A status code of 503 (SC_SERVICE_UNAVAILABLE) signifies that the server cannot respond because of maintenance or overloading. For example, a servlet might return this header if some thread or database connection pool is currently full. The server can supply a Retry-After header to tell the client when to try again.

504 (Gateway Timeout)

A value of 504 (SC_GATEWAY_TIMEOUT) is used by servers that act as proxies or gateways; it indicates that the initial server didn't get a timely response from the remote server. This status code is new in HTTP 1.1.

505 (HTTP Version Not Supported)

The 505 (SC_HTTP_VERSION_NOT_SUPPORTED) code means that the server doesn't support the version of HTTP named in the request line. This status code is new in HTTP 1.1.

6.3　A Front End to Various Search Engines

Listing 6.1 presents an example that makes use of the two most common status codes other than 200 (OK): 302 (Found) and 404 (Not Found). The 302 code is set by the shorthand sendRedirect method of HttpServletResponse, and 404 is specified by sendError.

In this application, an HTML form (see Figure 6–1 and the source code in Listing 6.3) first displays a page that lets the user choose a search string, the number of results to show per page, and the search engine to use. When the form is submitted, the servlet extracts those three parameters, constructs a URL with the parameters embedded in a way appropriate to the search engine selected (see the SearchSpec class of Listing 6.2), and redirects the user to that URL (see Figure 6–2). If the user fails to choose a search engine or specify search terms, an error page informs the client of this fact (see Figures 6–3 and 6–4).

Listing 6.1   SearchEngines.java

```java
package coreservlets;

import java.io.*;
import javax.servlet.*;
import javax.servlet.http.*;
import java.net.*;

/** Servlet that takes a search string, number of results per
 *  page, and a search engine name, sending the query to
 *  that search engine. Illustrates manipulating
 *  the response status line. It sends a 302 response
 *  (via sendRedirect) if it gets a known search engine,
 *  and sends a 404 response (via sendError) otherwise.
 */

public class SearchEngines extends HttpServlet {
  public void doGet(HttpServletRequest request,
                    HttpServletResponse response)
      throws ServletException, IOException {
    String searchString = request.getParameter("searchString");
    if ((searchString == null) ||
        (searchString.length() == 0)) {
     reportProblem(response, "Missing search string.");
      return;

    }
    // The URLEncoder changes spaces to "+" signs and other
    // non-alphanumeric characters to "%XY", where XY is the
    // hex value of the ASCII (or ISO Latin-1) character.
    // Browsers always URL-encode form values, so the
    // getParameter method decodes automatically. But since
    // we're just passing this on to another server, we need to
    // re-encode it.  class in java.net package
    searchString = URLEncoder.encode(searchString);
    String numResults =      translates a string into x-www-form-
      request.getParameter("numResults");              urlencoded format
```

Listing 6.1 `SearchEngines.java` (continued)

```java
    if ((numResults == null) ||
        (numResults.equals("0")) ||
        (numResults.length() == 0)) {
      numResults = "10";
    }
    String searchEngine =
      request.getParameter("searchEngine");
    if (searchEngine == null) {
      reportProblem(response, "Missing search engine name.");
      return;
    }
    SearchSpec[] commonSpecs = SearchSpec.getCommonSpecs();
    for(int i=0; i<commonSpecs.length; i++) {
      SearchSpec searchSpec = commonSpecs[i];
      if (searchSpec.getName().equals(searchEngine)) {
        String url =
          searchSpec.makeURL(searchString, numResults);
        response.sendRedirect(url);
        return;
      }
    }
    reportProblem(response, "Unrecognized search engine.");
  }

  private void reportProblem(HttpServletResponse response,
                             String message)
      throws IOException {
    response.sendError(response.SC_NOT_FOUND,
                       "<H2>" + message + "</H2>");
  }

  public void doPost(HttpServletRequest request,
                     HttpServletResponse response)
      throws ServletException, IOException {
    doGet(request, response);
  }
}
```

Listing 6.2   `SearchSpec.java`

```java
package coreservlets;

/** Small class that encapsulates how to construct a
 *  search string for a particular search engine.
 */

class SearchSpec {
  private String name, baseURL, numResultsSuffix;

  private static SearchSpec[] commonSpecs =
    { new SearchSpec("google",
                     "http://www.google.com/search?q=",
                     "&num="),
      new SearchSpec("infoseek",
                     "http://infoseek.go.com/Titles?qt=",
                     "&nh="),
      new SearchSpec("lycos",
                     "http://lycospro.lycos.com/cgi-bin/" +
                         "pursuit?query=",
                     "&maxhits="),
      new SearchSpec("hotbot",
                     "http://www.hotbot.com/?MT=",
                     "&DC=")
    };

  public SearchSpec(String name,
                    String baseURL,
                    String numResultsSuffix) {
    this.name = name;
    this.baseURL = baseURL;
    this.numResultsSuffix = numResultsSuffix;
  }

  public String makeURL(String searchString,
                        String numResults) {
    return(baseURL + searchString +
           numResultsSuffix + numResults);
  }

  public String getName() {
    return(name);
  }

  public static SearchSpec[] getCommonSpecs() {
    return(commonSpecs);
  }
}
```

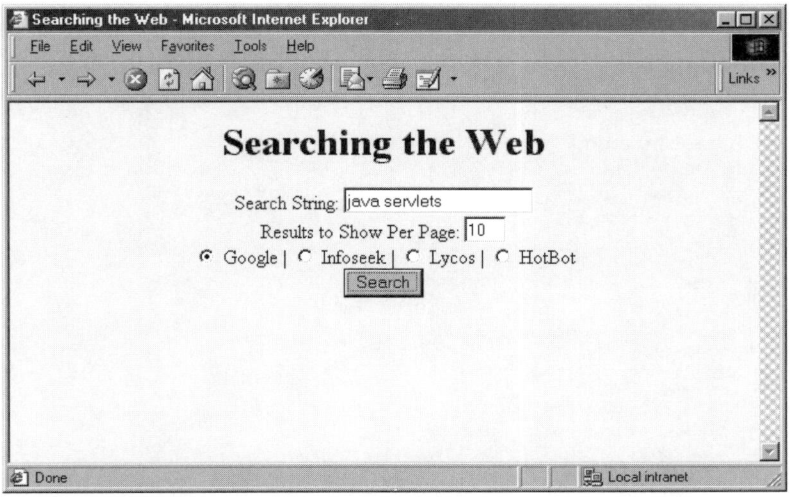

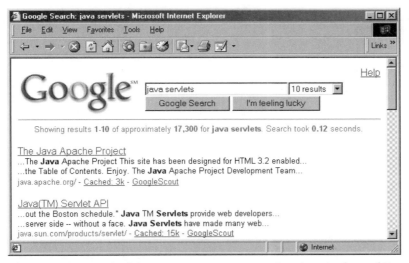

Figure 6–1   Front end to the `SearchEngines` servlet. See Listing 6.3 for the HTML source code.

Figure 6–2   Result of the `SearchEngines` servlet when the form of Figure 6–1 is submitted.

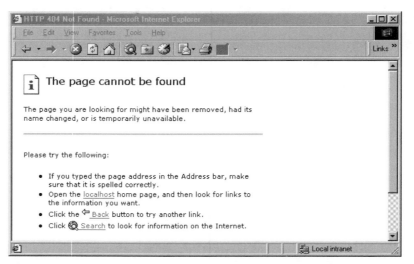

Figure 6–3   Result of `SearchEngines` servlet when no search string was specified. Internet Explorer 5 displays its own error page, even though the servlet generates one.

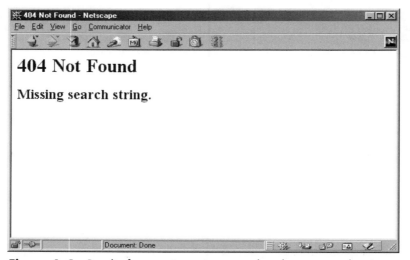

Figure 6–4   Result of `SearchEngines` servlet when no search string was specified. Netscape correctly displays the servlet-generated error page.

Listing 6.3   SearchEngines.html

```
<!DOCTYPE HTML PUBLIC "-//W3C//DTD HTML 4.0 Transitional//EN">
<HTML>
<HEAD>
  <TITLE>Searching the Web</TITLE>
</HEAD>

<BODY BGCOLOR="#FDF5E6">
<H1 ALIGN="CENTER">Searching the Web</H1>

<FORM ACTION="/servlet/coreservlets.SearchEngines">
  <CENTER>
    Search String:
    <INPUT TYPE="TEXT" NAME="searchString"><BR>
    Results to Show Per Page:
    <INPUT TYPE="TEXT" NAME="numResults"
                       VALUE=10 SIZE=3><BR>
    <INPUT TYPE="RADIO" NAME="searchEngine"
                        VALUE="google">
    Google |
    <INPUT TYPE="RADIO" NAME="searchEngine"
                        VALUE="infoseek">
    Infoseek |
    <INPUT TYPE="RADIO" NAME="searchEngine"
                        VALUE="lycos">
    Lycos |
    <INPUT TYPE="RADIO" NAME="searchEngine"
                        VALUE="hotbot">
    HotBot
    <BR>
    <INPUT TYPE="SUBMIT" VALUE="Search">
  </CENTER>
</FORM>

</BODY>
</HTML>
```

GENERATING THE SERVER RESPONSE: HTTP RESPONSE HEADERS

Topics in This Chapter

- Setting response headers from servlets
- The purpose of each of the HTTP 1.1 response headers
- Common MIME types
- A servlet that uses the `Refresh` header to repeatedly access ongoing computations
- Servlets that exploit persistent (keep-alive) HTTP connections
- Generating GIF images from servlets

Chapter 7

A response from a Web server normally consists of a status line, one or more response headers, a blank line, and the document. To get the most out of your servlets, you need to know how to use the status line and response headers effectively, not just how to generate the document.

Setting the HTTP response headers often goes hand in hand with setting the status codes in the status line, as discussed in the previous chapter. For example, all the "document moved" status codes (300 through 307) have an accompanying `Location` header, and a 401 (`Unauthorized`) code always includes an accompanying `WWW-Authenticate` header. However, specifying headers can also play a useful role even when no unusual status code is set. Response headers can be used to specify cookies, to supply the page modification date (for client-side caching), to instruct the browser to reload the page after a designated interval, to give the file size so that persistent HTTP connections can be used, to designate the type of document being generated, and to perform many other tasks.

7.1 Setting Response Headers from Servlets

The most general way to specify headers is to use the `setHeader` method of `HttpServletResponse`. This method takes two strings: the header name and the header value. As with setting status codes, you must specify headers *before* returning the actual document. With servlets version 2.1, this means that you must set the headers before the first use of the `PrintWriter` or raw `OutputStream` that transmits the document content. With servlets version 2.2 (the version in J2EE), the `PrintWriter` may use a buffer, so you can set headers until the first time the buffer is flushed. See Section 6.1 (Specifying Status Codes) for details.

Core Approach

*Be sure to set response headers **before** sending any document content to the client.*

In addition to the general-purpose `setHeader` method, `HttpServlet-Response` also has two specialized methods to set headers that contain dates and integers:

- **`setDateHeader(String header, long milliseconds)`**
  This method saves you the trouble of translating a Java date in milliseconds since 1970 (as returned by
  `System.currentTimeMillis`, `Date.getTime`, or
  `Calendar.getTimeInMillis`) into a GMT time string.
- **`setIntHeader(String header, int headerValue)`**
  This method spares you the minor inconvenience of converting an `int` to a `String` before inserting it into a header.

HTTP allows multiple occurrences of the same header name, and you sometimes want to add a new header rather than replace any existing header with the same name. For example, it is quite common to have multiple `Accept` and `Set-Cookie` headers that specify different supported MIME types and different cookies, respectively. With servlets version 2.1, `set-Header`, `setDateHeader` and `setIntHeader` always *add* new headers, so there is no way to "unset" headers that were set earlier (e.g., by an inherited method). With servlets version 2.2, `setHeader`, `setDateHeader`, and `setInt-Header` *replace* any existing headers of the same name, whereas `addHeader`, `addDateHeader`, and `addIntHeader` *add* a header regardless of whether a header of that name already exists. If it matters to you whether a specific header has already been set, use `containsHeader` to check.

Finally, `HttpServletResponse` also supplies a number of convenience methods for specifying common headers. These methods are summarized as follows.

- **setContentType**

  This method sets the `Content-Type` header and is used by the majority of servlets. See Section 7.5 (Using Servlets to Generate GIF Images) for an example of its use.

- **setContentLength**

  This method sets the `Content-Length` header, which is useful if the browser supports persistent (keep-alive) HTTP connections. See Section 7.4 for an example.

- **addCookie**

  This method inserts a cookie into the `Set-Cookie` header. There is no corresponding `setCookie` method, since it is normal to have multiple `Set-Cookie` lines. See Chapter 8 for a discussion of cookies.

- **sendRedirect**

  As discussed in the previous chapter, the `sendRedirect` method sets the `Location` header as well as setting the status code to 302. See Section 6.3 (A Front End to Various Search Engines) for an example.

7.2 HTTP 1.1 Response Headers and Their Meaning

Following is a summary of the HTTP 1.1 response headers. A good understanding of these headers can increase the effectiveness of your servlets, so you should at least skim the descriptions to see what options are at your disposal. You can come back to get details when you are ready to make use of the capabilities. Note that Appendix A (Servlet and JSP Quick Reference) presents a brief summary of these headers for use as a reminder.

These headers are a superset of those permitted in HTTP 1.0. For additional details on these headers, see the HTTP 1.1 specification, given in RFC 2616. There are a number of places the official RFCs are archived on-line; your best bet is to start at `http://www.rfc-editor.org/` to get a current list of the archive sites. Header names are not case sensitive, but are traditionally written with the first letter of each word capitalized.

Be cautious in writing servlets whose behavior depends on response headers that are only available in HTTP 1.1, especially if your servlet needs to run on the WWW "at large," rather than on an intranet—many older browsers support only HTTP 1.0. It is best to explicitly check the HTTP version with `request.getRequestProtocol` before using new headers.

Accept-Ranges

This header, which is new in HTTP 1.1, tells the client whether or not you accept `Range` request headers. You typically specify a value of `bytes` to indicate that you accept `Range` requests, and a value of `none` to indicate that you do not.

Age

This header is used by proxies to indicate how long ago the document was generated by the original server. It is new in HTTP 1.1 and is rarely used by servlets.

Allow

The `Allow` header specifies the request methods (`GET`, `POST`, etc.) that the server supports. It is required for 405 (`Method Not Allowed`) responses. The default `service` method of servlets automatically generates this header for `OPTIONS` requests.

Cache-Control

This useful header tells the browser or other client the circumstances in which the response document can safely be cached. It has the following possible values:

- `public`: Document is cacheable, even if normal rules (e.g., for password-protected pages) indicate that it shouldn't be.
- `private`: Document is for a single user and can only be stored in private (nonshared) caches.
- `no-cache`: Document should never be cached (i.e., used to satisfy a later request). The server can also specify "`no-cache="header1,header2,...,headerN"`" to indicate the headers that should be omitted if a cached response is later used. Browsers normally do not cache documents that were retrieved by requests that include form data. However, if a servlet generates different content for different requests even when the requests contain no form data, it is critical to tell the browser not to cache the response. Since older browsers use the `Pragma` header for this purpose, the typical servlet approach is to set *both* headers, as in the following example.

```
response.setHeader("Cache-Control", "no-cache");
response.setHeader("Pragma", "no-cache");
```

- `no-store`: Document should never be cached and should not even be stored in a temporary location on disk. This header is intended to prevent inadvertent copies of sensitive information.
- `must-revalidate`: Client must revalidate document with original server (not just intermediate proxies) each time it is used.
- `proxy-revalidate`: This is the same as `must-revalidate`, except that it applies only to shared caches.
- `max-age=xxx`: Document should be considered stale after *xxx* seconds. This is a convenient alternative to the `Expires` header, but only works with HTTP 1.1 clients. If both `max-age` and `Expires` are present in the response, the `max-age` value takes precedence.
- `s-max-age=xxx`: Shared caches should consider the document stale after *xxx* seconds.

The `Cache-Control` header is new in HTTP 1.1.

Connection

A value of `close` for this response header instructs the browser not to use persistent HTTP connections. Technically, persistent connections are the default when the client supports HTTP 1.1 and does *not* specify a "`Connection: close`" request header (or when an HTTP 1.0 client specifies "`Connection: keep-alive`"). However, since persistent connections require a `Content-Length` response header, there is no reason for a servlet to explicitly use the `Connection` header. Just omit the `Content-Length` header if you aren't using persistent connections. See Section 7.4 (Using Persistent HTTP Connections) for an example of the use of persistent HTTP connections from servlets.

Content-Encoding

This header indicates the way in which the page was encoded during transmission. The browser should reverse the encoding before deciding what to do with the document. Compressing the document with gzip can result in huge savings in transmission time; for an example, see Section 4.4 (Sending Compressed Web Pages).

Content-Language

The `Content-Language` header signifies the language in which the document is written. The value of the header should be one of the standard language codes such as en, en-us, da, etc. See RFC 1766 for details (you

can access RFCs on-line at one of the archive sites listed at
`http://www.rfc-editor.org/`).

Content-Length

This header indicates the number of bytes in the response. This information is needed only if the browser is using a persistent (keep-alive)
HTTP connection. See the `Connection` header for determining when
the browser supports persistent connections. If you want your servlet to
take advantage of persistent connections when the browser supports it,
your servlet should write the document into a `ByteArrayOutputStream`,
look up its size when done, put that into the `Content-Length` field with
`response.setContentLength`, then send the content via `byteArray-
Stream.writeTo(response.getOutputStream())`. For an example of
this approach, see Section 7.4.

Content-Location

This header supplies an alternative address for the requested document. `Content-Location` is informational; responses that include this
header also include the requested document, unlike the case with the
`Location` header. This header is new to HTTP 1.1.

Content-MD5

The `Content-MD5` response header provides an MD5 digest for the subsequent document. This digest provides a message integrity check for
clients that want to confirm they received the complete, unaltered
document. See RFC 1864 for details on MD5. This header is new in
HTTP 1.1.

Content-Range

This new HTTP 1.1 header is sent with partial-document responses and
specifies how much of the total document was sent. For example, a value
of "`bytes 500-999/2345`" means that the current response includes bytes
500 through 999 of a document that contains 2345 bytes in total.

Content-Type

The `Content-Type` header gives the MIME (Multipurpose Internet
Mail Extension) type of the response document. Setting this header is
so common that there is a special method in `HttpServletResponse` for
it: `setContentType`. MIME types are of the form `maintype/subtype` for
officially registered types, and of the form `maintype/x-subtype` for

unregistered types. The default MIME type for servlets is `text/plain`, but servlets usually explicitly specify `text/html`. They can, however, specify other types instead. For example, Section 7.5 (Using Servlets to Generate GIF Images) presents a servlet that builds a GIF image based upon input provided by specifying the `image/gif` content type, and Section 11.2 (The contentType Attribute) shows how servlets and JSP pages can generate Excel spreadsheets by specifying a content type of `application/vnd.ms-excel`.

Table 7.1 lists some the most common MIME types used by servlets.

For more detail, many of the common MIME types are listed in RFC 1521 and RFC 1522 (again, see `http://www.rfc-editor.org/` for a list of RFC archive sites). However, new MIME types are registered all the time, so a dynamic list is a better place to look. The officially registered types are listed at `http://www.isi.edu/in-notes/iana/assignments/media-types/media-types`. For common unregistered types, `http://www.ltsw.se/knbase/internet/mime.htp` is a good source.

Table 7.1	Common MIME Types

Type	*Meaning*
`application/msword`	Microsoft Word document
`application/octet-stream`	Unrecognized or binary data
`application/pdf`	Acrobat (.pdf) file
`application/postscript`	PostScript file
`application/vnd.lotus-notes`	Lotus Notes file
`application/vnd.ms-excel`	Excel spreadsheet
`application/vnd.ms-powerpoint`	Powerpoint presentation
`application/x-gzip`	Gzip archive
`application/x-java-archive`	JAR file
`application/x-java-serialized-object`	Serialized Java object
`application/x-java-vm`	Java bytecode (.class) file
`application/zip`	Zip archive

Table 7.1	Common MIME Types (continued)
audio/basic	Sound file in .au or .snd format
audio/x-aiff	AIFF sound file
audio/x-wav	Microsoft Windows sound file
audio/midi	MIDI sound file
text/css	HTML cascading style sheet
text/html	HTML document
text/plain	Plain text
image/gif	GIF image
image/jpeg	JPEG image
image/png	PNG image
image/tiff	TIFF image
image/x-xbitmap	X Window bitmap image
video/mpeg	MPEG video clip
video/quicktime	QuickTime video clip

Date

This header specifies the current date in GMT format. If you want to set the date from a servlet, use the setDateHeader method to specify it. That method saves you the trouble of formatting the date string properly, as would be necessary with response.setHeader("Date", "..."). However, most servers set this header automatically, so servlets don't usually need to.

ETag

This new HTTP 1.1 header gives names to returned documents so that they can be referred to by the client later (as with the If-Match request header).

Expires

This header stipulates the time at which the content should be considered out-of-date and thus no longer be cached. A servlet might use this for a document that changes relatively frequently, to prevent the browser from displaying a stale cached value. For example, the following would instruct the browser not to cache the document for longer than 10 minutes

```
long currentTime = System.currentTimeMillis();
long tenMinutes = 10*60*1000; // In milliseconds
response.setDateHeader("Expires",
                            currentTime + tenMinutes);
```

Also see the `max-age` value of the `Cache-Control` header.

Last-Modified

This very useful header indicates when the document was last changed. The client can then cache the document and supply a date by an `If-Mod-ified-Since` request header in later requests. This request is treated as a conditional `GET`, with the document only being returned if the `Last-Mod-ified` date is later than the one specified for `If-Modified-Since`. Otherwise, a 304 (`Not Modified`) status line is returned, and the client uses the cached document. If you set this header explicitly, use the `setDate-Header` method to save yourself the bother of formatting GMT date strings. However, in most cases you simply implement the `getLastModi-fied` method and let the standard `service` method handle `If-Modi-fied-Since` requests. For an example, see Section 2.8 (An Example Using Servlet Initialization and Page Modification Dates).

Location

This header, which should be included with all responses that have a status code in the 300s, notifies the browser of the document address. The browser automatically reconnects to this location and retrieves the new document. This header is usually set indirectly, along with a 302 status code, by the `sendRedirect` method of `HttpServletResponse`. An example is given in Section 6.3 (A Front End to Various Search Engines).

Pragma

Supplying this header with a value of `no-cache` instructs HTTP 1.0 clients not to cache the document. However, support for this header was inconsistent with HTTP 1.0 browsers. In HTTP 1.1, "`Cache-Control: no-cache`" is a more reliable replacement.

Refresh

This header indicates how soon (in seconds) the browser should ask for an updated page. For example, to tell the browser to ask for a new copy in 30 seconds, you would specify a value of 30 with

```
response.setIntHeader("Refresh", 30)
```

Note that `Refresh` does not stipulate continual updates; it just specifies when the *next* update should be. So, you have to continue to supply `Refresh` in all subsequent responses, and sending a 204 (`No Content`) status code stops the browser from reloading further. For an example, see Section 7.3 (Persistent Servlet State and Auto-Reloading Pages).

Instead of having the browser just reload the current page, you can specify the page to load. You do this by supplying a semicolon and a URL after the refresh time. For example, to tell the browser to go to `http://host/path` after 5 seconds, you would do the following.

```
response.setHeader("Refresh", "5; URL=http://host/path")
```

This setting is useful for "splash screens," where an introductory image or message is displayed briefly before the real page is loaded.

Note that this header is commonly set by

```
<META HTTP-EQUIV="Refresh"
      CONTENT="5; URL=http://host/path">
```

in the `HEAD` section of the HTML page, rather than as an explicit header from the server. That usage came about because automatic reloading or forwarding is something often desired by authors of static HTML pages. For servlets, however, setting the header directly is easier and clearer.

This header is not officially part of HTTP 1.1 but is an extension supported by both Netscape and Internet Explorer.

Retry-After

This header can be used in conjunction with a 503 (`Service Unavailable`) response to tell the client how soon it can repeat its request.

Server

This header identifies the Web server. Servlets don't usually set this; the Web server itself does.

Set-Cookie

The `Set-Cookie` header specifies a cookie associated with the page. Each cookie requires a separate `Set-Cookie` header. Servlets should not use `response.setHeader("Set-Cookie", ...)`, but instead should use the special-purpose `addCookie` method of `HttpServletResponse`. For details, see Chapter 8 (Handling Cookies). Technically, `Set-Cookie` is not part of HTTP 1.1. It was originally a Netscape extension but is now very widely supported, including in both Netscape and Internet Explorer.

Trailer

This new and rarely used HTTP 1.1 header identifies the header fields that are present in the trailer of a message that is sent with "chunked" transfer-coding. See Section 3.6 of the HTTP 1.1 specification (RFC 2616) for details. Recall that `http://www.rfc-editor.org/` maintains an up-to-date list of RFC archive sites.

Transfer-Encoding

Supplying this header with a value of `chunked` indicates "chunked" transfer-coding. See Section 3.6 of the HTTP 1.1 specification (RFC 2616) for details.

Upgrade

This header is used when the client first uses the `Upgrade` *request* header to ask the server to switch to one of several possible new protocols. If the server agrees, it sends a 101 (`Switching Protocols`) status code and includes an `Upgrade` *response* header with the specific protocol it is switching to. This protocol negotiation is usually carried on by the server itself, not by a servlet.

Vary

This rarely used new HTTP 1.1 header tells the client which headers can be used to determine if the response document can be cached.

Via

This header is used by gateways and proxies to list the intermediate sites the request passed through. It is new in HTTP 1.1.

Warning

This new and rarely used catchall header lets you warn clients about caching or content transformation errors.

WWW-Authenticate

This header is always included with a 401 (Unauthorized) status code. It tells the browser what authorization type and realm the client should supply in its Authorization header. Frequently, servlets let password-protected Web pages be handled by the Web server's specialized mechanisms (e.g., .htaccess) rather than handling them directly. For an example of servlets dealing directly with this header, see Section 4.5 (Restricting Access to Web Pages).

7.3 Persistent Servlet State and Auto-Reloading Pages

Here is an example that lets you ask for a list of some large, randomly chosen prime numbers. This computation may take some time for very large numbers (e.g., 150 digits), so the servlet immediately returns initial results but then keeps calculating, using a low-priority thread so that it won't degrade Web server performance. If the calculations are not complete, the servlet instructs the browser to ask for a new page in a few seconds by sending it a Refresh header.

In addition to illustrating the value of HTTP response headers, this example shows two other valuable servlet capabilities. First, it shows that the same servlet can handle multiple simultaneous connections, each with its own thread. So, while one thread is finishing a calculation for one client, another client can connect and still see partial results.

Second, this example shows how easy it is for servlets to maintain state between requests, something that is cumbersome to implement in traditional CGI and many CGI alternatives. Only a single instance of the servlet is created, and each request simply results in a new thread calling the servlet's service method (which calls doGet or doPost). So, shared data simply has to be placed in a regular instance variable (field) of the servlet. Thus, the servlet can access the appropriate ongoing calculation when the browser reloads the page and can keep a list of the N most recently requested results, returning them immediately if a new request specifies the same parameters as a recent one. Of course, the normal rules that require authors to synchronize multithreaded access to shared data still apply to servlets. Servlets can also store persistent data in the `Servlet-Context` object that is available through the `getServletContext` method. `ServletContext` has `setAttribute` and `getAttribute` methods that let you store arbitrary data associated with specified keys. The difference between storing data in instance variables and storing it in the `ServletContext` is that the `ServletContext` is shared by all servlets in the servlet engine (or in the Web application, if your server supports such a capability).

Listing 7.1 shows the main servlet class. First, it receives a request that specifies two parameters: `numPrimes` and `numDigits`. These values are normally collected from the user and sent to the servlet by means of a simple HTML form. Listing 7.2 shows the source code and Figure 7–1 shows the result. Next, these parameters are converted to integers by means of a simple utility that uses `Integer.parseInt` (see Listing 7.5). These values are then matched by the `findPrimeList` method to a `Vector` of recent or ongoing calculations to see if there is a previous computation corresponding to the same two values. If so, that previous value (of type `PrimeList`) is used; otherwise, a new `PrimeList` is created and stored in the ongoing-calculations `Vector`, potentially displacing the oldest previous list. Next, that `PrimeList` is checked to determine if it has finished finding all of its primes. If not, the client is sent a `Refresh` header to tell it to come back in five seconds for updated results. Either way, a bulleted list of the current values is returned to the client.

Listings 7.3 (`PrimeList.java`) and 7.4 (`Primes.java`) present auxiliary code used by the servlet. `PrimeList.java` handles the background thread for the creation of a list of primes for a specific set of values. `Primes.java` contains the low-level algorithms for choosing a random number of a specified length and then finding a prime at or above that value. It uses built-in methods in the `BigInteger` class; the algorithm for determining if the number is prime is a probabilistic one and thus has a chance of being mistaken. However, the probability of being wrong can be specified, and I use an error value of 100. Assuming that the algorithm used in most Java implementations is the Miller-Rabin test, the likelihood of falsely reporting a composite number as prime is provably less than 2^{100}. This is almost certainly smaller than the likelihood of a hardware error or random radiation causing an incorrect response in a deterministic algorithm, and thus the algorithm can be considered deterministic.

Listing 7.1   `PrimeNumbers.java`

```java
package coreservlets;

import java.io.*;
import javax.servlet.*;
import javax.servlet.http.*;
import java.util.*;

/** Servlet that processes a request to generate n
 *  prime numbers, each with at least m digits.
 *  It performs the calculations in a low-priority background
 *  thread, returning only the results it has found so far.
 *  If these results are not complete, it sends a Refresh
 *  header instructing the browser to ask for new results a
 *  little while later. It also maintains a list of a
 *  small number of previously calculated prime lists
 *  to return immediately to anyone who supplies the
 *  same n and m as a recent completed computation.
 */

public class PrimeNumbers extends HttpServlet {
  private Vector primeListVector = new Vector();
  private int maxPrimeLists = 30;

  public void doGet(HttpServletRequest request,
                    HttpServletResponse response)
      throws ServletException, IOException {
    int numPrimes =
      ServletUtilities.getIntParameter(request,
                                        "numPrimes", 50);
    int numDigits =
      ServletUtilities.getIntParameter(request,
                                        "numDigits", 120);
    PrimeList primeList =
      findPrimeList(primeListVector, numPrimes, numDigits);

    if (primeList == null) {
      primeList = new PrimeList(numPrimes, numDigits, true);
      // Multiple servlet request threads share the instance
      // variables (fields) of PrimeNumbers. So
      // synchronize all access to servlet fields.
      synchronized(primeListVector) {
        if (primeListVector.size() >= maxPrimeLists)
          primeListVector.removeElementAt(0);
        primeListVector.addElement(primeList);
      }
    }
    Vector currentPrimes = primeList.getPrimes();
    int numCurrentPrimes = currentPrimes.size();
    int numPrimesRemaining = (numPrimes - numCurrentPrimes);
    boolean isLastResult = (numPrimesRemaining == 0);
    if (!isLastResult) {
      response.setHeader("Refresh", "5");
    }
```

5 seconds

Listing 7.1   PrimeNumbers.java (continued)

```java
    response.setContentType("text/html");
    PrintWriter out = response.getWriter();
    String title = "Some " + numDigits + "-Digit Prime Numbers";
    out.println(ServletUtilities.headWithTitle(title) +
                "<BODY BGCOLOR=\"#FDF5E6\">\n" +
                "<H2 ALIGN=CENTER>" + title + "</H2>\n" +
                "<H3>Primes found with " + numDigits +
                " or more digits: " + numCurrentPrimes +
                ".</H3>");
    if (isLastResult)
      out.println("<B>Done searching.</B>");
    else
      out.println("<B>Still looking for " + numPrimesRemaining +
                  " more<BLINK>...</BLINK></B>");
    out.println("<OL>");
    for(int i=0; i<numCurrentPrimes; i++) {
      out.println("  <LI>" + currentPrimes.elementAt(i));
    }
    out.println("</OL>");
    out.println("</BODY></HTML>");
  }

  public void doPost(HttpServletRequest request,
                     HttpServletResponse response)
      throws ServletException, IOException {
    doGet(request, response);
  }

  // See if there is an existing ongoing or completed
  // calculation with the same number of primes and number
  // of digits per prime. If so, return those results instead
  // of starting a new background thread. Keep this list
  // small so that the Web server doesn't use too much memory.
  // Synchronize access to the list since there may be
  // multiple simultaneous requests.

  private PrimeList findPrimeList(Vector primeListVector,
                                  int numPrimes,
                                  int numDigits) {
    synchronized(primeListVector) {
      for(int i=0; i<primeListVector.size(); i++) {
        PrimeList primes =
          (PrimeList)primeListVector.elementAt(i);
        if ((numPrimes == primes.numPrimes()) &&
            (numDigits == primes.numDigits()))
          return(primes);
      }
      return(null);
    }
  }
}
```

Listing 7.2   PrimeNumbers.html

```
<!DOCTYPE HTML PUBLIC "-//W3C//DTD HTML 4.0 Transitional//EN">
<HTML>
<HEAD>
  <TITLE>Finding Large Prime Numbers</TITLE>
</HEAD>

<BODY BGCOLOR="#FDF5E6">
<H2 ALIGN="CENTER">Finding Large Prime Numbers</H2>
<BR><BR>
<CENTER>
<FORM ACTION="/servlet/coreservlets.PrimeNumbers">
  <B>Number of primes to calculate:</B>
  <INPUT TYPE="TEXT" NAME="numPrimes" VALUE=25 SIZE=4><BR>
  <B>Number of digits:</B>
  <INPUT TYPE="TEXT" NAME="numDigits" VALUE=150 SIZE=3><BR>
  <INPUT TYPE="SUBMIT" VALUE="Start Calculating">
</FORM>
</CENTER>
</BODY>
</HTML>
```

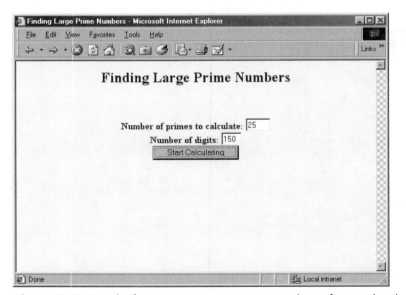

Figure 7-1   Result of `PrimeNumbers.html`, used as a front end to the `PrimeNumbers` servlet.

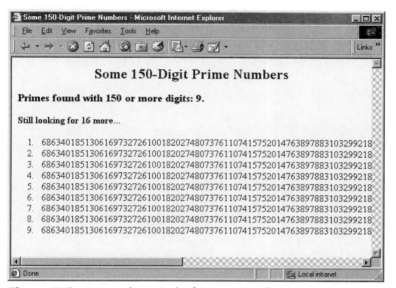

Figure 7-2 Intermediate result of a request to the `PrimeNumbers` servlet. This result can be obtained when the browser reloads automatically or when a different client independently enters the same parameters as those from an ongoing or recent request. Either way, the browser will automatically reload the page to get updated results.

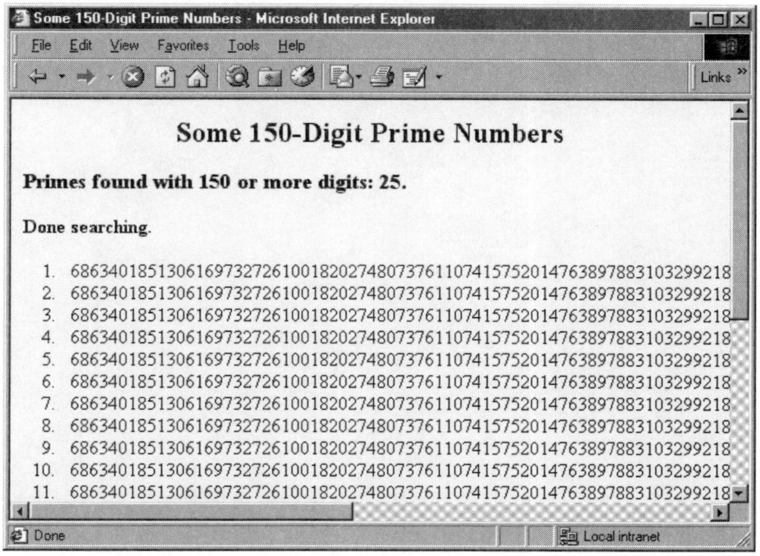

Figure 7-3 Final result of a request to the `PrimeNumbers` servlet. This result can be obtained when the browser reloads automatically or when a different client independently enters the same parameters as those from an ongoing or recent request. The browser will stop updating the page at this point.

Listing 7.3   `PrimeList.java`

```java
package coreservlets;

import java.util.*;
import java.math.BigInteger;

/** Creates a Vector of large prime numbers, usually in
 *  a low-priority background thread. Provides a few small
 *  thread-safe access methods.
 */

public class PrimeList implements Runnable {
  private Vector primesFound;
  private int numPrimes, numDigits;

  /** Finds numPrimes prime numbers, each of which are
   *  numDigits long or longer. You can set it to only
   *  return when done, or have it return immediately,
   *  and you can later poll it to see how far it
   *  has gotten.
   */
  public PrimeList(int numPrimes, int numDigits,
                   boolean runInBackground) {
    // Using Vector instead of ArrayList
    // to support JDK 1.1 servlet engines
    primesFound = new Vector(numPrimes);
    this.numPrimes = numPrimes;
    this.numDigits = numDigits;
    if (runInBackground) {
      Thread t = new Thread(this);
      // Use low priority so you don't slow down server.
      t.setPriority(Thread.MIN_PRIORITY);
      t.start();
    } else {
      run();
    }
  }

  public void run() {
    BigInteger start = Primes.random(numDigits);
    for(int i=0; i<numPrimes; i++) {
      start = Primes.nextPrime(start);
      synchronized(this) {
        primesFound.addElement(start);
      }
    }
  }

  public synchronized boolean isDone() {
    return(primesFound.size() == numPrimes);
  }
```

Listing 7.3   `PrimeList.java` (continued)

```java
  public synchronized Vector getPrimes() {
    if (isDone())
      return(primesFound);
    else
      return((Vector)primesFound.clone());
  }

  public int numDigits() {
    return(numDigits);
  }

  public int numPrimes() {
    return(numPrimes);
  }

  public synchronized int numCalculatedPrimes() {
    return(primesFound.size());
  }
}
```

Listing 7.4   `Primes.java`

```java
package coreservlets;

import java.math.BigInteger;

/** A few utilities to generate a large random BigInteger,
 *  and find the next prime number above a given BigInteger.
 */

public class Primes {
  // Note that BigInteger.ZERO was new in JDK 1.2, and 1.1
  // code is being used to support the most servlet engines.
  private static final BigInteger ZERO = new BigInteger("0");
  private static final BigInteger ONE = new BigInteger("1");
  private static final BigInteger TWO = new BigInteger("2");

  // Likelihood of false prime is less than 1/2^ERR_VAL
  // Assumedly BigInteger uses the Miller-Rabin test or
  // equivalent, and thus is NOT fooled by Carmichael numbers.
  // See section 33.8 of Cormen et al's Introduction to
  // Algorithms for details.
  private static final int ERR_VAL = 100;

  public static BigInteger nextPrime(BigInteger start) {
    if (isEven(start))
      start = start.add(ONE);
    else
```

Listing 7.4 `Primes.java` **(continued)**

```java
      start = start.add(TWO);
    if (start.isProbablePrime(ERR_VAL))
      return(start);
    else
      return(nextPrime(start));
  }

  private static boolean isEven(BigInteger n) {
    return(n.mod(TWO).equals(ZERO));
  }

  private static StringBuffer[] digits =
    { new StringBuffer("0"), new StringBuffer("1"),
      new StringBuffer("2"), new StringBuffer("3"),
      new StringBuffer("4"), new StringBuffer("5"),
      new StringBuffer("6"), new StringBuffer("7"),
      new StringBuffer("8"), new StringBuffer("9") };

  private static StringBuffer randomDigit() {
    int index = (int)Math.floor(Math.random() * 10);
    return(digits[index]);
  }

  public static BigInteger random(int numDigits) {
    StringBuffer s = new StringBuffer("");
    for(int i=0; i<numDigits; i++) {
      s.append(randomDigit());
    }
    return(new BigInteger(s.toString()));
  }

  /** Simple command-line program to test. Enter number
   *  of digits, and it picks a random number of that
   *  length and then prints the first 50 prime numbers
   *  above that.
   */

  public static void main(String[] args) {
    int numDigits;
    if (args.length > 0)
      numDigits = Integer.parseInt(args[0]);
    else
      numDigits = 150;
    BigInteger start = random(numDigits);
    for(int i=0; i<50; i++) {
      start = nextPrime(start);
      System.out.println("Prime " + i + " = " + start);
    }
  }
}
```

Listing 7.5   `ServletUtilities.java`

```
package coreservlets;

import javax.servlet.*;
import javax.servlet.http.*;


public class ServletUtilities {
  // ... Other utilities shown earlier

  /** Read a parameter with the specified name, convert it
   *  to an int, and return it. Return the designated default
   *  value if the parameter doesn't exist or if it is an
   *  illegal integer format.
   */

  public static int getIntParameter(HttpServletRequest request,
                                    String paramName,
                                    int defaultValue) {
    String paramString = request.getParameter(paramName);
    int paramValue;
    try {
      paramValue = Integer.parseInt(paramString);
    } catch(NumberFormatException nfe) { // null or bad format
      paramValue = defaultValue;
    }
    return(paramValue);
  }

  // ...
}
```

7.4 Using Persistent HTTP Connections

One of the problems with HTTP 1.0 was that it required a separate socket connection for each request. When a Web page that includes lots of small images or many applet classes is retrieved, the overhead of establishing all the connections could be significant compared to the actual download time of the documents. Many browsers and servers supported the "keep-alive" extension to address this problem. With this extension, the server tells the browser how many bytes are contained in the response, then leaves the connection open for a certain period of time after returning the document. The client detects that the document has finished loading by monitoring the number of bytes received, and reconnects on the same socket for further transactions. Persistent connections of this type became standard in HTTP 1.1, and compliant servers are supposed to use persistent connections unless the client explicitly instructs them not to (either by a "`Connection: close`" request header or indirectly by sending a request that specifies `HTTP/1.0` instead of `HTTP/1.1` and does *not* also stipulate "`Connection: keep-alive`").

Servlets can take advantage of persistent connections if the servlets are embedded in servers that support them. The server should handle most of the process, but it has no way to determine how large the returned document is. So the servlet needs to set the `Content-Length` response header by means of `response.setContentLength`. A servlet can determine the size of the returned document by buffering the output by means of a `ByteArrayOutput-Stream`, retrieving the number of bytes with the byte stream's `size` method, then sending the buffered output to the client by passing the servlet's output stream to the byte stream's `writeTo` method.

Using persistent connections is likely to pay off only for servlets that load a large number of small objects, where those objects are also servlet-generated and would thus not otherwise take advantage of the server's support for persistent connections. Even so, the advantage gained varies greatly from Web server to Web server and even from Web browser to Web browser. For example, the default configuration for Sun's Java Web Server is to permit only five connections on a single HTTP socket: a value that is too low for many applications. Those who use this server can raise the limit by going to the administration console, selecting "Web Service" then "Service Tuning," then entering a value in the "Connection Persistence" window.

Listing 7.6 shows a servlet that generates a page with 100 IMG tags (see Figure 7–4 for the result). Each of the IMG tags refers to another servlet (`ImageRetriever`, shown in Listing 7.7) that reads a GIF file from the server system and returns it to the client. Both the original servlet and the `Image-Retriever` servlet use persistent connections unless instructed not to do so by means of a parameter in the form data named `usePersistence` with a value of `no`. With Netscape 4.7 and a 28.8K dialup connection to talk to the Solaris version of Java Web Server 2.0 (with the connection limit raised above 100), the use of persistent connections reduced the average download time between 15 and 20 percent.

Listing 7.6 `PersistentConnection.java`

```java
package coreservlets;

import java.io.*;
import javax.servlet.*;
import javax.servlet.http.*;
import java.util.*;

/** Illustrates the value of persistent HTTP connections for
 *  pages that include many images, applet classes, or
 *  other auxiliary content that would otherwise require
 *  a separate connection to retrieve.
 */

public class PersistentConnection extends HttpServlet {
  public void doGet(HttpServletRequest request,
                    HttpServletResponse response)
      throws ServletException, IOException {
    response.setContentType("text/html");
    ByteArrayOutputStream byteStream =
      new ByteArrayOutputStream(7000);
    PrintWriter out = new PrintWriter(byteStream, true);
    String persistenceFlag =
      request.getParameter("usePersistence");
    boolean usePersistence =
      ((persistenceFlag == null) ||
       (!persistenceFlag.equals("no")));
    String title;
    if (usePersistence) {
      title = "Using Persistent Connection";
    } else {
      title = "Not Using Persistent Connection";
    }
    out.println(ServletUtilities.headWithTitle(title) +
                "<BODY BGCOLOR=\"#FDF5E6\">\n" +
                "<H1 ALIGN=\"CENTER\">" + title + "</H1>");
    int numImages = 100;
    for(int i=0; i<numImages; i++) {
      out.println(makeImage(i, usePersistence));
    }
    out.println("</BODY></HTML>");
    if (usePersistence) {
      response.setContentLength(byteStream.size());
    }
    byteStream.writeTo(response.getOutputStream());
  }

  private String makeImage(int n, boolean usePersistence) {
    String file =
      "/servlet/coreservlets.ImageRetriever?gifLocation=" +
      "/bullets/bullet" + n + ".gif";
    if (!usePersistence)
```

Listing 7.6   PersistentConnection.java (continued)

```
      file = file + "&usePersistence=no";
    return("<IMG SRC=\"" + file + "\"\n" +
           "      WIDTH=6 HEIGHT=6 ALT=\"\">");
  }

  public void doPost(HttpServletRequest request,
                     HttpServletResponse response)
      throws ServletException, IOException {
    doGet(request, response);
  }
}
```

Listing 7.7   ImageRetriever.java

```
package coreservlets;

import java.io.*;
import javax.servlet.*;
import javax.servlet.http.*;

/** A servlet that reads a GIF file off the local system
 *  and sends it to the client with the appropriate MIME type.
 *  Includes the Content-Length header to support the
 *  use of persistent HTTP connections unless explicitly
 *  instructed not to through "usePersistence=no".
 *  Used by the PersistentConnection servlet.
 */

public class ImageRetriever extends HttpServlet {
  public void doGet(HttpServletRequest request,
                    HttpServletResponse response)
      throws ServletException, IOException {
    String gifLocation = request.getParameter("gifLocation");
    if ((gifLocation == null) ||
        (gifLocation.length() == 0)) {
      reportError(response, "Image File Not Specified");
      return;
    }
    String file = getServletContext().getRealPath(gifLocation);
    try {
      BufferedInputStream in =
        new BufferedInputStream(new FileInputStream(file));
      ByteArrayOutputStream byteStream =
        new ByteArrayOutputStream(512);
      int imageByte;
```

Listing 7.7 `ImageRetriever.java` (continued)

```
      while((imageByte = in.read()) != -1) {
        byteStream.write(imageByte);
      }
      in.close();
      String persistenceFlag =
      request.getParameter("usePersistence");
      boolean usePersistence =
        ((persistenceFlag == null) ||
         (!persistenceFlag.equals("no")));
      response.setContentType("image/gif");
      if (usePersistence) {
        response.setContentLength(byteStream.size());
      }
      byteStream.writeTo(response.getOutputStream());
    } catch(IOException ioe) {
      reportError(response, "Error: " + ioe);
    }
  }

  public void reportError(HttpServletResponse response,
                          String message)
      throws IOException {
    response.sendError(response.SC_NOT_FOUND,
                       message);
  }
}
```

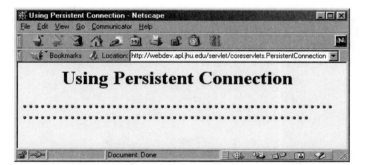

Figure 7-4 Result of the `PersistentConnection` servlet.

7.5 Using Servlets to Generate GIF Images

Although servlets often generate HTML output, they certainly don't *always* do so. For example, Section 11.2 (The contentType Attribute) shows a JSP page (which gets translated into a servlet) that builds Excel spreadsheets and returns them to the client. Here, I'll show you how to generate GIF images.

First, let me summarize the two main steps servlets have to perform in order to build multimedia content. First, they have to set the Content-Type response header by using the setContentType method of HttpServlet-Response. Second, they have to send the output in the appropriate format. This format varies among document types, of course, but in most cases you use send binary data, not strings as with HTML documents. Consequently, servlets will usually get the raw output stream by using the getOutputStream method, rather than getting a PrintWriter by using getWriter. Putting these two points together, servlets that generate non-HTML content usually have a section of their doGet or doPost method that looks like this:

```
response.setContentType("type/subtype");
OutputStream out = response.getOutputStream();
```

Those are the two general steps required to build non-HTML content. Next, let's look at the specific steps required to generate GIF images.

1. **Create an Image.**
   You create an Image object by using the createImage method of the Component class. Since server-side programs should not actually open any windows on the screen, they need to explicitly tell the system to create a native window system object, a process that normally occurs automatically when a window pops up. The addNotify method accomplishes this task. Putting this all together, here is the normal process:

   ```
   Frame f = new Frame();
   f.addNotify();
   int width = ...;
   int height = ...;
   Image img = f.createImage(width, height);
   ```

2. **Draw into the `Image`.**
    You accomplish this task by calling the `Image`'s `getGraphics`
    method and then using the resultant `Graphics` object in the
    usual manner. For example, with JDK 1.1, you would use vari-
    ous draw*Xxx* and fill*Xxx* methods of `Graphics` to draw images,
    strings, and shapes onto the `Image`. With the Java 2 platform,
    you would cast the `Graphics` object to `Graphics2D`, then make
    use of Java2D's much richer set of drawing operations, coordi-
    nate transformations, font settings, and fill patterns to perform
    the drawing. Here is a simple example:

    ```
    Graphics g = img.getGraphics();
    g.fillRect(...);
    g.drawString(...);
    ```

3. **Set the `Content-Type` response header.**
    As already discussed, you use the `setContentType` method of
    `HttpServletResponse` for this task. The MIME type for GIF
    images is `image/gif`.

    ```
    response.setContentType("image/gif");
    ```

4. **Get an output stream.**
    As discussed previously, if you are sending binary data, you
    should call the `getOutputStream` method of `HttpServlet-`
    `Response` rather than the `getWriter` method.

    ```
    OutputStream out = response.getOutputStream();
    ```

5. **Send the `Image` in GIF format to the output stream.**
    Accomplishing this task yourself requires quite a bit of work.
    Fortunately, there are several existing classes that perform this
    operation. One of the most popular ones is Jef Poskanzer's
    `GifEncoder` class, available free from
    `http://www.acme.com/java/`. Here is how you would use this
    class to send an `Image` in GIF format:

    ```
    try {
      new GifEncoder(img, out).encode();
    } catch(IOException ioe) {
      // Error message
    }
    ```

Listings 7.8 and 7.9 show a servlet that reads `message`, `fontName`, and
`fontSize` parameters and uses them to create a GIF image showing the

message in the designated face and size, with a gray, oblique shadowed version of the message shown behind the main string. This operation makes use of several facilities available only in the Java 2 platform. First, it makes use of any font that is installed on the server system, rather than limiting itself to the standard names (`Serif`, `SansSerif`, `Monospaced`, `Dialog`, and `DialogInput`) available to JDK 1.1 programs.

Second, it uses the `translate`, `scale`, and `shear` transformations to create the shadowed version of the main message. Consequently, the servlet will run *only* in servlet engines running on the Java 2 platform. You would expect this to be the case with engines supporting the servlet 2.2 specification, since that is the servlet version stipulated in J2EE.

Even if you are using a server that supports only version 2.1, you should still use the Java 2 platform if you can, since it tends to be significantly more efficient for server-side tasks. However, many servlet 2.1 engines come pre-configured to use JDK 1.1, and changing the Java version is not always simple. So, for example, Tomcat and the JSWDK automatically make use of whichever version of Java is first in your PATH, but the Java Web Server uses a bundled version of JDK 1.1.

Listing 7.10 shows an HTML form used as a front end to the servlet. Figures 7–5 through 7–8 show some possible results. Just to simplify experimentation, Listing 7.11 presents an interactive application that lets you specify the message, font name, and font size on the command line, popping up a JFrame that shows the same image as the servlet would return. Figure 7–9 shows one typical result.

Listing 7.8 `ShadowedText.java`

```
package coreservlets;

import java.io.*;
import javax.servlet.*;
import javax.servlet.http.*;
import java.awt.*;

/** Servlet that generates GIF images representing
 *  a designated message with an oblique shadowed
 *  version behind it.
 *  <P>
 *  <B>Only runs on servers that support Java 2, since
 *  it relies on Java2D to build the images.</B>
 */
public class ShadowedText extends HttpServlet {
  public void doGet(HttpServletRequest request,
                    HttpServletResponse response)
      throws ServletException, IOException {
    String message = request.getParameter("message");
    if ((message == null) || (message.length() == 0)) {
```

Listing 7.8   `ShadowedText.java` **(continued)**

```
      message = "Missing 'message' parameter";
    }
    String fontName = request.getParameter("fontName");
    if (fontName == null) {
      fontName = "Serif";
    }
    String fontSizeString = request.getParameter("fontSize");
    int fontSize;
    try {

      fontSize = Integer.parseInt(fontSizeString);
    } catch(NumberFormatException nfe) {
      fontSize = 90;
    }
    response.setContentType("image/gif");
    OutputStream out = response.getOutputStream();
    Image messageImage =
      MessageImage.makeMessageImage(message,
                                    fontName,
                                    fontSize);
    MessageImage.sendAsGIF(messageImage, out);
  }

  /** Allow form to send data via either GET or POST. */

  public void doPost(HttpServletRequest request,
                     HttpServletResponse response)
      throws ServletException, IOException {
    doGet(request, response);
  }
}
```

Listing 7.9   `MessageImage.java`

```
package coreservlets;

import java.awt.*;
import java.awt.geom.*;
import java.io.*;
import Acme.JPM.Encoders.GifEncoder;

/** Utilities for building images showing shadowed messages.
 *  Includes a routine that uses Jef Poskanzer's GifEncoder
 *  to return the result as a GIF.
 *  <P>
 *  <B>Does not run in JDK 1.1, since it relies on Java2D
 *  to build the images.</B>
 *  <P>
 */
```

Listing 7.9   `MessageImage.java` **(continued)**

```java
public class MessageImage {

  /** Creates an Image of a string with an oblique
   *  shadow behind it. Used by the ShadowedText servlet
   *  and the ShadowedTextFrame desktop application.
   */
  public static Image makeMessageImage(String message,
                                       String fontName,
                                       int fontSize) {
    Frame f = new Frame();
    // Connect to native screen resource for image creation.
    f.addNotify();
    // Make sure Java knows about local font names.
    GraphicsEnvironment env =
      GraphicsEnvironment.getLocalGraphicsEnvironment();
    env.getAvailableFontFamilyNames();
    Font font = new Font(fontName, Font.PLAIN, fontSize);
    FontMetrics metrics = f.getFontMetrics(font);
    int messageWidth = metrics.stringWidth(message);
    int baselineX = messageWidth/10;
    int width = messageWidth+2*(baselineX + fontSize);
    int height = fontSize*7/2;
    int baselineY = height*8/10;
    Image messageImage = f.createImage(width, height);
    Graphics2D g2d =
      (Graphics2D)messageImage.getGraphics();
    g2d.setFont(font);
    g2d.translate(baselineX, baselineY);
    g2d.setPaint(Color.lightGray);
    AffineTransform origTransform = g2d.getTransform();
    g2d.shear(-0.95, 0);
    g2d.scale(1, 3);
    g2d.drawString(message, 0, 0);
    g2d.setTransform(origTransform);
    g2d.setPaint(Color.black);
    g2d.drawString(message, 0, 0);
    return(messageImage);
  }

  /** Uses GifEncoder to send the Image down output stream
   *  in GIF89A format. See http://www.acme.com/java/ for
   *  the GifEncoder class.
   */

  public static void sendAsGIF(Image image, OutputStream out) {
    try {
      new GifEncoder(image, out).encode();
    } catch(IOException ioe) {
      System.err.println("Error outputting GIF: " + ioe);
    }

  }
}
```

Listing 7.10 ShadowedText.html

```
<!DOCTYPE HTML PUBLIC "-//W3C//DTD HTML 4.0 Transitional//EN">
<HTML>
<HEAD>
  <TITLE>GIF Generation Service</TITLE>
</HEAD>

<BODY BGCOLOR="#FDF5E6">
<H1 ALIGN="CENTER">GIF Generation Service</H1>
Welcome to the <I>free</I> trial edition of our GIF
generation service. Enter a message, a font name,
and a font size below, then submit the form. You will
be returned a GIF image showing the message in the
designated font, with an oblique "shadow" of the message
behind it. Once you get an image you are satisfied with, right
click on it (or click while holding down the SHIFT key) to save
it to your local disk.
<P>
The server is currently on Windows, so the font name must
be either a standard Java font name (e.g., Serif, SansSerif,
or Monospaced) or a Windows font name (e.g., Arial Black).
Unrecognized font names will revert to Serif.

<FORM ACTION="/servlet/coreservlets.ShadowedText">
  <CENTER>
    Message:
    <INPUT TYPE="TEXT" NAME="message"><BR>
    Font name:
    <INPUT TYPE="TEXT" NAME="fontName" VALUE="Serif"><BR>
    Font size:
    <INPUT TYPE="TEXT" NAME="fontSize" VALUE="90"><BR><BR>
    <Input TYPE="SUBMIT" VALUE="Build Image">
  </CENTER>
</FORM>

</BODY>
</HTML>
```

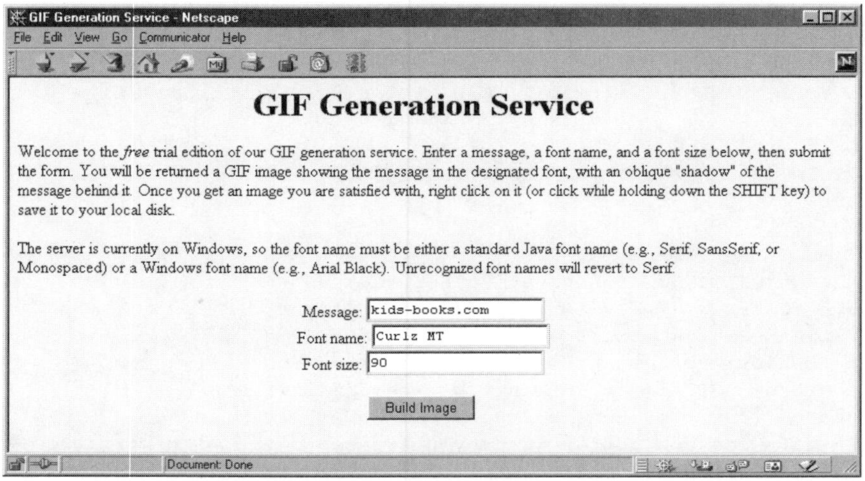

Figure 7–5   Front end to `ShadowedText` servlet.

Figure 7–6   Using the GIF-generation servlet to build the logo for a children's books Web site. (Result of submitting the form shown in Figure 7–5).

Figure 7–7   Using the GIF-generation servlet to build the title image for a site describing a local theater company.

Figure 7–8   Using the GIF-generation servlet to build an image for a page advertising a local carnival.

Listing 7.11 ShadowedTextFrame.java

```java
package coreservlets;

import java.awt.*;
import javax.swing.*;
import java.awt.geom.*;

/** Interactive interface to MessageImage class.
 *  Enter message, font name, and font size on the command
 *  line. Requires Java2.
 */

public class ShadowedTextFrame extends JPanel {
  private Image messageImage;

  public static void main(String[] args) {
    String message = "Shadowed Text";
    if (args.length > 0) {
      message = args[0];
    }
    String fontName = "Serif";
    if (args.length > 1) {
      fontName = args[1];
    }
    int fontSize = 90;
    if (args.length > 2) {
      try {
        fontSize = Integer.parseInt(args[2]);
      } catch(NumberFormatException nfe) {}
    }
    JFrame frame = new JFrame("Shadowed Text");
    frame.addWindowListener(new ExitListener());
    JPanel panel =
      new ShadowedTextFrame(message, fontName, fontSize);
    frame.setContentPane(panel);
    frame.pack();
    frame.setVisible(true);
  }

  public ShadowedTextFrame(String message,
                           String fontName,
                           int fontSize) {
    messageImage = MessageImage.makeMessageImage(message,
                                                 fontName,
                                                 fontSize);
    int width = messageImage.getWidth(this);
    int height = messageImage.getHeight(this);
    setPreferredSize(new Dimension(width, height));
  }
```

Listing 7.11 ShadowedTextFrame.java (continued)

```
public void paintComponent(Graphics g) {
    super.paintComponent(g);
    g.drawImage(messageImage, 0, 0, this);
  }
}
```

Figure 7-9   ShadowedTextFrame *application when invoked with* "java coreservlets.ShadowedTextFrame" Tom's Tools "Haettenschweiler100".

HANDLING COOKIES

Topics in This Chapter

- Purposes for cookies
- Problems with cookies
- The `Cookie` API
- A simple servlet that sets cookies
- A cookie-reporting servlet
- Some utilities that simplify cookie handling
- A customized search engine front end based upon cookies

Chapter 8

C ookies are small bits of textual information that a Web server sends to a browser and that the browser returns unchanged when later visiting the same Web site or domain. By letting the server read information it sent the client previously, the site can provide visitors with a number of conveniences such as presenting the site the way the visitor previously customized it or letting identifiable visitors in without their having to enter a password. Most browsers avoid caching documents associated with cookies, so the site can return different content each time.

This chapter discusses how to explicitly set and read cookies from within servlets, and the next chapter shows you how to use the servlet session tracking API (which can use cookies behind the scenes) to keep track of users as they move around to different pages within your site.

8.1 Benefits of Cookies

This section summarizes four typical ways in which cookies can add value to your site.

Identifying a User During an E-commerce Session

Many on-line stores use a "shopping cart" metaphor in which the user selects an item, adds it to his shopping cart, then continues shopping. Since the HTTP connection is usually closed after each page is sent, when the user selects a new item to add to the cart, how does the store know that it is the same user that put the previous item in the cart? Persistent (keep-alive) HTTP connections (see Section 7.4) do not solve this problem, since persistent connections generally apply only to requests made very close together in time, as when a browser asks for the images associated with a Web page. Besides, many servers and browsers lack support for persistent connections. Cookies, however, *can* solve this problem. In fact, this capability is so useful that servlets have an API specifically for session tracking, and servlet authors don't need to manipulate cookies directly to take advantage of it. Session tracking is discussed in Chapter 9.

Avoiding Username and Password

Many large sites require you to register in order to use their services, but it is inconvenient to remember and enter the username and password each time you visit. Cookies are a good alternative for low-security sites. When a user registers, a cookie containing a unique user ID is sent to him. When the client reconnects at a later date, the user ID is returned, the server looks it up, determines it belongs to a registered user, and permits access without an explicit username and password. The site may also remember the user's address, credit card number, and so forth, thus simplifying later transactions.

Customizing a Site

Many "portal" sites let you customize the look of the main page. They might let you pick which weather report you want to see, what stock and sports results you care about, how search results should be displayed, and so forth. Since it would be inconvenient for you to have to set up your page each time you visit their site, they use cookies to remember what you wanted. For simple settings, this customization could be accomplished by storing the page settings directly in the cookies. Section 8.6 gives an example of this. For more complex customization, however, the site just sends the client a unique identifier and keeps a server-side database that associates identifiers with page settings.

Focusing Advertising

Most advertiser-funded Web sites charge their advertisers much more for displaying "directed" ads than "random" ads. Advertisers are generally willing to pay much more to have their ads shown to people that are known to have some interest in the general product category. For example, if you go to a search engine and do a search on "Java Servlets," the search site can charge an advertiser much more for showing you an ad for a servlet development environment than for an ad for an on-line travel agent specializing in Indonesia. On the other hand, if the search had been for "Java Hotels," the situation would be reversed. Without cookies, the sites have to show a random ad when you first arrive and haven't yet performed a search, as well as when you search on something that doesn't match any ad categories. Cookies let them remember "Oh, that's the person who was searching for such and such previously" and display an appropriate (read "high priced") ad instead of a random (read "cheap") one.

8.2 Some Problems with Cookies

Providing convenience to the user and added value to the site owner is the purpose behind cookies. And despite much misinformation, cookies are not a serious security threat. Cookies are never interpreted or executed in any way and thus cannot be used to insert viruses or attack your system. Furthermore, since browsers generally only accept 20 cookies per site and 300 cookies total and since each cookie can be limited to 4 kilobytes, cookies cannot be used to fill up someone's disk or launch other denial of service attacks.

However, even though cookies don't present a serious *security* threat, they can present a significant threat to *privacy*. First, some people don't like the fact that search engines can remember that they're the user who usually does searches on certain topics. For example, they might search for job openings or sensitive health data and don't want some banner ad tipping off their coworkers next time they do a search. Even worse, two sites can share data on a user by each loading small images off the same third-party site, where that third party uses cookies and shares the data with both original sites. (Netscape, however, provides a nice feature that lets you refuse cookies from sites other than that to which you connected, but without disabling cookies altogether.) This trick of associating cookies with images can even be exploited via e-mail if you use an HTML-enabled e-mail reader that "supports" cookies and is associated with a browser. Thus, people could send you e-mail that loads images, attach cookies to those images, then identify you (e-mail address and all) if you subsequently visit their Web site. Boo.

A second privacy problem occurs when sites rely on cookies for overly sensitive data. For example, some of the big on-line bookstores use cookies to remember users and let you order without reentering much of your personal information. This is not a particular problem since they don't actually display the full credit card number and only let you send books to an address that was specified when you *did* enter the credit card in full or use the username and password. As a result, someone using your computer (or stealing your cookie file) could do no more harm than sending a big book order to your address, where the order could be refused. However, other companies might not be so careful, and an attacker who got access to someone's computer or cookie file could get on-line access to valuable personal information. Even worse, incompetent sites might embed credit card or other sensitive information directly in the cookies themselves, rather than using innocuous identifiers that are only linked to real users on the server. This is dangerous, since most users don't view leaving their computer unattended in their office as being tantamount to leaving their credit card sitting on their desk.

FOXTROT © 1998 Bill Amend. Reprinted with permission of UNIVERSAL PRESS SYNDICATE. All rights reserved

The point of all this is twofold. First, due to real and perceived privacy problems, some users turn off cookies. So, even when you use cookies to give added value to a site, your site shouldn't *depend* on them. Second, as the author of servlets that use cookies, you should be careful not to use cookies for particularly sensitive information, since this would open users up to risks if somebody accessed their computer or cookie files.

8.3 The Servlet Cookie API

To send cookies to the client, a servlet should create one or more cookies with designated names and values with `new Cookie(name, value)`, set any optional attributes with `cookie.setXxx` (readable later by `cookie.getXxx`), and insert the cookies into the response headers with `response.addCookie(cookie)`. To read incoming cookies, a servlet should call `request.getCookies`, which returns an array of `Cookie` objects corresponding to the cookies the browser has associated with your site (this is a zero-length but non-null array if there are no cookies in the request). In most cases, the servlet loops down this array until it finds the one whose name (`getName`) matches the name it had in mind, then calls `getValue` on that `Cookie` to see the value associated with that name. Each of these topics is discussed in more detail in the following sections.

Creating Cookies

You create a cookie by calling the `Cookie` constructor, which takes two strings: the cookie name and the cookie value. Neither the name nor the value should contain white space or any of the following characters:

```
[ ] ( ) = , " / ? @ : ;
```

Cookie Attributes

Before adding the cookie to the outgoing headers, you can set various characteristics of the cookie by using one of the following `setXxx` methods, where `Xxx` is the name of the attribute you want to specify. Each `setXxx` method has a corresponding `getXxx` method to retrieve the attribute value. Except for name and value, the cookie attributes apply only to *outgoing* cookies from the server to the client; they aren't set on cookies that come *from* the browser to the server. See Appendix A (Servlet and JSP Quick Reference) for a summarized version of this information.

public String getComment()
public void setComment(String comment)
These methods look up or specify a comment associated with the cookie. With version 0 cookies (see the upcoming subsection on

`getVersion` and `setVersion`), the comment is used purely for informational purposes on the server; it is not sent to the client.

public String getDomain()
public void setDomain(String domainPattern)

These methods get or set the domain to which the cookie applies. Normally, the browser only returns cookies to the exact same host-name that sent them. You can use `setDomain` method to instruct the browser to return them to other hosts within the same domain. To prevent servers setting cookies that apply to hosts outside their domain, the domain specified is required to start with a dot (e.g., `.prenhall.com`), and must contain two dots for noncountry domains like `.com`, `.edu` and `.gov`; and three dots for country domains like `.co.uk` and `.edu.es`. For instance, cookies sent from a servlet at `bali.vacations.com` would not normally get sent by the browser to pages at `mexico.vacations.com`. If the site wanted this to happen, the servlets could specify `cookie.setDomain(".vacations.com")`.

public int getMaxAge()
public void setMaxAge(int lifetime)

These methods tell how much time (in seconds) should elapse before the cookie expires. A negative value, which is the default, indicates that the cookie will last only for the current session (i.e., until the user quits the browser) and will not be stored on disk. See the `LongLivedCookie` class (Listing 8.4), which defines a subclass of `Cookie` with a maximum age automatically set one year in the future. Specifying a value of 0 instructs the browser to delete the cookie.

public String getName()
public void setName(String cookieName)

This pair of methods gets or sets the name of the cookie. The name and the value are the two pieces you virtually *always* care about. However, since the name is supplied to the `Cookie` constructor, you rarely need to call `setName`. On the other hand, `getName` is used on almost every cookie received on the server. Since the `getCookies` method of `HttpServlet-Request` returns an array of `Cookie` objects, it is common to loop down this array, calling `getName` until you have a particular name, then check the value with `getValue`. For an encapsulation of this process, see the `getCookieValue` method shown in Listing 8.3.

public String getPath()
public void setPath(String path)

These methods get or set the path to which the cookie applies. If you don't specify a path, the browser returns the cookie only to URLs in or below the directory containing the page that sent the cookie. For example, if the server sent the cookie from `http://ecommerce.site.com/toys/specials.html`, the browser would send the cookie back when connecting to `http://ecommerce.site.com/toys/bikes/beginners.html`, but not to `http://ecommerce.site.com/cds/classical.html`. The `setPath` method can be used to specify something more general. For example, `someCookie.setPath("/")` specifies that *all* pages on the server should receive the cookie. The path specified must include the current page; that is, you may specify a more general path than the default, but not a more specific one. So, for example, a servlet at `http://host/store/cust-service/request` could specify a path of `/store/` (since `/store/` includes `/store/cust-service/`) but not a path of `/store/cust-service/returns/` (since this directory does not include `/store/cust-service/`).

public boolean getSecure()
public void setSecure(boolean secureFlag)

This pair of methods gets or sets the boolean value indicating whether the cookie should only be sent over encrypted (i.e., SSL) connections. The default is `false`; the cookie should apply to all connections.

public String getValue()
public void setValue(String cookieValue)

The `getValue` method looks up the value associated with the cookie; the `setValue` method specifies it. Again, the name and the value are the two parts of a cookie that you almost *always* care about, although in a few cases, a name is used as a boolean flag and its value is ignored (i.e., the existence of a cookie with the designated name is all that matters).

public int getVersion()
public void setVersion(int version)

These methods get/set the cookie protocol version the cookie complies with. Version 0, the default, follows the original Netscape specification (`http://www.netscape.com/newsref/std/cookie_spec.html`) Version 1, not yet widely supported, adheres to RFC 2109 (retrieve RFCs from the archive sites listed at `http://www.rfc-editor.org/`).

Placing Cookies in the Response Headers

The cookie is inserted into a `Set-Cookie` HTTP response header by means of the `addCookie` method of `HttpServletResponse`. The method is called `addCookie`, not `setCookie`, because any previously specified `Set-Cookie` headers are left alone and a new header is set. Here's an example:

```
Cookie userCookie = new Cookie("user", "uid1234");
userCookie.setMaxAge(60*60*24*365); // 1 year
response.addCookie(userCookie);
```

Reading Cookies from the Client

To send cookies *to* the client, you create a `Cookie`, then use `addCookie` to send a `Set-Cookie` HTTP response header. To read the cookies that come back *from* the client, you call `getCookies` on the `HttpServletRequest`. This call returns an array of `Cookie` objects corresponding to the values that came in on the `Cookie` HTTP request header. If there are no cookies in the request, `get-Cookies` returns a zero-length array. Once you have this array, you typically loop down it, calling `getName` on each `Cookie` until you find one matching the name you have in mind. You then call `getValue` on the matching `Cookie` and finish with some processing specific to the resultant value. This is such a common process that Section 8.5 presents two utilities that simplify retrieving a cookie or cookie value that matches a designated cookie name.

8.4 Examples of Setting and Reading Cookies

Listing 8.1 and Figure 8–1 show the `SetCookies` servlet, a servlet that sets six cookies. Three have the default expiration date, meaning that they should apply only until the user next restarts the browser. The other three use `set-MaxAge` to stipulate that they should apply for the next hour, regardless of whether the user restarts the browser or reboots the computer to initiate a new browsing session.

Listing 8.2 shows a servlet that creates a table of all the cookies sent to it in the request. Figure 8–2 shows this servlet immediately after the `SetCookies` servlet is visited. Figure 8–3 shows it after `SetCookies` is visited then the browser is closed and restarted.

Listing 8.1   SetCookies.java

```java
package coreservlets;

import java.io.*;
import javax.servlet.*;
import javax.servlet.http.*;

/** Sets six cookies: three that apply only to the current
 *  session (regardless of how long that session lasts)
 *  and three that persist for an hour (regardless of
 *  whether the browser is restarted).
 */

public class SetCookies extends HttpServlet {
  public void doGet(HttpServletRequest request,
                    HttpServletResponse response)
      throws ServletException, IOException {
    for(int i=0; i<3; i++) {
      // Default maxAge is -1, indicating cookie
      // applies only to current browsing session.
      Cookie cookie = new Cookie("Session-Cookie " + i,
                                 "Cookie-Value-S" + i);
      response.addCookie(cookie);
      cookie = new Cookie("Persistent-Cookie " + i,
                          "Cookie-Value-P" + i);
      // Cookie is valid for an hour, regardless of whether
      // user quits browser, reboots computer, or whatever.
      cookie.setMaxAge(3600);
      response.addCookie(cookie);
    }
    response.setContentType("text/html");
    PrintWriter out = response.getWriter();
    String title = "Setting Cookies";
    out.println
      (ServletUtilities.headWithTitle(title) +
       "<BODY BGCOLOR=\"#FDF5E6\">\n" +
       "<H1 ALIGN=\"CENTER\">" + title + "</H1>\n" +
       "There are six cookies associated with this page.\n" +
       "To see them, visit the\n" +
       "<A HREF=\"/servlet/coreservlets.ShowCookies\">\n" +
       "<CODE>ShowCookies</CODE> servlet</A>.\n" +
       "<P>\n" +
       "Three of the cookies are associated only with the\n" +
       "current session, while three are persistent.\n" +
       "Quit the browser, restart, and return to the\n" +
       "<CODE>ShowCookies</CODE> servlet to verify that\n" +
       "the three long-lived ones persist across sessions.\n" +
       "</BODY></HTML>");
  }
}
```

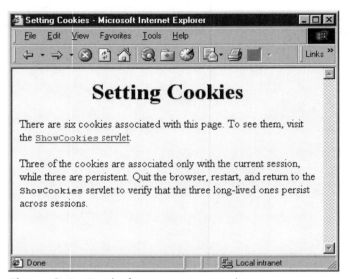

Figure 8–1 Result of `SetCookies` servlet.

Listing 8.2 `ShowCookies.java`

```
package coreservlets;

import java.io.*;
import javax.servlet.*;
import javax.servlet.http.*;

/** Creates a table of the cookies associated with
 *  the current page.
 */

public class ShowCookies extends HttpServlet {
  public void doGet(HttpServletRequest request,
                    HttpServletResponse response)
      throws ServletException, IOException {
    response.setContentType("text/html");
    PrintWriter out = response.getWriter();
    String title = "Active Cookies";
    out.println(ServletUtilities.headWithTitle(title) +
                "<BODY BGCOLOR=\"#FDF5E6\">\n" +
                "<H1 ALIGN=\"CENTER\">" + title + "</H1>\n" +
```

Listing 8.2   `ShowCookies.java` (continued)

```
                "<TABLE BORDER=1 ALIGN=\"CENTER\">\n" +
                "<TR BGCOLOR=\"#FFAD00\">\n" +
                "  <TH>Cookie Name\n" +
                "  <TH>Cookie Value");
    Cookie[] cookies = request.getCookies();
    Cookie cookie;
    for(int i=0; i<cookies.length; i++) {
      cookie = cookies[i];
      out.println("<TR>\n" +
                  "  <TD>" + cookie.getName() + "\n" +
                  "  <TD>" + cookie.getValue());
    }
    out.println("</TABLE></BODY></HTML>");
  }
}
```

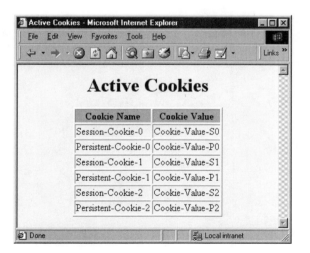

Figure 8–2   Result of visiting the `ShowCookies` servlet within an hour of visiting `SetCookies` in the same browser session.

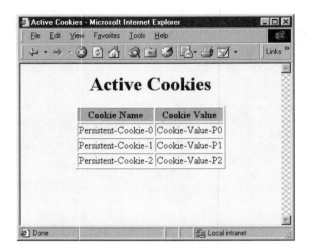

Figure 8–3   Result of visiting the ShowCookies servlet within an hour of visiting SetCookies in a different browser session.

8.5 Basic Cookie Utilities

This section presents some simple but useful utilities for dealing with cookies.

Finding Cookies with Specified Names

Listing 8.3 shows a section of ServletUtilities.java that simplifies the retrieval of a cookie or cookie value, given a cookie name. The getCookie-Value method loops through the array of available Cookie objects, returning the value of any Cookie whose name matches the input. If there is no match, the designated default value is returned. So, for example, my typical approach for dealing with cookies is as follows:

```
Cookie[] cookies = request.getCookies();
String color =
  ServletUtilities.getCookieValue(cookies, "color", "black");
String font =
  ServletUtilities.getCookieValue(cookies, "font", "Arial");
```

The getCookie method also loops through the array comparing names, but returns the actual Cookie object instead of just the value. That method is for cases when you want to do something with the Cookie other than just read its value.

Listing 8.3   `ServletUtilities.java`

```java
package coreservlets;

import javax.servlet.*;
import javax.servlet.http.*;

public class ServletUtilities {
  // Other methods in this class shown in earlier chapters.

  public static String getCookieValue(Cookie[] cookies,
                                      String cookieName,
                                      String defaultValue) {
    for(int i=0; i<cookies.length; i++) {
      Cookie cookie = cookies[i];
      if (cookieName.equals(cookie.getName()))
        return(cookie.getValue());
    }
    return(defaultValue);
  }

  public static Cookie getCookie(Cookie[] cookies,
                                 String cookieName) {
    for(int i=0; i<cookies.length; i++) {
      Cookie cookie = cookies[i];
      if (cookieName.equals(cookie.getName()))
        return(cookie);
    }
    return(null);
  }
}
```

Creating Long-Lived Cookies

Listing 8.4 shows a small class that you can use instead of `Cookie` if you want your cookie to automatically persist when the client quits the browser. See Listing 8.5 for a servlet that uses this class.

8.6   A Customized Search Engine Interface

Listing 8.5 shows the `CustomizedSearchEngines` servlet, a variation of the `SearchEngines` example previously shown in Section 6.3. Like the `Search-Engines` servlet (see Figure 8–5), the `CustomizedSearchEngines` servlet

Listing 8.4   `LongLivedCookie.java`

```java
package coreservlets;

import javax.servlet.http.*;

/** Cookie that persists 1 year. Default Cookie doesn't
 *  persist past current session.
 */

public class LongLivedCookie extends Cookie {
  public static final int SECONDS_PER_YEAR = 60*60*24*365;

  public LongLivedCookie(String name, String value) {
    super(name, value);
    setMaxAge(SECONDS_PER_YEAR);
  }
}
```

reads the user choices from the HTML front end and forwards them to the appropriate search engine. In addition, the `CustomizedSearchEngines` servlet returns to the client cookies that store the search values. Then, when the user comes back to the front-end servlet at a later time (even after quitting the browser and restarting), the front-end page is initialized with the values from the previous search.

To accomplish this customization, the front end is dynamically generated instead of coming from a static HTML file (see Listing 8.6 for the source code and Figure 8–4 for the result). The front-end servlet reads the cookie values and uses them for the initial values of the HTML form fields. Note that it would not have been possible for the front end to return the cookies directly to the client. That's because the search selections aren't known until the user interactively fills in the form and submits it, which cannot occur until after the servlet that generated the front end has finished executing.

This example uses the `LongLivedCookie` class, shown in the previous section, for creating a `Cookie` that automatically has a long-term expiration date, instructing the browser to use it beyond the current session.

Listing 8.5 `CustomizedSearchEngines.java`

```java
package coreservlets;

import java.io.*;
import javax.servlet.*;
import javax.servlet.http.*;
import java.net.*;

/** A variation of the SearchEngine servlet that uses
 *  cookies to remember users choices. These values
 *  are then used by the SearchEngineFrontEnd servlet
 *  to initialize the form-based front end.
 */

public class CustomizedSearchEngines extends HttpServlet {
  public void doGet(HttpServletRequest request,
                    HttpServletResponse response)
      throws ServletException, IOException {

    String searchString = request.getParameter("searchString");
    if ((searchString == null) ||
        (searchString.length() == 0)) {
      reportProblem(response, "Missing search string.");
      return;
    }
    Cookie searchStringCookie =
      new LongLivedCookie("searchString", searchString);
    response.addCookie(searchStringCookie);
    // The URLEncoder changes spaces to "+" signs and other
    // non-alphanumeric characters to "%XY", where XY is the
    // hex value of the ASCII (or ISO Latin-1) character.
    // Browsers always URL-encode form values, so the
    // getParameter method decodes automatically. But since
    // we're just passing this on to another server, we need to
    // re-encode it.
    searchString = URLEncoder.encode(searchString);
    String numResults = request.getParameter("numResults");
    if ((numResults == null) ||
        (numResults.equals("0")) ||
        (numResults.length() == 0)) {
      numResults = "10";
    }
    Cookie numResultsCookie =
      new LongLivedCookie("numResults", numResults);
    response.addCookie(numResultsCookie);
    String searchEngine = request.getParameter("searchEngine");
    if (searchEngine == null) {
      reportProblem(response, "Missing search engine name.");
      return;
    }
```

Listing 8.5 `CustomizedSearchEngines.java` **(continued)**

```java
  Cookie searchEngineCookie =
    new LongLivedCookie("searchEngine", searchEngine);
  response.addCookie(searchEngineCookie);
  SearchSpec[] commonSpecs = SearchSpec.getCommonSpecs();
  for(int i=0; i<commonSpecs.length; i++) {
    SearchSpec searchSpec = commonSpecs[i];
    if (searchSpec.getName().equals(searchEngine)) {
      String url =
        searchSpec.makeURL(searchString, numResults);
      response.sendRedirect(url);
      return;
    }
  }
  reportProblem(response, "Unrecognized search engine.");
}

private void reportProblem(HttpServletResponse response,
                           String message)
    throws IOException {
  response.sendError(response.SC_NOT_FOUND,
                     "<H2>" + message + "</H2>");
}

public void doPost(HttpServletRequest request,
                   HttpServletResponse response)
    throws ServletException, IOException {
  doGet(request, response);
}
}
```

Listing 8.6 `SearchEnginesFrontEnd.java`

```java
package coreservlets;

import java.io.*;
import javax.servlet.*;
import javax.servlet.http.*;
import java.net.*;

/** Dynamically generated variation of the
 *  SearchEngines.html front end that uses cookies
 *  to remember a user's preferences.
 */
```

Listing 8.6   `SearchEnginesFrontEnd.java` (continued)

```
public class SearchEnginesFrontEnd extends HttpServlet {
  public void doGet(HttpServletRequest request,
                    HttpServletResponse response)
     throws ServletException, IOException {
    Cookie[] cookies = request.getCookies();
    String searchString =
      ServletUtilities.getCookieValue(cookies,
                                      "searchString",
                                      "Java Programming");
    String numResults =
      ServletUtilities.getCookieValue(cookies,
                                      "numResults",
                                      "10");
    String searchEngine =
      ServletUtilities.getCookieValue(cookies,
                                      "searchEngine",
                                      "google");
    response.setContentType("text/html");
    PrintWriter out = response.getWriter();
    String title = "Searching the Web";
    out.println
      (ServletUtilities.headWithTitle(title) +
       "<BODY BGCOLOR=\"#FDF5E6\">\n" +
       "<H1 ALIGN=\"CENTER\">Searching the Web</H1>\n" +
       "\n" +
       "<FORM ACTION=\"/servlet/" +
         "coreservlets.CustomizedSearchEngines\">\n" +
       "<CENTER>\n" +
       "Search String:\n" +
       "<INPUT TYPE=\"TEXT\" NAME=\"searchString\"\n" +
       "       VALUE=\"" + searchString + "\"><BR>\n" +
       "Results to Show Per Page:\n" +
       "<INPUT TYPE=\"TEXT\" NAME=\"numResults\"\n" +
       "       VALUE=" + numResults + " SIZE=3><BR>\n" +
       "<INPUT TYPE=\"RADIO\" NAME=\"searchEngine\"\n" +
       "       VALUE=\"google\"" +
       checked("google", searchEngine) + ">\n" +
       "Google |\n" +
       "<INPUT TYPE=\"RADIO\" NAME=\"searchEngine\"\n" +
       "          VALUE=\"infoseek\"" +
       checked("infoseek", searchEngine) + ">\n" +
       "Infoseek |\n" +
       "<INPUT TYPE=\"RADIO\" NAME=\"searchEngine\"\n" +
       "       VALUE=\"lycos\"" +
       checked("lycos", searchEngine) + ">\n" +
       "Lycos |\n" +
       "<INPUT TYPE=\"RADIO\" NAME=\"searchEngine\"\n" +
       "       VALUE=\"hotbot\"" +
```

Listing 8.6   `SearchEnginesFrontEnd.java` (continued)

```java
           checked("hotbot", searchEngine) + ">\n" +
           "HotBot\n" +
           "<BR>\n" +
           "<INPUT TYPE=\"SUBMIT\" VALUE=\"Search\">\n" +
           "</CENTER>\n" +
           "</FORM>\n" +
           "\n" +
           "</BODY>\n" +
           "</HTML>\n");
    }

    private String checked(String name1, String name2) {
      if (name1.equals(name2))
        return(" CHECKED");
      else
        return("");
    }
}
```

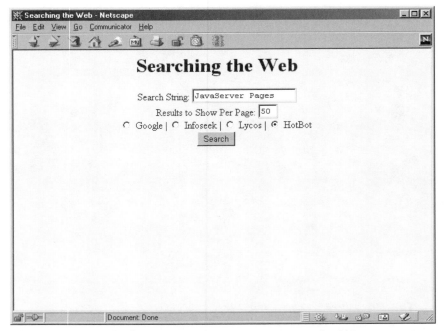

Figure 8–4   Result of `SearchEnginesFrontEnd` servlet. Whatever options you specify will be the initial choices next time you visit the same servlet.

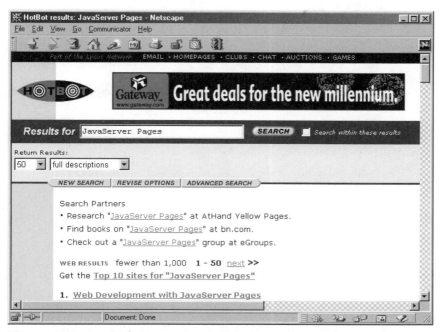

Figure 8–5   Result of `CustomizedSearchEngines` servlet.

SESSION
TRACKING

Topics in This Chapter

- The purpose of session tracking
- The servlet session tracking API
- A servlet that uses sessions to show per-client access counts
- A reusable shopping cart class
- An on-line store that uses session tracking, shopping carts, and pages automatically built from catalog entries

Chapter 9

This chapter shows you how to use the servlet session tracking API to keep track of visitors as they move around at your site.

9.1 The Need for Session Tracking

HTTP is a "stateless" protocol: each time a client retrieves a Web page, it opens a separate connection to the Web server, and the server does not automatically maintain contextual information about a client. Even with servers that support persistent (keep-alive) HTTP connections and keep a socket open for multiple client requests that occur close together in time (see Section 7.4), there is no built-in support for maintaining contextual information. This lack of context causes a number of difficulties. For example, when clients at an on-line store add an item to their shopping carts, how does the server know what's already in them? Similarly, when clients decide to proceed to checkout, how can the server determine which previously created shopping carts are theirs?

There are three typical solutions to this problem: cookies, URL-rewriting, and hidden form fields.

Cookies

You can use HTTP cookies to store information about a shopping session, and each subsequent connection can look up the current session and then extract information about that session from some location on the server machine. For example, a servlet could do something like the following:

```
String sessionID = makeUniqueString();
Hashtable sessionInfo = new Hashtable();
Hashtable globalTable = findTableStoringSessions();
globalTable.put(sessionID, sessionInfo);
Cookie sessionCookie = new Cookie("JSESSIONID", sessionID);
sessionCookie.setPath("/");
response.addCookie(sessionCookie);
```

Then, in later requests the server could use the `globalTable` hash table to associate a session ID from the `JSESSIONID` cookie with the `sessionInfo` hash table of data associated with that particular session. This is an excellent solution and is the most widely used approach for session handling. Still, it would be nice to have a higher-level API that handles some of these details. Even though servlets have a high-level and easy-to-use interface to cookies (see Chapter 8), a number of relatively tedious details still need to be handled in this case:

- Extracting the cookie that stores the session identifier from the other cookies (there may be many cookies, after all)
- Setting an appropriate expiration time for the cookie (sessions that are inactive for 24 hours probably should be reset)
- Associating the hash tables with each request
- Generating the unique session identifiers

Besides, due to real and perceived privacy concerns over cookies (see Section 8.2), some users disable them. So, it would be nice to have alternative implementation approaches in addition to a higher-level protocol.

URL-Rewriting

With this approach, the client appends some extra data on the end of each URL that identifies the session, and the server associates that identifier with data it has stored about that session. For example, with `http://host/path/file.html;jsessionid=1234`, the session information is attached as `jsessionid=1234`. This is also an excellent solution, and even has the advantage that it works when browsers don't support cookies or when the user has disabled them. However, it has most of the same problems as cookies, namely, that the server-side program has a lot of straightforward but tedious processing to do. In addition, you have to be very careful that every URL that references your site and is returned to the user (even by indirect means like `Location` fields in server redirects) has the extra information appended. And, if the user leaves the session and comes back via a bookmark or link, the session information can be lost.

Hidden Form Fields

HTML forms can have an entry that looks like the following:

```
<INPUT TYPE="HIDDEN" NAME="session" VALUE="...">
```

This entry means that, when the form is submitted, the specified name and value are included in the GET or POST data. For details, see Section 16.9 (Hidden Fields). This hidden field can be used to store information about the session but it has the major disadvantage that it only works if every page is dynamically generated.

Session Tracking in Servlets

Servlets provide an outstanding technical solution: the `HttpSession` API. This high-level interface is built on top of cookies or URL-rewriting. In fact, most servers use cookies if the browser supports them, but automatically revert to URL-rewriting when cookies are unsupported or explicitly disabled. But, the servlet author doesn't need to bother with many of the details, doesn't have to explicitly manipulate cookies or information appended to the URL, and is automatically given a convenient place to store arbitrary objects that are associated with each session.

9.2 The Session Tracking API

Using sessions in servlets is straightforward and involves looking up the session object associated with the current request, creating a new session object when necessary, looking up information associated with a session, storing information in a session, and discarding completed or abandoned sessions. Finally, if you return any URLs to the clients that reference your site and URL-rewriting is being used, you need to attach the session information to the URLs.

Looking Up the HttpSession Object Associated with the Current Request

You look up the `HttpSession` object by calling the `getSession` method of `HttpServletRequest`. Behind the scenes, the system extracts a user ID from a cookie or attached URL data, then uses that as a key into a table of previously created `HttpSession` objects. But this is all done transparently to the programmer: you just call `getSession`. If `getSession` returns `null`, this means that the user is not already participating in a session, so you can create a new session. Creating a new session in this case is so commonly done that there is an option to automatically create a new session if one doesn't already exist. Just pass `true` to `getSession`. Thus, your first step usually looks like this:

```
HttpSession session = request.getSession(true);
```

If you care whether the session existed previously or is newly created, you can use `isNew` to check.

Looking Up Information Associated with a Session

`HttpSession` objects live on the server; they're just automatically associated with the client by a behind-the-scenes mechanism like cookies or URL-rewriting. These session objects have a built-in data structure that lets you store any number of keys and associated values. In version 2.1 and earlier of the servlet API, you use `session.getValue("attribute")` to look up a previously stored value. The return type is `Object`, so you have to do a type-cast to whatever more specific type of data was associated with that attribute name in the session. The return value is `null` if there is no such attribute, so you need to check for `null` before calling methods on objects associated with sessions.

In version 2.2 of the servlet API, `getValue` is deprecated in favor of `get-Attribute` because of the better naming match with `setAttribute` (in version 2.1 the match for `getValue` is `putValue`, not `setValue`). Nevertheless, since not all commercial servlet engines yet support version 2.2, I'll use `getValue` in my examples.

Here's a representative example, assuming `ShoppingCart` is some class you've defined to store information on items being purchased (for an implementation, see Section 9.4 (An On-Line Store Using a Shopping Cart and Session Tracking)).

```
HttpSession session = request.getSession(true);
ShoppingCart cart =
  (ShoppingCart)session.getValue("shoppingCart");
if (cart == null) { // No cart already in session
  cart = new ShoppingCart();
  session.putValue("shoppingCart", cart);
}
doSomethingWith(cart);
```

In most cases, you have a specific attribute name in mind and want to find the value (if any) already associated with that name. However, you can also discover all the attribute names in a given session by calling getValueNames, which returns an array of strings. This method is your only option for finding attribute names in version 2.1, but in servlet engines supporting version 2.2 of the servlet specification, you can use getAttributeNames. That method is more consistent in that it returns an Enumeration, just like the getHeader-Names and getParameterNames methods of HttpServletRequest.

Although the data that was explicitly associated with a session is the part you care most about, there are some other pieces of information that are sometimes useful as well. Here is a summary of the methods available in the HttpSession class.

public Object getValue(String name)
public Object getAttribute(String name)
These methods extract a previously stored value from a session object. They return null if there is no value associated with the given name. Use getValue in version 2.1 of the servlet API. Version 2.2 supports both methods, but getAttribute is preferred and getValue is deprecated.

public void putValue(String name, Object value)
public void setAttribute(String name, Object value)
These methods associate a value with a name. Use putValue with version 2.1 servlets and either setAttribute (preferred) or putValue (deprecated) with version 2.2 servlets. If the object supplied to putValue or setAttribute implements the HttpSessionBinding-Listener interface, the object's valueBound method is called after it is stored in the session. Similarly, if the previous value implements HttpSessionBindingListener, its valueUnbound method is called.

public void removeValue(String name)
public void removeAttribute(String name)
These methods remove any values associated with the designated name. If the value being removed implements HttpSessionBindingListener,

its `valueUnbound` method is called. With version 2.1 servlets, use `removeValue`. In version 2.2, `removeAttribute` is preferred, but `removeValue` is still supported (albeit deprecated) for backward compatibility.

public String[] getValueNames()
public Enumeration getAttributeNames()

These methods return the names of all attributes in the session. Use `getValueNames` in version 2.1 of the servlet specification. In version 2.2, `getValueNames` is supported but deprecated; use `getAttributeNames` instead.

public String getId()

This method returns the unique identifier generated for each session. It is sometimes used as the key name when only a single value is associated with a session, or when information about sessions is being logged.

public boolean isNew()

This method returns `true` if the client (browser) has never seen the session, usually because it was just created rather than being referenced by an incoming client request. It returns `false` for preexisting sessions.

public long getCreationTime()

This method returns the time in milliseconds since midnight, January 1, 1970 (GMT) at which the session was first built. To get a value useful for printing out, pass the value to the `Date` constructor or the `setTimeInMillis` method of `GregorianCalendar`.

public long getLastAccessedTime()

This method returns the time in milliseconds since midnight, January 1, 1970 (GMT) at which the session was last sent from the client.

public int getMaxInactiveInterval()
public void setMaxInactiveInterval(int seconds)

These methods get or set the amount of time, in seconds, that a session should go without access before being automatically invalidated. A negative value indicates that the session should never time out. Note that the time out is maintained on the server and is *not* the same as the cookie expiration date, which is sent to the client.

public void invalidate()

This method invalidates the session and unbinds all objects associated with it.

Associating Information with a Session

As discussed in the previous section, you *read* information associated with a session by using getValue (in version 2.1 of the servlet specification) or getAttribute (in version 2.2). To *specify* information in version 2.1 servlets, you use putValue, supplying a key and a value. Use setAttribute in version 2.2. This is a more consistent name because it uses the get/set notation of JavaBeans. To let your values perform side effects when they are stored in a session, simply have the object you are associating with the session implement the HttpSessionBindingListener interface. Now, every time putValue or setAttribute is called on one of those objects, its valueBound method is called immediately afterward.

Be aware that putValue and setAttribute replace any previous values; if you want to remove a value without supplying a replacement, use remove-Value in version 2.1 and removeAttribute in version 2.2. These methods trigger the valueUnbound method of any values that implement Http-SessionBindingListener. Sometimes you just want to replace previous values; see the referringPage entry in the example below for an example. Other times, you want to retrieve a previous value and augment it; for an example, see the previousItems entry below. This example assumes a ShoppingCart class with an addItem method to store items being ordered, and a Catalog class with a static getItem method that returns an item, given an item identifier. For an implementation, see Section 9.4 (An On-Line Store Using a Shopping Cart and Session Tracking).

```
HttpSession session = request.getSession(true);
session.putValue("referringPage", request.getHeader("Referer"));
ShoppingCart cart =
  (ShoppingCart)session.getValue("previousItems");
if (cart == null) { // No cart already in session
  cart = new ShoppingCart();
  session.putValue("previousItems", cart);
}
String itemID = request.getParameter("itemID");
if (itemID != null) {
  cart.addItem(Catalog.getItem(itemID));
}
```

Terminating Sessions

Sessions will automatically become inactive when the amount of time between client accesses exceeds the interval specified by getMax-InactiveInterval. When this happens, any objects bound to the Http-Session object automatically get unbound. When this happens, your attached objects will automatically be notified if they implement the HttpSessionBindingListener interface.

Rather than waiting for sessions to time out, you can explicitly deactivate a session through the use of the session's invalidate method.

Encoding URLs Sent to the Client

If you are using URL-rewriting for session tracking and you send a URL that references your site to the client, you need to explicitly add on the session data. Since the servlet will automatically switch to URL-rewriting when cookies aren't supported by the client, you should routinely encode *all* URLs that reference your site. There are two possible places you might use URLs that refer to your own site. The first is when the URLs are embedded in the Web page that the servlet generates. These URLs should be passed through the encodeURL method of HttpServletResponse. The method will determine if URL-rewriting is currently in use and append the session information only if necessary. The URL is returned unchanged otherwise.

Here's an example:

```
String originalURL = someRelativeOrAbsoluteURL;
String encodedURL = response.encodeURL(originalURL);
out.println("<A HREF=\"" + encodedURL + "\">...</A>");
```

The second place you might use a URL that refers to your own site is in a sendRedirect call (i.e., placed into the Location response header). In this second situation, there are different rules for determining if session information needs to be attached, so you cannot use encodeURL. Fortunately, Http-ServletResponse supplies an encodeRedirectURL method to handle that case. Here's an example:

```
String originalURL = someURL; // Relative URL OK in version 2.2
String encodedURL = response.encodeRedirectURL(originalURL);
response.sendRedirect(encodedURL);
```

Since you often don't know if your servlet will later become part of a series of pages that use session tracking, it is good practice for servlets to plan ahead and encode URLs that reference their site.

Core Approach

Plan ahead: pass URLs that refer to your own site through `response.encodeURL`*or*`response.encodeRedirectURL`,*regardlessof whether your servlet is using session tracking.*

9.3 A Servlet Showing Per-Client Access Counts

Listing 9.1 presents a simple servlet that shows basic information about the client's session. When the client connects, the servlet uses `request.getSession(true)` to either retrieve the existing session or, if there was no session, to create a new one. The servlet then looks for an attribute of type `Integer` called `accessCount`. If it cannot find such an attribute, it uses 0 as the number of previous accesses. This value is then incremented and associated with the session by `putValue`. Finally, the servlet prints a small HTML table showing information about the session. Figures 9–1 and 9–2 show the servlet on the initial visit and after the page was reloaded several times.

Listing 9.1 `ShowSession.java`

```
import java.io.*;
import javax.servlet.*;
import javax.servlet.http.*;
import java.net.*;
import java.util.*;

/** Simple example of session tracking. See the shopping
 *  cart example for a more detailed one.
 */

public class ShowSession extends HttpServlet {
  public void doGet(HttpServletRequest request,
                    HttpServletResponse response)
      throws ServletException, IOException {
    response.setContentType("text/html");
    PrintWriter out = response.getWriter();
    String title = "Session Tracking Example";
    HttpSession session = request.getSession(true);
    String heading;
    // Use getAttribute instead of getValue in version 2.2.
    Integer accessCount =
```

Listing 9.1   `ShowSession.java` (continued)

```
        (Integer)session.getValue("accessCount");
  if (accessCount == null) {
    accessCount = new Integer(0);
    heading = "Welcome, Newcomer";
  } else {
    heading = "Welcome Back";
    accessCount = new Integer(accessCount.intValue() + 1);
  }
  // Use setAttribute instead of putValue in version 2.2.
  session.putValue("accessCount", accessCount);

  out.println(ServletUtilities.headWithTitle(title) +
              "<BODY BGCOLOR=\"#FDF5E6\">\n" +
              "<H1 ALIGN=\"CENTER\">" + heading + "</H1>\n" +
              "<H2>Information on Your Session:</H2>\n" +
              "<TABLE BORDER=1 ALIGN=\"CENTER\">\n" +
              "<TR BGCOLOR=\"#FFAD00\">\n" +
              "  <TH>Info Type<TH>Value\n" +
              "<TR>\n" +
              "  <TD>ID\n" +
              "  <TD>" + session.getId() + "\n" +
              "<TR>\n" +
              "  <TD>Creation Time\n" +
              "  <TD>" +
              new Date(session.getCreationTime()) + "\n" +
              "<TR>\n" +
              "  <TD>Time of Last Access\n" +
              "  <TD>" +
              new Date(session.getLastAccessedTime()) + "\n" +
              "<TR>\n" +
              "  <TD>Number of Previous Accesses\n" +
              "  <TD>" + accessCount + "\n" +
              "</TABLE>\n" +
              "</BODY></HTML>");

}


/** Handle GET and POST requests identically. */

public void doPost(HttpServletRequest request,
                   HttpServletResponse response)
    throws ServletException, IOException {
  doGet(request, response);
}
}
```

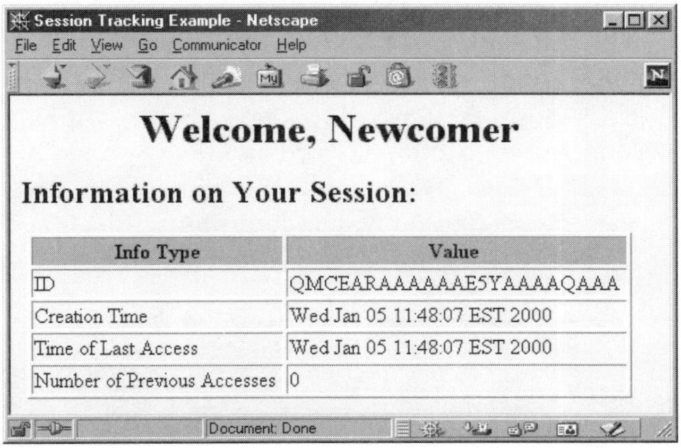

Figure 9–1 First visit to `ShowSession` servlet.

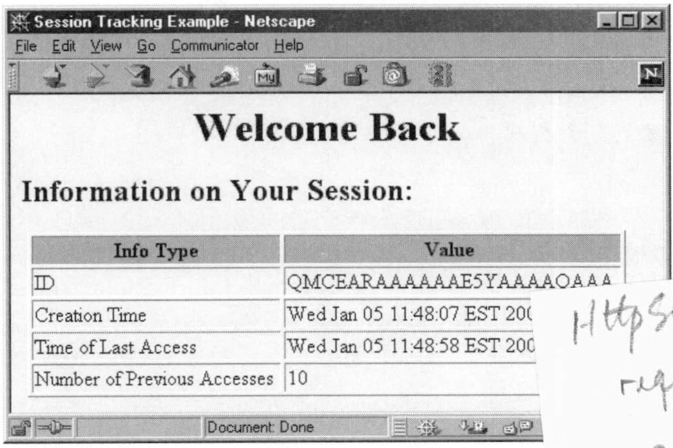

Figure 9–2 Eleventh visit to `ShowSession` se

HttpSession session = request.getSession(true);

request.getHeader("Referer")

9.4 An On-Line Store U Cart and Session Tr

This section gives an extended example of h store that uses session tracking. The first s pages that display items for sale. The code fo ... simply lists the page title and the identifiers of the items listed on the page. The actual page is then built automatically by methods in the parent class, based upon item descriptions stored in the catalog. The second subsection shows the page that handles the orders. It uses session tracking to associate a shopping cart with each user and permits the user to modify orders for any previously selected item. The third subsection presents the implementation of the shopping cart, the data structures representing individual items and orders, and the catalog.

DILBERT reprinted by permission of United Syndicate, Inc.

Building the Front End

Listing 9.2 presents an abstract base class used as a starting point for servlets that want to display items for sale. It takes the identifiers for the items for sale, looks them up in the catalog, and uses the descriptions and prices found there to present an order page to the user. Listing 9.3 (with the result shown in Figure 9–3) and Listing 9.4 (with the result shown in Figure 9–4) show how easy it is to build actual pages with this parent class.

Listing 9.2   `CatalogPage.java`

```
package coreservlets;

import java.io.*;
import javax.servlet.*;
import javax.servlet.http.*;
import java.util.*;

/** Base class for pages showing catalog entries.
 *   Servlets that extend this class must specify
 *   the catalog entries that they are selling and the page
 *   title <I>before</I> the servlet is ever accessed. This
```

Listing 9.2 `CatalogPage.java` **(continued)**

```
 *   is done by putting calls to setItems and setTitle
 *   in init.
 */

public abstract class CatalogPage extends HttpServlet {
  private Item[] items;
  private String[] itemIDs;
  private String title;

  /** Given an array of item IDs, look them up in the
   *  Catalog and put their corresponding Item entry
   *  into the items array. The Item contains a short
   *  description, a long description, and a price,
   *  using the item ID as the unique key.
   *  <P>
   *  Servlets that extend CatalogPage <B>must</B> call
   *  this method (usually from init) before the servlet
   *  is accessed.
   */

  protected void setItems(String[] itemIDs) {
    this.itemIDs = itemIDs;
    items = new Item[itemIDs.length];
    for(int i=0; i<items.length; i++) {
      items[i] = Catalog.getItem(itemIDs[i]);
    }
  }

  /** Sets the page title, which is displayed in
   *  an H1 heading in resultant page.
   *  <P>
   *  Servlets that extend CatalogPage <B>must</B> call
   *  this method (usually from init) before the servlet
   *  is accessed.
   */

  protected void setTitle(String title) {
    this.title = title;
  }

  /** First display title, then, for each catalog item,
   *  put its short description in a level-two (H2) heading
   *  with the price in parentheses and long description
   *  below. Below each entry, put an order button
   *  that submits info to the OrderPage servlet for
   *  the associated catalog entry.
   *  <P>
```

Listing 9.2 `CatalogPage.java` (continued)

```
 *   To see the HTML that results from this method, do
 *   "View Source" on KidsBooksPage or TechBooksPage, two
 *   concrete classes that extend this abstract class.
 */

public void doGet(HttpServletRequest request,
                  HttpServletResponse response)
    throws ServletException, IOException {
  response.setContentType("text/html");
  if (items == null) {
    response.sendError(response.SC_NOT_FOUND,
                       "Missing Items.");
    return;
  }
  PrintWriter out = response.getWriter();
  out.println(ServletUtilities.headWithTitle(title) +
              "<BODY BGCOLOR=\"#FDF5E6\">\n" +
              "<H1 ALIGN=\"CENTER\">" + title + "</H1>");
  Item item;
  for(int i=0; i<items.length; i++) {
    out.println("<HR>");
    item = items[i];
    // Show error message if subclass lists item ID
    // that's not in the catalog.
    if (item == null) {
      out.println("<FONT COLOR=\"RED\">" +
                  "Unknown item ID " + itemIDs[i] +
                  "</FONT>");
    } else {
      out.println();
      String formURL =
        "/servlet/coreservlets.OrderPage";
      // Pass URLs that reference own site through encodeURL.
      formURL = response.encodeURL(formURL);
      out.println
        ("<FORM ACTION=\"" + formURL + "\">\n" +
        "<INPUT TYPE=\"HIDDEN\" NAME=\"itemID\" " +
        "       VALUE=\"" + item.getItemID() + "\">\n" +
        "<H2>" + item.getShortDescription() +
        " ($" + item.getCost() + ")</H2>\n" +
        item.getLongDescription() + "\n" +
        "<P>\n<CENTER>\n" +
        "<INPUT TYPE=\"SUBMIT\" " +
        "VALUE=\"Add to Shopping Cart\">\n" +
        "</CENTER>\n<P>\n</FORM>");
    }
  }
  out.println("<HR>\n</BODY></HTML>");
}
```

Listing 9.2 `CatalogPage.java` **(continued)**

```java
/** POST and GET requests handled identically. */

public void doPost(HttpServletRequest request,
                   HttpServletResponse response)
    throws ServletException, IOException {
  doGet(request, response);
}
}
```

Listing 9.3 `KidsBooksPage.java`

```java
package coreservlets;

/** A specialization of the CatalogPage servlet that
 *  displays a page selling three famous kids-book series.
 *  Orders are sent to the OrderPage servlet.
 */

public class KidsBooksPage extends CatalogPage {
  public void init() {
    String[] ids = { "lewis001", "alexander001", "rowling001" };
    setItems(ids);
    setTitle("All-Time Best Children's Fantasy Books");
  }
}
```

Listing 9.4 `TechBooksPage.java`

```java
package coreservlets;

/** A specialization of the CatalogPage servlet that
 *  displays a page selling two famous computer books.
 *  Orders are sent to the OrderPage servlet.
 */

public class TechBooksPage extends CatalogPage {
  public void init() {
    String[] ids = { "hall001", "hall002" };
    setItems(ids);
    setTitle("All-Time Best Computer Books");
  }
}
```

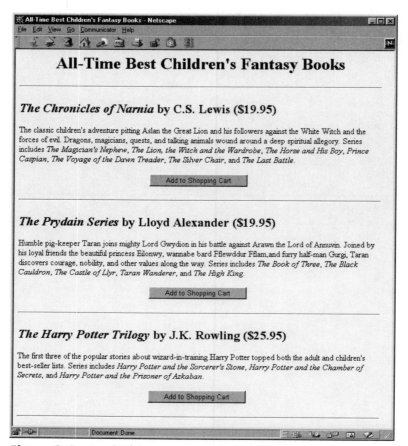

Figure 9–3   Result of the `KidsBooksPage` servlet.

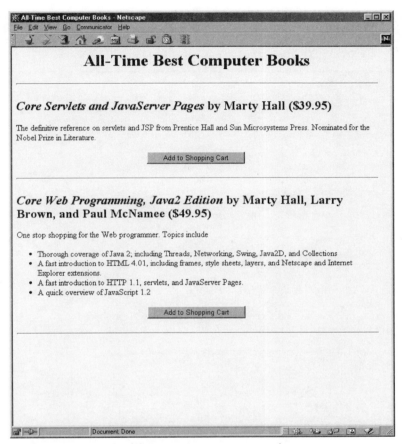

Figure 9–4   Result of the `TechBooksPage` servlet.

Handling the Orders

Listing 9.5 shows the servlet that handles the orders coming from the various catalog pages shown in the previous subsection. It uses session tracking to associate a shopping cart with each user. Since each user has a separate session, it is unlikely that multiple threads will be accessing the same shopping cart simultaneously. However, if you were paranoid, you could conceive of a few circumstances where concurrent access could occur, such as when a single user has multiple browser windows open and sends updates from more than one very close together in time. So, just to be safe, the code synchronizes access based upon the session object. This prevents other threads that

use the same session from accessing the data concurrently, while still allowing simultaneous requests from different users to proceed. Figures 9–5 and
9–6 show some typical results.

Listing 9.5   `OrderPage.java`

```
package coreservlets;

import java.io.*;
import javax.servlet.*;
import javax.servlet.http.*;
import java.util.*;
import java.text.NumberFormat;

/** Shows all items currently in ShoppingCart. Clients
 *  have their own session that keeps track of which
 *  ShoppingCart is theirs. If this is their first visit
 *  to the order page, a new shopping cart is created.
 *  Usually, people come to this page by way of a page
 *  showing catalog entries, so this page adds an additional
 *  item to the shopping cart. But users can also
 *  bookmark this page, access it from their history list,
 *  or be sent back to it by clicking on the "Update Order"
 *  button after changing the number of items ordered.
 */

public class OrderPage extends HttpServlet {
  public void doGet(HttpServletRequest request,
                    HttpServletResponse response)
      throws ServletException, IOException {
    HttpSession session = request.getSession(true);
    ShoppingCart cart;
    synchronized(session) {
      cart = (ShoppingCart)session.getValue("shoppingCart");
      // New visitors get a fresh shopping cart.
      // Previous visitors keep using their existing cart.
      if (cart == null) {
        cart = new ShoppingCart();
        session.putValue("shoppingCart", cart);
      }
      String itemID = request.getParameter("itemID");
      if (itemID != null) {
        String numItemsString =
          request.getParameter("numItems");
        if (numItemsString == null) {
          // If request specified an ID but no number,
          // then customers came here via an "Add Item to Cart"
          // button on a catalog page.
          cart.addItem(itemID);
        } else {
          // If request specified an ID and number, then
```

Listing 9.5 `OrderPage.java` (continued)

```java
      // customers came here via an "Update Order" button
      // after changing the number of items in order.
      // Note that specifying a number of 0 results
      // in item being deleted from cart.
      int numItems;
      try {
        numItems = Integer.parseInt(numItemsString);
      } catch(NumberFormatException nfe) {
        numItems = 1;
      }
      cart.setNumOrdered(itemID, numItems);
    }
  }
}
// Whether or not the customer changed the order, show
// order status.
response.setContentType("text/html");
PrintWriter out = response.getWriter();
String title = "Status of Your Order";
out.println(ServletUtilities.headWithTitle(title) +
            "<BODY BGCOLOR=\"#FDF5E6\">\n" +
            "<H1 ALIGN=\"CENTER\">" + title + "</H1>");
synchronized(session) {
  Vector itemsOrdered = cart.getItemsOrdered();
  if (itemsOrdered.size() == 0) {
    out.println("<H2><I>No items in your cart...</I></H2>");
  } else {
    // If there is at least one item in cart, show table
    // of items ordered.
    out.println
      ("<TABLE BORDER=1 ALIGN=\"CENTER\">\n" +
       "<TR BGCOLOR=\"#FFAD00\">\n" +
       "  <TH>Item ID<TH>Description\n" +
       "  <TH>Unit Cost<TH>Number<TH>Total Cost");
    ItemOrder order;

    // Rounds to two decimal places, inserts dollar
    // sign (or other currency symbol), etc., as
    // appropriate in current Locale.
    NumberFormat formatter =
      NumberFormat.getCurrencyInstance();

    String formURL =
      "/servlet/coreservlets.OrderPage";
    // Pass URLs that reference own site through encodeURL.
    formURL = response.encodeURL(formURL);

    // For each entry in shopping cart, make
    // table row showing ID, description, per-item
    // cost, number ordered, and total cost.
```

Listing 9.5 `OrderPage.java` (continued)

```java
          // Put number ordered in textfield that user
          // can change, with "Update Order" button next
          // to it, which resubmits to this same page
          // but specifying a different number of items.
          for(int i=0; i<itemsOrdered.size(); i++) {
            order = (ItemOrder)itemsOrdered.elementAt(i);
            out.println
              ("<TR>\n" +
               "  <TD>" + order.getItemID() + "\n" +
               "  <TD>" + order.getShortDescription() + "\n" +
               "  <TD>" +
               formatter.format(order.getUnitCost()) + "\n" +
               "  <TD>" +
               "<FORM ACTION=\"" + formURL + "\">\n" +
               "<INPUT TYPE=\"HIDDEN\" NAME=\"itemID\"\n" +
               "       VALUE=\"" + order.getItemID() + "\">\n" +
               "<INPUT TYPE=\"TEXT\" NAME=\"numItems\"\n" +
               "       SIZE=3 VALUE=\"" +
               order.getNumItems() + "\">\n" +
               "<SMALL>\n" +
               "<INPUT TYPE=\"SUBMIT\"\n " +
               "       VALUE=\"Update Order\">\n" +
               "</SMALL>\n" +
               "</FORM>\n" +
               "  <TD>" +
               formatter.format(order.getTotalCost()));
          }
          String checkoutURL =
            response.encodeURL("/Checkout.html");
          // "Proceed to Checkout" button below table
          out.println
            ("</TABLE>\n" +
             "<FORM ACTION=\"" + checkoutURL + "\">\n" +
             "<BIG><CENTER>\n" +
             "<INPUT TYPE=\"SUBMIT\"\n" +
             "       VALUE=\"Proceed to Checkout\">\n" +
             "</CENTER></BIG></FORM>");
        }
        out.println("</BODY></HTML>");
      }
  }

  /** POST and GET requests handled identically. */

  public void doPost(HttpServletRequest request,
                     HttpServletResponse response)
      throws ServletException, IOException {
    doGet(request, response);
  }
}
```

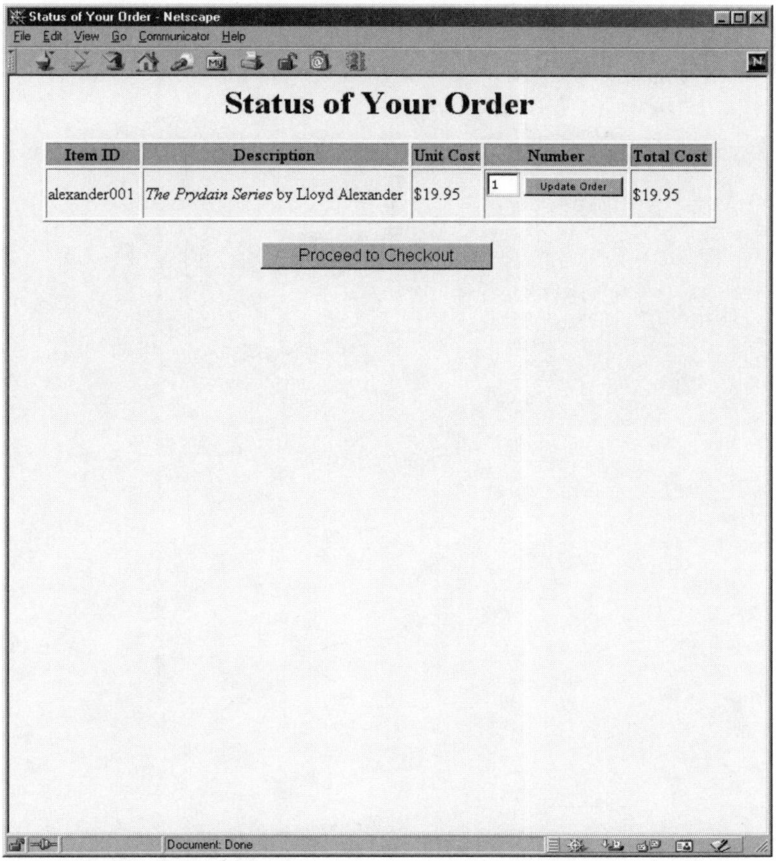

Figure 9–5   Result of `OrderPage` servlet after user clicks on "Add to Shopping Cart" in `KidsBooksPage`.

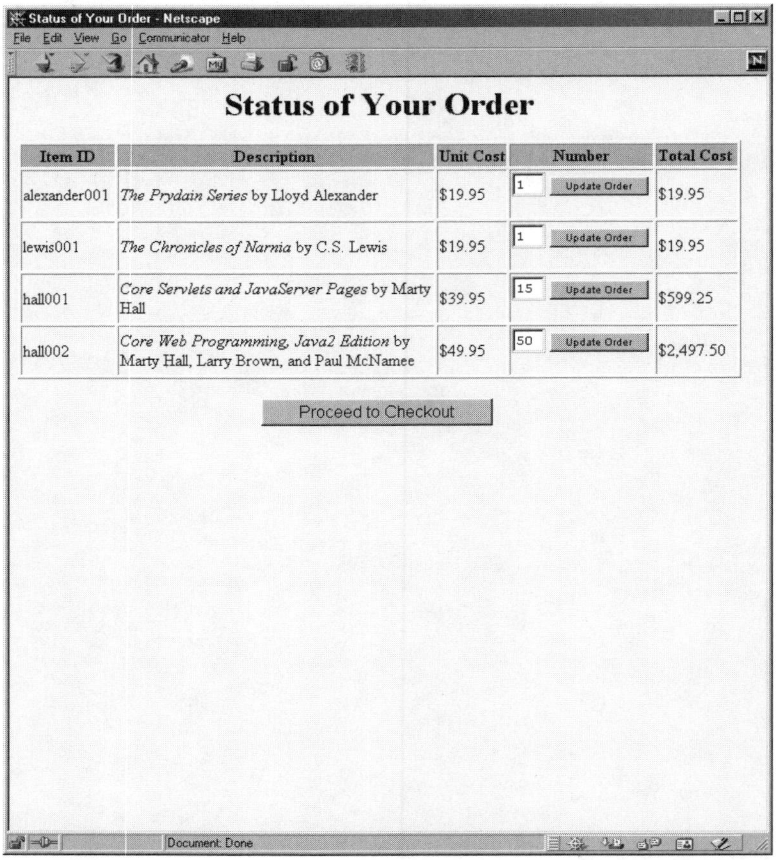

Figure 9–6 Result of `OrderPage` servlet after several additions and changes to the order.

Behind the Scenes: Implementing the Shopping Cart and Catalog Items

Listing 9.6 gives the shopping cart implementation. It simply maintains a `Vector` of orders, with methods to add and update these orders. Listing 9.7 shows the code for the individual catalog item, Listing 9.8 presents the class representing the order status of a particular item, and Listing 9.9 gives the catalog implementation.

Listing 9.6 ShoppingCart.java

```java
package coreservlets;

import java.util.*;

/** A shopping cart data structure used to track orders.
 *  The OrderPage servlet associates one of these carts
 *  with each user session.
 */

public class ShoppingCart {
  private Vector itemsOrdered;

  /** Builds an empty shopping cart. */

  public ShoppingCart() {
    itemsOrdered = new Vector();
  }

  /** Returns Vector of ItemOrder entries giving
   *  Item and number ordered.
   */

  public Vector getItemsOrdered() {
    return(itemsOrdered);
  }

  /** Looks through cart to see if it already contains
   *  an order entry corresponding to item ID. If it does,
   *  increments the number ordered. If not, looks up
   *  Item in catalog and adds an order entry for it.
   */

  public synchronized void addItem(String itemID) {
    ItemOrder order;
    for(int i=0; i<itemsOrdered.size(); i++) {
      order = (ItemOrder)itemsOrdered.elementAt(i);
      if (order.getItemID().equals(itemID)) {
        order.incrementNumItems();
        return;
      }
    }
    ItemOrder newOrder = new ItemOrder(Catalog.getItem(itemID));
    itemsOrdered.addElement(newOrder);
  }

  /** Looks through cart to find order entry corresponding
   *  to item ID listed. If the designated number
```

Listing 9.6   `ShoppingCart.java` (continued)

```
 *    is positive, sets it. If designated number is 0
 *    (or, negative due to a user input error), deletes
 *    item from cart.
 */

public synchronized void setNumOrdered(String itemID,
                                       int numOrdered) {
  ItemOrder order;
  for(int i=0; i<itemsOrdered.size(); i++) {
    order = (ItemOrder)itemsOrdered.elementAt(i);
    if (order.getItemID().equals(itemID)) {
      if (numOrdered <= 0) {
        itemsOrdered.removeElementAt(i);
      } else {
        order.setNumItems(numOrdered);
      }
      return;
    }
  }
  ItemOrder newOrder =
    new ItemOrder(Catalog.getItem(itemID));
  itemsOrdered.addElement(newOrder);
}
}
```

Listing 9.7   `Item.java`

```
package coreservlets;

/** Describes a catalog item for on-line store. The itemID
 *  uniquely identifies the item, the short description
 *  gives brief info like the book title and author,
 *  the long description describes the item in a couple
 *  of sentences, and the cost gives the current per-item price.
 *  Both the short and long descriptions can contain HTML
 *  markup.
 */

public class Item {
  private String itemID;
  private String shortDescription;
  private String longDescription;
  private double cost;
```

Listing 9.7 `Item.java` (continued)

```java
public Item(String itemID, String shortDescription,
            String longDescription, double cost) {
  setItemID(itemID);
  setShortDescription(shortDescription);
  setLongDescription(longDescription);
  setCost(cost);
}

public String getItemID() {
  return(itemID);
}

protected void setItemID(String itemID) {
  this.itemID = itemID;
}

public String getShortDescription() {
  return(shortDescription);
}

protected void setShortDescription(String shortDescription) {
  this.shortDescription = shortDescription;
}

public String getLongDescription() {
  return(longDescription);
}

protected void setLongDescription(String longDescription) {
  this.longDescription = longDescription;
}

public double getCost() {
  return(cost);
}

protected void setCost(double cost) {
  this.cost = cost;
}
}
```

Listing 9.8   `ItemOrder.java`

```java
package coreservlets;

/** Associates a catalog Item with a specific order by
 *  keeping track of the number ordered and the total price.
 *  Also provides some convenience methods to get at the
 *  Item data without first extracting the Item separately.
 */

public class ItemOrder {
  private Item item;
  private int numItems;

  public ItemOrder(Item item) {
    setItem(item);
    setNumItems(1);
  }

  public Item getItem() {
    return(item);
  }

  protected void setItem(Item item) {
    this.item = item;
  }

  public String getItemID() {
    return(getItem().getItemID());
  }

  public String getShortDescription() {
    return(getItem().getShortDescription());
  }

  public String getLongDescription() {
    return(getItem().getLongDescription());
  }

  public double getUnitCost() {
    return(getItem().getCost());
  }

  public int getNumItems() {
    return(numItems);
  }

  public void setNumItems(int n) {
    this.numItems = n;
  }
```

Listing 9.8 `ItemOrder.java` **(continued)**

```java
  public void incrementNumItems() {
    setNumItems(getNumItems() + 1);
  }

  public void cancelOrder() {
    setNumItems(0);
  }

  public double getTotalCost() {
    return(getNumItems() * getUnitCost());
  }
}
```

Listing 9.9 `Catalog.java`

```java
package coreservlets;

/** A catalog listing the items available in inventory. */

public class Catalog {
  // This would come from a database in real life
  private static Item[] items =
    { new Item("hall001",
               "<I>Core Servlets and JavaServer Pages</I> " +
                 " by Marty Hall",
               "The definitive reference on servlets " +
                 "and JSP from Prentice Hall and \n" +
                 "Sun Microsystems Press. Nominated for " +
                 "the Nobel Prize in Literature.",
               39.95),
      new Item("hall002",
               "<I>Core Web Programming, Java2 Edition</I> " +
                 "by Marty Hall, Larry Brown, and " +
                 "Paul McNamee",
               "One stop shopping for the Web programmer. " +
                 "Topics include \n" +
                 "<UL><LI>Thorough coverage of Java 2; " +
                 "including Threads, Networking, Swing, \n" +
                 "Java2D, and Collections\n" +
                 "<LI>A fast introduction to HTML 4.01, " +
                 "including frames, style sheets, layers,\n" +
                 "and Netscape and Internet Explorer " +
                 "extensions.\n" +
                 "<LI>A fast introduction to HTTP 1.1, " +
                 "servlets, and JavaServer Pages.\n" +
```

Listing 9.9 `Catalog.java` (continued)

```
                    "<LI>A quick overview of JavaScript 1.2\n" +
                    "</UL>",
                49.95),
        new Item("lewis001",
                    "<I>The Chronicles of Narnia</I> by C.S. Lewis",
                    "The classic children's adventure pitting " +
                    "Aslan the Great Lion and his followers\n" +
                    "against the White Witch and the forces " +
                    "of evil. Dragons, magicians, quests, \n" +
                    "and talking animals wound around a deep " +
                    "spiritual allegory. Series includes\n" +
                    "<I>The Magician's Nephew</I>,\n" +
                    "<I>The Lion, the Witch and the " +
                      "Wardrobe</I>,\n" +
                    "<I>The Horse and His Boy</I>,\n" +
                    "<I>Prince Caspian</I>,\n" +
                    "<I>The Voyage of the Dawn " +
                      "Treader</I>,\n" +
                    "<I>The Silver Chair</I>, and \n" +
                    "<I>The Last Battle</I>.",
                19.95),
        new Item("alexander001",
                    "<I>The Prydain Series</I> by Lloyd Alexander",
                    "Humble pig-keeper Taran joins mighty " +
                    "Lord Gwydion in his battle against\n" +
                    "Arawn the Lord of Annuvin. Joined by " +
                    "his loyal friends the beautiful princess\n" +
                    "Eilonwy, wannabe bard Fflewddur Fflam," +
                    "and furry half-man Gurgi, Taran discovers " +
                    "courage, nobility, and other values along\n" +
                    "the way. Series includes\n" +
                    "<I>The Book of Three</I>,\n" +
                    "<I>The Black Cauldron</I>,\n" +
                    "<I>The Castle of Llyr</I>,\n" +
                    "<I>Taran Wanderer</I>, and\n" +
                    "<I>The High King</I>.",
                19.95),
        new Item("rowling001",
                    "<I>The Harry Potter Trilogy</I> by " +
                    "J.K. Rowling",
                    "The first three of the popular stories " +
                    "about wizard-in-training Harry Potter\n" +
                    "topped both the adult and children's " +
                    "best-seller lists. Series includes\n" +
                    "<I>Harry Potter and the " +
                      "Sorcerer's Stone</I>,\n" +
                    "<I>Harry Potter and the " +
```

Listing 9.9   `Catalog.java` **(continued)**

```
                    "Chamber of Secrets</I>, and\n" +
                  "<I>Harry Potter and the " +
                  "Prisoner of Azkaban</I>.",
              25.95)
    };

  public static Item getItem(String itemID) {
    Item item;
    if (itemID == null) {
      return(null);
    }
    for(int i=0; i<items.length; i++) {
      item = items[i];
      if (itemID.equals(item.getItemID())) {
        return(item);
      }
    }
    return(null);
  }
}
```

Part 2

JAVASERVER PAGES

JSP SCRIPTING ELEMENTS

Topics in This Chapter

- The purpose of JSP

- How JSP pages are invoked

- Using JSP expressions to insert dynamic results directly into the output page

- Using JSP scriptlets to insert Java code into the method that handles requests for the page

- Using JSP declarations to add methods and field declarations to the servlet that corresponds to the JSP page

- Predefined variables that can be used within expressions and scriptlets

Chapter 10

JavaServer Pages (JSP) technology enables you to mix regular, static HTML with dynamically generated content from servlets. You simply write the regular HTML in the normal manner, using familiar Web-page-building tools. You then enclose the code for the dynamic parts in special tags, most of which start with `<%` and end with `%>`. For example, here is a section of a JSP page that results in "Thanks for ordering *Core Web Programming*" for a URL of `http://host/OrderConfirmation.jsp?title=Core+Web+Programming`:

```
Thanks for ordering <I><%= request.getParameter("title") %></I>
```

Separating the static HTML from the dynamic content provides a number of benefits over servlets alone, and the approach used in JavaServer Pages offers several advantages over competing technologies such as ASP, PHP, or ColdFusion. Section 1.4 (The Advantages of JSP) gives some details on these advantages, but they basically boil down to two facts: that JSP is widely supported and thus doesn't lock you into a particular operating system or Web server and that JSP gives you full access to servlet and Java technology for the dynamic part, rather than requiring you to use an unfamiliar and weaker special-purpose language.

The process of making JavaServer Pages accessible on the Web is much simpler than that for servlets. Assuming you have a Web server that supports JSP, you give your file a `.jsp` extension and simply install it in any place you could put a normal Web page: no compiling, no packages, and no user CLASSPATH settings. However, although your personal *environment* doesn't need any special settings, the *server* still has to be set up with access to the servlet and JSP class files and the Java compiler. For details, see your server's documentation or Section 1.5 (Installation and Setup).

Although what you write often looks more like a regular HTML file than a servlet, behind the scenes, the JSP page is automatically converted to a normal servlet, with the static HTML simply being printed to the output stream associated with the servlet's service method. This translation is normally done the first time the page is requested. To ensure that the first real user doesn't get a momentary delay when the JSP page is translated into a servlet and compiled, developers can simply request the page themselves after first installing it. Many Web servers also let you define aliases so that a URL that appears to reference an HTML file really points to a servlet or JSP page.

Depending on how your server is set up, you can even look at the source code for servlets generated from your JSP pages. With Tomcat 3.0, you need to change the isWorkDirPersistent attribute from false to true in *install_dir*/server.xml. After that, the code can be found in *install_dir*/work/*port-number*. With the JSWDK 1.0.1, you need to change the workDirIsPersistent attribute from false to true in *install_dir*/webserver.xml. After that, the code can be found in *install_dir*/work/%3A*port-number*%2F. With the Java Web Server, 2.0 the default setting is to save source code for automatically generated servlets. They can be found in *install_dir*/tmpdir/default/pagecompile/jsp/_JSP.

One warning about the automatic translation process is in order. If you make an error in the dynamic portion of your JSP page, the system may not be able to properly translate it into a servlet. If your page has such a fatal translation-time error, the server will present an HTML error page describing the problem to the client. Internet Explorer 5, however, typically replaces server-generated error messages with a canned page that it considers friendlier. You will need to turn off this "feature" when debugging JSP pages. To do so with Internet Explorer 5, go to the Tools menu, select Internet Options, choose the Advanced tab, and make sure "Show friendly HTTP error messages" box is not checked.

Core Warning

When debugging JSP pages, be sure to turn off Internet Explorer's "friendly" HTTP error messages.

Aside from the regular HTML, there are three main types of JSP constructs that you embed in a page: *scripting elements*, *directives*, and *actions*. Scripting elements let you specify Java code that will become part of the resultant servlet, directives let you control the overall structure of the servlet, and actions let you specify existing components that should be used and otherwise control the behavior of the JSP engine. To simplify the scripting elements, you have access to a number of predefined variables, such as `request` in the code snippet just shown (see Section 10.5 for more details). Scripting elements are covered in this chapter, and directives and actions are explained in the following chapters. You can also refer to Appendix (Servlet and JSP Quick Reference) for a thumbnail guide summarizing JSP syntax.

This book covers versions 1.0 and 1.1 of the JavaServer Pages specification. JSP changed dramatically from version 0.92 to version 1.0, and although these changes are very much for the better, you should note that newer JSP pages are almost totally incompatible with the early 0.92 JSP engines, and older JSP pages are equally incompatible with 1.0 JSP engines. The changes from version 1.0 to 1.1 are much less dramatic: the main additions in version 1.1 are the ability to portably define new tags and the use of the servlet 2.2 specification for the underlying servlets. JSP 1.1 pages that do not use custom tags or explicitly call 2.2-specific statements are compatible with JSP 1.0 engines, and JSP 1.0 pages are totally upward compatible with JSP 1.1 engines.

10.1 Scripting Elements

JSP scripting elements let you insert code into the servlet that will be generated from the JSP page. There are three forms:

1. *Expressions* of the form `<%= expression %>`, which are evaluated and inserted into the servlet's output

2. *Scriptlets* of the form `<% code %>`, which are inserted into the servlet's `_jspService` method (called by `service`)

3. *Declarations* of the form `<%! code %>`, which are inserted into the body of the servlet class, outside of any existing methods

Each of these scripting elements is described in more detail in the following sections.

Template Text

In many cases, a large percentage of your JSP page just consists of static HTML, known as *template text*. In almost all respects, this HTML looks just like normal HTML, follows all the same syntax rules, and is simply "passed through" to the client by the servlet created to handle the page. Not only does the HTML look normal, it can be created by whatever tools you already are using for building Web pages. For example, I used Allaire's HomeSite for most of the JSP pages in this book.

There are two minor exceptions to the "template text is passed straight through" rule. First, if you want to have `<%` in the output, you need to put `<\%` in the template text. Second, if you want a comment to appear in the JSP page but not in the resultant document, use

```
<%-- JSP Comment --%>
```

HTML comments of the form

```
<!-- HTML Comment -->
```

are passed through to the resultant HTML normally.

10.2 JSP Expressions

A JSP expression is used to insert values directly into the output. It has the following form:

```
<%= Java Expression %>
```

The expression is evaluated, converted to a string, and inserted in the page. This evaluation is performed at run time (when the page is requested) and thus has full access to information about the request. For example, the following shows the date/time that the page was requested:

```
Current time: <%= new java.util.Date() %>
```

Predefined Variables

To simplify these expressions, you can use a number of predefined variables. These implicit objects are discussed in more detail in Section 10.5, but for the purpose of expressions, the most important ones are:

* **request**, the HttpServletRequest
* **response**, the HttpServletResponse

- **session**, the HttpSession associated with the request (unless disabled with the session attribute of the page directive — see Section 11.4)
- **out**, the PrintWriter (a buffered version called JspWriter) used to send output to the client

Here is an example:

```
Your hostname: <%= request.getRemoteHost() %>
```

XML Syntax for Expressions

XML authors can use the following alternative syntax for JSP expressions:

```
<jsp:expression>
Java Expression
</jsp:expression>
```

Note that XML elements, unlike HTML ones, are case sensitive, so be sure to use jsp:expression in lower case.

Using Expressions as Attribute Values

As we will see later, JSP includes a number of elements that use XML syntax to specify various parameters. For example, the following example passes "Marty" to the setFirstName method of the object bound to the author variable. Don't worry if you don't understand the details of this code; it is discussed in detail in Chapter 13 (Using JavaBeans with JSP). My purpose here is simply to point out the use of the name, property, and value attributes.

```
<jsp:setProperty name="author"
                 property="firstName"
                 value="Marty" />
```

Most attributes require the value to be a fixed string enclosed in either single or double quotes, as in the example above. A few attributes, however, permit you to use a JSP expression that is computed at request time. The value attribute of jsp:setProperty is one such example, so the following code is perfectly legal:

```
<jsp:setProperty name="user"
                 property="id"
                 value='<%= "UserID" + Math.random() %>' />
```

Table 10.1 lists the attributes that permit a request-time value as in this example.

Table 10.1 Attributes That Permit JSP Expressions	
Element Name	*Attribute Name(s)*
`jsp:setProperty` (see Section 13.3, "Setting Bean Properties")	name value
`jsp:include` (see Chapter 12, "Including Files and Applets in JSP Documents")	page
`jsp:forward` (see Chapter 15, "Integrating Servlets and JSP")	page
`jsp:param` (see Chapter 12, "Including Files and Applets in JSP Documents")	value

Example

Listing 10.1 gives an example JSP page; Figure 10–1 shows the result. Notice that I included META tags and a style sheet link in the HEAD section of the HTML page. It is good practice to include these elements, but there are two reasons why they are often omitted from pages generated by normal servlets. First, with servlets, it is tedious to generate the required `println` statements. With JSP, however, the format is simpler and you can make use of the code reuse options in your usual HTML building tool. Second, servlets cannot use the simplest form of relative URLs (ones that refer to files in the same directory as the current page) since the servlet directories are not mapped to URLs in the same manner as are URLs for normal Web pages. JSP pages, on the other hand, are installed in the normal Web page hierarchy on the server, and relative URLs are resolved properly. Thus, style sheets and JSP pages can be kept together in the same directory. The source code for the style sheet, like all code shown or referenced in the book, can be downloaded from `http://www.coreservlets.com/`.

Listing 10.1 `Expressions.jsp`

```
<!DOCTYPE HTML PUBLIC "-//W3C//DTD HTML 4.0 Transitional//EN">
<HTML>
<HEAD>
<TITLE>JSP Expressions</TITLE>
<META NAME="author" CONTENT="Marty Hall">
<META NAME="keywords"
      CONTENT="JSP,expressions,JavaServer,Pages,servlets">
<META NAME="description"
      CONTENT="A quick example of JSP expressions.">
<LINK REL=STYLESHEET
      HREF="JSP-Styles.css"
      TYPE="text/css">
</HEAD>

<BODY>
<H2>JSP Expressions</H2>
<UL>
  <LI>Current time: <%= new java.util.Date() %>
  <LI>Your hostname: <%= request.getRemoteHost() %>
  <LI>Your session ID: <%= session.getId() %>
  <LI>The <CODE>testParam</CODE> form parameter:
      <%= request.getParameter("testParam") %>
</UL>
</BODY>
</HTML>
```

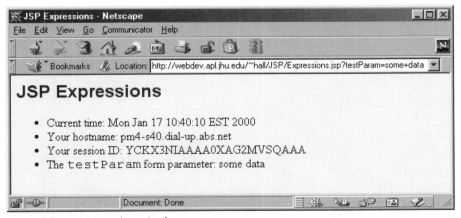

Figure 10–1 Typical result of `Expressions.jsp`.

10.3 JSP Scriptlets

If you want to do something more complex than insert a simple expression, JSP scriptlets let you insert arbitrary code into the servlet's _jspService method (which is called by service). Scriptlets have the following form:

```
<% Java Code %>
```

Scriptlets have access to the same automatically defined variables as expressions (request, response, session, out, etc.; see Section 10.5). So, for example, if you want output to appear in the resultant page, you would use the out variable, as in the following example.

```
<%
String queryData = request.getQueryString();
out.println("Attached GET data: " + queryData);
%>
```

In this particular instance, you could have accomplished the same effect more easily by using the following JSP expression:

```
Attached GET data: <%= request.getQueryString() %>
```

In general, however, scriptlets can perform a number of tasks that cannot be accomplished with expressions alone. These tasks include setting response headers and status codes, invoking side effects such as writing to the server log or updating a database, or executing code that contains loops, conditionals, or other complex constructs. For instance, the following snippet specifies that the current page is sent to the client as plain text, not as HTML (which is the default).

```
<% response.setContentType("text/plain"); %>
```

It is important to note that you can set response headers or status codes at various places within a JSP page, even though this capability appears to violate the rule that this type of response data needs to be specified before any document content is sent to the client. Setting headers and status codes is permitted because servlets that result from JSP pages use a special type of PrintWriter (of the more specific class JspWriter) that buffers the document before sending it. This buffering behavior can be changed, however; see Section 11.6 for a discussion of the autoflush attribute of the page directive.

As an example of executing code that is too complex for a JSP expression, Listing 10.2 presents a JSP page that uses the bgColor request parameter to set the background color of the page. Some results are shown in Figures 10–2, 10–3, and 10–4.

Listing 10.2 `BGColor.jsp`

```
<!DOCTYPE HTML PUBLIC "-//W3C//DTD HTML 4.0 Transitional//EN">
<HTML>
<HEAD>
  <TITLE>Color Testing</TITLE>
</HEAD>

<%
String bgColor = request.getParameter("bgColor");
boolean hasExplicitColor;
if (bgColor != null) {
  hasExplicitColor = true;
} else {
  hasExplicitColor = false;
  bgColor = "WHITE";
}
%>
<BODY BGCOLOR="<%= bgColor %>">
<H2 ALIGN="CENTER">Color Testing</H2>

<%
if (hasExplicitColor) {
  out.println("You supplied an explicit background color of " +
              bgColor + ".");
} else {
  out.println("Using default background color of WHITE. " +
              "Supply the bgColor request attribute to try " +
              "a standard color, an RRGGBB value, or to see " +
              "if your browser supports X11 color names.");
}
%>

</BODY>
</HTML>
```

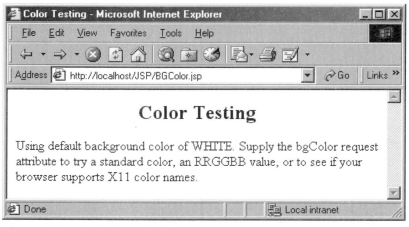

Figure 10–2 Default result of BGColor.jsp.

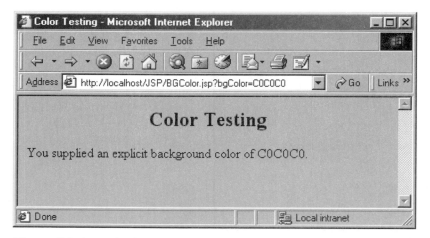

Figure 10–3 Result of BGColor.jsp when accessed with a bgColor parameter having the RGB value C0C0C0.

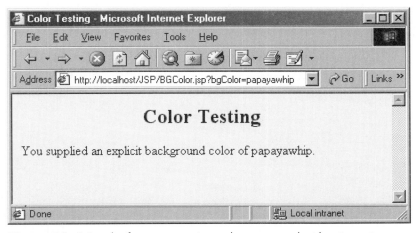

Figure 10–4 Result of `BGColor.jsp` when accessed with a `bgColor` parameter having the X11 color value `papayawhip`.

Using Scriptlets to Make Parts of the JSP File Conditional

Another use of scriptlets is to conditionally include standard HTML and JSP constructs. The key to this approach is the fact that code inside a scriptlet gets inserted into the resultant servlet's `_jspService` method (called by `service`) *exactly* as written, and any static HTML (template text) before or after a scriptlet gets converted to `print` statements. This means that scriptlets need not contain complete Java statements, and blocks left open can affect the static HTML or JSP outside of the scriptlets. For example, consider the following JSP fragment containing mixed template text and scriptlets.

```
<% if (Math.random() < 0.5) { %>
Have a <B>nice</B> day!
<% } else { %>
Have a <B>lousy</B> day!
<% } %>
```

When converted to a servlet by the JSP engine, this fragment will result in something similar to the following.

```
if (Math.random() < 0.5) {
  out.println("Have a <B>nice</B> day!");
} else {
  out.println("Have a <B>lousy</B> day!");
}
```

Special Scriptlet Syntax

There are two special constructs you should take note of. First, if you want to use the characters %> inside a scriptlet, enter %\> instead. Second, the XML equivalent of <% Code %> is

```
<jsp:scriptlet>
Code
</jsp:scriptlet>
```

The two forms are treated identically by JSP engines.

10.4 JSP Declarations

A JSP declaration lets you define methods or fields that get inserted into the main body of the servlet class (*outside* of the _jspService method that is called by service to process the request). A declaration has the following form:

```
<%! Java Code %>
```

Since declarations do not generate any output, they are normally used in conjunction with JSP expressions or scriptlets. For example, here is a JSP fragment that prints the number of times the current page has been requested since the server was booted (or the servlet class was changed and reloaded). Recall that multiple client requests to the same servlet result only in multiple threads calling the service method of a single servlet instance. They do *not* result in the creation of multiple servlet instances except possibly when the servlet implements SingleThreadModel. For a discussion of SingleThreadModel, see Section 2.6 (The Servlet Life Cycle) and Section 11.3 (The isThreadSafe Attribute). Thus, instance variables (fields) of a servlet are shared by multiple requests and accessCount does not have to be declared static below.

```
<%! private int accessCount = 0; %>
Accesses to page since server reboot:
<%= ++accessCount %>
```

Listing 10.3 shows the full JSP page; Figure 10–5 shows a representative result.

Listing 10.3 `AccessCounts.jsp`

```
<!DOCTYPE HTML PUBLIC "-//W3C//DTD HTML 4.0 Transitional//EN">
<HTML>
<HEAD>
<TITLE>JSP Declarations</TITLE>
<META NAME="author" CONTENT="Marty Hall">
<META NAME="keywords"
      CONTENT="JSP,declarations,JavaServer,Pages,servlets">
<META NAME="description"
      CONTENT="A quick example of JSP declarations.">
<LINK REL=STYLESHEET
      HREF="JSP-Styles.css"
      TYPE="text/css">
</HEAD>

<BODY>
<H1>JSP Declarations</H1>

<%! private int accessCount = 0; %>
<H2>Accesses to page since server reboot:
<%= ++accessCount %></H2>

</BODY>
</HTML>
```

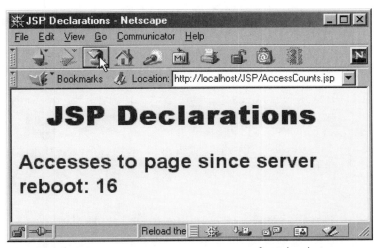

Figure 10–5 Visiting `AccessCounts.jsp` after it has been requested 15 times by the same or different clients.

Special Declaration Syntax

As with scriptlets, if you want to use the characters %>, enter %\> instead. Finally, note that the XML equivalent of <%! *Code* %> is

```
<jsp:declaration>
Code
</jsp:declaration>
```

10.5 Predefined Variables

To simplify code in JSP expressions and scriptlets, you are supplied with eight automatically defined variables, sometimes called *implicit objects*. Since JSP declarations (see Section 10.4) result in code that appears outside of the _jspService method, these variables are not accessible in declarations. The available variables are request, response, out, session, application, config, pageContext, and page. Details for each are given below.

request
This variable is the HttpServletRequest associated with the request; it gives you access to the request parameters, the request type (e.g., GET or POST), and the incoming HTTP headers (e.g., cookies). Strictly speaking, if the protocol in the request is something other than HTTP, request is allowed to be a subclass of ServletRequest other than HttpServletRequest. However, few, if any, JSP servers currently support non-HTTP servlets.

response
This variable is the HttpServletResponse associated with the response to the client. Note that since the output stream (see out) is normally buffered, it is legal to set HTTP status codes and response headers in JSP pages, even though the setting of headers or status codes is not permitted in servlets once any output has been sent to the client.

out
This is the PrintWriter used to send output to the client. However, to make the response object useful, this is a buffered version of PrintWriter called JspWriter. You can adjust the buffer size through use of the buffer attribute of the page directive (see Section 11.5). Also note

that out is used almost exclusively in scriptlets, since JSP expressions are automatically placed in the output stream and thus rarely need to refer to out explicitly.

session

This variable is the HttpSession object associated with the request. Recall that sessions are created automatically, so this variable is bound even if there is no incoming session reference. The one exception is if you use the session attribute of the page directive (see Section 11.4) to turn sessions off. In that case, attempts to reference the session variable cause errors at the time the JSP page is translated into a servlet.

application

This variable is the ServletContext as obtained via getServletConfig().getContext(). Servlets and JSP pages can store persistent data in the ServletContext object rather than in instance variables. ServletContext has setAttribute and getAttribute methods that let you store arbitrary data associated with specified keys. The difference between storing data in instance variables and storing it in the ServletContext is that the ServletContext is shared by all servlets in the servlet engine (or in the Web application, if your server supports such a capability). For more information on the use of the ServletContext, see Section 13.4 (Sharing Beans) and Chapter 15 (Integrating Servlets and JSP).

config

This variable is the ServletConfig object for this page.

pageContext

JSP introduced a new class called PageContext to give a single point of access to many of the page attributes and to provide a convenient place to store shared data. The pageContext variable stores the value of the PageContext object associated with the current page. See Section 13.4 (Sharing Beans) for a discussion of its use.

page

This variable is simply a synonym for this and is not very useful in the Java programming language. It was created as a place holder for the time when the scripting language could be something other than Java.

THE JSP PAGE DIRECTIVE: STRUCTURING GENERATED SERVLETS

Topics in This Chapter

- The purpose of the `page` directive
- Designating which classes are imported
- Using custom classes
- Specifying the MIME type of the page
- Generating Excel documents
- Controlling threading behavior
- Participating in sessions
- Setting the size and behavior of the output buffer
- Designating pages to process JSP errors
- XML-compatible syntax for directives

Chapter 11

A JSP *directive* affects the overall structure of the servlet that results from the JSP page. The following templates show the two possible forms for directives. Single quotes can be substituted for the double quotes around the attribute values, but the quotation marks cannot be omitted altogether. To obtain quote marks within an attribute value, precede them with a back slash, using \' for ' and \" for ".

```
<%@ directive attribute="value" %>
<%@ directive attribute1="value1"
              attribute2="value2"
              ...
              attributeN="valueN" %>
```

In JSP, there are three types of directives: `page`, `include`, and `taglib`. The `page` directive lets you control the structure of the servlet by importing classes, customizing the servlet superclass, setting the content type, and the like. A `page` directive can be placed anywhere within the document; its use is the topic of this chapter. The second directive, `include`, lets you insert a file into the servlet class at the time the JSP file is translated into a servlet. An `include` directive should be placed in the document at the point at which you want the file to be inserted; it is discussed in Chapter 12 (Including Files and Applets in JSP Documents) for inserting files into JSP pages. JSP 1.1 introduces a third directive, `taglib`, which can be used to define custom markup tags; it is discussed in Chapter 14 (Creating Custom JSP Tag Libraries).

The page directive lets you define one or more of the following case-sensitive attributes: import, contentType, isThreadSafe, session, buffer, autoflush, extends, info, errorPage, isErrorPage, and language. These attributes are explained in the following sections.

11.1 The import Attribute

The import attribute of the page directive lets you specify the packages that should be imported by the servlet into which the JSP page gets translated. If you don't explicitly specify any classes to import, the servlet imports java.lang.*, javax.servlet.*, javax.servlet.jsp.*, javax.servlet.http.*, and possibly some number of server-specific entries. Never write JSP code that relies on any server-specific classes being imported automatically. Use of the import attribute takes one of the following two forms:

```
<%@ page import="package.class" %>
<%@ page import="package.class1,...,package.classN" %>
```

For example, the following directive signifies that all classes in the java.util package should be available to use without explicit package identifiers.

```
<%@ page import="java.util.*" %>
```

The import attribute is the only page attribute that is allowed to appear multiple times within the same document. Although page directives can appear anywhere within the document, it is traditional to place import statements either near the top of the document or just before the first place that the referenced package is used.

Directories for Custom Classes

If you import classes that are not in any of the standard java or javax.servlet packages, you need to be sure that those classes have been properly installed on your server. In particular, most servers that support automatic servlet reloading do not permit classes that are in the auto-reloading directories to be referenced by JSP pages. The particular locations used for servlet classes vary from server to server, so you should consult your server's documentation for definitive guidance. The locations used by Apache Tomcat 3.0, the JSWDK 1.0.1, and the Java Web Server 2.0 are summarized in Table

11.1. All three of these servers also make use of JAR files in the `lib` subdirectory, and in all three cases you must restart the server whenever you change files in this directory.

Table 11.1   Class Installation Directories

Server	Location Relative to Installation Directory	Use	Automatically Reloaded When Class Changes?	Available from JSP Pages?
Tomcat 3.0	`webpages/WEB-INF/classes`	Standard location for servlet classes	No	Yes
Tomcat 3.0	`classes`	Alternative location for servlet classes	No	Yes
JSWDK 1.0.1	`webpages/WEB-INF/servlets`	Standard location for servlet classes	No	Yes
JSWDK 1.0.1	`classes`	Alternative location for servlet classes	No	Yes
Java Web Server 2.0	`servlets`	Location for frequently changing servlet classes	**Yes**	**No**
Java Web Server 2.0	`classes`	Location for infrequently changing servlet classes	No	Yes

Example

Listing 11.1 presents a page that uses three classes not in the standard JSP import list: `java.util.Date`, `coreservlets.ServletUtilities` (see Listing 8.3), and `coreservlets.LongLivedCookie` (see Listing 8.4). To simplify references to these classes, the JSP page uses

```
<%@ page import="java.util.*,coreservlets.*" %>
```

Figures 11–1 and 11–2 show some typical results.

Listing 11.1 `ImportAttribute.jsp`

```
<!DOCTYPE HTML PUBLIC "-//W3C//DTD HTML 4.0 Transitional//EN">
<HTML>
<HEAD>
<TITLE>The import Attribute</TITLE>
<LINK REL=STYLESHEET
      HREF="JSP-Styles.css"
      TYPE="text/css">
</HEAD>

<BODY>
<H2>The import Attribute</H2>
<%-- JSP page directive --%>
<%@ page import="java.util.*,coreservlets.*" %>

<%-- JSP Declaration (see Section 10.4) --%>
<%!
private String randomID() {
  int num = (int)(Math.random()*10000000.0);
  return("id" + num);
}

private final String NO_VALUE = "<I>No Value</I>";
%>

<%-- JSP Scriptlet (see Section 10.3) --%>
<%
Cookie[] cookies = request.getCookies();
String oldID =
  ServletUtilities.getCookieValue(cookies, "userID", NO_VALUE);
String newID;
if (oldID.equals(NO_VALUE)) {
  newID = randomID();
} else {
  newID = oldID;
}
LongLivedCookie cookie = new LongLivedCookie("userID", newID);
response.addCookie(cookie);
%>

<%-- JSP Expressions (see Section 10.2) --%>
This page was accessed at <%= new Date() %> with a userID
cookie of <%= oldID %>.

</BODY>
</HTML>
```

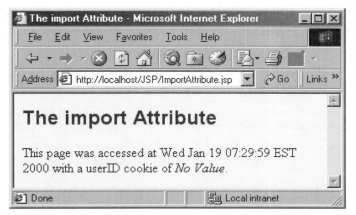

Figure 11–1 ImportAttribute.jsp when first accessed.

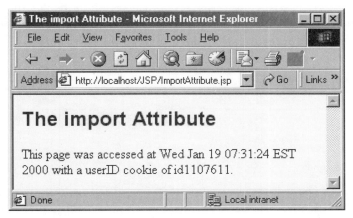

Figure 11–2 ImportAttribute.jsp when accessed in a subsequent visit.

11.2 The contentType Attribute

The contentType attribute sets the Content-Type response header, indicating the MIME type of the document being sent to the client. For more information on MIME types, see Table 7.1 (Common MIME Types) in Section 7.2 (HTTP 1.1 Response Headers and Their Meaning).

Use of the `contentType` attribute takes one of the following two forms:

```
<%@ page contentType="MIME-Type" %>
<%@ page contentType="MIME-Type; charset=Character-Set" %>
```

For example, the directive

```
<%@ page contentType="text/plain" %>
```

has the same effect as the scriptlet

```
<% response.setContentType("text/plain"); %>
```

Unlike regular servlets, where the default MIME type is `text/plain`, the default for JSP pages is `text/html` (with a default character set of `ISO-8859-1`).

Generating Plain Text Documents

Listing 11.2 shows a document that appears to be HTML but has a `content-Type` of `text/plain`. Strictly speaking, browsers are supposed to display the raw HTML content in such a case, as shown in Netscape in Figure 11–3. Internet Explorer, however, interprets the document as though it were of type `text/html`, as shown in Figure 11–4.

Listing 11.2 `ContentType.jsp`

```
<!DOCTYPE HTML PUBLIC "-//W3C//DTD HTML 4.0 Transitional//EN">
<HTML>
<HEAD>
<TITLE>The contentType Attribute</TITLE>
</HEAD>
<BODY>

<H2>The contentType Attribute</H2>
<%@ page contentType="text/plain" %>
This should be rendered as plain text,
<B>not</B> as HTML.

</BODY>
</HTML>
```

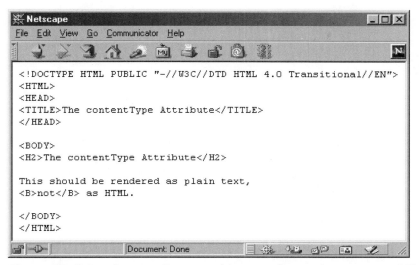

Figure 11–3 For plain text documents, Netscape does not try to interpret HTML tags.

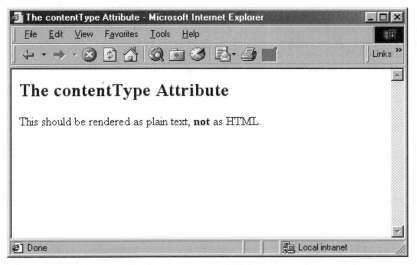

Figure 11–4 Internet Explorer interprets HTML tags in plain text documents.

Generating Excel Spreadsheets

You can create simple Microsoft Excel spreadsheets by specifying `applica-tion/vnd.ms-excel` as the content type and then formatting the spreadsheet entries in one of two ways.

One way to format the content is to put rows on separate lines of the document and to use tabs between each of the columns. Listing 11.3 shows a simple example, and Figures 11–5 and 11–6 show the results of loading the page in Netscape on a system with Excel installed. Of course, in a real application, the entries would probably be generated dynamically, perhaps by a JSP expression or scriptlet that refers to database values that were accessed with JDBC (see Chapter 18).

Listing 11.3 `Excel.jsp`

```
<%@ page contentType="application/vnd.ms-excel" %>
<%-- Note that there are tabs, not spaces, between columns. --%>
1997    1998    1999    2000    2001 (Anticipated)
12.3    13.4    14.5    15.6    16.7
```

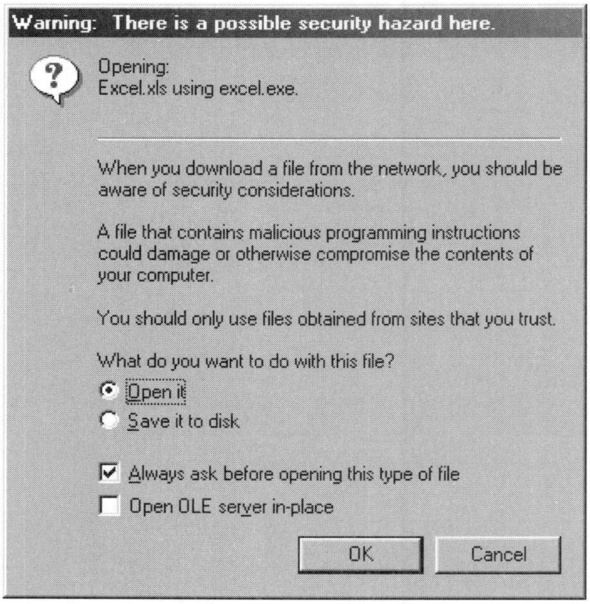

Figure 11–5 With the default browser settings, Netscape prompts you before allowing Excel content.

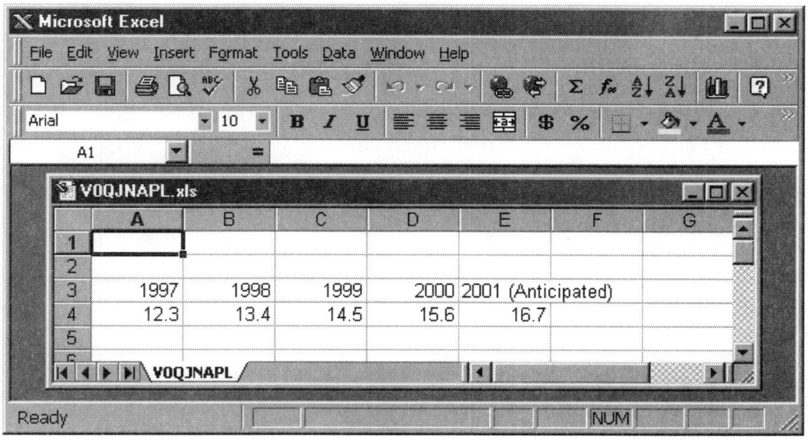

Figure 11–6 Result of `Excel.jsp` on system that has Excel installed.

A second way to format Excel content is to use a normal HTML table, which recent versions of Excel can interpret properly as long as the page is marked with the proper MIME type. This capability suggests a simple method of returning either HTML or Excel content, depending on which the user prefers: just use an HTML table and set the content type to `application/vnd.ms-excel` only if the user requests the results in Excel. Unfortunately, this approach brings to light a small deficiency in the `page` directive: attribute values cannot be computed at run time, nor can `page` directives be conditionally inserted as can template text. So, the following attempt results in Excel content regardless of the result of the `checkUser-Request` method.

```
<% boolean usingExcel = checkUserRequest(request); %>
<% if (usingExcel) { %>
<%@ page contentType="application/vnd.ms-excel" %>
<% } %>
```

Fortunately, there is a simple solution to the problem of conditionally setting the content type: just use scriptlets and the normal servlet approach of `response.setContentType`, as in the following snippet:

```
<%
String format = request.getParameter("format");
if ((format != null) && (format.equals("excel"))) {
  response.setContentType("application/vnd.ms-excel");
}
%>
```

Listing 11.4 shows a page that uses this approach; Figures 11–7 and 11–8 show the results in Internet Explorer. Again, in a real application the data would almost certainly be dynamically generated. For example, see Section 18.3 (Some JDBC Utilities) for some very simple methods to create an HTML table (usable in HTML or as an Excel spreadsheet) from a database query.

Listing 11.4 `ApplesAndOranges.jsp`

```
<!DOCTYPE HTML PUBLIC "-//W3C//DTD HTML 4.0 Transitional//EN">
<HTML>
<HEAD>
<TITLE>Comparing Apples and Oranges</TITLE>
<LINK REL=STYLESHEET
      HREF="JSP-Styles.css"
      TYPE="text/css">
</HEAD>

<BODY>
<CENTER>
<H2>Comparing Apples and Oranges</H2>

<%
String format = request.getParameter("format");
if ((format != null) && (format.equals("excel"))) {
  response.setContentType("application/vnd.ms-excel");
}
%>

<TABLE BORDER=1>
  <TR><TH></TH><TH>Apples<TH>Oranges
  <TR><TH>First Quarter<TD>2307<TD>4706
  <TR><TH>Second Quarter<TD>2982<TD>5104
  <TR><TH>Third Quarter<TD>3011<TD>5220
  <TR><TH>Fourth Quarter<TD>3055<TD>5287
</TABLE>

</CENTER>
</BODY>
</HTML>
```

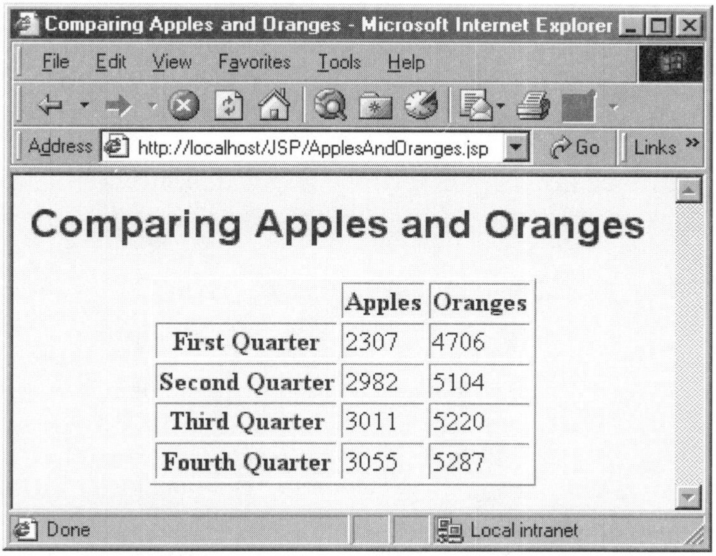

Figure 11–7 The default result of `ApplesAndOranges.jsp` is HTML content.

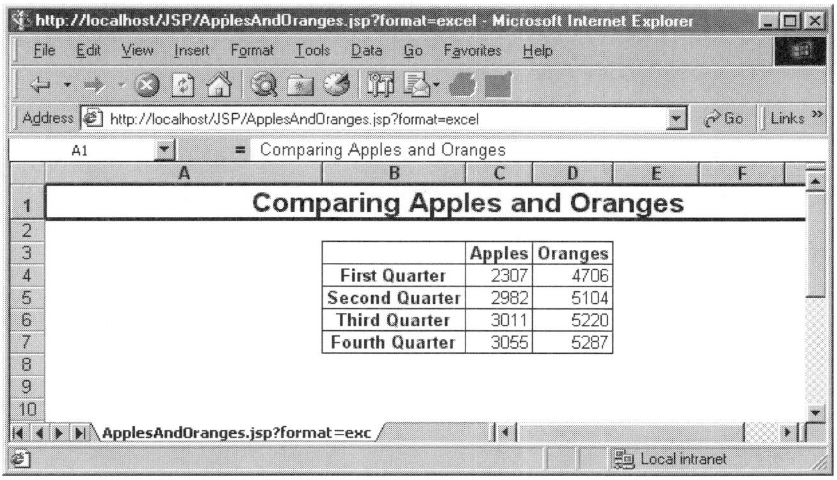

Figure 11–8 Specifying `format=excel` for `ApplesAndOranges.jsp` results in Excel content.

11.3 The isThreadSafe Attribute

The `isThreadSafe` attribute controls whether or not the servlet that results from the JSP page will implement the `SingleThreadModel` interface. Use of the `isThreadSafe` attribute takes one of the following two forms:

```
<%@ page isThreadSafe="true" %> <%!-- Default --%>
<%@ page isThreadSafe="false" %>
```

With normal servlets, simultaneous user requests result in multiple threads concurrently accessing the `service` method of the same servlet instance. This behavior assumes that the servlet is *thread safe*; that is, that the servlet synchronizes access to data in its fields so that inconsistent values will not result from an unexpected ordering of thread execution. In some cases (such as page access counts), you may not care if two visitors occasionally get the same value, but in other cases (such as user IDs), identical values can spell disaster. For example, the following snippet is not thread safe since a thread could be preempted after reading `idNum` but before updating it, yielding two users with the same user ID.

```
<%! private int idNum = 0; %>
<%
String userID = "userID" + idNum;
out.println("Your ID is " + userID + ".");
idNum = idNum + 1;
%>
```

The code should have used a `synchronized` block. This construct is written

```
synchronized(someObject) { ... }
```

and means that once a thread enters the block of code, no other thread can enter the same block (or any other block marked with the same object reference) until the first thread exits. So, the previous snippet should have been written in the following manner.

```
<%! private int idNum = 0; %>
<%
synchronized(this) {
  String userID = "userID" + idNum;
  out.println("Your ID is " + userID + ".");
  idNum = idNum + 1;
}
%>
```

That's the normal servlet behavior: multiple simultaneous requests are dispatched to multiple threads concurrently accessing the same servlet instance. However, if a servlet implements the `SingleThreadModel` interface, the system guarantees that there will not be simultaneous access to the same servlet instance. The system can satisfy this guarantee either by queuing up all requests and passing them to the same servlet instance or by creating a pool of instances, each of which handles a single request at a time.

You use `<%@ page isThreadSafe="false" %>` to indicate that your code is *not* thread safe and thus that the resulting servlet should implement `Sin-gleThreadModel`. (See Section 2.6 (The Servlet Life Cycle.) The default value is `true`, which means that the system assumes you made your code thread safe, and it can consequently use the higher-performance approach of multiple simultaneous threads accessing a single servlet instance. Be careful about using `isThreadSafe="false"` when your servlet has instance variables (fields) that maintain persistent data. In particular, note that servlet engines are permitted (but not required) to create multiple servlet instances in such a case and thus instance variables are not necessarily unique. You could still use `static` fields in such a case, however.

11.4 The session Attribute

The `session` attribute controls whether or not the page participates in HTTP sessions. Use of this attribute takes one of the following two forms:

```
<%@ page session="true" %> <%-- Default --%>
<%@ page session="false" %>
```

A value of `true` (the default) indicates that the predefined variable `session` (of type `HttpSession`) should be bound to the existing session if one exists; otherwise, a new session should be created and bound to `session`. A value of `false` means that no sessions will be used automatically and attempts to access the variable `session` will result in errors at the time the JSP page is translated into a servlet.

11.5 The buffer Attribute

The `buffer` attribute specifies the size of the buffer used by the `out` variable, which is of type `JspWriter` (a subclass of `PrintWriter`). Use of this attribute takes one of two forms:

```
<%@ page buffer="sizekb" %>
<%@ page buffer="none" %>
```

Servers can use a larger buffer than you specify, but not a smaller one. For example, `<%@ page buffer="32kb" %>` means the document content should be buffered and not sent to the client until at least 32 kilobytes have been accumulated or the page is completed. The default buffer size is server specific, but must be at least 8 kilobytes. Be cautious about turning off buffering; doing so requires JSP entries that set headers or status codes to appear at the top of the file, before any HTML content.

11.6 The autoflush Attribute

The `autoflush` attribute controls whether the output buffer should be automatically flushed when it is full or whether an exception should be raised when the buffer overflows. Use of this attribute takes one of the following two forms:

```
<%@ page autoflush="true" %> <%-- Default --%>
<%@ page autoflush="false" %>
```

A value of `false` is illegal when also using `buffer="none"`.

11.7 The extends Attribute

The `extends` attribute indicates the superclass of the servlet that will be generated for the JSP page and takes the following form:

```
<%@ page extends="package.class" %>
```

Use this attribute with extreme caution since the server may be using a custom superclass already.

11.8 The info Attribute

The `info` attribute defines a string that can be retrieved from the servlet by means of the `getServletInfo` method. Use of `info` takes the following form:

```
<%@ page info="Some Message" %>
```

11.9 The errorPage Attribute

The `errorPage` attribute specifies a JSP page that should process any exceptions (i.e., something of type `Throwable`) thrown but not caught in the current page. It is used as follows:

```
<%@ page errorPage="Relative URL" %>
```

The exception thrown will be automatically available to the designated error page by means of the `exception` variable. See Listings 11.5 and 11.6 for examples.

11.10 The isErrorPage Attribute

The `isErrorPage` attribute indicates whether or not the current page can act as the error page for another JSP page. Use of `isErrorPage` takes one of the following two forms:

```
<%@ page isErrorPage="true" %>
<%@ page isErrorPage="false" %> <%!-- Default --%>
```

For example, Listing 11.5 shows a JSP page to compute speed based upon distance and time parameters. The page neglects to check if the input parameters are missing or malformed, so an error could easily occur at run time. However, the page designated `SpeedErrors.jsp` (Listing 11.6) as the page to handle errors that occur in `ComputeSpeed.jsp`, so the user does not receive the typical terse JSP error messages. Figures 11–9 and 11–10 show results when good and bad input parameters are received, respectively.

Listing 11.5 `ComputeSpeed.jsp`

```
<!DOCTYPE HTML PUBLIC "-//W3C//DTD HTML 4.0 Transitional//EN">
<HTML>
<HEAD>
<TITLE>Computing Speed</TITLE>
<LINK REL=STYLESHEET
      HREF="JSP-Styles.css"
      TYPE="text/css">
</HEAD>

<BODY>

<%@ page errorPage="SpeedErrors.jsp" %>
```

Listing 11.5 ComputeSpeed.jsp **(continued)**

```
<TABLE BORDER=5 ALIGN="CENTER">
  <TR><TH CLASS="TITLE">
      Computing Speed</TABLE>

<%!
// Note lack of try/catch for NumberFormatException if
// value is null or malformed.

private double toDouble(String value) {
  return(Double.valueOf(value).doubleValue());
}
%>

<%
double furlongs = toDouble(request.getParameter("furlongs"));
double fortnights = toDouble(request.getParameter("fortnights"));
double speed = furlongs/fortnights;
%>

<UL>
  <LI>Distance: <%= furlongs %> furlongs.
  <LI>Time: <%= fortnights %> fortnights.
  <LI>Speed: <%= speed %> furlongs per fortnight.
</UL>

</BODY>
</HTML>
```

Listing 11.6 SpeedErrors.jsp

```
<!DOCTYPE HTML PUBLIC "-//W3C//DTD HTML 4.0 Transitional//EN">
<HTML>
<HEAD>
<TITLE>Error Computing Speed</TITLE>
<LINK REL=STYLESHEET
      HREF="JSP-Styles.css"
      TYPE="text/css">
</HEAD>

<BODY>

<%@ page isErrorPage="true" %>

<TABLE BORDER=5 ALIGN="CENTER">
```

Listing 11.6 `SpeedErrors.jsp` (continued)

```
  <TR><TH CLASS="TITLE">
      Error Computing Speed</TABLE>
<P>
ComputeSpeed.jsp reported the following error:
<I><%= exception %></I>. This problem occurred in the
following place:
<PRE>
<% exception.printStackTrace(new PrintWriter(out)); %>
</PRE>

</BODY>
</HTML>
```

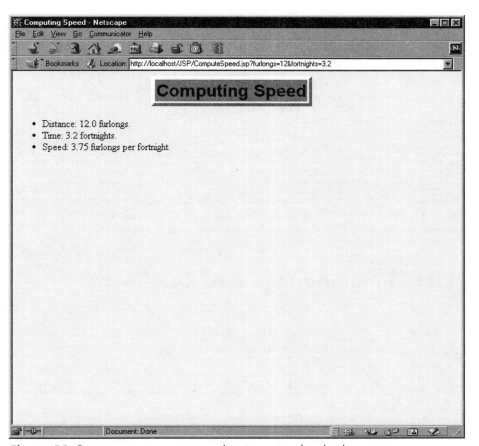

Figure 11-9 `ComputeSpeed.jsp` when it receives legal values.

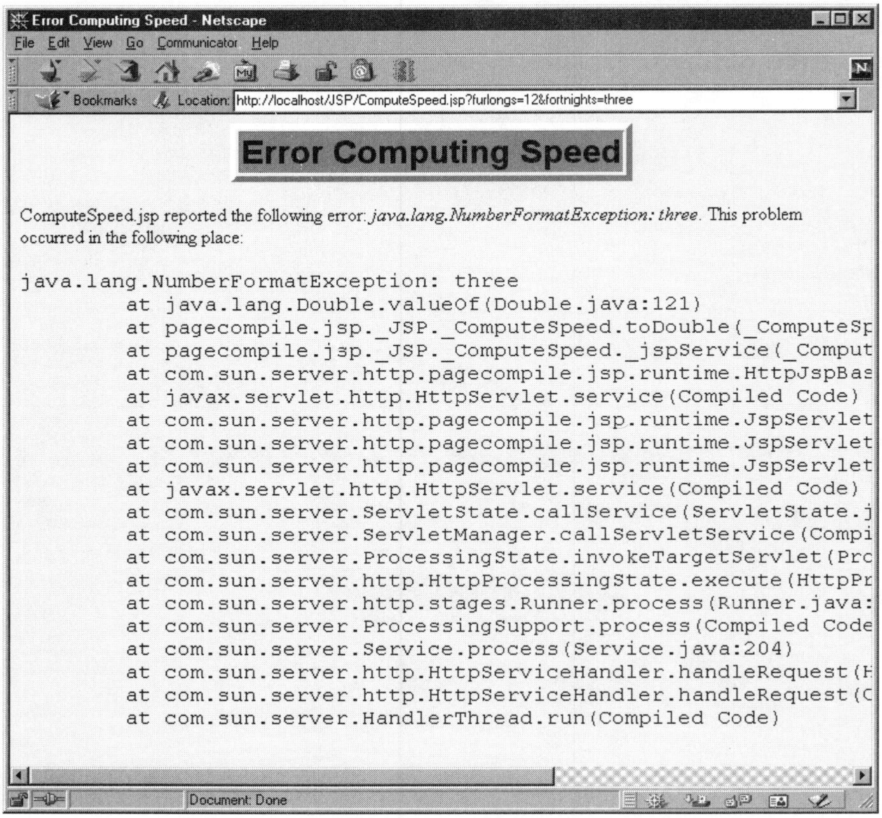

Figure 11-10 `ComputeSpeed.jsp` when it receives illegal values.

11.11 The language Attribute

At some point, the `language` attribute is intended to specify the underlying programming language being used, as below.

```
<%@ page language="cobol" %>
```

For now, don't bother with this attribute since `java` is both the default and the only legal choice.

11.12 XML Syntax for Directives

JSP permits you to use an alternative XML-compatible syntax for directives. These constructs take the following form:

```
<jsp:directive.directiveType attribute="value" />
```

For example, the XML equivalent of

```
<%@ page import="java.util.*" %>
```

is

```
<jsp:directive.page import="java.util.*" />
```

INCLUDING FILES AND APPLETS IN JSP DOCUMENTS

Topics in This Chapter

- Including JSP files at the time the main page is translated into a servlet
- Including HTML or plain text files at the time the client requests the page
- Including applets that use the Java Plug-In

Chapter 12

JSP has three main capabilities for including external pieces into a JSP document.

The `include` directive lets you reuse navigation bars, tables, and other elements in multiple pages. The included elements can contain JSP code and thus are inserted into the page before the page is translated into a servlet. This capability is discussed in Section 12.1.

Although including external pieces that use JSP is a powerful capability, other times you would rather sacrifice some power for the convenience of being able to change the included documents without updating the main JSP page. For example, my family's church has a Web page on which it posts snow cancellation announcements. This page is updated by 6:30 AM on Sundays when there is a cancellation. It is hardly reasonable to expect the Web developer to post this update; he probably sleeps in and barely makes the late-late service. Instead, a simple plain text file could be uploaded with the announcement, and the main page could use the `jsp:include` element to insert the announcement into the home page. This capability is discussed in Section 12.2.

Although this book is primarily about server-side Java, client-side Java in the form of Web-embedded applets continues to play a role, especially within fast corporate intranets. The `jsp:plugin` element is used to insert applets that use the Java Plug-In into JSP pages. This capability is discussed in Section 12.3.

12.1 Including Files at Page Translation Time

You use the `include` directive to include a file in the main JSP document at the time the document is translated into a servlet (which is typically the first time it is accessed). The syntax is as follows:

```
<%@ include file="Relative URL" %>
```

There are two ramifications of the fact that the included file is inserted at page translation time, not at request time as with `jsp:include` (Section 12.2).

First, the included file is permitted to contain JSP code, not just static HTML. This capability lets you create reusable navigation bars, contact information sections, page counts, and other elements that use both HTML and JSP and would otherwise need to be repeated on multiple pages.

Second, if the included file changes, all the JSP files that use it need to be updated. Unfortunately, although servers are *allowed* to support a mechanism for detecting when an included file has changed (and then recompiling the servlet), they are not *required* to do so. In practice, few servers support this capability. Furthermore, there is not a simple and portable "retranslate this JSP page now" command. Instead, you have to update the modification date of the JSP page. Some operating systems have commands that update the modification date without your actually editing the file (e.g., the Unix `touch` command), but a simple portable alternative is to include a JSP comment in the top-level page. Update the comment whenever the included file changes. For example, you might put the modification date of the included file in the comment, as below.

```
<%-- Navbar.jsp modified 3/1/00 --%>
<%@ include file="Navbar.jsp" %>
```

Core Warning

If you change an included JSP file, you must update the modification dates of all JSP files that use it.

For example, Listing 12.1 shows a page fragment that gives corporate contact information and some per-page access statistics appropriate to be included at the bottom of multiple pages within a site. Listing 12.2 shows a page that makes use of it, and Figure 12–1 shows the result.

Listing 12.1 `ContactSection.jsp`

```jsp
<%@ page import="java.util.Date" %>

<%-- The following become fields in each servlet that
     results from a JSP page that includes this file. --%>
<%!
private int accessCount = 0;
private Date accessDate = new Date();
private String accessHost = "<I>No previous access</I>";
%>

<P>
<HR>
This page &copy; 2000
<A HREF="http//www.my-company.com/">my-company.com</A>.
This page has been accessed <%= ++accessCount %>
times since server reboot. It was last accessed from
<%= accessHost %> at <%= accessDate %>.

<% accessHost = request.getRemoteHost(); %>
<% accessDate = new Date(); %>
```

Listing 12.2 `SomeRandomPage.jsp`

```jsp
<!DOCTYPE HTML PUBLIC "-//W3C//DTD HTML 4.0 Transitional//EN">
<HTML>
<HEAD>
<TITLE>Some Random Page</TITLE>
<META NAME="author" CONTENT="J. Random Hacker">
<META NAME="keywords"
      CONTENT="foo,bar,baz,quux">
<META NAME="description"
      CONTENT="Some random Web page.">
<LINK REL=STYLESHEET
      HREF="JSP-Styles.css"
      TYPE="text/css">
</HEAD>

<BODY>
<TABLE BORDER=5 ALIGN="CENTER">
  <TR><TH CLASS="TITLE">
      Some Random Page</TABLE>
<P>
Information about our products and services.
<P>
Blah, blah, blah.
<P>
Yadda, yadda, yadda.

<%@ include file="ContactSection.jsp" %>

</BODY>
</HTML>
```

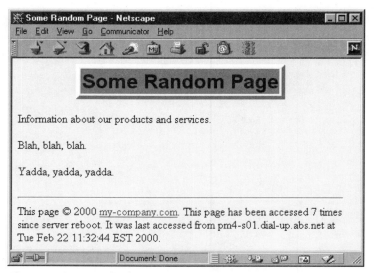

Figure 12–1 Result of `SomeRandomPage.jsp`.

12.2 Including Files at Request Time

The `include` directive (Section 12.1) lets you include documents that contain JSP code into multiple different pages. Including JSP content is a useful capability, but the `include` directive requires you to update the modification date of the page whenever the included file changes, which is a significant inconvenience. The `jsp:include` action includes files at the time of the client request and thus does not require you to update the main file when an included file changes. On the other hand, the page has already been translated into a servlet by request time, so the included files cannot contain JSP.

Core Approach

Use the `include` *directive if included files will use JSP constructs. Otherwise, use* `jsp:include`.

Although the included files cannot *contain* JSP, they can be the result of resources that *use* JSP to create the output. That is, the URL that refers to the included resource is interpreted in the normal manner by the server and thus can be a servlet or JSP page. This is precisely the behavior of the `include` method of the `RequestDispatcher` class, which is what servlets use if they want to do this type of file inclusion. See Section 15.3 (Including Static or Dynamic Content) for details.

The `jsp:include` element has two required attributes, as shown in the sample below: `page` (a relative URL referencing the file to be included) and `flush` (which *must* have the value `true`).

```
<jsp:include page="Relative URL" flush="true" />
```

Although you typically include HTML or plain text documents, there is no requirement that the included files have any particular file extension. However, the Java Web Server 2.0 has a bug that causes it to terminate page processing when it tries to include a file that does not have a `.html` or `.htm` extension (e.g., `somefile.txt`). Tomcat, the JSWDK, and most commercial servers have no such restrictions.

Core Warning

*Due to a bug, you must use `.html` or `.htm` **extensions for included files** used with the Java Web Server.*

As an example, consider the simple news summary page shown in Listing 12.3. Page developers can change the news items in the files `Item1.html` through `Item4.html` (Listings 12.4 through 12.7) without having to update the main news page. Figure 12–2 shows the result.

Listing 12.3 `WhatsNew.jsp`

```
<!DOCTYPE HTML PUBLIC "-//W3C//DTD HTML 4.0 Transitional//EN">
<HTML>
<HEAD>
<TITLE>What's New</TITLE>
<LINK REL=STYLESHEET
      HREF="JSP-Styles.css"
      TYPE="text/css">
</HEAD>

<BODY>
```

Listing 12.3 `WhatsNew.jsp` (continued)

```
<CENTER>
<TABLE BORDER=5>
  <TR><TH CLASS="TITLE">
      What's New at JspNews.com</TABLE>
</CENTER>
<P>

Here is a summary of our four most recent news stories:
<OL>
  <LI><jsp:include page="news/Item1.html" flush="true" />
  <LI><jsp:include page="news/Item2.html" flush="true" />
  <LI><jsp:include page="news/Item3.html" flush="true" />
  <LI><jsp:include page="news/Item4.html" flush="true" />
</OL>
</BODY>
</HTML>
```

Listing 12.4 `Item1.html`

```
<B>Bill Gates acts humble.</B> In a startling and unexpected
development, Microsoft big wig Bill Gates put on an open act of
humility yesterday.
<A HREF="http://www.microsoft.com/Never.html">More details...</A>
```

Listing 12.5 `Item2.html`

```
<B>Scott McNealy acts serious.</B> In an unexpected twist,
wisecracking Sun head Scott McNealy was sober and subdued at
yesterday's meeting.
<A HREF="http://www.sun.com/Imposter.html">More details...</A>
```

Listing 12.6 `Item3.html`

```
<B>Larry Ellison acts conciliatory.</B> Catching his competitors
off guard yesterday, Oracle prez Larry Ellison referred to his
rivals in friendly and respectful terms.
<A HREF="http://www.oracle.com/Mistake.html">More details...</A>
```

Listing 12.7 `Item4.html`

```
<B>Sportscaster uses "literally" correctly.</B> In an apparent
slip of the tongue, a popular television commentator was
heard to use the word "literally" when he did <I>not</I>
mean "figuratively."
<A HREF="http://www.espn.com/Slip.html">More details...</A>
```

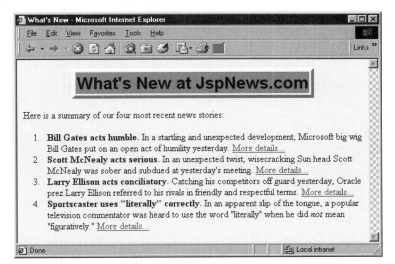

Figure 12–2 Result of `WhatsNew.jsp`.

12.3 Including Applets for the Java Plug-In

With JSP, you don't need any special syntax to include ordinary applets: just use the normal HTML APPLET tag. However, these applets must use JDK 1.1 or JDK 1.02 since neither Netscape 4.x nor Internet Explorer 5.x support the Java 2 platform (i.e., JDK 1.2). This lack of support imposes several restrictions on applets:

- In order to use Swing, you must send the Swing files over the network. This process is time consuming and fails in Internet Explorer 3 and Netscape 3.x and 4.01-4.05 (which only support JDK 1.02), since Swing depends on JDK 1.1.
- You cannot use Java 2D.
- You cannot use the Java 2 collections package.
- Your code runs more slowly, since most compilers for the Java 2 platform are significantly improved over their 1.1 predecessors.

Furthermore, early browser releases had a number of inconsistencies in the way they supported various AWT components, making testing and delivery of complex user interfaces more burdensome than it ought to have been. To address this problem, Sun developed a browser plug-in for Netscape and Internet Explorer that lets you use the Java 2 platform for applets in a variety of browsers. This plug-in is available at `http://java.sun.com/products/plugin/`, and also comes bundled with JDK 1.2.2 and later. Since the plug-in is quite large (several megabytes), it is not reasonable to expect users on the WWW at large to download and install it just to run your applets. On the other hand, it is a reasonable alternative for fast corporate intranets, especially since applets can automatically prompt browsers that lack the plug-in to download it.

Unfortunately, however, the normal APPLET tag will not work with the plug-in, since browsers are specifically designed to use only their built-in virtual machine when they see APPLET. Instead, you have to use a long and messy OBJECT tag for Internet Explorer and an equally long EMBED tag for Netscape. Furthermore, since you typically don't know which browser type will be accessing your page, you have to either include both OBJECT and EMBED (placing the EMBED within the COMMENT section of OBJECT) or identify the browser type at the time of the request and conditionally build the right tag. This process is straightforward but tedious and time consuming.

The `jsp:plugin` element instructs the server to build a tag appropriate for applets that use the plug-in. Servers are permitted some leeway in exactly how they implement this support, but most simply include both OBJECT and EMBED.

The jsp:plugin Element

The simplest way to use `jsp:plugin` is to supply four attributes: `type`, `code`, `width`, and `height`. You supply a value of `applet` for the `type` attribute and use the other three attributes in exactly the same way as with the APPLET element, with two exceptions: the attribute names are case sensitive, and single or double quotes are always required around the attribute values. So, for example, you could replace

```
<APPLET CODE="MyApplet.class"
        WIDTH=475 HEIGHT=350>
</APPLET>
```

with

```
<jsp:plugin type="applet"
            code="MyApplet.class"
            width="475" height="350">
</jsp:plugin>
```

The `jsp:plugin` element has a number of other optional attributes. Most, but not all, parallel attributes of the APPLET element. Here is a full list.

- **type**
  For applets, this attribute should have a value of `applet`. However, the Java Plug-In also permits you to embed JavaBeans elements in Web pages. Use a value of `bean` in such a case.

- **code**
  This attribute is used identically to the CODE attribute of APPLET, specifying the top-level applet class file that extends `Applet` or `JApplet`. Just remember that the name `code` must be lower case with `jsp:plugin` (since it follows XML syntax), whereas with APPLET, case did not matter (since HTML attribute names are never case sensitive).

- **width**
  This attribute is used identically to the WIDTH attribute of APPLET, specifying the width in pixels to be reserved for the applet. Just remember that you must enclose the value in single or double quotes.

- **height**
  This attribute is used identically to the HEIGHT attribute of
  APPLET, specifying the height in pixels to be reserved for the
  applet. Just remember that you must enclose the value in single
  or double quotes.

- **codebase**
  This attribute is used identically to the CODEBASE attribute of
  APPLET, specifying the base directory for the applets. The code
  attribute is interpreted relative to this directory. As with the
  APPLET element, if you omit this attribute, the directory of the
  current page is used as the default. In the case of JSP, this
  default location is the directory where the original JSP file
  resided, not the system-specific location of the servlet that
  results from the JSP file.

- **align**
  This attribute is used identically to the ALIGN attribute of
  APPLET and IMG, specifying the alignment of the applet within
  the Web page. Legal values are left, right, top, bottom, and
  middle. With jsp:plugin, don't forget to include these values in
  single or double quotes, even though quotes are optional for
  APPLET and IMG.

- **hspace**
  This attribute is used identically to the HSPACE attribute of
  APPLET, specifying empty space in pixels reserved on the left
  and right of the applet. Just remember that you must enclose
  the value in single or double quotes.

- **vspace**
  This attribute is used identically to the VSPACE attribute of
  APPLET, specifying empty space in pixels reserved on the top
  and bottom of the applet. Just remember that you must enclose
  the value in single or double quotes.

- **archive**
  This attribute is used identically to the ARCHIVE attribute of
  APPLET, specifying a JAR file from which classes and images
  should be loaded.

- **name**
  This attribute is used identically to the NAME attribute of APPLET,
  specifying a name to use for inter-applet communication or for
  identifying the applet to scripting languages like JavaScript.

- **title**
  This attribute is used identically to the very rarely used TITLE attribute of APPLET (and virtually all other HTML elements in HTML 4.0), specifying a title that could be used for a tool-tip or for indexing.
- **jreversion**
  This attribute identifies the version of the Java Runtime Environment (JRE) that is required. The default is 1.1.
- **iepluginurl**
  This attribute designates a URL from which the plug-in for Internet Explorer can be downloaded. Users who don't already have the plug-in installed will be prompted to download it from this location. The default value will direct the user to the Sun site, but for intranet use you might want to direct the user to a local copy.
- **nspluginurl**
  This attribute designates a URL from which the plug-in for Netscape can be downloaded. The default value will direct the user to the Sun site, but for intranet use you might want to direct the user to a local copy.

The jsp:param and jsp:params Elements

The jsp:param element is used with jsp:plugin in a manner similar to the way that PARAM is used with APPLET, specifying a name and value that are accessed from within the applet by getParameter. There are two main differences, however. First, since jsp:param follows XML syntax, attribute names must be lower case, attribute values must be enclosed in single or double quotes, and the element must end with />, not just >. Second, all jsp:param entries must be enclosed within a jsp:params element.

So, for example, you would replace

```
<APPLET CODE="MyApplet.class"
        WIDTH=475 HEIGHT=350>
  <PARAM NAME="PARAM1" VALUE="VALUE1">
  <PARAM NAME="PARAM2" VALUE="VALUE2">
</APPLET>
```

with

```
<jsp:plugin type="applet"
            code="MyApplet.class"
            width="475" height="350">
  <jsp:params>
    <jsp:param name="PARAM1" value="VALUE1" />
```

```
        <jsp:param name="PARAM2" value="VALUE2" />
    </jsp:params>
</jsp:plugin>
```

The jsp:fallback Element

The jsp:fallback element provides alternative text to browsers that do not support OBJECT or EMBED. You use this element in almost the same way as you would use alternative text placed within an APPLET element. So, for example, you would replace

```
<APPLET CODE="MyApplet.class"
        WIDTH=475 HEIGHT=350>
  <B>Error: this example requires Java.</B>
</APPLET>
```

with

```
<jsp:plugin type="applet"
            code="MyApplet.class"
            width="475" height="350">
  <jsp:fallback>
    <B>Error: this example requires Java.</B>
  </jsp:fallback>
</jsp:plugin>
```

However, you should note that the Java Web Server 2.0 has a bug that causes it to fail when translating pages that include jsp:fallback elements. Tomcat, the JSWDK, and most commercial servers handle jsp:fallback properly.

Core Warning

The Java Web Server does not properly handle jsp:fallback.

Example: Building Shadowed Text

In Section 7.5 (Using Servlets to Generate GIF Images), Listings 7.9 and 7.11 show a JFrame that uses Java 2D to create shadowed text in the size and font of the user's choosing. Listings 12.10 and 12.11 present an applet that uses Swing components to control this frame.

Since the applet uses Swing and Java 2D, it can run only with the Java Plug-In. Listing 12.8 shows a page that uses jsp:plugin to load the applet. Listing 12.9 shows the HTML that results from this page (I added some line breaks for readability) and Figures 12–3 through 12–6 show some typical output.

Listing 12.8 ShadowedTextApplet.jsp

```
<!DOCTYPE HTML PUBLIC "-//W3C//DTD HTML 4.0 Transitional//EN">
<HTML>
<HEAD>
<TITLE>Using jsp:plugin</TITLE>
<LINK REL=STYLESHEET
      HREF="JSP-Styles.css"
      TYPE="text/css">
</HEAD>

<BODY>

<TABLE BORDER=5 ALIGN="CENTER">
  <TR><TH CLASS="TITLE">

      Using jsp:plugin</TABLE>
<P>
<CENTER>
<jsp:plugin type="applet"
            code="coreservlets.ShadowedTextApplet.class"
            width="475" height="350">
  <jsp:params>
    <jsp:param name="MESSAGE" value="Your Message Here" />
  </jsp:params>
</jsp:plugin>
</CENTER>

</BODY>
</HTML>
```

Listing 12.9 HTML resulting from `ShadowedTextApplet.jsp`.

```
<!DOCTYPE HTML PUBLIC "-//W3C//DTD HTML 4.0 Transitional//EN">
<HTML>
<HEAD>
<TITLE>Using jsp:plugin</TITLE>
<LINK REL=STYLESHEET
      HREF="JSP-Styles.css"
      TYPE="text/css">
</HEAD>

<BODY>

<TABLE BORDER=5 ALIGN="CENTER">
  <TR><TH CLASS="TITLE">
      Using jsp:plugin</TABLE>
<P>
<CENTER>
<OBJECT classid="clsid:8AD9C840-044E-11D1-B3E9-00805F499D93"
        width="475"  height="350"
        codebase="http://java.sun.com/products/plugin/1.2.2/jin-
stall-1_2_2-win.cab#Version=1,2,2,0">
<PARAM name="java_code"
       value="coreservlets.ShadowedTextApplet.class">
<PARAM name="type" value="application/x-java-applet;">
<PARAM name="MESSAGE" value="Your Message Here">
<COMMENT>
<EMBED type="application/x-java-applet;"
       width="475"  height="350"
       pluginspage="http://java.sun.com/products/plugin/"
       java_code="coreservlets.ShadowedTextApplet.class"

       MESSAGE="Your Message Here" >
<NOEMBED>
</COMMENT>
</NOEMBED></EMBED>
</OBJECT>

</CENTER>

</BODY>
</HTML>
```

Listing 12.10 ShadowedTextApplet.java

```java
package coreservlets;

import java.awt.*;
import javax.swing.*;
import java.awt.event.*;

/** Applet interface to the ShadowedTextFrame
 *  class. Requires Swing and Java 2D.
 */

public class ShadowedTextApplet extends JApplet
                                implements ActionListener {
  private JTextField messageField;
  private JComboBox fontBox;
  private JSlider fontSizeSlider;
  private JButton showFrameButton;

  public void init() {
    WindowUtilities.setNativeLookAndFeel();
    Color bgColor = new Color(0xFD, 0xF5, 0xE6);
    Font font = new Font("Serif", Font.PLAIN, 16);
    Container contentPane = getContentPane();
    contentPane.setLayout(new GridLayout(4, 1));
    contentPane.setBackground(bgColor);

    // Use a JTextField to gather the text for the message.
    // If the MESSAGE parameter is in the HTML,
    // use it as the initial value of this text field.
    messageField = new JTextField(20);
    String message = getParameter("MESSAGE");
    if (message != null) {
      messageField.setText(message);

    }
    JPanel messagePanel =
      new LabelPanel("Message:", "Message to Display",
                     bgColor, font, messageField);
    contentPane.add(messagePanel);

    // Use a JComboBox to let users choose any
    // font available on their system.
    GraphicsEnvironment env =
      GraphicsEnvironment.getLocalGraphicsEnvironment();
    String[] fontNames = env.getAvailableFontFamilyNames();
```

Listing 12.10 `ShadowedTextApplet.java` **(continued)**

```java
      fontBox = new JComboBox(fontNames);
      fontBox.setEditable(false);
      JPanel fontPanel =
        new LabelPanel("Font:", "Font to Use",
                        bgColor, font, fontBox);
      contentPane.add(fontPanel);

      // Use a JSlider to select the font size.
      fontSizeSlider = new JSlider(0, 150);
      fontSizeSlider.setBackground(bgColor);
      fontSizeSlider.setMajorTickSpacing(50);
      fontSizeSlider.setMinorTickSpacing(25);
      fontSizeSlider.setPaintTicks(true);
      fontSizeSlider.setPaintLabels(true);
      JPanel fontSizePanel =
        new LabelPanel("Font Size:", "Font Size to Use",
                        bgColor, font, fontSizeSlider);
      contentPane.add(fontSizePanel);

      // Pressing the button will open the frame
      // that shows the shadowed text.
      showFrameButton = new JButton("Open Frame");
      showFrameButton.addActionListener(this);
      JPanel buttonPanel =
        new LabelPanel("Show Shadowed Text:",
                        "Open JFrame to Show Shadowed Text",
                        bgColor, font, showFrameButton);
      contentPane.add(buttonPanel);
  }

  public void actionPerformed(ActionEvent event) {
    String message = messageField.getText();
    if (message.length() == 0) {
      message = "No Message";
    }

    String fontName = (String)fontBox.getSelectedItem();
    int fontSize = fontSizeSlider.getValue();
    JFrame frame = new JFrame("Shadowed Text");
    JPanel panel =
      new ShadowedTextFrame(message, fontName, fontSize);
    frame.setContentPane(panel);
    frame.pack();
    frame.setVisible(true);
  }
}
```

Listing 12.11 LabelPanel.java

```java
package coreservlets;

import java.awt.*;
import javax.swing.*;

/** A small JPanel that includes a JLabel to the left
 *  of a designated component. Also puts a titled border
 *  around the panel.
 */

public class LabelPanel extends JPanel {
  public LabelPanel(String labelMessage, String title,
                    Color bgColor, Font font,
                    JComponent component) {
    setBackground(bgColor);
    setFont(font);
    setBorder(BorderFactory.createTitledBorder(title));
    JLabel label = new JLabel(labelMessage);
    label.setFont(font);
    add(label);
    component.setFont(font);
    add(component);
  }
}
```

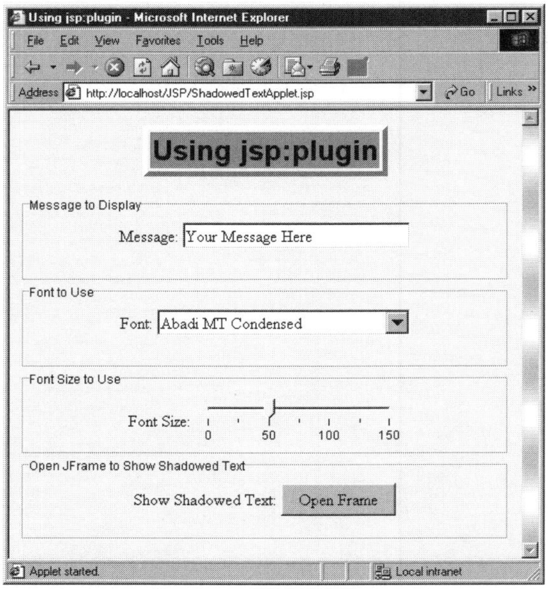

Figure 12–3 Initial result of `ShadowedTextApplet.jsp` in a browser that has the JDK 1.2 plug-in installed.

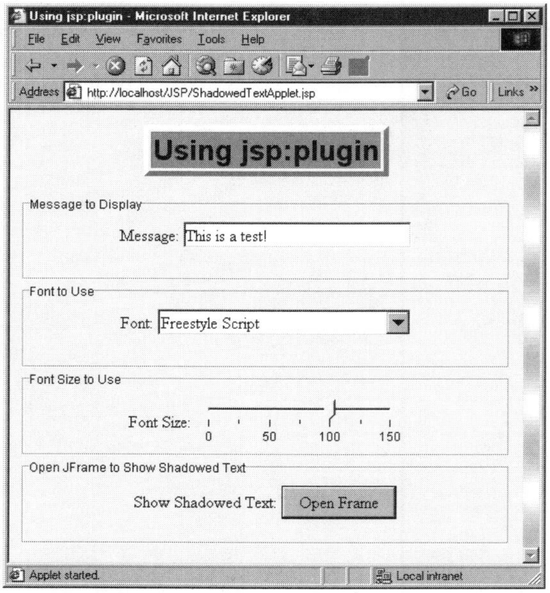

Figure 12–4 `ShadowedTextApplet.jsp` after changing the message, font, and size entries.

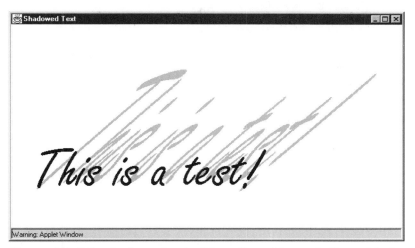

Figure 12–5 Result of pressing the "Open Frame" button in Figure 12–4.

Figure 12–6 Another possible frame built by `ShadowedTextApplet.jsp`.

USING JAVABEANS WITH JSP

Topics in This Chapter

- Creating and accessing beans
- Installing bean classes on your server
- Setting bean properties explicitly
- Associating bean properties with input parameters
- Automatic conversion of bean property types
- Sharing beans among multiple JSP pages and servlets

Chapter 13

The JavaBeans API provides a standard format for Java classes. Visual
manipulation tools and other programs can automatically discover
information about classes that follow this format and can then create
and manipulate the classes without the user having to explicitly write any code.

Full coverage of JavaBeans is beyond the scope of this book. If you want
details, pick up one of the many books on the subject or see the documentation and tutorials at `http://java.sun.com/beans/docs/`. For the purposes of this chapter, all you need to know about beans are three simple
points:

1. **A bean class must have a zero-argument (empty) constructor.** You can satisfy this requirement either by explicitly
defining such a constructor or by omitting all constructors, which
results in an empty constructor being created automatically. The
empty constructor will be called when JSP elements create beans.

2. **A bean class should have no public instance variables
(fields).** I hope you already follow this practice and use accessor
methods instead of allowing direct access to the instance variables. Use of accessor methods lets you impose constraints on
variable values (e.g., have the `setSpeed` method of your `Car`
class disallow negative speeds), allows you to change your internal data structures without changing the class interface (e.g.,

change from English units to metric units internally, but still have `getSpeedInMPH` and `getSpeedInKPH` methods), and automatically perform side effects when values change (e.g., update the user interface when `setPosition` is called).

3. **Persistent values should be accessed through methods called `getXxx` and `setXxx`.** For example, if your `Car` class stores the current number of passengers, you might have methods named `getNumPassengers` (which takes no arguments and returns an `int`) and `setNumPassengers` (which takes an `int` and has a `void` return type). In such a case, the `Car` class is said to have a *property* named `numPassengers` (notice the lowercase n in the property name, but the uppercase N in the method names). If the class has a `getXxx` method but no corresponding `setXxx`, the class is said to have a read-only property named `xxx`.

The one exception to this naming convention is with boolean properties: they use a method called `isXxx` to look up their values. So, for example, your `Car` class might have methods called `isLeased` (which takes no arguments and returns a `boolean`) and `setLeased` (which takes a `boolean` and has a `void` return type), and would be said to have a `boolean` property named `leased` (again, notice the lowercase leading letter in the property name).

Although you can use JSP scriptlets or expressions to access arbitrary methods of a class, standard JSP actions for accessing beans can only make use of methods that use the `getXxx`/`setXxx` or `isXxx`/`setXxx` design pattern.

13.1 Basic Bean Use

The `jsp:useBean` action lets you load a bean to be used in the JSP page. Beans provide a very useful capability because they let you exploit the reusability of Java classes without sacrificing the convenience that JSP adds over servlets alone.

The simplest syntax for specifying that a bean should be used is:

```
<jsp:useBean id="name" class="package.Class" />
```

This usually means "instantiate an object of the class specified by `Class`, and bind it to a variable with the name specified by `id`." So, for example, the JSP action

```
<jsp:useBean id="book1" class="coreservlets.Book" />
```

can normally be thought of as equivalent to the scriptlet

```
<% coreservlets.Book book1 = new coreservlets.Book(); %>
```

Although it is convenient to think of jsp:useBean as being equivalent to building an object, jsp:useBean has additional options that make it more powerful. As we'll see in Section 13.4 (Sharing Beans), you can specify a scope attribute that makes the bean associated with more than just the current page. If beans can be shared, it is useful to obtain references to existing beans, so the jsp:useBean action specifies that a new object is instantiated only if there is no existing one with the same id and scope.

Rather than using the class attribute, you are permitted to use beanName instead. The difference is that beanName can refer either to a class or to a file containing a serialized bean object. The value of the beanName attribute is passed to the instantiate method of java.beans.Bean.

In most cases, you want the local variable to have the same type as the object being created. In a few cases, however, you might want the variable to be declared to have a type that is a superclass of the actual bean type or is an interface that the bean implements. Use the type attribute to control this, as in the following example:

```
<jsp:useBean id="thread1" class="MyClass" type="Runnable" />
```

This use results in code similar to the following being inserted into the _jspService method:

```
Runnable thread1 = new MyClass();
```

Note that since jsp:useBean uses XML syntax, the format differs in three ways from HTML syntax: the attribute names are case sensitive, either single or double quotes can be used (but one or the other *must* be used), and the end of the tag is marked with />, not just >. The first two syntactic differences apply to all JSP elements that look like jsp:*xxx*. The third difference applies unless the element is a container with a separate start and end tag.

Core Warning

Syntax for jsp:*xxx* *elements differs in three ways from HTML syntax: attribute names are case sensitive, you must enclose the value in single or double quotes, and noncontainer elements should end the tag with* />, *not just* >.

There are also a few character sequences that require special handling in order to appear inside attribute values:

- To get ′ within an attribute value, use \′.
- To get " within an attribute value, use \".
- To get \ within an attribute value, use \\.
- To get %> within an attribute value, use %\>.
- To get <% within an attribute value, use <\%.

Accessing Bean Properties

Once you have a bean, you can access its properties with jsp:getProperty, which takes a name attribute that should match the id given in jsp:useBean and a property attribute that names the property of interest. Alternatively, you could use a JSP expression and explicitly call a method on the object that has the variable name specified with the id attribute. For example, assuming that the Book class has a String property called title and that you've created an instance called book1 by using the jsp:useBean example just given, you could insert the value of the title property into the JSP page in either of the following two ways:

```
<jsp:getProperty name="book1" property="title" />
<%= book1.getTitle() %>
```

The first approach is preferable in this case, since the syntax is more accessible to Web page designers who are not familiar with the Java programming language. However, direct access to the variable is useful when you are using loops, conditional statements, and methods not represented as properties.

If you are not familiar with the concept of bean properties, the standard interpretation of the statement "this bean has a property of type T called foo" is "this class has a method called getFoo that returns something of type T and has another method called setFoo that takes a T as an argument and stores it for later access by getFoo."

Setting Bean Properties: Simple Case

To modify bean properties, you normally use jsp:setProperty. This action has several different forms, but with the simplest form you just supply three attributes: name (which should match the id given by jsp:useBean), property (the name of the property to change), and value (the new value). Section 13.3 (Setting Bean Properties) discusses some alternate forms of jsp:setProperty that let you automatically associate a property with a request parameter. That section also explains how to supply values that are computed at request time (rather than fixed strings) and discusses the type conversion conventions that let you supply string values for parameters that expect numbers, characters, or boolean values.

An alternative to using the jsp:setProperty action is to use a scriptlet that explicitly calls methods on the bean object. For example, given the book1 object shown earlier in this section, you could use either of the following two forms to modify the title property:

```
<jsp:setProperty name="book1"
                 property="title"
                 value="Core Servlets and JavaServer Pages" />
<% book1.setTitle("Core Servlets and JavaServer Pages"); %>
```

Using jsp:setProperty has the advantage that it is more accessible to the nonprogrammer, but direct access to the object lets you perform more complex operations such as setting the value conditionally or calling methods other than getXxx or setXxx on the object.

Installing Bean Classes

The class specified for the bean must be in the server's regular class path, not the part reserved for classes that get automatically reloaded when they change. For example, in the Java Web Server, the main bean class and all the auxiliary classes it uses should go in the install_dir/classes directory or be in a JAR file in install_dir/lib, not in install_dir/servlets. Since Tomcat and the JSWDK don't support auto-reloading servlets, bean classes can be installed in any of the normal servlet directories. For Tomcat 3.0, assuming you haven't defined your own Web application, the primary directory for servlet class files is install_dir/webpages/WEB-INF/classes; for the JSWDK, the default location is install_dir/webpages/WEB-INF/servlets. With all three servers, remember that a package name corresponds to a subdirectory. So, for example, a bean called Fordhook that declares "package lima;" would typically be installed in the following locations:

- **Tomcat 3.0:**
  install_dir/webpages/WEB-INF/classes/lima/Fordhook.class
- **JSWDK 1.0.1:**
  install_dir/webpages/WEB-INF/servlets/lima/Fordhook.class
- **Java Web Server 2.o:**
  install_dir/classes/lima/Fordhook.class

The JSP files that *use* bean classes don't need to be installed anywhere special, however. As is usual with JSP files on a JSP-capable server, they can be placed anywhere that normal Web pages can be.

13.2 Example: StringBean

Listing 13.1 presents a simple class called StringBean that is in the core-servlets package. Because the class has no public instance variables (fields) and has a zero-argument constructor since it doesn't declare any explicit constructors, it satisfies the basic criteria for being a bean. Since StringBean has a method called getMessage that returns a String and another method called setMessage that takes a String as an argument, in beans terminology the class is said to have a String parameter called message.

Listing 13.2 shows a JSP file that uses the StringBean class. First, an instance of StringBean is created with the jsp:useBean action as follows:

```
<jsp:useBean id="stringBean" class="coreservlets.StringBean" />
```

After this, the message property can be inserted into the page in either of the following two ways:

```
<jsp:getProperty name="stringBean" property="message" />
<%= stringBean.getMessage() %>
```

The message property can be modified in either of the following two ways:

```
<jsp:setProperty name="stringBean"
                 property="message"
                 value="some message" />
<% stringBean.setMessage("some message"); %>
```

Figure 13–1 shows the result.

Listing 13.1 StringBean.java

```java
package coreservlets;

/** A simple bean that has a single String property
 *  called message.
 */

public class StringBean {
  private String message = "No message specified";

  public String getMessage() {
    return(message);
  }

  public void setMessage(String message) {
    this.message = message;
  }
}
```

Listing 13.2 `StringBean.jsp`

```
<!DOCTYPE HTML PUBLIC "-//W3C//DTD HTML 4.0 Transitional//EN">
<HTML>
<HEAD>
<TITLE>Using JavaBeans with JSP</TITLE>
<LINK REL=STYLESHEET
      HREF="JSP-Styles.css"
      TYPE="text/css">
</HEAD>

<BODY>

<TABLE BORDER=5 ALIGN="CENTER">
  <TR><TH CLASS="TITLE">
      Using JavaBeans with JSP</TABLE>

<jsp:useBean id="stringBean" class="coreservlets.StringBean" />

<OL>
<LI>Initial value (getProperty):
    <I><jsp:getProperty name="stringBean"
                        property="message" /></I>

<LI>Initial value (JSP expression):
    <I><%= stringBean.getMessage() %></I>
<LI><jsp:setProperty name="stringBean"
                     property="message"
                     value="Best string bean: Fortex" />
    Value after setting property with setProperty:
    <I><jsp:getProperty name="stringBean"
                        property="message" /></I>

<LI><% stringBean.setMessage("My favorite: Kentucky Wonder"); %>
    Value after setting property with scriptlet:
    <I><%= stringBean.getMessage() %></I>
</OL>

</BODY>
</HTML>
```

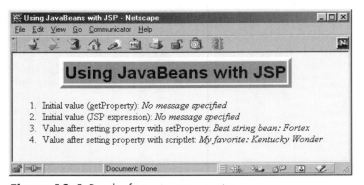

Figure 13-1 Result of `StringBean.jsp`.

13.3 Setting Bean Properties

You normally use `jsp:setProperty` to set bean properties. The simplest form of this action takes three attributes: `name` (which should match the `id` given by `jsp:useBean`), `property` (the name of the property to change), and `value` (the new value).

For example, the `SaleEntry` class shown in Listing 13.3 has an `itemID` property (a `String`), a `numItems` property (an `int`), a `discountCode` property (a `double`), and two read-only properties `itemCost` and `totalCost` (each of type `double`). Listing 13.4 shows a JSP file that builds an instance of the `SaleEntry` class by means of:

```
<jsp:useBean id="entry" class="coreservlets.SaleEntry" />
```

The results are shown in Figure 13–2.

Once the bean is instantiated, using an input parameter to set the `itemID` is straightforward, as shown below:

```
<jsp:setProperty
    name="entry"
    property="itemID"
    value='<%= request.getParameter("itemID") %>' />
```

Notice that I used a JSP expression for the `value` parameter. Most JSP attribute values have to be fixed strings, but the `value` and `name` attributes of `jsp:setProperty` are permitted to be request-time expressions. If the expression uses double quotes internally, recall that single quotes can be used instead of double quotes around attribute values and that `\'` and `\"` can be used to represent single or double quotes within an attribute value.

Listing 13.3 SaleEntry.java

```java
package coreservlets;

/** Simple bean to illustrate the various forms
 *  of jsp:setProperty.
 */

public class SaleEntry {
  private String itemID = "unknown";
  private double discountCode = 1.0;
  private int numItems = 0;

  public String getItemID() {
    return(itemID);
  }

  public void setItemID(String itemID) {
    if (itemID != null) {
      this.itemID = itemID;
    } else {
      this.itemID = "unknown";
    }
  }

  public double getDiscountCode() {
    return(discountCode);
  }

  public void setDiscountCode(double discountCode) {
    this.discountCode = discountCode;
  }

  public int getNumItems() {
    return(numItems);
  }

  public void setNumItems(int numItems) {
    this.numItems = numItems;
  }

  // Replace this with real database lookup.

  public double getItemCost() {
    double cost;
    if (itemID.equals("a1234")) {
      cost = 12.99*getDiscountCode();
    } else {
      cost = -9999;
```

Listing 13.3 `SaleEntry.java` **(continued)**

```
  }
  return(roundToPennies(cost));
}

private double roundToPennies(double cost) {
  return(Math.floor(cost*100)/100.0);
}

public double getTotalCost() {
  return(getItemCost() * getNumItems());
}
}
```

Listing 13.4 `SaleEntry1.jsp`

```
<!DOCTYPE HTML PUBLIC "-//W3C//DTD HTML 4.0 Transitional//EN">
<HTML>
<HEAD>
<TITLE>Using jsp:setProperty</TITLE>
<LINK REL=STYLESHEET
      HREF="JSP-Styles.css"
      TYPE="text/css">
</HEAD>

<BODY>

<TABLE BORDER=5 ALIGN="CENTER">
  <TR><TH CLASS="TITLE">
      Using jsp:setProperty</TABLE>

<jsp:useBean id="entry" class="coreservlets.SaleEntry" />

<jsp:setProperty
    name="entry"
    property="itemID"
    value='<%= request.getParameter("itemID") %>' />

<%
int numItemsOrdered = 1;
try {
  numItemsOrdered =
    Integer.parseInt(request.getParameter("numItems"));
} catch(NumberFormatException nfe) {}
%>
```

Listing 13.4 `SaleEntry1.jsp` (continued)

```
<jsp:setProperty
    name="entry"
    property="numItems"
    value="<%= numItemsOrdered %>" />

<%
double discountCode = 1.0;
try {
  String discountString =
    request.getParameter("discountCode");
  // Double.parseDouble not available in JDK 1.1.
  discountCode =
    Double.valueOf(discountString).doubleValue();
} catch(NumberFormatException nfe) {}
%>
<jsp:setProperty
    name="entry"
    property="discountCode"
    value="<%= discountCode %>" />

<BR>
<TABLE ALIGN="CENTER" BORDER=1>
<TR CLASS="COLORED">
  <TH>Item ID<TH>Unit Price<TH>Number Ordered<TH>Total Price
<TR ALIGN="RIGHT">
  <TD><jsp:getProperty name="entry" property="itemID" />
  <TD>$<jsp:getProperty name="entry" property="itemCost" />
  <TD><jsp:getProperty name="entry" property="numItems" />
  <TD>$<jsp:getProperty name="entry" property="totalCost" />
</TABLE>

</BODY>
</HTML>
```

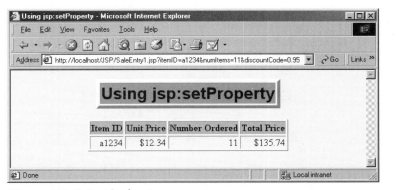

Figure 13–2 Result of `SaleEntry1.jsp`.

Associating Individual Properties with Input Parameters

Setting the `itemID` property was easy since its value is a `String`. Setting the `numItems` and `discountCode` properties is a bit more problematic since their values must be numbers and `getParameter` returns a `String`. Here is the somewhat cumbersome code required to set `numItems`:

```
<%
int numItemsOrdered = 1;
try {
  numItemsOrdered =
    Integer.parseInt(request.getParameter("numItems"));
} catch(NumberFormatException nfe) {}
%>
<jsp:setProperty
    name="entry"
    property="numItems"
    value="<%= numItemsOrdered %>" />
```

Fortunately, JSP has a nice solution to this problem that lets you associate a property with a request parameter and that automatically performs type conversion from strings to numbers, characters, and boolean values. Instead of using the `value` attribute, you use `param` to name an input parameter. The value of this parameter is automatically used as the value of the property, and simple type conversions are performed automatically. If the specified input parameter is missing from the request, no action is taken (the system does not pass `null` to the associated property). So, for example, setting the `numItems` property can be simplified to:

```
<jsp:setProperty
    name="entry"
    property="numItems"
    param="numItems" />
```

Listing 13.5 shows the entire JSP page reworked in this manner.

Listing 13.5 `SaleEntry2.jsp`

```
<!DOCTYPE HTML PUBLIC "-//W3C//DTD HTML 4.0 Transitional//EN">
<HTML>
<HEAD>
<TITLE>Using jsp:setProperty</TITLE>
<LINK REL=STYLESHEET
      HREF="JSP-Styles.css"
      TYPE="text/css">
</HEAD>

<BODY>

<TABLE BORDER=5 ALIGN="CENTER">
  <TR><TH CLASS="TITLE">
      Using jsp:setProperty</TABLE>

<jsp:useBean id="entry" class="coreservlets.SaleEntry" />

<jsp:setProperty
    name="entry"
    property="itemID"
    param="itemID" />

<jsp:setProperty
    name="entry"
    property="numItems"
    param="numItems" />

<%-- WARNING! Both the JSWDK 1.0.1 and the Java Web Server
              have a bug that makes them fail on double
              type conversions of the following sort.
--%>
<jsp:setProperty
    name="entry"
    property="discountCode"
    param="discountCode" />

<BR>
<TABLE ALIGN="CENTER" BORDER=1>
<TR CLASS="COLORED">
  <TH>Item ID<TH>Unit Price<TH>Number Ordered<TH>Total Price
<TR ALIGN="RIGHT">
  <TD><jsp:getProperty name="entry" property="itemID" />
  <TD>$<jsp:getProperty name="entry" property="itemCost" />
  <TD><jsp:getProperty name="entry" property="numItems" />
  <TD>$<jsp:getProperty name="entry" property="totalCost" />
</TABLE>

</BODY>
</HTML>
```

Automatic Type Conversions

Table 13.1 summarizes the automatic type conversions performed when a bean property is automatically associated with an input parameter. One warning is in order, however: both JSWDK 1.0.1 and the Java Web Server 2.0 have a bug that causes them to crash at page translation time for pages that try to perform automatic type conversions for properties that expect `double` values. Tomcat and most commercial servers work as expected.

Core Warning

With the JSWDK and the Java Web Server, you cannot associate properties that expect double-precision values with input parameters.

Table 13.1   Type Conversions When Properties Are Associated with Input Parameters

Property Type	Conversion Routine
boolean	Boolean.valueOf(paramString).booleanValue()
Boolean	Boolean.valueOf(paramString)
byte	Byte.valueOf(paramString).byteValue()
Byte	Byte.valueOf(paramString)
char	Character.valueOf(paramString).charValue()
Character	Character.valueOf(paramString)
double	Double.valueOf(paramString).doubleValue()
Double	Double.valueOf(paramString)
int	Integer.valueOf(paramString).intValue()
Integer	Integer.valueOf(paramString)
float	Float.valueOf(paramString).floatValue()
Float	Float.valueOf(paramString)
long	Long.valueOf(paramString).longValue()
Long	Long.valueOf(paramString)

Associating All Properties with Input Parameters

Associating a property with an input parameter saves you the bother of performing conversions for many of the simple built-in types. JSP lets you take the process one step further by associating *all* properties with identically named input parameters. All you have to do is to supply "*" for the property parameter. So, for example, all three of the jsp:setProperty statements of Listing 13.5 can be replaced by the following simple line. Listing 13.6 shows the complete page.

```
<jsp:setProperty name="entry" property="*" />
```

Although this approach is simple, four small warnings are in order. First, as with individually associated properties, no action is taken when an input parameter is missing. In particular, the system does not supply null as the property value. Second, the JSWDK and the Java Web Server both fail for conversions to properties that expect double values. Third, automatic type conversion does not guard against illegal values as effectively as does manual type conversion. So you might consider error pages (see Sections 11.9 and 11.10) when using automatic type conversion. Fourth, since both property names and input parameters are case sensitive, the property name and input parameter must match exactly.

Core Warning

*In order for all properties to be associated with input parameters, the property names must match the parameter names **exactly**, including case.*

Listing 13.6 `SaleEntry3.jsp`

```html
<!DOCTYPE HTML PUBLIC "-//W3C//DTD HTML 4.0 Transitional//EN">
<HTML>
<HEAD>
<TITLE>Using jsp:setProperty</TITLE>
<LINK REL=STYLESHEET
      HREF="JSP-Styles.css"
      TYPE="text/css">
</HEAD>

<BODY>
```

Listing 13.6 `SaleEntry3.jsp` **(continued)**

```
<TABLE BORDER=5 ALIGN="CENTER">
  <TR><TH CLASS="TITLE">
      Using jsp:setProperty</TABLE>

<jsp:useBean id="entry" class="coreservlets.SaleEntry" />
<%-- WARNING! Both the JSWDK 1.0.1 and the Java Web Server
            have a bug that makes them fail on automatic
            type conversions to double values.
--%>
<jsp:setProperty name="entry" property="*" />

<BR>
<TABLE ALIGN="CENTER" BORDER=1>
<TR CLASS="COLORED">
  <TH>Item ID<TH>Unit Price<TH>Number Ordered<TH>Total Price
<TR ALIGN="RIGHT">
  <TD><jsp:getProperty name="entry" property="itemID" />
  <TD>$<jsp:getProperty name="entry" property="itemCost" />
  <TD><jsp:getProperty name="entry" property="numItems" />
  <TD>$<jsp:getProperty name="entry" property="totalCost" />
</TABLE>

</BODY>
</HTML>
```

13.4 Sharing Beans

Up to this point, I have treated the objects that were created with `jsp:use-Bean` as though they were simply bound to local variables in the `_jspService` method (which is called by the `service` method of the servlet that is generated from the page). Although the beans are indeed bound to local variables, that is not the only behavior. They are also stored in one of four different locations, depending on the value of the optional `scope` attribute of `jsp:use-Bean`. The `scope` attribute has the following possible values:

- **page**

  This is the default value. It indicates that, in addition to being bound to a local variable, the bean object should be placed in the `PageContext` object for the duration of the current request. In principle, storing the object there means that servlet code can access it by calling `getAttribute` on the predefined `pageContext` variable. In practice, beans created with `page` scope are almost always accessed by `jsp:getProperty`, `jsp:setProperty`, scriptlets, or expressions later in the same page.

- **application**

  This very useful value means that, in addition to being bound to a local variable, the bean will be stored in the shared `ServletContext` available through the predefined `application` variable or by a call to `getServletContext()`. The `ServletContext` is shared by all servlets in the same Web application (or all servlets in the same server or servlet engine if no explicit Web applications are defined). Values in the `ServletContext` can be retrieved by the `getAttribute` method. This sharing has a couple of ramifications.

  First, it provides a simple mechanism for multiple servlets and JSP pages to access the same object. See the following subsection (Conditional Bean Creation) for details and an example.

  Second, it lets a servlet *create* a bean that will be used in JSP pages, not just *access* one that was previously created. This approach lets a servlet handle complex user requests by setting up beans, storing them in the `ServletContext`, then forwarding the request to one of several possible JSP pages to present results appropriate to the request data. For details on this approach, see Chapter 15 (Integrating Servlets and JSP).

- **session**

  This value means that, in addition to being bound to a local variable, the bean will be stored in the `HttpSession` object associated with the current request, where it can be retrieved with `getValue`. Attempting to use `scope="session"` causes an error at page translation time when the `page` directive stipulates that the current page is not participating in sessions. (See Section 11.4, "The session Attribute.")

- **request**

  This value signifies that, in addition to being bound to a local variable, the bean object should be placed in the `ServletRequest` object for the duration of the current request, where it is available by means of the `getAttribute` method. This value is only a slight variation of the per-request scope provided by `scope="page"` (or by default when no `scope` is specified).

Conditional Bean Creation

To make bean sharing more convenient, there are two situations where bean-related elements are evaluated conditionally.

First, a `jsp:useBean` element results in a new bean being instantiated only if no bean with the same `id` and `scope` can be found. If a bean with the same `id` and `scope` *is* found, the preexisting bean is simply bound to the variable referenced by `id`. A typecast is performed if the preexisting bean is of a more specific type than the bean being declared, and a `ClassCastException` results if this typecast is illegal.

Second, instead of

```
<jsp:useBean ... />
```

you can use

```
<jsp:useBean ...>
  statements
</jsp:useBean>
```

The point of using the second form is that the statements between the `jsp:useBean` start and end tags are executed *only* if a new bean is created, *not* if an existing bean is used. This conditional execution is convenient for setting initial bean properties for beans that are shared by multiple pages. Since you don't know which page will be accessed first, you don't know which page should contain the initialization code. No problem: they can all contain the code, but only the page first accessed actually executes it. For example, Listing 13.7 shows a simple bean that can be used to record cumulative access counts to any of a set of related pages. It also stores the name of the first page that was accessed. Since there is no way to predict which page in a set will be accessed first, each page that uses the shared counter has statements like the following:

```
<jsp:useBean id="counter"
             class="coreservlets.AccessCountBean"
             scope="application">
  <jsp:setProperty name="counter"
                   property="firstPage"
                   value="Current Page Name" />
</jsp:useBean>
```

Collectively, the pages using the counter have been accessed `<jsp:getProperty name="counter" property="accessCount" />` times.

Listing 13.8 shows the first of three pages that use this approach. The source code archive at `http://www.coreservlets.com/` contains the other two nearly identical pages. Figure 13–3 shows a typical result.

Listing 13.7 `AccessCountBean.java`

```
package coreservlets;

/** Simple bean to illustrate sharing beans through
 *  use of the scope attribute of jsp:useBean.
 */

public class AccessCountBean {
  private String firstPage;
  private int accessCount = 1;

  public String getFirstPage() {
    return(firstPage);
  }

  public void setFirstPage(String firstPage) {
    this.firstPage = firstPage;
  }

  public int getAccessCount() {
    return(accessCount++);
  }
}
```

Listing 13.8 SharedCounts1.jsp

```
<!DOCTYPE HTML PUBLIC "-//W3C//DTD HTML 4.0 Transitional//EN">
<HTML>
<HEAD>
<TITLE>Shared Access Counts: Page 1</TITLE>
<LINK REL=STYLESHEET
      HREF="JSP-Styles.css"
      TYPE="text/css">
</HEAD>

<BODY>

<TABLE BORDER=5 ALIGN="CENTER">
  <TR><TH CLASS="TITLE">
      Shared Access Counts: Page 1</TABLE>
<P>
<jsp:useBean id="counter"
             class="coreservlets.AccessCountBean"
             scope="application">
  <jsp:setProperty name="counter"
                   property="firstPage"
                   value="SharedCounts1.jsp" />
</jsp:useBean>

Of SharedCounts1.jsp (this page),
<A HREF="SharedCounts2.jsp">SharedCounts2.jsp</A>, and
<A HREF="SharedCounts3.jsp">SharedCounts3.jsp</A>,
<jsp:getProperty name="counter" property="firstPage" />
was the first page accessed.
<P>
Collectively, the three pages have been accessed
<jsp:getProperty name="counter" property="accessCount" />
times.

</BODY>
</HTML>
```

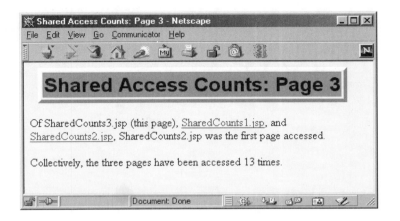

Figure 13–3 Result of a user visiting `SharedCounts3.jsp`. The first page visited by any user was `SharedCounts2.jsp`. `SharedCounts1.jsp`, `SharedCounts2.jsp`, and `SharedCounts3.jsp` were collectively visited a total of twelve times after the server was last started but prior to the visit shown in this figure.

CREATING CUSTOM JSP TAG LIBRARIES

Topics in This Chapter

- Tag handler classes
- Tag library descriptor files
- The JSP `taglib` directive
- Simple tags
- Tags that use attributes
- Tags that use the body content between their start and end tags
- Tags that modify their body content
- Looping tags
- Nested tags

Chapter 14

J SP 1.1 introduced an extremely valuable new capability: the ability to define your own JSP tags. You define how the tag, its attributes, and its body are interpreted, then group your tags into collections called *tag libraries* that can be used in any number of JSP files. The ability to define tag libraries in this way permits Java developers to boil down complex server-side behaviors into simple and easy-to-use elements that content developers can easily incorporate into their JSP pages.

Custom tags accomplish some of the same goals as beans that are accessed with `jsp:useBean` (see Chapter 13, "Using JavaBeans with JSP")—encapsulating complex behaviors into simple and accessible forms. There are several differences, however. First, beans cannot manipulate JSP content; custom tags can. Second, complex operations can be reduced to a significantly simpler form with custom tags than with beans. Third, custom tags require quite a bit more work to set up than do beans. Fourth, beans are often defined in one servlet and then used in a different servlet or JSP page (see Chapter 15, "Integrating Servlets and JSP"), whereas custom tags usually define more self-contained behavior. Finally, custom tags are available only in JSP 1.1, but beans can be used in both JSP 1.0 and 1.1.

At the time this book went to press, no official release of Tomcat 3.0 properly supported custom tags, so the examples in this chapter use the beta version of Tomcat 3.1. Other than the support for custom tags and a few efficiency improvements and minor bug fixes, there is little difference in the behavior of the two versions. However, Tomcat 3.1 uses a slightly different directory structure, as summarized Table 14.1.

Table 14.1 Standard Tomcat Directories		
	Tomcat 3.0	*Tomcat 3.1*
Location of `startup` and `shutdown` Scripts	`install_dir`	`install_dir`/bin
Standard Top-Level Directory for Servlets and Supporting Classes	`install_dir`/webpages/ `WEB-INF`/classes	`install_dir`/webapps/ `ROOT/WEB-INF`/classes
Standard Top-Level Directory for HTML and JSP Files	`install_dir`/webpages	`install_dir`/webapps/ `ROOT`

14.1 The Components That Make Up a Tag Library

In order to use custom JSP tags, you need to define three separate components: the tag handler class that defines the tag's behavior, the tag library descriptor file that maps the XML element names to the tag implementations, and the JSP file that uses the tag library. The rest of this section gives an overview of each of these components and the following sections give details on how to build these components for various different styles of tags.

The Tag Handler Class

When defining a new tag, your first task is to define a Java class that tells the system what to do when it sees the tag. This class must implement the `javax.servlet.jsp.tagext.Tag` interface. This is usually accomplished by extending the `TagSupport` or `BodyTagSupport` class. Listing 14.1 is an example of a simple tag that just inserts "`Custom tag example (coreserv-lets.tags.ExampleTag)`" into the JSP page wherever the corresponding tag is used. Don't worry about understanding the exact behavior of this class; that will be made clear in the next section. For now, just note that it is in the coreservlets.tags class and is called ExampleTag. Thus, with Tomcat 3.1, the class file would be in *install_dir*/webapps/ROOT/WEB-INF/classes/core-servlets/tags/ExampleTag.class.

Listing 14.1 ExampleTag.java

```java
package coreservlets.tags;

import javax.servlet.jsp.*;
import javax.servlet.jsp.tagext.*;
import java.io.*;

/** Very simple JSP tag that just inserts a string
 *  ("Custom tag example...") into the output.
 *  The actual name of the tag is not defined here;
 *  that is given by the Tag Library Descriptor (TLD)
 *  file that is referenced by the taglib directive
 *  in the JSP file.
 */

public class ExampleTag extends TagSupport {
  public int doStartTag() {
    try {
      JspWriter out = pageContext.getOut();
      out.print("Custom tag example " +
                "(coreservlets.tags.ExampleTag)");
    } catch(IOException ioe) {
      System.out.println("Error in ExampleTag: " + ioe);
    }
    return(SKIP_BODY);
  }
}
```

The Tag Library Descriptor File

Once you have defined a tag handler, your next task is to identify the class to the server and to associate it with a particular XML tag name. This task is accomplished by means of a tag library descriptor file (in XML format) like the one shown in Listing 14.2. This file contains some fixed information, an arbitrary short name for your library, a short description, and a series of tag descriptions. The nonbold part of the listing is the same in virtually all tag library descriptors and can be copied verbatim from the source code archive at http://www.coreservlets.com/ or from the Tomcat 3.1 standard examples (*install_dir*/webapps/examples/WEB-INF/jsp).

The format of tag descriptions will be described in later sections. For now, just note that the `tag` element defines the main name of the tag (really tag suffix, as will be seen shortly) and identifies the class that handles the tag. Since the tag handler class is in the `coreservlets.tags` package, the fully qualified class name of `coreservlets.tags.ExampleTag` is used. Note that this is a class name, not a URL or relative path name. The class can be installed anywhere on the server that beans or other supporting classes can be put. With Tomcat 3.1, the standard base location is *install_dir*/webapps/ROOT/WEB-INF/classes, so `ExampleTag` would be in *install_dir*/webapps/ROOT/WEB-INF/classes/coreservlets/tags. Although it is always a good idea to put your servlet classes in packages, a surprising feature of Tomcat 3.1 is that tag handlers are *required* to be in packages.

Listing 14.2 `csajsp-taglib.tld`

```xml
<?xml version="1.0" encoding="ISO-8859-1" ?>
<!DOCTYPE taglib
  PUBLIC "-//Sun Microsystems, Inc.//DTD JSP Tag Library 1.1//EN"
  "http://java.sun.com/j2ee/dtds/web-jsptaglibrary_1_1.dtd">

<!-- a tag library descriptor -->

<taglib>
  <!-- after this the default space is
       "http://java.sun.com/j2ee/dtds/jsptaglibrary_1_2.dtd"
   -->

  <tlibversion>1.0</tlibversion>
  <jspversion>1.1</jspversion>
  <shortname>csajsp</shortname>
  <urn></urn>
  <info>
    A tag library from Core Servlets and JavaServer Pages,
    http://www.coreservlets.com/.
  </info>

  <tag>
    <name>example</name>
    <tagclass>coreservlets.tags.ExampleTag</tagclass>
    <info>Simplest example: inserts one line of output</info>
    <bodycontent>EMPTY</bodycontent>
  </tag>
  <!-- Other tags defined later... -->

</taglib>
```

The JSP File

Once you have a tag handler implementation and a tag library description, you are ready to write a JSP file that makes use of the tag. Listing 14.3 gives an example. Somewhere before the first use of your tag, you need to use the `taglib` directive. This directive has the following form:

```
<%@ taglib uri="..." prefix="..." %>
```

The required `uri` attribute can be either an absolute or relative URL referring to a tag library descriptor file like the one shown in Listing 14.2. To complicate matters a little, however, Tomcat 3.1 uses a `web.xml` file that maps an absolute URL for a tag library descriptor to a file on the local system. I don't recommend that you use this approach, but you should be aware of it in case you look at the Apache examples and wonder why it works when they specify a nonexistent URL for the `uri` attribute of the `taglib` directive.

The `prefix` attribute, also required, specifies a prefix that will be used in front of whatever tag name the tag library descriptor defined. For example, if the TLD file defines a tag named `tag1` and the `prefix` attribute has a value of `test`, the actual tag name would be `test:tag1`. This tag could be used in either of the following two ways, depending on whether it is defined to be a container that makes use of the tag body:

```
<test:tag1>
Arbitrary JSP
</test:tag1>
```

or just

```
<test:tag1 />
```

To illustrate, the descriptor file of Listing 14.2 is called `csajsp-taglib.tld`, and resides in the same directory as the JSP file shown in Listing 14.3. Thus, the `taglib` directive in the JSP file uses a simple relative URL giving just the filename, as shown below.

```
<%@ taglib uri="csajsp-taglib.tld" prefix="csajsp" %>
```

Furthermore, since the `prefix` attribute is `csajsp` (for *Core Servlets and JavaServer Pages*), the rest of the JSP page uses `csajsp:example` to refer to the `example` tag defined in the descriptor file. Figure 14–1 shows the result.

Listing 14.3 `SimpleExample.jsp`

```
<!DOCTYPE HTML PUBLIC "-//W3C//DTD HTML 4.0 Transitional//EN">
<HTML>
<HEAD>

<%@ taglib uri="csajsp-taglib.tld" prefix="csajsp" %>

<TITLE><csajsp:example /></TITLE>
<LINK REL=STYLESHEET
      HREF="JSP-Styles.css"
      TYPE="text/css">
</HEAD>

<BODY>
<H1><csajsp:example /></H1>
<csajsp:example />

</BODY>
</HTML>
```

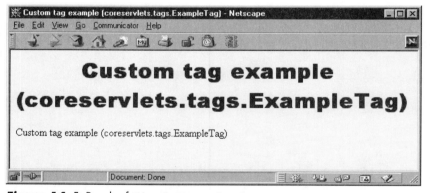

Figure 14–1 Result of `SimpleExample.jsp`.

14.2 Defining a Basic Tag

This section gives details on defining simple tags without attributes or tag
bodies; the tags are thus of the form `<prefix:tagname />`.

The Tag Handler Class

Tags that either have no body or that merely include the body verbatim should extend the `TagSupport` class. This is a built-in class in the `javax.servlet.jsp.tagext` package that implements the `Tag` interface and contains much of the standard functionality basic tags need. Because of other classes you will use, your tag should normally import classes in the `javax.servlet.jsp` and `java.io` packages as well. So, most tag implementations contain the following `import` statements after the package declaration:

```
import javax.servlet.jsp.*;
import javax.servlet.jsp.tagext.*;
import java.io.*;
```

I recommend that you download an example from `http://www.core-servlets.com/` and use it as the starting point for your own implementations.

For a tag without attributes or body, all you need to do is override the `doStartTag` method, which defines code that gets called *at request time* where the element's start tag is found. To generate output, the method should obtain the `JspWriter` (the specialized `PrintWriter` available in JSP pages through use of the predefined `out` variable) from the `pageContext` field by means of `getOut`. In addition to the `getOut` method, the `pageContext` field (of type `PageContext`) has methods for obtaining other data structures associated with the request. The most important ones are `getRequest`, `getResponse`, `getServletContext`, and `getSession`.

Since the `print` method of `JspWriter` throws `IOException`, the `print` statements should be inside a `try`/`catch` block. To report other types of errors to the client, you can declare that your `doStartTag` method throws a `JspException` and then throw one when the error occurs.

If your tag does not have a body, your `doStartTag` should return the `SKIP_BODY` constant. This instructs the system to ignore any content between the tag's start and end tags. As we will see in Section 14.5 (Optionally Including the Tag Body), `SKIP_BODY` is sometimes useful even when there is a tag body, but the simple tag we're developing here will be used as a stand-alone tag (`<prefix:tagname />`) and thus does not have body content.

Listing 14.4 shows a tag implementation that uses this approach to generate a random 50-digit prime through use of the `Primes` class developed in Chapter 7 (Generating the Server Response: HTTP Response Headers) — see Listing 7.4.

Listing 14.4 `SimplePrimeTag.java`

```java
package coreservlets.tags;

import javax.servlet.jsp.*;
import javax.servlet.jsp.tagext.*;
import java.io.*;
import java.math.*;
import coreservlets.*;

/** Generates a prime of approximately 50 digits.
 *  (50 is actually the length of the random number
 *  generated -- the first prime above that number will
 *  be returned.)
 */

public class SimplePrimeTag extends TagSupport {
  protected int len = 50;

  public int doStartTag() {
    try {
      JspWriter out = pageContext.getOut();
      BigInteger prime = Primes.nextPrime(Primes.random(len));
      out.print(prime);
    } catch(IOException ioe) {
      System.out.println("Error generating prime: " + ioe);
    }
    return(SKIP_BODY);
  }
}
```

The Tag Library Descriptor File

The general format of a descriptor file is almost always the same: it should contain an XML version identifier followed by a DOCTYPE declaration followed by a `taglib` container element. To get started, just download a sample from `http://www.coreservlets.com/`. The important part to understand is what goes *in* the `taglib` element: the `tag` element. For tags without attributes, the `tag` element should contain four elements between `<tag>` and `</tag>`:

1. **name**, whose body defines the base tag name to which the prefix of the `taglib` directive will be attached. In this case, I use
   `<name>simplePrime</name>`
   to assign a base tag name of `simplePrime`.

2. **tagclass**, which gives the fully qualified class name of the tag handler. In this case, I use

   ```
   <tagclass>coreservlets.tags.SimplePrimeTag
   </tagclass>
   ```

3. **info**, which gives a short description. Here, I use

   ```
   <info>Outputs a random 50-digit prime.</info>
   ```

4. **bodycontent**, which should have the value EMPTY for tags without bodies. Tags with normal bodies that might be interpreted as normal JSP use a value of JSP, and the rare tags whose handlers completely process the body themselves use a value of TAGDEPENDENT. For the SimplePrimeTag discussed here, I use EMPTY as below:

   ```
   <bodycontent>EMPTY</bodycontent>
   ```

Listing 14.5 shows the full TLD file.

Listing 14.5 `csajsp-taglib.tld`

```
<?xml version="1.0" encoding="ISO-8859-1" ?>
<!DOCTYPE taglib
 PUBLIC "-//Sun Microsystems, Inc.//DTD JSP Tag Library 1.1//EN"
 "http://java.sun.com/j2ee/dtds/web-jsptaglibrary_1_1.dtd">

<!-- a tag library descriptor -->

<taglib>
  <!-- after this the default space is
       "http://java.sun.com/j2ee/dtds/jsptaglibrary_1_2.dtd"
   -->

  <tlibversion>1.0</tlibversion>
  <jspversion>1.1</jspversion>
  <shortname>csajsp</shortname>
  <urn></urn>
  <info>
    A tag library from Core Servlets and JavaServer Pages,
    http://www.coreservlets.com/.
  </info>

  <!-- Other tags defined earlier... -->
```

Listing 14.5 `csajsp-taglib.tld` (continued)

```
  <tag>
    <name>simplePrime</name>
    <tagclass>coreservlets.tags.SimplePrimeTag</tagclass>
    <info>Outputs a random 50-digit prime.</info>
    <bodycontent>EMPTY</bodycontent>
  </tag>

</taglib>
```

The JSP File

JSP documents that make use of custom tags need to use the `taglib` directive, supplying a `uri` attribute that gives the location of the tag library descriptor file and a `prefix` attribute that specifies a short string that will be attached (along with a colon) to the main tag name. Listing 14.6 shows a JSP document that uses

```
    <%@ taglib uri="csajsp-taglib.tld" prefix="csajsp" %>
```

to use the TLD file just shown in Listing 14.5 with a prefix of `csajsp`. Since the base tag name is `simplePrime`, the full tag used is

```
    <csajsp:simplePrime />
```

Figure 14–2 shows the result.

Listing 14.6 `SimplePrimeExample.jsp`

```
<!DOCTYPE HTML PUBLIC "-//W3C//DTD HTML 4.0 Transitional//EN">
<HTML>
<HEAD>
<TITLE>Some 50-Digit Primes</TITLE>
<LINK REL=STYLESHEET
      HREF="JSP-Styles.css"
      TYPE="text/css">
</HEAD>

<BODY>
<H1>Some 50-Digit Primes</H1>

<%@ taglib uri="csajsp-taglib.tld" prefix="csajsp" %>

<UL>
  <LI><csajsp:simplePrime />
  <LI><csajsp:simplePrime />
  <LI><csajsp:simplePrime />
  <LI><csajsp:simplePrime />
</UL>

</BODY>
</HTML>
```

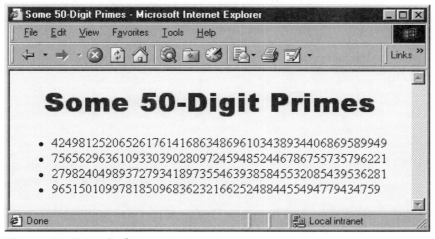

Figure 14–2 Result of `SimplePrimeExample.jsp`.

14.3 Assigning Attributes to Tags

Allowing tags like

```
<prefix:name attribute1="value1" attribute2="value2" ... />
```

adds significant flexibility to your tag library. This section explains how to add attribute support to your tags.

The Tag Handler Class

Providing support for attributes is straightforward. Use of an attribute called `attribute1` simply results in a call to a method called `setAttribute1` in your class that extends `TagSupport` (or otherwise implements the `Tag` interface). The attribute value is supplied to the method as a `String`. Consequently, adding support for an attribute named `attribute1` is merely a matter of implementing the following method:

```
public void setAttribute1(String value1) {
    doSomethingWith(value1);
}
```

Note that an attribute of `attributeName` (lowercase a) corresponds to a method called `setAttributeName` (uppercase A).

One of the most common things to do in the attribute handler is to simply store the attribute in a field that will later be used by `doStartTag` or a similar method. For example, following is a section of a tag implementation that adds support for the `message` attribute.

```
private String message = "Default Message";

public void setMessage(String message) {
  this.message = message;
}
```

If the tag handler will be accessed from other classes, it is a good idea to provide a `getAttributeName` method in addition to the `setAttributeName` method. Only `setAttributeName` is required, however.

Listing 14.7 shows a subclass of `SimplePrimeTag` that adds support for the `length` attribute. When such an attribute is supplied, it results in a call to `setLength`, which converts the input `String` to an `int` and stores it in the `len` field already used by the `doStartTag` method in the parent class.

Listing 14.7 `PrimeTag.java`

```
package coreservlets.tags;

import javax.servlet.jsp.*;
import javax.servlet.jsp.tagext.*;
import java.io.*;
import java.math.*;
import coreservlets.*;

/** Generates an N-digit random prime (default N = 50).
 *  Extends SimplePrimeTag, adding a length attribute
 *  to set the size of the prime. The doStartTag
 *  method of the parent class uses the len field
 *  to determine the approximate length of the prime.
 */

public class PrimeTag extends SimplePrimeTag {
  public void setLength(String length) {
    try {
      len = Integer.parseInt(length);
    } catch(NumberFormatException nfe) {
      len = 50;
    }
  }
}
```

The Tag Library Descriptor File

Tag attributes must be declared inside the tag element by means of an attribute element. The attribute element has three nested elements that can appear between <attribute> and </attribute>.

1. **name**, a required element that defines the case-sensitive attribute name. In this case, I use

   ```
   <name>length</name>
   ```

2. **required**, a required element that stipulates whether the attribute must always be supplied (true) or is optional (false). In this case, to indicate that length is optional, I use

   ```
   <required>false</required>
   ```
   If you omit the attribute, no call is made to the setAttribute-Name method. So, be sure to give default values to the fields that the method sets.

3. **rtexprvalue**, an optional attribute that indicates whether the attribute value can be a JSP expression like

   ```
   <%= expression %>
   ```
   (true) or whether it must be a fixed string (false). The default value is false, so this element is usually omitted except when you want to allow attributes to have values determined at request time.

Listing 14.8 shows the complete tag element within the tag library descriptor file. In addition to supplying an attribute element to describe the length attribute, the tag element also contains the standard name (prime), tagclass (coreservlets.tags.PrimeTag), info (short description), and bodycontent (EMPTY) elements.

Listing 14.8 `csajsp-taglib.tld`

```
<?xml version="1.0" encoding="ISO-8859-1" ?>
<!DOCTYPE taglib
  PUBLIC "-//Sun Microsystems, Inc.//DTD JSP Tag Library 1.1//EN"
  "http://java.sun.com/j2ee/dtds/web-jsptaglibrary_1_1.dtd">

<!-- a tag library descriptor -->

<taglib>
  <!-- after this the default space is
       "http://java.sun.com/j2ee/dtds/jsptaglibrary_1_2.dtd"
  -->
```

Listing 14.8 `csajsp-taglib.tld` (continued)

```
<tlibversion>1.0</tlibversion>
<jspversion>1.1</jspversion>
<shortname>csajsp</shortname>
<urn></urn>
<info>
  A tag library from Core Servlets and JavaServer Pages,
  http://www.coreservlets.com/.
</info>

<!-- Other tag defined earlier... -->

<tag>
  <name>prime</name>
  <tagclass>coreservlets.tags.PrimeTag</tagclass>
  <info>Outputs a random N-digit prime.</info>
  <bodycontent>EMPTY</bodycontent>
  <attribute>
    <name>length</name>
    <required>false</required>
  </attribute>
</tag>

</taglib>
```

The JSP File

Listing 14.9 shows a JSP document that uses the `taglib` directive to load the tag library descriptor file and to specify a prefix of `csajsp`. Since the `prime` tag is defined to permit a `length` attribute, Listing 14.9 uses

```
<csajsp:prime length="xxx" />
```

Remember that custom tags follow XML syntax, which requires attribute values to be enclosed in either single or double quotes. Also, since the `length` attribute is not required, it is permissible to use

```
<csajsp:prime />
```

The tag handler is responsible for using a reasonable default value in such a case.

Figure 14–3 shows the result of Listing 14.9.

Listing 14.9 `PrimeExample.jsp`

```
<!DOCTYPE HTML PUBLIC "-//W3C//DTD HTML 4.0 Transitional//EN">
<HTML>
<HEAD>
<TITLE>Some N-Digit Primes</TITLE>
<LINK REL=STYLESHEET
      HREF="JSP-Styles.css"
      TYPE="text/css">
</HEAD>

<BODY>
<H1>Some N-Digit Primes</H1>

<%@ taglib uri="csajsp-taglib.tld" prefix="csajsp" %>

<UL>
  <LI>20-digit: <csajsp:prime length="20" />
  <LI>40-digit: <csajsp:prime length="40" />
  <LI>80-digit: <csajsp:prime length="80" />
  <LI>Default (50-digit): <csajsp:prime />
</UL>

</BODY>
</HTML>
```

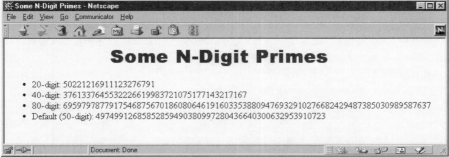

Figure 14–3 Result of `PrimeExample.jsp`.

14.4 Including the Tag Body

Up to this point, all of the custom tags you have seen ignore the tag body and thus are used as stand-alone tags of the form

```
<prefix:tagname />
```

In this section, we see how to define tags that use their body content, and are thus used in the following manner:

```
<prefix:tagname>body</prefix:tagname>
```

The Tag Handler Class

In the previous examples, the tag handlers defined a doStartTag method that returned SKIP_BODY. To instruct the system to make use of the body that occurs between the new element's start and end tags, your doStartTag method should return EVAL_BODY_INCLUDE instead. The body content can contain JSP scripting elements, directives, and actions, just like the rest of the page. The JSP constructs are translated into servlet code at page translation time, and that code is invoked at request time.

If you make use of a tag body, then you might want to take some action *after* the body as well as before it. Use the doEndTag method to specify this action. In almost all cases, you want to continue with the rest of the page after finishing with your tag, so the doEndTag method should return EVAL_PAGE. If you want to abort the processing of the rest of the page, you can return SKIP_PAGE instead.

Listing 14.10 defines a tag for a heading element that is more flexible than the standard HTML H1 through H6 elements. This new element allows a precise font size, a list of preferred font names (the first entry that is available on the client system will be used), a foreground color, a background color, a border, and an alignment (LEFT, CENTER, RIGHT). Only the alignment capability is available with the H1 through H6 elements. The heading is implemented through use of a one-cell table enclosing a SPAN element that has embedded style sheet attributes. The doStartTag method generates the TABLE and SPAN start tags, then returns EVAL_BODY_INCLUDE to instruct the system to include the tag body. The doEndTag method generates the </SPAN> and </TABLE> tags, then returns EVAL_PAGE to continue with normal page processing. Various setAttributeName methods are used to handle the attributes like bgColor and fontSize.

Listing 14.10 `HeadingTag.java`

```java
package coreservlets.tags;

import javax.servlet.jsp.*;
import javax.servlet.jsp.tagext.*;
import java.io.*;

/** Generates an HTML heading with the specified background
 *  color, foreground color, alignment, font, and font size.
 *  You can also turn on a border around it, which normally
 *  just barely encloses the heading, but which can also
 *  stretch wider. All attributes except the background
 *  color are optional.
 */

public class HeadingTag extends TagSupport {
  private String bgColor; // The one required attribute
  private String color = null;
  private String align="CENTER";
  private String fontSize="36";
  private String fontList="Arial, Helvetica, sans-serif";
  private String border="0";
  private String width=null;

  public void setBgColor(String bgColor) {
    this.bgColor = bgColor;
  }

  public void setColor(String color) {
    this.color = color;
  }

  public void setAlign(String align) {
    this.align = align;
  }

  public void setFontSize(String fontSize) {
    this.fontSize = fontSize;
  }

  public void setFontList(String fontList) {
    this.fontList = fontList;
  }

  public void setBorder(String border) {
    this.border = border;
  }

  public void setWidth(String width) {
    this.width = width;
  }
```

Listing 14.10 `HeadingTag.java` (continued)

```java
public int doStartTag() {
  try {
    JspWriter out = pageContext.getOut();
    out.print("<TABLE BORDER=" + border +
              " BGCOLOR=\"" + bgColor + "\"" +
              " ALIGN=\"" + align + "\"");
    if (width != null) {
      out.print(" WIDTH=\"" + width + "\"");
    }
    out.print("><TR><TH>");
    out.print("<SPAN STYLE=\"" +
              "font-size: " + fontSize + "px; " +
              "font-family: " + fontList + "; ");
    if (color != null) {
      out.println("color: " + color + ";");
    }
    out.print("\"> "); // End of <SPAN ...>
  } catch(IOException ioe) {
    System.out.println("Error in HeadingTag: " + ioe);
  }
  return(EVAL_BODY_INCLUDE); // Include tag body
}

public int doEndTag() {
  try {
    JspWriter out = pageContext.getOut();
    out.print("</SPAN></TABLE>");
  } catch(IOException ioe) {
    System.out.println("Error in HeadingTag: " + ioe);
  }
  return(EVAL_PAGE); // Continue with rest of JSP page
}
}
```

The Tag Library Descriptor File

There is only one new feature in the use of the `tag` element for tags that use body content: the `bodycontent` element should contain the value `JSP` as below.

```
<bodycontent>JSP</bodycontent>
```

The `name`, `tagclass`, `info`, and `attribute` elements are used in the same manner as described previously. Listing 14.11 gives the code.

Listing 14.11 `csajsp-taglib.tld`

```xml
<?xml version="1.0" encoding="ISO-8859-1" ?>
<!DOCTYPE taglib
 PUBLIC "-//Sun Microsystems, Inc.//DTD JSP Tag Library 1.1//EN"
 "http://java.sun.com/j2ee/dtds/web-jsptaglibrary_1_1.dtd">

<!-- a tag library descriptor -->

<taglib>
  <!-- after this the default space is
       "http://java.sun.com/j2ee/dtds/jsptaglibrary_1_2.dtd"
   -->

  <tlibversion>1.0</tlibversion>
  <jspversion>1.1</jspversion>
  <shortname>csajsp</shortname>
  <urn></urn>
  <info>
    A tag library from Core Servlets and JavaServer Pages,
    http://www.coreservlets.com/.
  </info>

  <!-- Other tags defined earlier... -->

  <tag>
    <name>heading</name>
    <tagclass>coreservlets.tags.HeadingTag</tagclass>
    <info>Outputs a 1-cell table used as a heading.</info>
    <bodycontent>JSP</bodycontent>
    <attribute>
      <name>bgColor</name>
      <required>true</required> <!-- bgColor is required -->
    </attribute>
    <attribute>
      <name>color</name>
      <required>false</required>
    </attribute>
    <attribute>
      <name>align</name>
      <required>false</required>
    </attribute>
    <attribute>
      <name>fontSize</name>
      <required>false</required>
    </attribute>
    <attribute>
      <name>fontList</name>
      <required>false</required>
    </attribute>
    <attribute>
      <name>border</name>
      <required>false</required>
    </attribute>
```

Listing 14.11 `csajsp-taglib.tld` (continued)

```
    <attribute>
      <name>width</name>
      <required>false</required>
    </attribute>
  </tag>

</taglib>
```

The JSP File

Listing 14.12 shows a document that uses the `heading` tag just defined. Since the `bgColor` attribute was defined to be required, all uses of the tag include it. Figure 14–4 shows the result.

Listing 14.12 `HeadingExample.jsp`

```
<!DOCTYPE HTML PUBLIC "-//W3C//DTD HTML 4.0 Transitional//EN">
<HTML>
<HEAD>
<TITLE>Some Tag-Generated Headings</TITLE>
</HEAD>

<BODY>
<%@ taglib uri="csajsp-taglib.tld" prefix="csajsp" %>

<csajsp:heading bgColor="#C0C0C0">
Default Heading
</csajsp:heading>
<P>
<csajsp:heading bgColor="BLACK" color="WHITE">
White on Black Heading
</csajsp:heading>
<P>
<csajsp:heading bgColor="#EF8429" fontSize="60" border="5">
Large Bordered Heading
</csajsp:heading>
<P>
<csajsp:heading bgColor="CYAN" width="100%">
Heading with Full-Width Background
</csajsp:heading>
<P>
<csajsp:heading bgColor="CYAN" fontSize="60"
                fontList="Brush Script MT, Times, serif">
Heading with Non-Standard Font
</csajsp:heading>
<P>
</BODY>
</HTML>
```

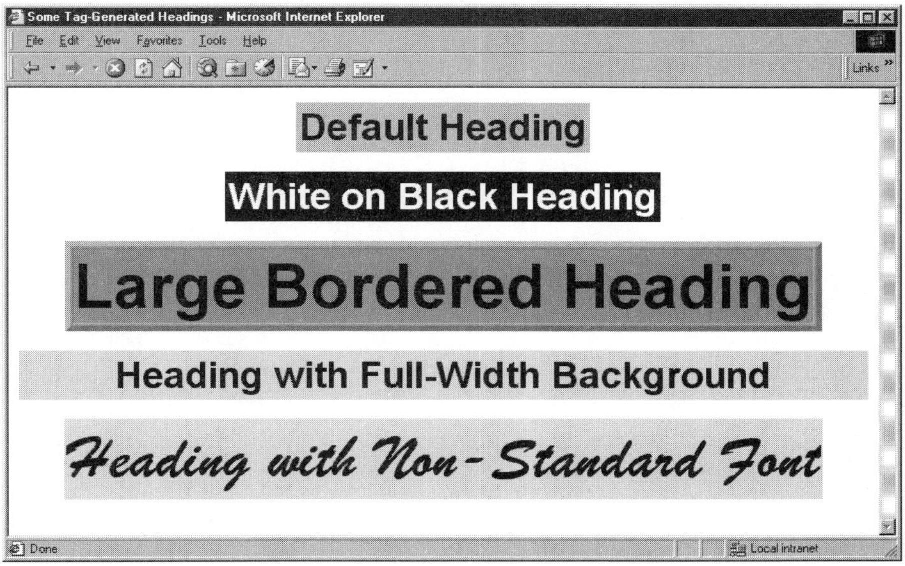

Figure 14–4 The custom `csajsp:heading` element gives you much more control over heading format than does the standard `H1` through `H6` elements in HTML.

14.5 Optionally Including the Tag Body

Most tags either *never* make use of body content or *always* do so. This section shows you how to use request time information to decide whether or not to include the tag body. Although the body can contain JSP that is interpreted at page translation time, the result of that translation is servlet code that can be invoked or ignored at request time.

The Tag Handler Class

Optionally including the tag body is a trivial exercise: just return `EVAL_BODY_INCLUDE` or `SKIP_BODY` depending on the value of some request time expression. The important thing to know is how to discover that request time information, since `doStartTag` does not have `Http-ServletRequest` and `HttpServletResponse` arguments as do `service`, _jspService, doGet, and doPost. The solution to this dilemma is to use getRequest to obtain the HttpServletRequest from the automatically defined pageContext field of TagSupport. Strictly speaking, the return type of getRequest is ServletRequest, so you have to do a typecast to HttpServletRequest if you want to call a method that is not inherited from ServletRequest. However, in this case I just use getParameter, so no typecast is required.

Listing 14.13 defines a tag that ignores its body unless a request time debug parameter is supplied. Such a tag provides a useful capability whereby you embed debugging information directly in the JSP page during development, but activate it only when a problem occurs.

Listing 14.13 DebugTag.java

```java
package coreservlets.tags;

import javax.servlet.jsp.*;
import javax.servlet.jsp.tagext.*;
import java.io.*;
import javax.servlet.*;

/** A tag that includes the body content only if
 *  the "debug" request parameter is set.
 */

public class DebugTag extends TagSupport {
  public int doStartTag() {
    ServletRequest request = pageContext.getRequest();
    String debugFlag = request.getParameter("debug");
    if ((debugFlag != null) &&
        (!debugFlag.equalsIgnoreCase("false"))) {
      return(EVAL_BODY_INCLUDE);
    } else {
      return(SKIP_BODY);
    }
  }
}
```

The Tag Library Descriptor File

If your tag *ever* makes use of its body, you must provide the value JSP inside the bodycontent element. Other than that, all the elements within tag are used in the same way as described previously. Listing 14.14 shows the entries needed for DebugTag.

Listing 14.14 csajsp-taglib.tld

```
<?xml version="1.0" encoding="ISO-8859-1" ?>
<!DOCTYPE taglib
  PUBLIC "-//Sun Microsystems, Inc.//DTD JSP Tag Library 1.1//EN"
  "http://java.sun.com/j2ee/dtds/web-jsptaglibrary_1_1.dtd">

<!-- a tag library descriptor -->

<taglib>
  <!-- after this the default space is
       "http://java.sun.com/j2ee/dtds/jsptaglibrary_1_2.dtd"
   -->

  <tlibversion>1.0</tlibversion>
  <jspversion>1.1</jspversion>
  <shortname>csajsp</shortname>
  <urn></urn>
  <info>
    A tag library from Core Servlets and JavaServer Pages,
    http://www.coreservlets.com/.
  </info>

  <!-- Other tags defined earlier... -->

  <tag>
    <name>debug</name>
    <tagclass>coreservlets.tags.DebugTag</tagclass>
    <info>Includes body only if debug param is set.</info>
    <bodycontent>JSP</bodycontent>
  </tag>

</taglib>
```

The JSP File

Listing 14.15 shows a page that encloses debugging information between
`<csajsp:debug>` and `</csajsp:debug>`. Figures 14–5 and 14–6 show the
normal result and the result when a request time `debug` parameter is supplied, respectively.

Listing 14.15 `DebugExample.jsp`

```
<!DOCTYPE HTML PUBLIC "-//W3C//DTD HTML 4.0 Transitional//EN">
<HTML>
<HEAD>
<TITLE>Using the Debug Tag</TITLE>
<LINK REL=STYLESHEET
      HREF="JSP-Styles.css"
      TYPE="text/css">
</HEAD>

<BODY>
<H1>Using the Debug Tag</H1>

<%@ taglib uri="csajsp-taglib.tld" prefix="csajsp" %>

Top of regular page. Blah, blah, blah. Yadda, yadda, yadda.
<P>

<csajsp:debug>
<B>Debug:</B>
<UL>
  <LI>Current time: <%= new java.util.Date() %>
  <LI>Requesting hostname: <%= request.getRemoteHost() %>
  <LI>Session ID: <%= session.getId() %>
</UL>
</csajsp:debug>

<P>
Bottom of regular page. Blah, blah, blah. Yadda, yadda, yadda.

</BODY>
</HTML>
```

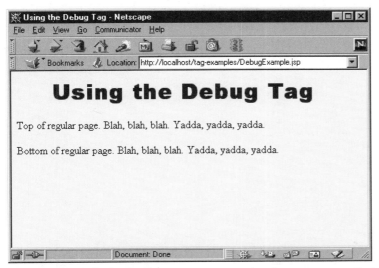

Figure 14–5 The body of the `csajsp:debug` element is normally ignored.

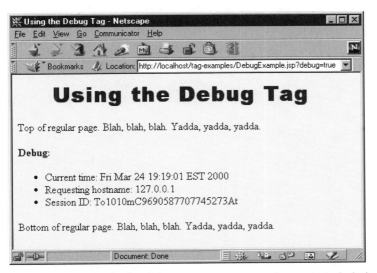

Figure 14–6 The body of the `csajsp:debug` element is included when a `debug` request parameter is supplied.

14.6 Manipulating the Tag Body

The `csajsp:prime` element (Section 14.3) ignored any body content, the `csajsp:heading` element (Section 14.4) used body content, and the `csa-jsp:debug` element (Section 14.5) ignored or used it depending on a request time parameter. The common thread among these elements is that the tag body was never modified; it was either ignored or included verbatim (after JSP translation). This section shows you how to process the tag body.

The Tag Handler Class

Up to this point, all of the tag handlers have extended the `TagSupport` class. This is a good standard starting point, as it implements the required `Tag` interface and performs a number of useful setup operations like storing the `PageContext` reference in the `pageContext` field. However, `TagSupport` is not powerful enough for tag implementations that need to manipulate their body content, and `BodyTagSupport` should be used instead.

`BodyTagSupport` extends `TagSupport`, so the `doStartTag` and `doEndTag` methods are used in the same way as before. The two important new methods defined by `BodyTagSupport` are:

1. **doAfterBody**, a method that you should override to handle the manipulation of the tag body. This method should normally return `SKIP_BODY` when it is done, indicating that no further body processing should be performed.
2. **getBodyContent**, a method that returns an object of type `BodyContent` that encapsulates information about the tag body.

The `BodyContent` class has three important methods:

1. **getEnclosingWriter**, a method that returns the `JspWriter` being used by `doStartTag` and `doEndTag`.
2. **getReader**, a method that returns a `Reader` that can read the tag's body.
3. **getString**, a method that returns a `String` containing the entire tag body.

In Section 3.4 (Example: Reading All Parameters), we saw a static `filter` method that would take a string and replace <, >, ", and & with <, >,

", and &, respectively. This method is useful when servlets output strings that might contain characters that would interfere with the HTML structure of the page in which the strings are embedded. Listing 14.16 shows a tag implementation that gives this filtering functionality to a custom JSP tag.

Listing 14.16 `FilterTag.java`

```java
package coreservlets.tags;

import javax.servlet.jsp.*;
import javax.servlet.jsp.tagext.*;
import java.io.*;
import coreservlets.*;

/** A tag that replaces <, >, ", and & with their HTML
 *  character entities (&lt;, &gt;, &quot;, and &amp;).
 *  After filtering, arbitrary strings can be placed
 *  in either the page body or in HTML attributes.
 */

public class FilterTag extends BodyTagSupport {
  public int doAfterBody() {
    BodyContent body = getBodyContent();
    String filteredBody =
      ServletUtilities.filter(body.getString());
    try {
      JspWriter out = body.getEnclosingWriter();
      out.print(filteredBody);
    } catch(IOException ioe) {
      System.out.println("Error in FilterTag: " + ioe);
    }
    // SKIP_BODY means I'm done. If I wanted to evaluate
    // and handle the body again, I'd return EVAL_BODY_TAG.
    return(SKIP_BODY);
  }
}
```

The Tag Library Descriptor File

Tags that manipulate their body content should use the `bodycontent` element the same way as tags that simply include it verbatim; they should supply a value of JSP. Other than that, nothing new is required in the descriptor file, as you can see by examining Listing 14.17.

Listing 14.17 `csajsp-taglib.tld`

```xml
<?xml version="1.0" encoding="ISO-8859-1" ?>
<!DOCTYPE taglib
  PUBLIC "-//Sun Microsystems, Inc.//DTD JSP Tag Library 1.1//EN"
  "http://java.sun.com/j2ee/dtds/web-jsptaglibrary_1_1.dtd">

<!-- a tag library descriptor -->

<taglib>
  <!-- after this the default space is
         "http://java.sun.com/j2ee/dtds/jsptaglibrary_1_2.dtd"
    -->

  <tlibversion>1.0</tlibversion>
  <jspversion>1.1</jspversion>
  <shortname>csajsp</shortname>
  <urn></urn>
  <info>
    A tag library from Core Servlets and JavaServer Pages,
    http://www.coreservlets.com/.
  </info>

  <!-- Other tags defined earlier... -->

  <tag>
    <name>filter</name>
    <tagclass>coreservlets.tags.FilterTag</tagclass>
    <info>Replaces HTML-specific characters in body.</info>
    <bodycontent>JSP</bodycontent>
  </tag>

</taglib>
```

The JSP File

Listing 14.18 shows a page that uses a table to show some sample HTML and its result. Creating this table would be tedious in regular HTML since the table cell that shows the original HTML would have to change all the < and > characters to < and >. Doing so is particularly onerous during development when the sample HTML is frequently changing. Use of the <csa-jsp:filter> tag greatly simplifies the process, as Listing 14.18 illustrates. Figure 14–7 shows the result.

Listing 14.18 `FilterExample.jsp`

```
<!DOCTYPE HTML PUBLIC "-//W3C//DTD HTML 4.0 Transitional//EN">
<HTML>
<HEAD>
<TITLE>HTML Logical Character Styles</TITLE>
<LINK REL=STYLESHEET
      HREF="JSP-Styles.css"
      TYPE="text/css">
</HEAD>

<BODY>
<H1>HTML Logical Character Styles</H1>
Physical character styles (B, I, etc.) are rendered consistently
in different browsers. Logical character styles, however,
may be rendered differently by different browsers.
Here's how your browser
(<%= request.getHeader("User-Agent") %>)
renders the HTML 4.0 logical character styles:
<P>

<%@ taglib uri="csajsp-taglib.tld" prefix="csajsp" %>

<TABLE BORDER=1 ALIGN="CENTER">
<TR CLASS="COLORED"><TH>Example<TH>Result
<TR>

<TD><PRE><csajsp:filter>
<EM>Some emphasized text.</EM><BR>
<STRONG>Some strongly emphasized text.</STRONG><BR>
<CODE>Some code.</CODE><BR>
<SAMP>Some sample text.</SAMP><BR>
<KBD>Some keyboard text.</KBD><BR>
<DFN>A term being defined.</DFN><BR>
<VAR>A variable.</VAR><BR>
<CITE>A citation or reference.</CITE>
</csajsp:filter></PRE>

<TD>
<EM>Some emphasized text.</EM><BR>
<STRONG>Some strongly emphasized text.</STRONG><BR>
<CODE>Some code.</CODE><BR>
<SAMP>Some sample text.</SAMP><BR>
<KBD>Some keyboard text.</KBD><BR>
<DFN>A term being defined.</DFN><BR>
<VAR>A variable.</VAR><BR>
<CITE>A citation or reference.</CITE>

</TABLE>
</BODY>
</HTML>
```

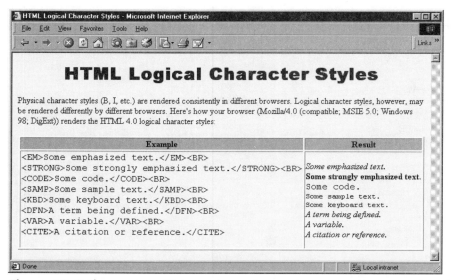

Figure 14–7 The `csajsp:filter` element lets you insert text without worrying about it containing special HTML characters.

14.7 Including or Manipulating the Tag Body Multiple Times

Rather than just including or processing the body of the tag a single time, you sometimes want to do so more than once. The ability to support multiple body inclusion lets you define a variety of iteration tags that repeat JSP fragments a variable number of times, repeat them until a certain condition occurs, and so forth. This section shows you how to build such tags.

The Tag Handler Class

Tags that process the body content multiple times should start by extending `BodyTagSupport` and implementing `doStartTag`, `doEndTag`, and, most importantly, `doAfterBody` as before. The difference lies in the return value of `doAfterBody`. If this method returns `EVAL_BODY_TAG`, the tag body is evaluated again, resulting in a new call to `doAfterBody`. This process continues until `doAfterBody` returns `SKIP_BODY`.

Listing 14.19 defines a tag that repeats the body content the number of times specified by the `reps` attribute. Since the body content can contain JSP (which gets made into servlet code at page translation time but invoked at request time), each repetition does not necessarily result in the same output to the client.

Listing 14.19 `RepeatTag.java`

```java
package coreservlets.tags;

import javax.servlet.jsp.*;
import javax.servlet.jsp.tagext.*;
import java.io.*;

/** A tag that repeats the body the specified
 *  number of times.
 */

public class RepeatTag extends BodyTagSupport {
  private int reps;

  public void setReps(String repeats) {
    try {
      reps = Integer.parseInt(repeats);
    } catch(NumberFormatException nfe) {
      reps = 1;
    }
  }

  public int doAfterBody() {
    if (reps-- >= 1) {
      BodyContent body = getBodyContent();
      try {
        JspWriter out = body.getEnclosingWriter();
        out.println(body.getString());
        body.clearBody(); // Clear for next evaluation
      } catch(IOException ioe) {
        System.out.println("Error in RepeatTag: " + ioe);
      }
      return(EVAL_BODY_TAG);
    } else {
      return(SKIP_BODY);
    }
  }
}
```

The Tag Library Descriptor File

Listing 14.20 shows a TLD file that gives the name `csajsp:repeat` to the
tag just defined. To accommodate request time values in the `reps` attribute,
the file uses an `rtexprvalue` element (enclosing a value of `true`) within the
`attribute` element.

Listing 14.20 `csajsp-taglib.tld`

```xml
<?xml version="1.0" encoding="ISO-8859-1" ?>
<!DOCTYPE taglib
  PUBLIC "-//Sun Microsystems, Inc.//DTD JSP Tag Library 1.1//EN"
  "http://java.sun.com/j2ee/dtds/web-jsptaglibrary_1_1.dtd">

<!-- a tag library descriptor -->

<taglib>
  <!-- after this the default space is
        "http://java.sun.com/j2ee/dtds/jsptaglibrary_1_2.dtd"
    -->

  <tlibversion>1.0</tlibversion>
  <jspversion>1.1</jspversion>
  <shortname>csajsp</shortname>
  <urn></urn>
  <info>
    A tag library from Core Servlets and JavaServer Pages,
    http://www.coreservlets.com/.
  </info>

  <!-- Other tags defined earlier... -->

  <tag>
    <name>repeat</name>
    <tagclass>coreservlets.tags.RepeatTag</tagclass>
    <info>Repeats body the specified number of times.</info>
    <bodycontent>JSP</bodycontent>
    <attribute>
      <name>reps</name>
      <required>true</required>
      <!-- rtexprvalue indicates whether attribute
          can be a JSP expression. -->
      <rtexprvalue>true</rtexprvalue>
    </attribute>
  </tag>

</taglib>
```

The JSP File

Listing 14.21 shows a JSP document that creates a numbered list of prime numbers. The number of primes in the list is taken from the request time `repeats` parameter. Figure 14–8 shows one possible result.

Listing 14.21 `RepeatExample.jsp`

```
<!DOCTYPE HTML PUBLIC "-//W3C//DTD HTML 4.0 Transitional//EN">
<HTML>
<HEAD>
<TITLE>Some 40-Digit Primes</TITLE>
<LINK REL=STYLESHEET
      HREF="JSP-Styles.css"
      TYPE="text/css">
</HEAD>

<BODY>
<H1>Some 40-Digit Primes</H1>
Each entry in the following list is the first prime number
higher than a randomly selected 40-digit number.

<%@ taglib uri="csajsp-taglib.tld" prefix="csajsp" %>

<OL>
<!-- Repeats N times. A null reps value means repeat once. -->
<csajsp:repeat reps='<%= request.getParameter("repeats") %>'>
  <LI><csajsp:prime length="40" />
</csajsp:repeat>
</OL>

</BODY>
</HTML>
```

14.8 Using Nested Tags

Although Listing 14.21 places the `csajsp:prime` element within the `csajsp:repeat` element, the two elements are independent of each other. The first generates a prime number regardless of where it is used, and the second repeats the enclosed content regardless of whether that content uses a `csajsp:prime` element.

Some tags, however, depend on a particular nesting. For example, in standard HTML, the `TD` and `TH` elements can only appear within `TR`, which in turn

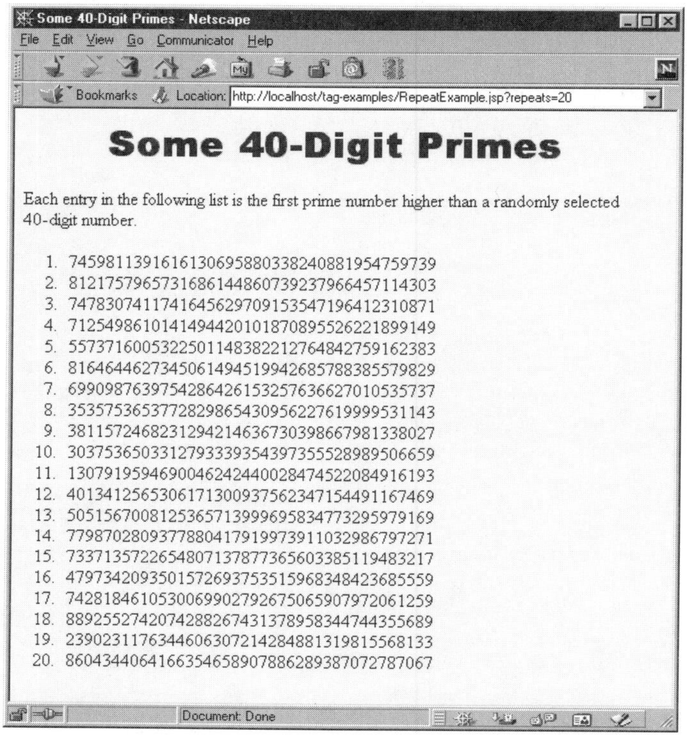

Figure 14–8 Result of `RepeatExample.jsp` when accessed with a `repeats` parameter of 20.

can only appear within TABLE. The color and alignment settings of TABLE are inherited by TR, and the values of TR affect how TD and TH behave. So, the nested elements cannot act in isolation even when nested properly. Similarly, the tag library descriptor file makes use of a number of elements like taglib, tag, attribute and required where a strict nesting hierarchy is imposed.

This section shows you how to define tags that depend on a particular nesting order and where the behavior of certain tags depends on values supplied by earlier ones.

The Tag Handler Classes

Class definitions for nested tags can extend *either* TagSupport or BodyTag-Support, depending on whether they need to manipulate their body content (these extend BodyTagSupport) or, more commonly, just ignore it or include it verbatim (these extend TagSupport).

There are two key new approaches for nested tags, however. First, nested tags can use findAncestorWithClass to find the tag in which they are nested. This method takes a reference to the current class (e.g., this) and the Class object of the enclosing class (e.g., EnclosingTag.class) as arguments. If no enclosing class is found, the method in the nested class can throw a JspTagException that reports the problem. Second, if one tag wants to store data that a later tag will use, it can place that data in the instance of the enclosing tag. The definition of the enclosing tag should provide methods for storing and accessing this data. Listing 14.22 outlines this approach.

Listing 14.22 Template for Nested Tags

```
public class OuterTag extends TagSupport {
  public void setSomeValue(SomeClass arg) { ... }
  public SomeClass getSomeValue() { ... }
}

public class FirstInnerTag extends BodyTagSupport {
  public int doStartTag() throws JspTagException {
    OuterTag parent =
      (OuterTag)findAncestorWithClass(this, OuterTag.class);
    if (parent == null) {
      throw new JspTagException("nesting error");
    } else {
      parent.setSomeValue(...);
    }
    return(EVAL_BODY_TAG);
  }
  ...
}

public class SecondInnerTag extends BodyTagSupport {
  public int doStartTag() throws JspTagException {
    OuterTag parent =
      (OuterTag)findAncestorWithClass(this, OuterTag.class);
    if (parent == null) {
      throw new JspTagException("nesting error");
    } else {
      SomeClass value = parent.getSomeValue();
      doSomethingWith(value);
    }
    return(EVAL_BODY_TAG);
  }
  ...
}
```

Now, suppose that we want to define a set of tags that would be used like this:

```
<csajsp:if>
  <csajsp:condition><%= someExpression %></csajsp:condition>
  <csajsp:then>JSP to include if condition is true</csajsp:then>
  <csajsp:else>JSP to include if condition is false</csajsp:else>
</csajsp:if>
```

To accomplish this task, the first step is to define an `IfTag` class to handle the `csajsp:if` tag. This handler should have methods to specify and check whether the condition is true or false (`setCondition` and `getCondition`) as well as methods to designate and check if the condition has ever been explicitly set (`setHasCondition` and `getHasCondition`), since we want to disallow `csajsp:if` tags that contain no `csajsp:condition` entry. Listing 14.23 shows the code for `IfTag`.

The second step is to define a tag handler for `csajsp:condition`. This class, called `IfConditionTag`, defines a `doStartTag` method that merely checks if the tag appears within `IfTag`. It returns `EVAL_BODY_TAG` if so and throws an exception if not. The handler's `doAfterBody` method looks up the body content (`getBodyContent`), converts it to a `String` (`getString`), and compares that to `"true"`. This approach means that an explicit value of `true` can be substituted for a JSP expression like `<%= expression %>` if, during initial page development, you want to temporarily designate that the `then` portion should always be used. Using a comparison to `"true"` also means that *any* other value will be considered "false." Once this comparison is performed, the result is stored in the enclosing tag by means of the `setCondition` method of `IfTag`. The code for `IfConditionTag` is shown in Listing 14.24.

The third step is to define a class to handle the `csajsp:then` tag. The `doStartTag` method of this class verifies that it is inside `IfTag` and also checks that an explicit condition has been set (i.e., that the `IfConditionTag` has already appeared within the `IfTag`). The `doAfterBody` method checks for the condition in the `IfTag` class, and, if it is true, looks up the body content and prints it. Listing 14.25 shows the code.

The final step in defining tag handlers is to define a class for `csajsp:else`. This class is very similar to the one to handle the `then` part of the tag, except that this handler only prints the tag body from `doAfterBody` if the condition from the surrounding `IfTag` is false. The code is shown in Listing 14.26.

Listing 14.23 `IfTag.java`

```java
package coreservlets.tags;

import javax.servlet.jsp.*;
import javax.servlet.jsp.tagext.*;
import java.io.*;
import javax.servlet.*;

/** A tag that acts like an if/then/else.
 */

public class IfTag extends TagSupport {
  private boolean condition;
  private boolean hasCondition = false;

  public void setCondition(boolean condition) {
    this.condition = condition;
    hasCondition = true;
  }

  public boolean getCondition() {
    return(condition);
  }

  public void setHasCondition(boolean flag) {
    this.hasCondition = flag;
  }

  /** Has the condition field been explicitly set? */

  public boolean hasCondition() {
    return(hasCondition);
  }

  public int doStartTag() {
    return(EVAL_BODY_INCLUDE);
  }
}
```

Listing 14.24 `IfConditionTag.java`

```java
package coreservlets.tags;

import javax.servlet.jsp.*;
import javax.servlet.jsp.tagext.*;
import java.io.*;
import javax.servlet.*;

/** The condition part of an if tag.
 */

public class IfConditionTag extends BodyTagSupport {
  public int doStartTag() throws JspTagException {
    IfTag parent =
      (IfTag)findAncestorWithClass(this, IfTag.class);
    if (parent == null) {
      throw new JspTagException("condition not inside if");
    }
    return(EVAL_BODY_TAG);
  }

  public int doAfterBody() {
    IfTag parent =
      (IfTag)findAncestorWithClass(this, IfTag.class);
    String bodyString = getBodyContent().getString();
    if (bodyString.trim().equals("true")) {
      parent.setCondition(true);
    } else {
      parent.setCondition(false);
    }
    return(SKIP_BODY);
  }
}
```

Listing 14.25 IfThenTag.java

```java
package coreservlets.tags;

import javax.servlet.jsp.*;
import javax.servlet.jsp.tagext.*;
import java.io.*;
import javax.servlet.*;

/** The then part of an if tag.
 */

public class IfThenTag extends BodyTagSupport {
  public int doStartTag() throws JspTagException {
    IfTag parent =
      (IfTag)findAncestorWithClass(this, IfTag.class);
    if (parent == null) {
      throw new JspTagException("then not inside if");
    } else if (!parent.hasCondition()) {
      String warning =
        "condition tag must come before then tag";
      throw new JspTagException(warning);
    }
    return(EVAL_BODY_TAG);
  }

  public int doAfterBody() {
    IfTag parent =
      (IfTag)findAncestorWithClass(this, IfTag.class);
    if (parent.getCondition()) {
      try {
        BodyContent body = getBodyContent();
        JspWriter out = body.getEnclosingWriter();
        out.print(body.getString());
      } catch(IOException ioe) {
        System.out.println("Error in IfThenTag: " + ioe);
      }
    }
    return(SKIP_BODY);
  }
}
```

Listing 14.26 `IfElseTag.java`

```java
package coreservlets.tags;

import javax.servlet.jsp.*;
import javax.servlet.jsp.tagext.*;
import java.io.*;
import javax.servlet.*;

/** The else part of an if tag.
 */

public class IfElseTag extends BodyTagSupport {
  public int doStartTag() throws JspTagException {
    IfTag parent =
      (IfTag)findAncestorWithClass(this, IfTag.class);
    if (parent == null) {
      throw new JspTagException("else not inside if");
    } else if (!parent.hasCondition()) {
      String warning =
        "condition tag must come before else tag";
      throw new JspTagException(warning);
    }
    return(EVAL_BODY_TAG);
  }

  public int doAfterBody() {
    IfTag parent =
      (IfTag)findAncestorWithClass(this, IfTag.class);
    if (!parent.getCondition()) {
      try {
        BodyContent body = getBodyContent();
        JspWriter out = body.getEnclosingWriter();
        out.print(body.getString());
      } catch(IOException ioe) {
        System.out.println("Error in IfElseTag: " + ioe);
      }
    }
    return(SKIP_BODY);
  }
}
```

The Tag Library Descriptor File

Even though there is an explicit required nesting structure for the tags just defined, the tags must be declared separately in the TLD file. This means that nesting validation is performed only at request time, not at page translation time. In principle, you could instruct the system to do some validation at page translation time by using a `TagExtraInfo` class. This class has a `get-VariableInfo` method that you can use to check that attributes exist and where they are used. Once you have defined a subclass of `TagExtraInfo`, you associate it with your tag in the tag library descriptor file by means of the `teiclass` element, which is used just like `tagclass`. In practice, however, `TagExtraInfo` is poorly documented and cumbersome to use.

Listing 14.27 `csajsp-taglib.tld`

```
<?xml version="1.0" encoding="ISO-8859-1" ?>
<!DOCTYPE taglib
 PUBLIC "-//Sun Microsystems, Inc.//DTD JSP Tag Library 1.1//EN"
 "http://java.sun.com/j2ee/dtds/web-jsptaglibrary_1_1.dtd">

<!-- a tag library descriptor -->

<taglib>
  <!-- after this the default space is
        "http://java.sun.com/j2ee/dtds/jsptaglibrary_1_2.dtd"
   -->

  <tlibversion>1.0</tlibversion>
  <jspversion>1.1</jspversion>
  <shortname>csajsp</shortname>
  <urn></urn>
  <info>
    A tag library from Core Servlets and JavaServer Pages,
    http://www.coreservlets.com/.
  </info>

  <!-- Other tags defined earlier... -->

  <tag>
    <name>if</name>
    <tagclass>coreservlets.tags.IfTag</tagclass>
    <info>if/condition/then/else tag.</info>
    <bodycontent>JSP</bodycontent>
  </tag>

  <tag>
    <name>condition</name>
    <tagclass>coreservlets.tags.IfConditionTag</tagclass>
    <info>condition part of if/condition/then/else tag.</info>
    <bodycontent>JSP</bodycontent>
  </tag>
```

Listing 14.27 `csajsp-taglib.tld` (continued)

```
<tag>
  <name>then</name>
  <tagclass>coreservlets.tags.IfThenTag</tagclass>
  <info>then part of if/condition/then/else tag.</info>
  <bodycontent>JSP</bodycontent>
</tag>

<tag>
  <name>else</name>
  <tagclass>coreservlets.tags.IfElseTag</tagclass>
  <info>else part of if/condition/then/else tag.</info>
  <bodycontent>JSP</bodycontent>
</tag>

</taglib>
```

The JSP File

Listing 14.28 shows a page that uses the `csajsp:if` tag three different ways. In the first instance, a value of `true` is hardcoded for the condition. In the second instance, a parameter from the HTTP request is used for the condition, and in the third case, a random number is generated and compared to a fixed cutoff. Figure 14–9 shows a typical result.

Listing 14.28 `IfExample.jsp`

```
<!DOCTYPE HTML PUBLIC "-//W3C//DTD HTML 4.0 Transitional//EN">
<HTML>
<HEAD>
<TITLE>If Tag Example</TITLE>
<LINK REL=STYLESHEET
      HREF="JSP-Styles.css"
      TYPE="text/css">
</HEAD>

<BODY>
<H1>If Tag Example</H1>

<%@ taglib uri="csajsp-taglib.tld" prefix="csajsp" %>

<csajsp:if>
  <csajsp:condition>true</csajsp:condition>
  <csajsp:then>Condition was true</csajsp:then>
  <csajsp:else>Condition was false</csajsp:else>
</csajsp:if>
```

Listing 14.28 `IfExample.jsp` (continued)

```
<P>
<csajsp:if>
  <csajsp:condition><%= request.isSecure() %></csajsp:condition>
  <csajsp:then>Request is using SSL (https)</csajsp:then>
  <csajsp:else>Request is not using SSL</csajsp:else>
</csajsp:if>
<P>
Some coin tosses:<BR>
<csajsp:repeat reps="20">
  <csajsp:if>
    <csajsp:condition>
      <%= Math.random() > 0.5 %>
    </csajsp:condition>
    <csajsp:then><B>Heads</B><BR></csajsp:then>
    <csajsp:else><B>Tails</B><BR></csajsp:else>
  </csajsp:if>
</csajsp:repeat>

</BODY>
</HTML>
```

Figure 14–9 Result of
`IfExample.jsp`.

INTEGRATING SERVLETS AND JSP

Chapter 15

Servlets are great when your application requires a lot of real programming to accomplish its task. As you've seen elsewhere in the book, servlets can manipulate HTTP status codes and headers, use cookies, track sessions, save information between requests, compress pages, access databases, generate GIF images on-the-fly, and perform many other tasks flexibly and efficiently. But, generating HTML with servlets can be tedious and can yield a result that is hard to modify. That's where JSP comes in; it lets you separate much of the presentation from the dynamic content. That way, you can write the HTML in the normal manner, even using HTML-specific tools and putting your Web content developers to work on your JSP documents. JSP expressions, scriptlets, and declarations let you insert simple Java code into the servlet that results from the JSP page, and directives let you control the overall layout of the page. For more complex requirements, you can wrap up Java code inside beans or define your own JSP tags.

Great. We have everything we need, right? Well, no, not quite. The assumption behind a JSP document is that it provides a *single* overall presentation. What if you want to give totally different results depending on the data that you receive? Beans and custom tags, although extremely powerful and flexible, don't overcome the limitation that the JSP page defines a relatively fixed top-level page appearance. The solution is to use *both* servlets and JavaServer Pages. If you have a complicated application that may require several substantially different presentations, a servlet can handle the initial

353

request, partially process the data, set up beans, then forward the results to one of a number of different JSP pages, depending on the circumstances. In early JSP specifications, this approach was known as the *model 2* approach to JSP. Rather than completely forwarding the request, the servlet can generate part of the output itself, then include the output of one or more JSP pages to obtain the final result.

15.1   Forwarding Requests

The key to letting servlets forward requests or include external content is to use a `RequestDispatcher`. You obtain a `RequestDispatcher` by calling the `getRequestDispatcher` method of `ServletContext`, supplying a URL relative to the server root. For example, to obtain a `RequestDispatcher` associated with `http://yourhost/presentations/presentation1.jsp`, you would do the following:

```
String url = "/presentations/presentation1.jsp";
RequestDispatcher dispatcher =
  getServletContext().getRequestDispatcher(url);
```

Once you have a `RequestDispatcher`, you use `forward` to completely transfer control to the associated URL and use `include` to output the associated URL's content. In both cases, you supply the `HttpServletRequest` and `HttpServletResponse` as arguments. Both methods throw `Servlet-Exception` and `IOException`. For example, Listing 15.1 shows a portion of a servlet that forwards the request to one of three different JSP pages, depending on the value of the `operation` parameter. To avoid repeating the `getRequestDispatcher` call, I use a utility method called `gotoPage` that takes the URL, the `HttpServletRequest` and the `HttpServletResponse`; gets a `RequestDispatcher`; and then calls `forward` on it.

Using Static Resources

In most cases, you forward requests to a JSP page or another servlet. In some cases, however, you might want to send the request to a static HTML page. In an e-commerce site, for example, requests that indicate that the user does not have a valid account name might be forwarded to an account application page that uses HTML forms to gather the requisite information. With GET requests, forwarding requests to a static HTML page is perfectly legal and requires no special syntax; just supply the address of the HTML page as the

Listing 15.1 Request Forwarding Example

```
public void doGet(HttpServletRequest request,
                  HttpServletResponse response)
    throws ServletException, IOException {
  String operation = request.getParameter("operation");
  if (operation == null) {
    operation = "unknown";
  }
  if (operation.equals("operation1")) {
    gotoPage("/operations/presentation1.jsp",
             request, response);
  } else if (operation.equals("operation2")) {
    gotoPage("/operations/presentation2.jsp",
             request, response);
  } else {
    gotoPage("/operations/unknownRequestHandler.jsp",
             request, response);
  }
}

private void gotoPage(String address,
                      HttpServletRequest request,
                      HttpServletResponse response)
    throws ServletException, IOException {
  RequestDispatcher dispatcher =
    getServletContext().getRequestDispatcher(address);
  dispatcher.forward(request, response);
}
```

argument to `getRequestDispatcher`. However, since forwarded requests use the same request method as the original request, POST requests cannot be forwarded to normal HTML pages. The solution to this problem is to simply rename the HTML page to have a `.jsp` extension. Renaming `some-file.html` to `somefile.jsp` does not change its output for GET requests, but `somefile.html` cannot handle POST requests, whereas `somefile.jsp` gives an identical response for both GET and POST.

Supplying Information to the Destination Pages

To forward the request to a JSP page, a servlet merely needs to obtain a `RequestDispatcher` by calling the `getRequestDispatcher` method of `ServletContext`, then call `forward` on the result, supplying the `Http-ServletRequest` and `HttpServletResponse` as arguments. That's fine as far as it goes, but this approach requires the destination page to read the information it needs out of the `HttpServletRequest`. There are two reasons why it might not be a good idea to have the destination page look up and process all the data itself. First, complicated programming is easier in a servlet than in a JSP page. Second, multiple JSP pages may require the same data, so it would be wasteful for each JSP page to have to set up the same data. A better approach is for the original servlet to set up the information that the destination pages need, then store it somewhere that the destination pages can easily access.

There are two main places for the servlet to store the data that the JSP pages will use: in the `HttpServletRequest` and as a bean in the location specific to the `scope` attribute of `jsp:useBean` (see Section 13.4, "Sharing Beans").

The originating servlet would store arbitrary objects in the `HttpServlet-Request` by using

```
request.setAttribute("key1", value1);
```

The destination page would access the value by using a JSP scripting element to call

```
Type1 value1 = (Type1)request.getAttribute("key1");
```

For complex values, an even better approach is to represent the value as a bean and store it in the location used by `jsp:useBean` for shared beans. For example, a `scope` of `application` means that the value is stored in the `ServletContext`, and `ServletContext` uses `setAttribute` to store values. Thus, to make a bean accessible to all servlets or JSP pages in the server or Web application, the originating servlet would do the following:

```
Type1 value1 = computeValueFromRequest(request);
getServletContext().setAttribute("key1", value1);
```

The destination JSP page would normally access the previously stored value by using `jsp:useBean` as follows:

```
<jsp:useBean id="key1" class="Type1" scope="application" />
```

Alternatively, the destination page could use a scripting element to explicitly call `application.getAttribute("key1")` and cast the result to `Type1`.

For a servlet to make data specific to a user session rather than globally accessible, the servlet would store the value in the `HttpSession` in the normal manner, as below:

```
Type1 value1 = computeValueFromRequest(request);
HttpSession session = request.getSession(true);
session.putValue("key1", value1);
```

The destination page would then access the value by means of

```
<jsp:useBean id="key1" class="Type1" scope="session" />
```

The Servlet 2.2 specification adds a third way to send data to the destination page when using GET requests: simply append the query data to the URL. For example,

```
String address = "/path/resource.jsp?newParam=value";
RequestDispatcher dispatcher =
  getServletContext().getRequestDispatcher(address);
dispatcher.forward(request, response);
```

This technique results in an *additional* request parameter of newParam (with a value of value) being added to whatever request parameters already existed. The new parameter is added to the beginning of the query data so that it will replace existing values if the destination page uses getParameter (use the first occurrence of the named parameter) rather than getParameterValues (use all occurrences of the named parameter).

Interpreting Relative URLs in the Destination Page

Although a servlet can forward the request to arbitrary locations on the same server, the process is quite different from that of using the sendRedirect method of HttpServletResponse (see Section 6.1). First, sendRedirect requires the client to reconnect to the new resource, whereas the forward method of RequestDispatcher is handled completely on the server. Second, sendRedirect does not automatically preserve all of the request data; forward does. Third, sendRedirect results in a different final URL, whereas with forward, the URL of the original servlet is maintained.

This final point means that, if the destination page uses relative URLs for images or style sheets, it needs to make them relative to the server root, not to the destination page's actual location. For example, consider the following style sheet entry:

```
<LINK REL=STYLESHEET
      HREF="my-styles.css"
      TYPE="text/css">
```

If the JSP page containing this entry is accessed by means of a forwarded request, my-styles.css will be interpreted relative to the URL of the originating servlet, not relative to the JSP page itself, almost certainly resulting in an error. The solution is to give the full server path to the style sheet file, as follows:

```
<LINK REL=STYLESHEET
      HREF="/path/my-styles.css"
      TYPE="text/css">
```

The same approach is required for addresses used in `<IMG SRC=...>` and `<A HREF=...>`.

Alternative Means of Getting a RequestDispatcher

In servers that support version 2.2 of the servlet specification, there are two additional ways of obtaining a `RequestDispatcher` besides the `get-RequestDispatcher` method of `ServletContext`.

First, since most servers let you give explicit names to servlets or JSP pages, it makes sense to access them by name rather than by path. Use the `getNamedDispatcher` method of `ServletContext` for this task.

Second, you might want to access a resource by a path relative to the current servlet's location, rather than relative to the server root. This approach is not common when servlets are accessed in the standard manner (`http://host/servlet/ServletName`), because JSP files would not be accessible by means of `http://host/servlet/...` since that URL is reserved especially for servlets. However, it is common to register servlets under another path, and in such a case you can use the `getRequest-Dispatcher` method of `HttpServletRequest` rather than the one from `ServletContext`. For example, if the originating servlet is at `http://host/travel/TopLevel`,

```
getServletContext().getRequestDispatcher("/travel/cruises.jsp")
```

could be replaced by

```
request.getRequestDispatcher("cruises.jsp");
```

15.2 Example: An On-Line Travel Agent

Consider the case of an on-line travel agent that has a quick-search page, as shown in Figure 15–1 and Listing 15.2. Users need to enter their e-mail address and password to associate the request with their previously established customer account. Each request also includes a trip origin, trip destination, start date, and end date. However, the action that will result will vary substantially based upon the action requested. For example, pressing the "Book Flights" button should show a list of available flights on the dates specified, ordered by price (see Figure 15–1). The user's real name, frequent flyer information, and credit card number should be used to generate the page. On the other hand, selecting "Edit Account" should show any previously entered customer information, letting the user modify values or add entries. Likewise, the actions resulting from choosing "Rent Cars" or "Find Hotels" will share much of the same customer data but will have a totally different presentation.

To accomplish the desired behavior, the front end (Listing 15.2) submits the request to the top-level travel servlet shown in Listing 15.3. This servlet looks up the customer information (see Listings 15.5 through 15.9), puts it in the HttpSession object associating the value (of type coreservlets.TravelCustomer) with the name customer, and then forwards the request to a different JSP page corresponding to each of the possible actions. The destination page (see Listing 15.4 and the result in Figure 15–2) looks up the customer information by means of

```
<jsp:useBean id="customer"
            class="coreservlets.TravelCustomer"
            scope="session" />
```

then uses jsp:getProperty to insert customer information into various parts of the page. You should note two things about the TravelCustomer class (Listing 15.5).

First, the class spends a considerable amount of effort making the customer information accessible as plain strings or even HTML-formatted strings through simple properties. Almost every task that requires any substantial amount of programming at all is spun off into the bean, rather than being performed in the JSP page itself. This is typical of servlet/JSP integration—the use of JSP does not *entirely* obviate the need to format data as strings or HTML in Java code. Significant up-front effort to make the data conveniently available to JSP more than pays for itself when multiple JSP pages access the same type of data.

Second, remember that many servers that automatically reload servlets when their class files change do not allow bean classes used by JSP to be in the auto-reloading directories. Thus, with the Java Web Server for example, TravelCustomer and its supporting classes must be in *install_dir/*classes/coreservlets/, not *install_dir*/servlets/coreservlets/. Tomcat 3.0 and the JSWDK 1.0.1 do not support auto-reloading servlets, so TravelCustomer can be installed in the normal location.

Figure 15–1 Front end to travel servlet (see Listing 15.2).

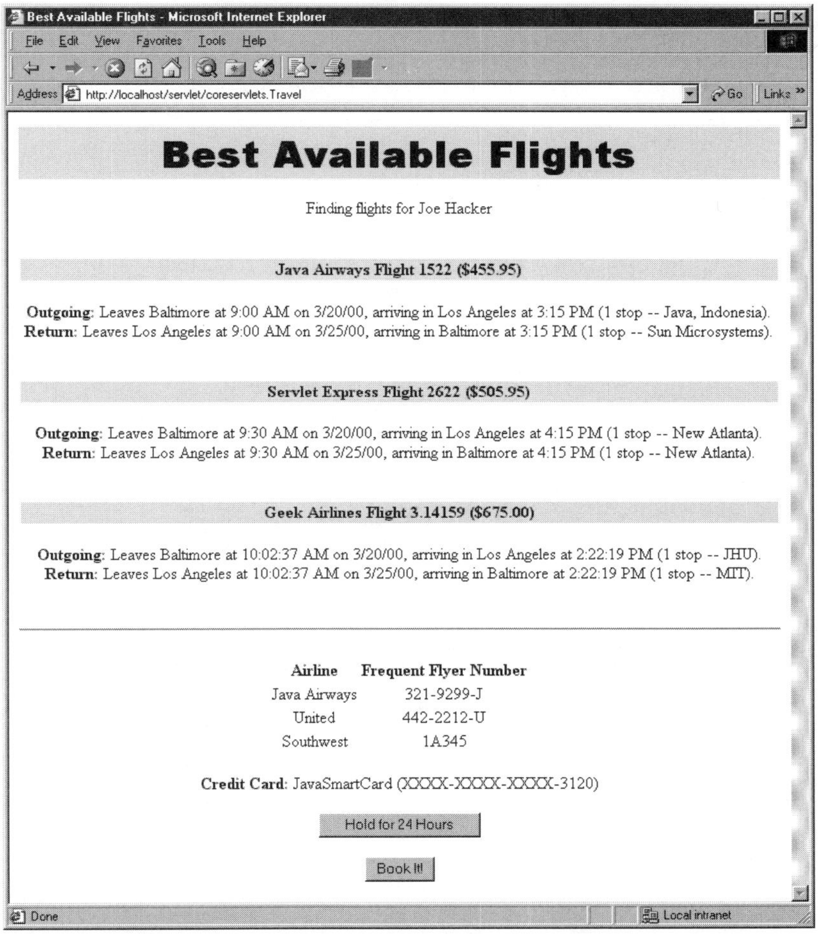

Figure 15–2 Result of travel servlet (Listing 15.3) dispatching request to BookFlights.jsp (Listing 15.4).

Listing 15.2 /travel/quick-search.html

```
<!DOCTYPE HTML PUBLIC "-//W3C//DTD HTML 4.0 Transitional//EN">
<HTML>
<HEAD>
  <TITLE>Online Travel Quick Search</TITLE>
  <LINK REL=STYLESHEET
        HREF="travel-styles.css"
        TYPE="text/css">
</HEAD>
```

Listing 15.2 `/travel/quick-search.html` **(continued)**

```
<BODY>
<BR>
<H1>Online Travel Quick Search</H1>

<FORM ACTION="/servlet/coreservlets.Travel" METHOD="POST">
<CENTER>
Email address: <INPUT TYPE="TEXT" NAME="emailAddress"><BR>
Password: <INPUT TYPE="PASSWORD" NAME="password" SIZE=10><BR>
Origin: <INPUT TYPE="TEXT" NAME="origin"><BR>
Destination: <INPUT TYPE="TEXT" NAME="destination"><BR>
Start date (MM/DD/YY):
  <INPUT TYPE="TEXT" NAME="startDate" SIZE=8><BR>
End date (MM/DD/YY):
  <INPUT TYPE="TEXT" NAME="endDate" SIZE=8><BR>
<P>
<TABLE CELLSPACING=1>
<TR>
  <TH> <IMG SRC="airplane.gif" WIDTH=100 HEIGHT=29
              ALIGN="TOP" ALT="Book Flight"> 
  <TH> <IMG SRC="car.gif" WIDTH=100 HEIGHT=31
              ALIGN="MIDDLE" ALT="Rent Car"> 
  <TH> <IMG SRC="bed.gif" WIDTH=100 HEIGHT=85
              ALIGN="MIDDLE" ALT="Find Hotel"> 
  <TH> <IMG SRC="passport.gif" WIDTH=71 HEIGHT=100
              ALIGN="MIDDLE" ALT="Edit Account"> 
<TR>
  <TH><SMALL>
      <INPUT TYPE="SUBMIT" NAME="flights" VALUE="Book Flight">
      </SMALL>
  <TH><SMALL>
      <INPUT TYPE="SUBMIT" NAME="cars" VALUE="Rent Car">
      </SMALL>
  <TH><SMALL>
      <INPUT TYPE="SUBMIT" NAME="hotels" VALUE="Find Hotel">
      </SMALL>
  <TH><SMALL>
      <INPUT TYPE="SUBMIT" NAME="account" VALUE="Edit Account">
      </SMALL>
</TABLE>
</CENTER>
</FORM>
<BR>
<P ALIGN="CENTER">
<B>Not yet a member? Get a free account
<A HREF="accounts.jsp">here</A>.</B></P>
</BODY>
</HTML>
```

Listing 15.3 `Travel.java`

```java
package coreservlets;

import java.io.*;
import javax.servlet.*;
import javax.servlet.http.*;

/** Top-level travel-processing servlet. This servlet sets up
 *  the customer data as a bean, then forwards the request
 *  to the airline booking page, the rental car reservation
 *  page, the hotel page, the existing account modification
 *  page, or the new account page.
 */

public class Travel extends HttpServlet {
  private TravelCustomer[] travelData;

  public void init() {
    travelData = TravelData.getTravelData();
  }

  /** Since password is being sent, use POST only. However,
   *  the use of POST means that you cannot forward
   *  the request to a static HTML page, since the forwarded
   *  request uses the same request method as the original
   *  one, and static pages cannot handle POST. Solution:
   *  have the "static" page be a JSP file that contains
   *  HTML only. That's what accounts.jsp is. The other
   *  JSP files really need to be dynamically generated,
   *  since they make use of the customer data.
   */

  public void doPost(HttpServletRequest request,
                     HttpServletResponse response)
      throws ServletException, IOException {
    String emailAddress = request.getParameter("emailAddress");
    String password = request.getParameter("password");
    TravelCustomer customer =
      TravelCustomer.findCustomer(emailAddress, travelData);
    if ((customer == null) || (password == null) ||
        (!password.equals(customer.getPassword()))) {
      gotoPage("/travel/accounts.jsp", request, response);
    }
    // The methods that use the following parameters will
    // check for missing or malformed values.
    customer.setStartDate(request.getParameter("startDate"));
    customer.setEndDate(request.getParameter("endDate"));
    customer.setOrigin(request.getParameter("origin"));
```

Listing 15.3 `Travel.java` (continued)

```java
    customer.setDestination(request.getParameter
                              ("destination"));
    HttpSession session = request.getSession(true);
    session.putValue("customer", customer);
    if (request.getParameter("flights") != null) {
      gotoPage("/travel/BookFlights.jsp",
               request, response);
    } else if (request.getParameter("cars") != null) {
      gotoPage("/travel/RentCars.jsp",
               request, response);
    } else if (request.getParameter("hotels") != null) {
      gotoPage("/travel/FindHotels.jsp",
               request, response);
    } else if (request.getParameter("cars") != null) {
      gotoPage("/travel/EditAccounts.jsp",
               request, response);
    } else {
      gotoPage("/travel/IllegalRequest.jsp",
               request, response);
    }
  }

  private void gotoPage(String address,
                        HttpServletRequest request,
                        HttpServletResponse response)
      throws ServletException, IOException {
    RequestDispatcher dispatcher =
      getServletContext().getRequestDispatcher(address);
    dispatcher.forward(request, response);
  }
}
```

Listing 15.4 `BookFlights.jsp`

```
<!DOCTYPE HTML PUBLIC "-//W3C//DTD HTML 4.0 Transitional//EN">
<HTML>
<HEAD>
  <TITLE>Best Available Flights</TITLE>
  <LINK REL=STYLESHEET
        HREF="/travel/travel-styles.css"
        TYPE="text/css">
</HEAD>

<BODY>
<H1>Best Available Flights</H1>
<CENTER>
<jsp:useBean id="customer"
             class="coreservlets.TravelCustomer"
             scope="session" />
Finding flights for
<jsp:getProperty name="customer" property="fullName" />
<P>
<jsp:getProperty name="customer" property="flights" />

<P>
<BR>
<HR>
<BR>
<FORM ACTION="/servlet/BookFlight">
<jsp:getProperty name="customer"
                 property="frequentFlyerTable" />
<P>
<B>Credit Card:</B>
<jsp:getProperty name="customer" property="creditCard" />
<P>
<INPUT TYPE="SUBMIT" NAME="holdButton" VALUE="Hold for 24 Hours">
<P>
<INPUT TYPE="SUBMIT" NAME="bookItButton" VALUE="Book It!">
</FORM>
</CENTER>

</BODY>
</HTML>
```

Listing 15.5 `TravelCustomer.java`

```java
package coreservlets;

import java.util.*;
import java.text.*;

/** Describes a travel services customer. Implemented
 *  as a bean with some methods that return data in HTML
 *  format, suitable for access from JSP.
 */

public class TravelCustomer {
  private String emailAddress, password, firstName, lastName;
  private String creditCardName, creditCardNumber;
  private String phoneNumber, homeAddress;
  private String startDate, endDate;
  private String origin, destination;
  private FrequentFlyerInfo[] frequentFlyerData;
  private RentalCarInfo[] rentalCarData;
  private HotelInfo[] hotelData;

  public TravelCustomer(String emailAddress,
                        String password,
                        String firstName,
                        String lastName,
                        String creditCardName,
                        String creditCardNumber,
                        String phoneNumber,
                        String homeAddress,
                        FrequentFlyerInfo[] frequentFlyerData,
                        RentalCarInfo[] rentalCarData,
                        HotelInfo[] hotelData) {
    setEmailAddress(emailAddress);
    setPassword(password);
    setFirstName(firstName);
    setLastName(lastName);
    setCreditCardName(creditCardName);
    setCreditCardNumber(creditCardNumber);
    setPhoneNumber(phoneNumber);
    setHomeAddress(homeAddress);
    setStartDate(startDate);
    setEndDate(endDate);
    setFrequentFlyerData(frequentFlyerData);
    setRentalCarData(rentalCarData);
    setHotelData(hotelData);
  }
```

> **Listing 15.5** `TravelCustomer.java` **(continued)**

```java
  public String getEmailAddress() {
    return(emailAddress);
  }

  public void setEmailAddress(String emailAddress) {
    this.emailAddress = emailAddress;
  }

  public String getPassword() {
    return(password);
  }

  public void setPassword(String password) {
    this.password = password;
  }

  public String getFirstName() {
    return(firstName);
  }

  public void setFirstName(String firstName) {
    this.firstName = firstName;
  }

  public String getLastName() {
    return(lastName);
  }

  public void setLastName(String lastName) {
    this.lastName = lastName;
  }

  public String getFullName() {
    return(getFirstName() + " " + getLastName());
  }

  public String getCreditCardName() {
    return(creditCardName);
  }

  public void setCreditCardName(String creditCardName) {
    this.creditCardName = creditCardName;
  }

  public String getCreditCardNumber() {
    return(creditCardNumber);
  }
```

Listing 15.5 `TravelCustomer.java` (continued)

```java
public void setCreditCardNumber(String creditCardNumber) {
  this.creditCardNumber = creditCardNumber;
}

public String getCreditCard() {
  String cardName = getCreditCardName();
  String cardNum = getCreditCardNumber();
  cardNum = cardNum.substring(cardNum.length() - 4);
  return(cardName + " (XXXX-XXXX-XXXX-" + cardNum + ")");
}

public String getPhoneNumber() {
  return(phoneNumber);
}

public void setPhoneNumber(String phoneNumber) {
  this.phoneNumber = phoneNumber;
}

public String getHomeAddress() {
  return(homeAddress);
}

public void setHomeAddress(String homeAddress) {
  this.homeAddress = homeAddress;
}

public String getStartDate() {
  return(startDate);
}

public void setStartDate(String startDate) {
  this.startDate = startDate;
}

public String getEndDate() {
  return(endDate);
}

public void setEndDate(String endDate) {
  this.endDate = endDate;
}

public String getOrigin() {
  return(origin);
}
```

Listing 15.5 `TravelCustomer.java` **(continued)**

```java
public void setOrigin(String origin) {
  this.origin = origin;
}

public String getDestination() {
  return(destination);
}

public void setDestination(String destination) {
  this.destination = destination;
}

public FrequentFlyerInfo[] getFrequentFlyerData() {
  return(frequentFlyerData);
}

public void setFrequentFlyerData(FrequentFlyerInfo[]
                                 frequentFlyerData) {
  this.frequentFlyerData = frequentFlyerData;
}

public String getFrequentFlyerTable() {
  FrequentFlyerInfo[] frequentFlyerData =
    getFrequentFlyerData();
  if (frequentFlyerData.length == 0) {
    return("<I>No frequent flyer data recorded.</I>");
  } else {
    String table =
      "<TABLE>\n" +
      "  <TR><TH>Airline<TH>Frequent Flyer Number\n";
    for(int i=0; i<frequentFlyerData.length; i++) {
      FrequentFlyerInfo info = frequentFlyerData[i];
      table = table +
              "<TR ALIGN=\"CENTER\">" +
              "<TD>" + info.getAirlineName() +
              "<TD>" + info.getFrequentFlyerNumber() + "\n";
    }
    table = table + "</TABLE>\n";
    return(table);
  }
}

public RentalCarInfo[] getRentalCarData() {
  return(rentalCarData);
}
```

Listing 15.5 `TravelCustomer.java` (continued)

```java
public void setRentalCarData(RentalCarInfo[] rentalCarData) {
  this.rentalCarData = rentalCarData;
}

public HotelInfo[] getHotelData() {
  return(hotelData);
}

public void setHotelData(HotelInfo[] hotelData) {
  this.hotelData = hotelData;
}

// This would be replaced by a database lookup
// in a real application.

public String getFlights() {
  String flightOrigin =
    replaceIfMissing(getOrigin(), "Nowhere");
  String flightDestination =
    replaceIfMissing(getDestination(), "Nowhere");
  Date today = new Date();
  DateFormat formatter =
    DateFormat.getDateInstance(DateFormat.MEDIUM);
  String dateString = formatter.format(today);
  String flightStartDate =
    replaceIfMissing(getStartDate(), dateString);
  String flightEndDate =
    replaceIfMissing(getEndDate(), dateString);
  String [][] flights =
    { { "Java Airways", "1522", "455.95", "Java, Indonesia",
        "Sun Microsystems", "9:00", "3:15" },
      { "Servlet Express", "2622", "505.95", "New Atlanta",
        "New Atlanta", "9:30", "4:15" },
      { "Geek Airlines", "3.14159", "675.00", "JHU",
        "MIT", "10:02:37", "2:22:19" } };
  String flightString = "";
  for(int i=0; i<flights.length; i++) {
    String[] flightInfo = flights[i];
```

Listing 15.5 `TravelCustomer.java` (continued)

```java
      flightString =
        flightString + getFlightDescription(flightInfo[0],
                                             flightInfo[1],
                                             flightInfo[2],
                                             flightInfo[3],
                                             flightInfo[4],
                                             flightInfo[5],
                                             flightInfo[6],
                                             flightOrigin,
                                             flightDestination,
                                             flightStartDate,
                                             flightEndDate);
    }
    return(flightString);
  }

  private String getFlightDescription(String airline,
                                      String flightNum,
                                      String price,
                                      String stop1,
                                      String stop2,
                                      String time1,
                                      String time2,
                                      String flightOrigin,
                                      String flightDestination,
                                      String flightStartDate,
                                      String flightEndDate) {
    String flight =
      "<P><BR>\n" +
      "<TABLE WIDTH=\"100%\"><TR><TH CLASS=\"COLORED\">\n" +
      "<B>" + airline + " Flight " + flightNum +
      " ($" + price + ")</B></TABLE><BR>\n" +
      "<B>Outgoing:</B> Leaves " + flightOrigin +
      " at " + time1 + " AM on " + flightStartDate +
      ", arriving in " + flightDestination +
      " at " + time2 + " PM (1 stop -- " + stop1 + ").\n" +
      "<BR>\n" +
      "<B>Return:</B> Leaves " + flightDestination +
      " at " + time1 + " AM on " + flightEndDate +
      ", arriving in " + flightOrigin +
      " at " + time2 + " PM (1 stop -- " + stop2 + ").\n";
    return(flight);
  }
```

Listing 15.5 `TravelCustomer.java` **(continued)**

```java
  private String replaceIfMissing(String value,
                                  String defaultValue) {
    if ((value != null) && (value.length() > 0)) {
      return(value);
    } else {
      return(defaultValue);
    }
  }

  public static TravelCustomer findCustomer
                              (String emailAddress,
                               TravelCustomer[] customers) {
    if (emailAddress == null) {
      return(null);
    }
    for(int i=0; i<customers.length; i++) {
      String custEmail = customers[i].getEmailAddress();
      if (emailAddress.equalsIgnoreCase(custEmail)) {
        return(customers[i]);
      }
    }
    return(null);
  }
}
```

Listing 15.6 `TravelData.java`

```java
package coreservlets;

/** This class simply sets up some static data to
 *  describe some supposed preexisting customers.
 *  Use a database call in a real application. See
 *  CSAJSP Chapter 18 for many examples of the use
 *  of JDBC from servlets.
 */

public class TravelData {
  private static FrequentFlyerInfo[] janeFrequentFlyerData =
    { new FrequentFlyerInfo("Java Airways", "123-4567-J"),
      new FrequentFlyerInfo("Delta", "234-6578-D") };
  private static RentalCarInfo[] janeRentalCarData =
    { new RentalCarInfo("Alamo", "345-AA"),
      new RentalCarInfo("Hertz", "456-QQ-H"),
      new RentalCarInfo("Avis", "V84-N8699") };
```

Listing 15.6 `TravelData.java` (continued)

```java
  private static HotelInfo[] janeHotelData =
   { new HotelInfo("Marriot", "MAR-666B"),
     new HotelInfo("Holiday Inn", "HI-228-555") };
  private static FrequentFlyerInfo[] joeFrequentFlyerData =
    { new FrequentFlyerInfo("Java Airways", "321-9299-J"),
      new FrequentFlyerInfo("United", "442-2212-U"),
      new FrequentFlyerInfo("Southwest", "1A345") };
  private static RentalCarInfo[] joeRentalCarData =
    { new RentalCarInfo("National", "NAT00067822") };
  private static HotelInfo[] joeHotelData =
   { new HotelInfo("Red Roof Inn", "RRI-PREF-236B"),
     new HotelInfo("Ritz Carlton", "AA0012") };
  private static TravelCustomer[] travelData =
    { new TravelCustomer("jane@somehost.com",
                          "tarzan52",
                          "Jane",
                          "Programmer",
                          "Visa",
                          "1111-2222-3333-6755",
                          "(123) 555-1212",
                          "6 Cherry Tree Lane\n" +
                            "Sometown, CA 22118",
                          janeFrequentFlyerData,
                          janeRentalCarData,
                          janeHotelData),
       new TravelCustomer("joe@somehost.com",
                          "qWeRtY",
                          "Joe",
                          "Hacker",
                          "JavaSmartCard",
                          "000-1111-2222-3120",
                          "(999) 555-1212",
                          "55 25th St., Apt 2J\n" +
                            "New York, NY 12345",
                          joeFrequentFlyerData,
                          joeRentalCarData,
                          joeHotelData)
    };

  public static TravelCustomer[] getTravelData() {
    return(travelData);
  }
}
```

Listing 15.7 `FrequentFlyerInfo.java`

```java
package coreservlets;

/** Simple class describing an airline and associated
 *  frequent flyer number, used from the TravelData class
 *  (where an array of FrequentFlyerInfo is associated with
 *  each customer).
 */

public class FrequentFlyerInfo {
  private String airlineName, frequentFlyerNumber;

  public FrequentFlyerInfo(String airlineName,
                           String frequentFlyerNumber) {
    this.airlineName = airlineName;
    this.frequentFlyerNumber = frequentFlyerNumber;
  }

  public String getAirlineName() {
    return(airlineName);
  }

  public String getFrequentFlyerNumber() {
    return(frequentFlyerNumber);
  }
}
```

Listing 15.8 `RentalCarInfo.java`

```java
package coreservlets;

/** Simple class describing a car company and associated
 *  frequent renter number, used from the TravelData class
 *  (where an array of RentalCarInfo is associated with
 *  each customer).
 */

public class RentalCarInfo {
  private String rentalCarCompany, rentalCarNumber;

  public RentalCarInfo(String rentalCarCompany,
                       String rentalCarNumber) {
    this.rentalCarCompany = rentalCarCompany;
    this.rentalCarNumber = rentalCarNumber;
  }

  public String getRentalCarCompany() {
    return(rentalCarCompany);
  }

  public String getRentalCarNumber() {
    return(rentalCarNumber);
  }
}
```

Listing 15.9 `HotelInfo.java`

```java
package coreservlets;

/** Simple class describing a hotel name and associated
 *  frequent guest number, used from the TravelData class
 *  (where an array of HotelInfo is associated with
 *  each customer).
 */

public class HotelInfo {
  private String hotelName, frequentGuestNumber;

  public HotelInfo(String hotelName,
                   String frequentGuestNumber) {
    this.hotelName = hotelName;
    this.frequentGuestNumber = frequentGuestNumber;
  }

  public String getHotelName() {
    return(hotelName);
  }

  public String getfrequentGuestNumber() {
    return(frequentGuestNumber);
  }
}
```

15.3 Including Static or Dynamic Content

If a servlet uses the `forward` method of `RequestDispatcher`, it cannot actually send any output to the client—it must leave that entirely to the destination page. If the servlet wants to generate some of the content itself but use a JSP page or static HTML document for other parts of the result, the servlet can use the `include` method of `RequestDispatcher` instead. The process is very similar to that for forwarding requests: call the `getRequestDispatcher` method of `ServletContext` with an address relative to the server root, then call `include` with the `HttpServletRequest` and `HttpServletResponse`. The two differences when `include` is used are that you can send content to the browser before making the call and that control is returned to the servlet after the `include` call finishes. Although the included pages (servlets, JSP pages, or even static HTML) can send output to the client, they should not try to set HTTP response headers. Here is an example:

```
response.setContentType("text/html");
PrintWriter out = response.getWriter();
out.println("...");
RequestDispatcher dispatcher =
  getServletContext().getRequestDispatcher("/path/resource");
dispatcher.include(request, response);
out.println("...");
```

The `include` method has many of the same features as the `forward` method. If the original method uses POST, so does the forwarded request. Whatever request data was associated with the original request is also associated with the auxiliary request, and you can add new parameters (in version 2.2 only) by appending them to the URL supplied to `getRequestDispatcher`. Also supported in version 2.2 is the ability to get a `RequestDispatcher` by name (`getNamedDispatcher`) or by using a relative URL (use the `getRequestDispatcher` method of the `HttpServletRequest`); see Section 15.1 (Forwarding Requests) for details. However, `include` does one thing that `forward` does not: it automatically sets up attributes in the `HttpServletRequest` object that describe the original request path in case the included servlet or JSP page needs that information. These attributes, available to the included resource by calling `getAttribute` on the `HttpServletRequest`, are listed below:

- `javax.servlet.include.request_uri`
- `javax.servlet.include.context_path`
- `javax.servlet.include.servlet_path`
- `javax.servlet.include.path_info`
- `javax.servlet.include.query_string`

Note that this type of file inclusion is not the same as the nonstandard *servlet chaining* supported as an extension by several early servlet engines. With servlet chaining, each servlet in a series of requests can see (and modify) the output of the servlet before it. With the `include` method of `RequestDispatcher`, the included resource cannot see the output generated by the original servlet. In fact, there is no standard construct in the servlet specification that reproduces the behavior of servlet chaining.

Also note that this type of file inclusion differs from that supported by the JSP `include` directive discussed in Section 12.1 (Including Files at Page Translation Time). There, the actual *source code* of JSP files was included in the page by use of the `include` directive, whereas the `include` method of `RequestDispatcher` just includes the *result* of the specified resource. On the other hand, the `jsp:include` action discussed in Section 12.2 (Including Files at Request Time) has behavior similar to that of the `include` method, except that `jsp:include` is available only from JSP pages, not from servlets.

15.4 Example: Showing Raw Servlet and JSP Output

When you are debugging servlets or JSP pages, it is often useful to see the raw HTML they generate. To do this, you can choose "View Source" from the browser menu after seeing the result. Alternatively, to set HTTP request headers and see the HTTP response headers in addition to HTML source, use the `WebClient` program shown in Section 2.10 (WebClient: Talking to Web Servers Interactively). For quick debugging, another option is available: create a servlet that takes a URL as input and creates an output page showing the HTML source code. Accomplishing this task relies on the fact that the HTML `TEXTAREA` element ignores all HTML markup other than the `</TEXTAREA>` tag. So, the original servlet generates the top of a Web page, up to a `<TEXTAREA>` tag. Then, it includes the output of whatever URL was specified in the query data. Next, it continues with the Web page, starting with a `</TEXTAREA>` tag. Of course, the servlet will fail if it tries to display a resource that contains the `</TEXTAREA>` tag, but the point here is the process of including files.

Listing 15.10 shows the servlet that accomplishes this task, and Listing 15.11 shows an HTML form that gathers input and sends it to the servlet. Figures 15–3 and 15–4 show the results of the HTML form and servlet, respectively.

Listing 15.10 ShowPage.java

```java
package coreservlets;

import java.io.*;
import javax.servlet.*;
import javax.servlet.http.*;

/** Example of the include method of RequestDispatcher.
 *  Given a URI on the same system as this servlet, the
 *  servlet shows you its raw HTML output.
 */

public class ShowPage extends HttpServlet {
  public void doGet(HttpServletRequest request,
                    HttpServletResponse response)
      throws ServletException, IOException {
    response.setContentType("text/html");
    PrintWriter out = response.getWriter();
    String url = request.getParameter("url");
    out.println(ServletUtilities.headWithTitle(url) +
                "<BODY BGCOLOR=\"#FDF5E6\">\n" +
                "<H1 ALIGN=CENTER>" + url + "</H1>\n" +
                "<FORM><CENTER>\n" +
                "<TEXTAREA ROWS=30 COLS=70>");
    if ((url == null) || (url.length() == 0)) {
      out.println("No URL specified.");
    } else {
      // Attaching data works only in version 2.2.
      String data = request.getParameter("data");
      if ((data != null) && (data.length() > 0)) {
        url = url + "?" + data;
      }
      RequestDispatcher dispatcher =
        getServletContext().getRequestDispatcher(url);
      dispatcher.include(request, response);
    }
    out.println("</TEXTAREA>\n" +
                "</CENTER></FORM>\n" +
                "</BODY></HTML>");
  }

  /** Handle GET and POST identically. */

  public void doPost(HttpServletRequest request,
                     HttpServletResponse response)
      throws ServletException, IOException {
    doGet(request, response);
  }
}
```

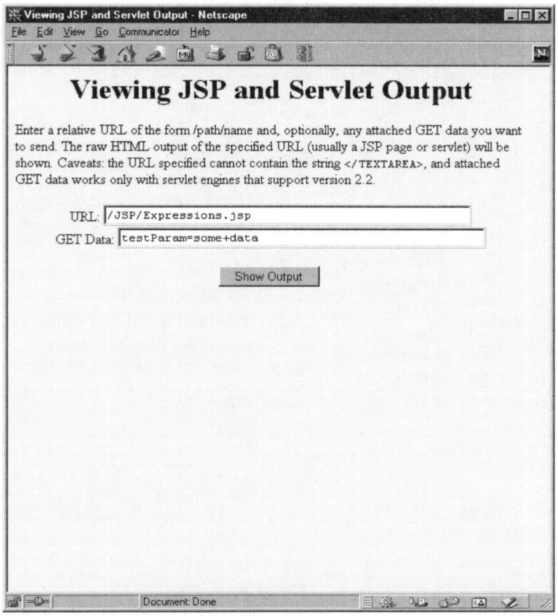

Figure 15–3 Front end to `ShowPage` servlet. See Listing 15.11 for the HTML source.

Figure 15–4 Result of `ShowPage` servlet when given a URL referring to `Expressions.jsp` (see Listing 10.1 in Section 10.2).

Listing 15.11 `ShowPage.html`

```html
<!DOCTYPE HTML PUBLIC "-//W3C//DTD HTML 4.0 Transitional//EN">
<HTML>
<HEAD>
  <TITLE>Viewing JSP and Servlet Output</TITLE>
</HEAD>

<BODY BGCOLOR="#FDF5E6">
<H1 ALIGN="CENTER">Viewing JSP and Servlet Output</H1>
Enter a relative URL of the form /path/name and, optionally,
any attached GET data you want to send. The raw HTML output
of the specified URL (usually a JSP page or servlet) will be
shown. Caveats: the URL specified cannot contain the string
<CODE>&lt;/TEXTAREA&gt;</CODE>, and attached GET data works
only with servlet engines that support version 2.2.

<FORM ACTION="/servlet/coreservlets.ShowPage">
  <CENTER>
    URL:
    <INPUT TYPE="TEXT" NAME="url" SIZE=50 VALUE="/"><BR>
    GET Data:
    <INPUT TYPE="TEXT" NAME="data" SIZE=50><BR><BR>
    <Input TYPE="SUBMIT" VALUE="Show Output">
  </CENTER>
</FORM>

</BODY>
</HTML>
```

15.5 Forwarding Requests From JSP Pages

The most common request forwarding scenario is that the request first comes to a servlet and the servlet forwards the request to a JSP page. The reason a servlet usually handles the original request is that checking request parameters and setting up beans requires a lot of programming, and it is more convenient to do this programming in a servlet than in a JSP document. The reason that the destination page is usually a JSP document is that JSP simplifies the process of creating the HTML content.

However, just because this is the *usual* approach doesn't mean that it is the *only* way of doing things. It is certainly possible for the destination page to be a servlet. Similarly, it is quite possible for a JSP page to forward requests elsewhere. For example, a request might go to a JSP page that normally presents results of a certain type and that forwards the request elsewhere only when it receives unexpected values.

Sending requests to servlets instead of JSP pages requires no changes whatsoever in the use of the `RequestDispatcher`. However, there is special syntactic support for forwarding requests from JSP pages. In JSP, the `jsp:forward` action is simpler and easier to use than wrapping up `Request-Dispatcher` code in a scriptlet. This action takes the following form:

```
<jsp:forward page="Relative URL" />
```

The `page` attribute is allowed to contain JSP expressions so that the destination can be computed at request time. For example, the following sends about half the visitors to `http://host/examples/page1.jsp` and the others to `http://host/examples/page2.jsp`.

```
<% String destination;
   if (Math.random() > 0.5) {
     destination = "/examples/page1.jsp";
   } else {
     destination = "/examples/page2.jsp";
   }
%>
<jsp:forward page="<%= destination %>" />
```

Part 3

SUPPORTING TECHNOLOGIES

USING HTML FORMS

Topics in This Chapter

Chapter 16

This chapter discusses using HTML forms as front ends to servlets or other server-side programs. These forms provide simple and reliable user interface controls to collect data from the user and transmit it to the servlet. The following chapter discusses the use of applets as servlet front ends. Using applets in this role requires considerably more effort and has some security limitations. However, it permits a much richer user interface and can support significantly more efficient and flexible network communication.

To use forms, you'll need to know where to place regular HTML files in order to make them accessible to the Web server. This location varies from server to server, but with the JSWDK and Tomcat, you place an HTML file in `install_dir/webpages/path/file.html` and then access it via `http://localhost/path/file.html` (replace `localhost` with the real hostname if running remotely).

16.1 How HTML Forms Transmit Data

HTML forms let you create a variety of user interface controls to collect input on a Web page. Each of the controls typically has a name and a value, where the name is specified in the HTML and the value comes either from the HTML or by means of user input. The entire form is associated with the

URL of a program that will process the data, and when the user submits the form (usually by pressing a button), the names and values of the controls are sent to the designated URL as a string of the form

```
Name1=Value1&Name2=Value2...NameN=ValueN
```

This string can be sent to the designated program in one of two ways. The first, which uses the HTTP GET method, appends the string to the end of the specified URL, after a question mark. The second way data can be sent is by the HTTP POST method. Here, the POST request line, the HTTP request headers, and a blank line are first sent to the server, and then the data string is sent on the following line.

For example, Listing 16.1 (HTML code) and Figure 16–1 (typical result) show a simple form with two textfields. The HTML elements that make up this form are discussed in detail in the rest of this chapter, but for now note a couple of things. First, observe that one text field has a name of firstName and the other has a name of lastName. Second, note that the GUI controls are considered text-level (inline) elements, so you need to use explicit HTML formatting to make sure that the controls appear next to the text describing them. Finally, notice that the FORM element designates http://local-host:8088/SomeProgram as the URL to which the data will be sent.

Before submitting the form, I start a server program called EchoServer on port 8088 of my local machine. EchoServer, shown in Section 16.12, is a mini "Web server" used for debugging. No matter what URL is specified and what data is sent to it, it merely returns a Web page showing all the HTTP information sent by the browser. As shown in Figure 16–2, when the form is submitted with Joe in the first textfield and Hacker in the second, the browser simply requests the URL http://localhost:8088/Some-Program?firstName=Joe&lastName=Hacker. Listing 16.2 (HTML code) and Figure 16–3 (typical result) show a variation that uses POST instead of GET. As shown in Figure 16–4, submitting the form with textfield values of Joe and Hacker results in the line firstName=Joe&lastName=Hacker being sent to the browser on a separate line after the HTTP request headers and a blank line.

That's the general idea behind HTML forms: GUI controls gather data from the user, each control has a name and a value, and a string containing all the name/value pairs is sent to the server when the form is submitted. Extracting the names and values on the server is straightforward in servlets: that was covered in Chapter 3 (Handling the Client Request: Form Data). The remainder of this chapter covers options in setting up forms and the various GUI controls you can put in them.

Listing 16.1 `GetForm.html`

```html
<!DOCTYPE HTML PUBLIC "-//W3C//DTD HTML 4.0 Transitional//EN">
<HTML>
<HEAD>
  <TITLE>A Sample Form Using GET</TITLE>
</HEAD>

<BODY BGCOLOR="#FDF5E6">
<H2 ALIGN="CENTER">A Sample Form Using GET</H2>

<FORM ACTION="http://localhost:8088/SomeProgram">
  <CENTER>
  First name:
  <INPUT TYPE="TEXT" NAME="firstName" VALUE="Joe"><BR>
  Last name:
  <INPUT TYPE="TEXT" NAME="lastName" VALUE="Hacker"><P>
  <INPUT TYPE="SUBMIT"> <!-- Press this button to submit form -->
  </CENTER>
</FORM>

</BODY>
</HTML>
```

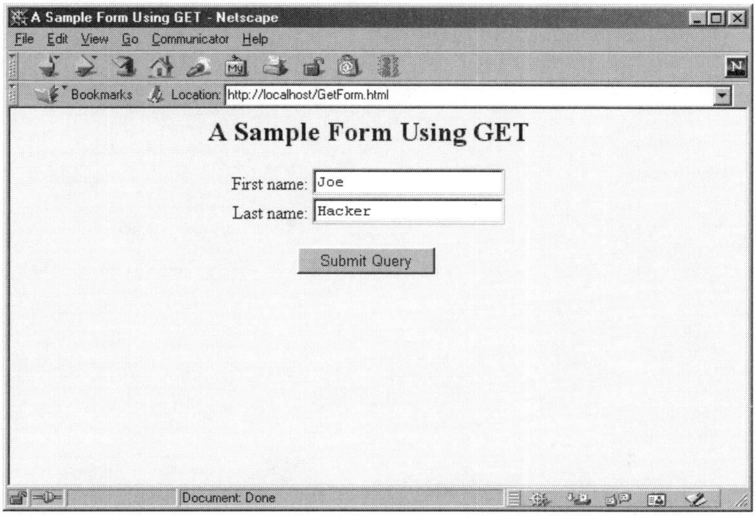

Figure 16–1 Initial result of `GetForm.html`.

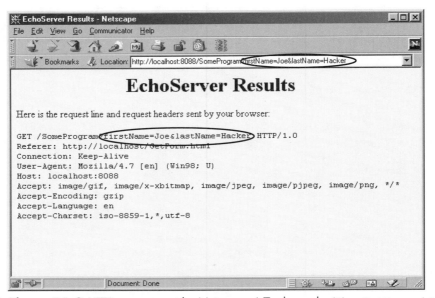

Figure 16-2 HTTP request sent by Netscape 4.7 when submitting `GetForm.html`.

Listing 16.2 `PostForm.html`

```html
<!DOCTYPE HTML PUBLIC "-//W3C//DTD HTML 4.0 Transitional//EN">
<HTML>
<HEAD>
  <TITLE>A Sample Form Using POST</TITLE>
</HEAD>

<BODY BGCOLOR="#FDF5E6">
<H2 ALIGN="CENTER">A Sample Form Using POST</H2>

<FORM ACTION="http://localhost:8088/SomeProgram"
      METHOD="POST">
  <CENTER>
  First name:
  <INPUT TYPE="TEXT" NAME="firstName" VALUE="Joe"><BR>
  Last name:
  <INPUT TYPE="TEXT" NAME="lastName" VALUE="Hacker"><P>
  <INPUT TYPE="SUBMIT">
  </CENTER>
</FORM>

</BODY>
</HTML>
```

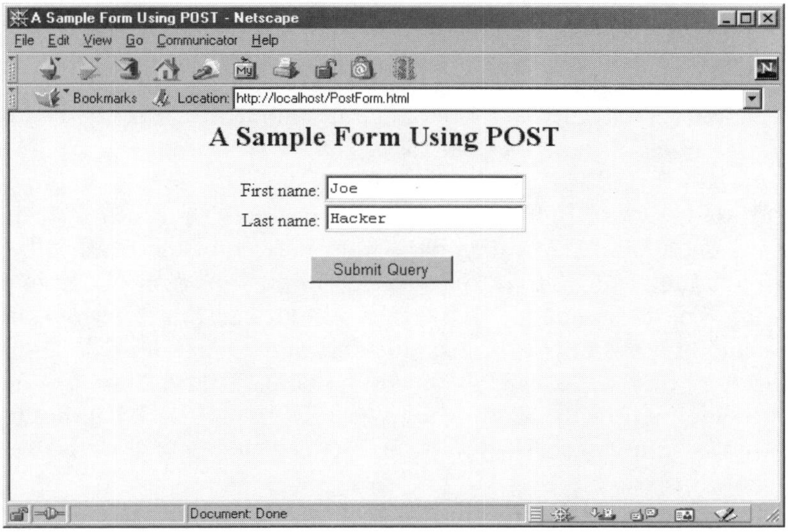

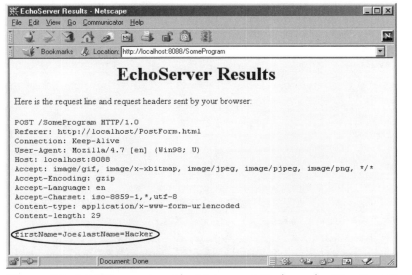

Figure 16–3 Initial result of `PostForm.html`.

Figure 16–4 HTTP request sent by Netscape 4.7 when submitting `PostForm.html`.

16.2 The FORM Element

HTML forms allow you to create a set of data input elements associated with a particular URL. Each of these elements is typically given a name and has a value based on the original HTML or user input. When the form is submitted, the names and values of all active elements are collected into a string with = between each name and value and with & between each name/value pair. This string is then transmitted to the URL designated by the FORM element. The string is either appended to the URL after a question mark or sent on a separate line after the HTTP request headers and a blank line, depending on whether GET or POST is used as the submission method. This section covers the FORM element itself, used primarily to designate the URL and to choose the submission method. The following sections cover the various user interface controls that can be used within forms.

HTML Element: `<FORM ACTION="URL" ...> ... </FORM>`
Attributes: ACTION (required), METHOD, ENCTYPE, TARGET, ONSUBMIT,
            ONRESET, ACCEPT, ACCEPT-CHARSET

The FORM element creates an area for data input elements and designates the URL to which any collected data will be transmitted. For example:

```
<FORM ACTION="http://some.isp.com/servlet/SomeServlet">
  FORM input elements and regular HTML
</FORM>
```

The rest of this section explains the attributes that apply to the FORM element: ACTION, METHOD, ENCTYPE, TARGET, ONSUBMIT, ONRESET, ACCEPT, and ACCEPT-CHARSET. Note that I am not discussing attributes like STYLE, CLASS, and LANG that apply to general HTML elements, but only those that are specific to the FORM element.

ACTION

The ACTION attribute specifies the URL of the servlet or CGI program that will process the FORM data (e.g., `http://cgi.whitehouse.gov/bin/schedule-fund-raiser`) or an email address where the FORM data will be sent (e.g., `mailto:audit@irs.gov`). Some ISPs do not allow ordinary users to create servlets or CGI programs, or they charge extra for this privilege. In such a case, sending the data by email is a convenient option when you create pages that need to collect data but not return results (e.g., for accepting orders for products). You must use the POST method (see METHOD in the following subsection) when using a `mailto` URL.

METHOD

The METHOD attribute specifies how the data will be transmitted to the HTTP server. When GET is used, the data is appended to the end of the designated URL after a question mark. For an example, see Section 16.1 (How HTML Forms Transmit Data). GET is the default and is also the method that is used when a browser requests a normal URL. When POST is used, the data is sent on a separate line.

The advantages of using the GET method are twofold: the method is simple; and with servlets that use GET, users can access those servlets for testing and debugging without creating a form, simply by entering a URL with the proper data appended. On the other hand, due to URL size restrictions on some browsers, GET requests have limits on the amount of data that can be appended, whereas POST requests do not. Another disadvantage of GET is that most browsers show the URL, including the attached data string, in an address field at the top of the browser. This display makes GET inappropriate for sending sensitive data if your computer is in a relatively public place.

ENCTYPE

This attribute specifies the way in which the data will be encoded before being transmitted. The default is `application/x-www-form-urlencoded`, which means that the client converts each space into a plus sign (+) and every other nonalphanumeric character into a percent sign (%) followed by the two hexadecimal digits representing that character (e.g., in ASCII or ISO Latin-1). Those transformations are in addition to placing an equal sign (=) between entry names and values and an ampersand (&) between entries.

For example, Figure 16–5 shows a version of the `GetForm.html` page (Listing 16.1) where "`Marty (Java Hacker?)`" is entered for the first name. As can be seen in Figure 16–6, this entry gets sent as "`Marty+%28Java+Hacker%3F%29`". That's because spaces become plus signs, 28 is the ASCII value (in hex) for a left parenthesis, 3F is the ASCII value of a question mark, and 29 is a right parenthesis.

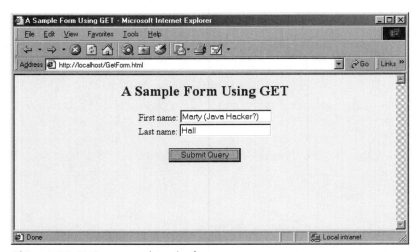

Figure 16–5 Customized result of `GetForm.html`.

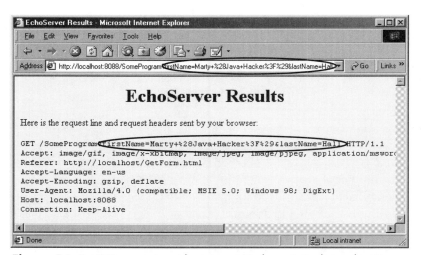

Figure 16–6 HTTP request sent by Internet Explorer 5.0 when submitting `GetForm.html` with the data shown in Figure 16–5.

Most recent browsers support an additional ENCTYPE of multipart/ form-data. This encoding transmits each of the fields as separate parts of a MIME-compatible document and automatically uses POST to submit them. This encoding sometimes makes it easier for the server-side program to handle complex data and is required when using file upload controls to send entire documents (see Section 16.7). For example, Listing 16.3 shows a form that differs from GetForm.html (Listing 16.1) only in that

```
<FORM ACTION="http://localhost:8088/SomeProgram">
```

has been changed to

```
<FORM ACTION="http://localhost:8088/SomeProgram"
      ENCTYPE="multipart/form-data">
```

Figures 16–7 and 16–8 show the results.

Listing 16.3 MultipartForm.html

```
<!DOCTYPE HTML PUBLIC "-//W3C//DTD HTML 4.0 Transitional//EN">
<HTML>
<HEAD>
  <TITLE>Using ENCTYPE="multipart/form-data"</TITLE>
</HEAD>

<BODY BGCOLOR="#FDF5E6">
<H2 ALIGN="CENTER">Using ENCTYPE="multipart/form-data"</H2>

<FORM ACTION="http://localhost:8088/SomeProgram"
      ENCTYPE="multipart/form-data">
  <CENTER>
  First name:
  <INPUT TYPE="TEXT" NAME="firstName" VALUE="Joe"><BR>
  Last name:
  <INPUT TYPE="TEXT" NAME="lastName" VALUE="Hacker"><P>
  <INPUT TYPE="SUBMIT">
  </CENTER>
</FORM>

</BODY>
</HTML>
```

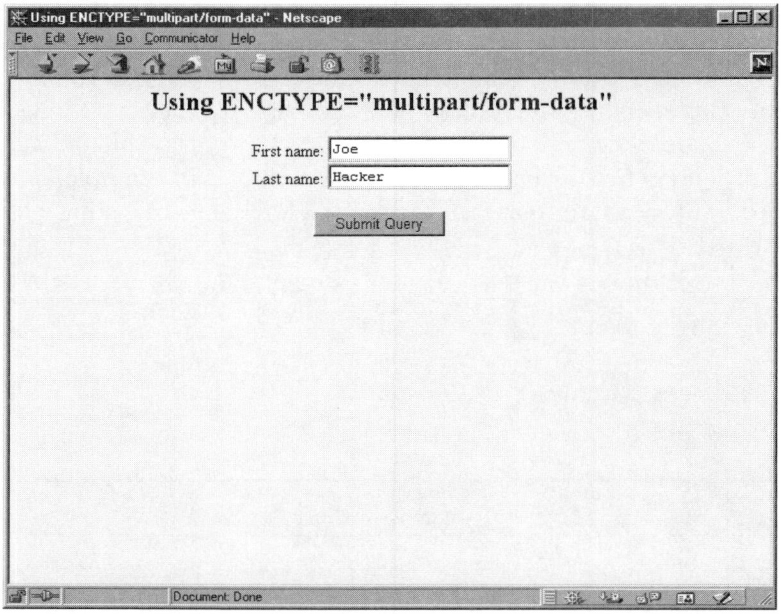

Figure 16–7 Initial result of `MultipartForm.html`.

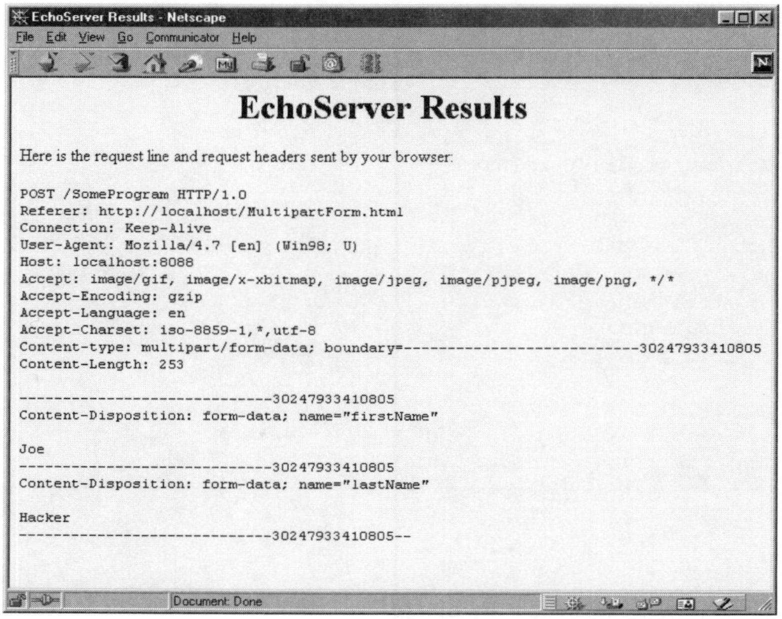

Figure 16–8 HTTP request sent by Netscape 4.7 when submitting
`MultipartForm.html`.

TARGET

The TARGET attribute is used by frame-capable browsers to determine which frame cell should be used to display the results of the servlet or other program handling the form submission. The default is to display the results in whatever frame contains the form being submitted.

ONSUBMIT and ONRESET

These attributes are used by JavaScript to attach code that should be evaluated when the form is submitted or reset. For ONSUBMIT, if the expression evaluates to false, the form is not submitted. This case lets you invoke JavaScript code on the client that checks the format of the form field values before they are submitted, prompting the user for missing or illegal entries.

ACCEPT and ACCEPT-CHARSET

These attributes are new in HTML 4.0 and specify the MIME types (ACCEPT) and character encodings (ACCEPT-CHARSET) that must be accepted by the servlet or other program processing the form data. The MIME types listed in ACCEPT could also be used by the client to limit which file types are displayed to the user for file upload elements.

16.3 Text Controls

HTML supports three types of text-input elements: textfields, password fields, and text areas. Each is given a name, and the value is taken from the content of the control. The name and value are sent to the server when the form is submitted, which is typically done by means of a submit button (see Section 16.4).

Textfields

HTML Element: `<INPUT TYPE="TEXT" NAME="..." ...>`
     (No End Tag)

Attributes: NAME (required), VALUE, SIZE, MAXLENGTH,
    ONCHANGE, ONSELECT, ONFOCUS, ONBLUR, ONKEYDOWN,
    ONKEYPRESS, ONKEYUP

This element creates a single-line input field where the user can enter text, as illustrated earlier in Listings 16.1, 16.2, and 16.3. For multiline fields, see

TEXTAREA in the following subsection. TEXT is the default TYPE in INPUT forms, although it is recommended that TEXT be supplied explicitly. You should remember that the normal browser word wrapping applies inside FORM elements, so be careful to make sure the browser will not separate the descriptive text from the associated textfield.

Core Approach

Use explicit HTML constructs to group textfields with their descriptive text.

Some browsers submit the form when the user presses Enter when the cursor is in a textfield, but you should avoid depending on this behavior because it is not standard. For instance, Netscape submits the form when the user types a carriage return only if the current form has a single textfield, regardless of the number of forms on the page. Internet Explorer submits the form on Enter only when there is a single form on the page, regardless of the number of textfields in the form. Mosaic submits the form on Enter only when the cursor is in the last textfield on the entire page.

Core Warning

Don't rely on the browser submitting the form when the user presses Enter when in a textfield. Always include a button or image map that submits the form explicitly.

The following subsections describe the attributes that apply specifically to textfields. Attributes that apply to general HTML elements (e.g., STYLE, CLASS, ID) are not discussed. The TABINDEX attribute, which applies to *all* form elements, is discussed in Section 16.11 (Controlling Tab Order).

NAME
The NAME attribute identifies the textfield when the form is submitted. In standard HTML the attribute is required. Because data is always sent to the server in the form of name/value pairs, no data is sent from form controls that have no NAME.

VALUE
A VALUE attribute, if supplied, specifies the *initial* contents of the textfield. When the form is submitted, the *current* contents are sent; these can reflect user input. If the textfield is empty when the form is submit-

ted, the form data simply consists of the name and an equal sign (e.g., `other-data&`**`textfieldname=`**`&other-data`).

SIZE

This attribute specifies the width of the textfield, based on the average character width of the font being used. If text beyond this size is entered, the textfield scrolls to accommodate it. This could happen if the user enters more characters than the `SIZE` or enters `SIZE` number of wide characters (e.g., capital W) if a proportional-width font is being used. Netscape automatically uses a proportional font in textfields. Internet Explorer, unfortunately, does not, and you cannot change the font by embedding the `INPUT` element in a `FONT` or `CODE` element.

MAXLENGTH

`MAXLENGTH` gives the maximum number of *allowable* characters. This number is in contrast to the number of *visible* characters, which is specified via `SIZE`.

ONCHANGE, ONSELECT, ONFOCUS, ONBLUR, ONDBLDOWN, ONKEYPRESS, and ONKEYUP

These attributes are used only by browsers that support JavaScript. They specify the action to take when the mouse leaves the textfield after a change has occurred, when the user selects text in the textfield, when the textfield gets the input focus, when it loses the input focus, and when individual keys are pressed.

Password Fields

HTML Element: `<INPUT TYPE="PASSWORD" NAME="..." ...>`
                      (No End Tag)
Attributes: `NAME` (required), `VALUE`, `SIZE`, `MAXLENGTH`,
                   `ONCHANGE`, `ONSELECT`, `ONFOCUS`, `ONBLUR`, `ONKEYDOWN`,
                   `ONKEYPRESS`, `ONKEYUP`

Password fields are created and used just like textfields, except that when the user enters text, the input is not echoed but instead some obscuring character, usually an asterisk, is displayed (see Figure 16–9). Obscured input is useful for collecting data such as credit card numbers or passwords that the user would not want shown to people who may be near his computer. The regular, unobscured text is transmitted as the value of the field when the form is submitted. Since `GET` data is appended to the URL after a question mark, you will want to use the POST method when using a password field so that a bystander cannot read the unobscured password from the URL display at the top of the browser.

Core Approach

To protect the user's privacy, always use POST *when creating forms with password fields.*

NAME, VALUE, SIZE, MAXLENGTH, ONCHANGE, ONSELECT, ONFOCUS, ONBLUR, ONKEYDOWN, ONKEY-PRESS, and ONKEYUP

Attributes for password fields are used in exactly the same manner as with textfields.

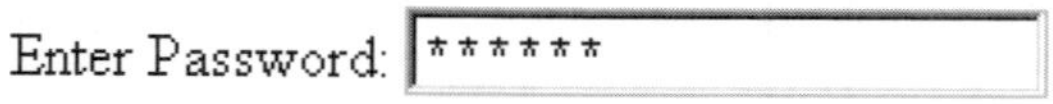

Enter Password: [******]

Figure 16–9 A password field created by means of `<INPUT TYPE="PASSWORD" ...>`.

Text Areas

HTML Element: `<TEXTAREA NAME="..."`
                            `ROWS=xxx COLS=yyy> ...`
            `</TEXTAREA>`

Attributes: NAME (required), ROWS (required), COLS (required), WRAP (nonstandard), ONCHANGE, ONSELECT, ONFOCUS, ONBLUR, ONKEYDOWN, ONKEYPRESS, ONKEYUP

The TEXTAREA element creates a multiline text area; see Figure 16–10. There is no VALUE attribute; instead, text between the start and end tags is used as the initial contents of the text area. The initial text between `<TEXTAREA ...>` and `</TEXTAREA>` is treated similarly to text inside the now-obsolete XMP element. That is, white space in this initial text is maintained and HTML markup between the start and end tags is taken literally, except for character entities such as <, ©, and so forth, which are interpreted normally. Unless a custom ENCTYPE is used in the form (see Section 16.2, "The FORM

Element"), characters, including those generated from character entities, are URL-encoded before being transmitted. That is, spaces become plus signs and other nonalphanumeric characters become %*XX*, where *XX* is the numeric value of the character in hex.

NAME

This attribute specifies the name that will be sent to the server.

ROWS

ROWS specifies the number of visible lines of text. If more lines of text are entered, a vertical scrollbar will be added to the text area.

COLS

COLS specifies the visible width of the text area, based on the average width of characters in the font being used. If the text on a single line contains more characters than the specified width allows, the result is browser dependent. In Netscape, horizontal scrollbars are added (but see the WRAP attribute, described next, to change this behavior). In Internet Explorer, the word wraps around to the next line.

WRAP

The Netscape-specific WRAP attribute specifies what to do with lines that are longer than the size specified by COLS. A value of OFF disables word wrap and is the default. The user can still enter explicit line breaks in such a case. A value of HARD causes words to wrap in the text area *and* the associated line breaks to be transmitted when the form is submitted. Finally, a value of SOFT causes the words to wrap in the text area but no extra line breaks to be transmitted when the form is submitted.

ONCHANGE, ONSELECT, ONFOCUS, ONBLUR, ONKEY-DOWN, ONKEYPRESS, and ONKEYUP

These attributes apply only to browsers that support JavaScript; they specify code to be executed when certain conditions arise. ONCHANGE handles the situation when the input focus leaves the text area after it has changed, ONSELECT describes what to do when text in the text area is selected by the user, ONFOCUS and ONBLUR specify what to do when the text area acquires or loses the input focus, and the remaining attributes determine what to do when individual keys are typed.

The following example creates a text area with 5 visible rows that can hold about 30 characters per row. The result is shown in Figure 16–10.

```
<CENTER>
<P>
Enter some HTML:<BR>
<TEXTAREA NAME="HTML" ROWS=5 COLS=30>
Delete this text and replace
with some HTML to validate.
</TEXTAREA>
<CENTER>
```

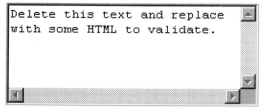

Figure 16–10 A text area.

16.4 Push Buttons

Push buttons are used for two main purposes in HTML forms: to submit forms and to reset the controls to the values specified in the original HTML. Browsers that use JavaScript can also use buttons for a third purpose: to trigger arbitrary JavaScript code.

Traditionally, buttons have been created by the INPUT element used with a TYPE attribute of SUBMIT, RESET, or BUTTON. In HTML 4.0, the BUTTON element was introduced but is currently supported only by Internet Explorer. This new element lets you create buttons with multiline labels, images, font changes, and the like, so is preferred if you are sure your users will all be using browsers that support it (e.g., in a corporate intranet). Since the element is not supported by Netscape, at least as of Netscape version 4.7, for now you should reserve BUTTON for intranets that use Internet Explorer exclusively.

Core Warning

Netscape does not support the BUTTON *element.*

Submit Buttons

HTML Element: `<INPUT TYPE="SUBMIT" ...>` (No End Tag)
Attributes: NAME, VALUE, ONCLICK, ONDBLCLICK, ONFOCUS, ONBLUR

When a submit button is clicked, the form is sent to the servlet or other server-side program designated by the ACTION parameter of the FORM. Although the action can be triggered other ways, such as the user clicking on an image map, most forms have at least one submit button. Submit buttons, like other form controls, adopt the look and feel of the client operating system, so will look slightly different on different platforms. Figure 16–11 shows a submit button on Windows 98, created by

```
<INPUT TYPE="SUBMIT">
```

Figure 16–11 A submit button with the default label.

NAME and VALUE

Most input elements have a name and an associated value. When the form is submitted, the names and values of active elements are concatenated to form the data string. If a submit button is used simply to initiate the submission of the form, its name can be omitted and then it does not contribute to the data string that is sent. If a name *is* supplied, then only the name and value of the button that was actually clicked are sent. The label is used as the value that is transmitted. Supplying an explicit VALUE will change the default label. For instance, the following code snippet creates a textfield and two submit buttons, shown in Figure 16–12. If, for example, the first button is selected, the data string sent to the server would be

```
Item=256MB+SIMM&Add=Add+Item+to+Cart.
```

```
<CENTER>
Item:
<INPUT TYPE="TEXT" NAME="Item" VALUE="256MB SIMM"><BR>
```

```
<INPUT TYPE="SUBMIT" NAME="Add"
       VALUE="Add Item to Cart">
<INPUT TYPE="SUBMIT" NAME="Delete"
       VALUE="Delete Item from Cart">
</CENTER>
```

Figure 16–12 Submit buttons with user-defined labels.

ONCLICK, ONDBLCLICK, ONFOCUS, and ONBLUR

These nonstandard attributes are used by JavaScript-capable browsers to associate JavaScript code with the button. The ONCLICK and ONDBL-CLICK code is executed when the button is pressed, the ONFOCUS code when the button gets the input focus, and the ONBLUR code when the button loses the focus. If the code attached to a button returns false, the submission of the form is suppressed. HTML attributes are not case sensitive, and these attributes are traditionally called onClick, onDblClick, onFocus, and onBlur by JavaScript programmers.

HTML Element:
```
<BUTTON TYPE="SUBMIT" ...>
HTML Markup
</BUTTON>
```
Attributes: NAME, VALUE, ONCLICK, ONDBLCLICK, ONFOCUS, ONBLUR

This alternative way of creating submit buttons, supported only by Internet Explorer, lets you use arbitrary HTML markup for the content of the button. This element lets you to have multiline button labels, button labels with font changes, image buttons, and so forth. Listing 16.4 gives a few examples, with results shown in Figure 16–13.

NAME, VALUE, ONCLICK, ONDBLCLICK, ONFOCUS, and ONBLUR

These attributes are used in the same way as with
```
<INPUT TYPE="SUBMIT" ...>.
```

Listing 16.4 `ButtonElement.html`

```
<!DOCTYPE HTML PUBLIC "-//W3C//DTD HTML 4.0 Transitional//EN">
<HTML>
<HEAD>
  <TITLE>The BUTTON Element</TITLE>
</HEAD>
<BODY BGCOLOR="WHITE">
<H2 ALIGN="CENTER">The BUTTON Element</H2>

<FORM ACTION="http://localhost:8088/SomeProgram">
<CENTER>
<BUTTON TYPE="SUBMIT">Single-line Label</BUTTON>
  
<BUTTON TYPE="SUBMIT">Multi-line<BR>label</BUTTON>
<P>
<BUTTON TYPE="SUBMIT">
<B>Label</B> with <I>font</I> changes.
</BUTTON>
<P>
<BUTTON TYPE="SUBMIT">
<IMG SRC="images/Java-Logo.gif" WIDTH=110 HEIGHT=101
     ALIGN="LEFT" ALT="Java Cup Logo">
Label<BR>with image
</BUTTON>
</CENTER>
</FORM>

</BODY>
</HTML>
```

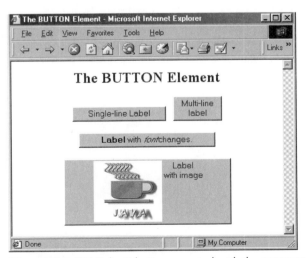

Figure 16–13 Submit buttons created with the BUTTON element.

Reset Buttons

HTML Element: `<INPUT TYPE="RESET" ...>` (No End Tag)
Attributes: VALUE, NAME, ONCLICK, ONDBLCLICK, ONFOCUS, ONBLUR

Reset buttons serve to reset the values of all items in the FORM to those specified in the original VALUE parameters. Their value is never transmitted as part of the form's contents.

VALUE
The VALUE attribute specifies the button label; "Reset" is the default.

NAME
Because reset buttons do not contribute to the data string transmitted when the form is submitted, they are not named in standard HTML. However, JavaScript permits a NAME attribute to be used to simplify reference to the element.

ONCLICK, ONDBLCLICK, ONFOCUS, and ONBLUR
These nonstandard attributes are used by JavaScript-capable browsers to associate JavaScript code with the button. The ONCLICK and ONDBL-CLICK code is executed when the button is pressed, the ONFOCUS code when the button gets the input focus, and the ONBLUR code when it loses the focus. HTML attributes are not case sensitive, and these attributes are traditionally called onClick, onDblClick, onFocus, and onBlur by JavaScript programmers.

HTML Element: `<BUTTON TYPE="RESET" ...>`
`HTML Markup`
`</BUTTON>`
Attributes: VALUE, NAME, ONCLICK, ONDBLCLICK, ONFOCUS, ONBLUR

This alternative way of creating reset buttons, supported only by Internet Explorer, lets you use arbitrary HTML markup for the content of the button. All attributes are used identically to those in `<INPUT TYPE="RESET" ...>`.

JavaScript Buttons

HTML Element: `<INPUT TYPE="BUTTON" ...>` (No End Tag)
Attributes: NAME, VALUE, ONCLICK, ONDBLCLICK, ONFOCUS, ONBLUR

The BUTTON element is recognized only by browsers that support JavaScript. It creates a button with the same visual appearance as a SUBMIT or RESET button and allows the author to attach JavaScript code to the ONCLICK, ONDBLCLICK, ONFOCUS, or ONBLUR attributes. The name/value pair associated with a JavaScript button is not transmitted as part of the data when the form is submitted. Arbitrary code can be associated with the button, but one of the most common uses is to verify that all input elements are in the proper format before the form is submitted to the server. For instance, the following would create a button where the user-defined validateForm function would be called whenever the button is activated.

```
<INPUT TYPE="BUTTON" VALUE="Check Values"
       onClick="validateForm()">
```

HTML Element: `<BUTTON TYPE="BUTTON" ...>`
                   `HTML Markup`
                   `</BUTTON>`
Attributes: NAME, VALUE, ONCLICK, ONDBLCLICK, ONFOCUS, ONBLUR

This alternative way of creating JavaScript buttons, supported only by Internet Explorer, lets you use arbitrary HTML markup for the content of the button. All attributes are used identically to those in `<INPUT TYPE="BUTTON" ...>`.

16.5 Check Boxes and Radio Buttons

Check boxes and radio buttons are useful controls for allowing the user to select among a set of predefined choices. While each individual check box can be selected or deselected individually, radio buttons can be grouped so that only a single member of the group can be selected at a time.

Check boxes

HTML Element: `<INPUT TYPE="CHECKBOX" NAME="..." ...>`
(No End Tag)
Attributes: NAME (required), VALUE, CHECKED, ONCLICK, ONFOCUS, ONBLUR

This input element creates a check box whose name/value pair is transmitted *only* if the check box is checked when the form is submitted. For instance, the following code results in the check box shown in Figure 16–14.

```
<P>
<INPUT TYPE="CHECKBOX" NAME="noEmail" CHECKED>
Check here if you do <I>not</I> want to
get our email newsletter
```

☑ Check here if you do *not* want to get our email newsletter

Figure 16–14 An HTML check box.

Note that the descriptive text associated with the check box is normal HTML, and care should be taken to guarantee that it appears next to the check box. Thus, the `<P>` in the preceding example ensures that the check box isn't part of the previous paragraph.

Core Approach

Paragraphs inside a FORM *are filled and wrapped just like regular paragraphs. So, be sure to insert explicit HTML markup to keep input elements with the text that describes them.*

NAME

This attribute supplies the name that is sent to the server. It is required for standard HTML check boxes but optional when used with JavaScript.

VALUE

The VALUE attribute is optional and defaults to on. Recall that the name and value are only sent to the server if the check box is checked when the form is submitted. For instance, in the preceding example, noEmail=on would be added to the data string since the box is checked, but nothing would be added if the box was unchecked. As a result, servlets or CGI programs often check only for the existence of the check box name, ignoring its value.

CHECKED

If the CHECKED attribute is supplied, then the check box is initially checked when the associated Web page is loaded. Otherwise, it is initially unchecked.

ONCLICK, ONFOCUS, and ONBLUR

These attributes supply JavaScript code to be executed when the button is clicked, receives the input focus, and loses the focus, respectively.

Radio Buttons

HTML Element: `<INPUT TYPE="RADIO" NAME="..."`
                                    `VALUE="..." ...>` (No End Tag)
Attributes: NAME (required), VALUE (required), CHECKED, ONCLICK, ONFOCUS, ONBLUR

Radio buttons differ from check boxes in that only a single radio button in a given group can be selected at any one time. You indicate a group of radio buttons by providing all of them with the same NAME. Only one button in a group can be depressed at a time; selecting a new button when one is already selected results in the previous choice becoming deselected. The value of the one selected is sent when the form is submitted. Although radio buttons technically need not appear near to each other, this proximity is almost always recommended.

An example of a radio button group follows. Because input elements are wrapped as part of normal paragraphs, a DL list is used to make sure that the buttons appear under each other in the resultant page and are indented from the heading above them. Figure 16–15 shows the result. In this case, credit-Card=java would get sent as part of the form data when the form is submitted.

```
<DL>
  <DT>Credit Card:
  <DD><INPUT TYPE="RADIO" NAME="creditCard" VALUE="visa">
      Visa
  <DD><INPUT TYPE="RADIO" NAME="creditCard" VALUE="mastercard">
      Master Card
  <DD><INPUT TYPE="RADIO" NAME="creditCard"
           VALUE="java" CHECKED>
      Java Smart Card
  <DD><INPUT TYPE="RADIO" NAME="creditCard" VALUE="amex">
      American Express
  <DD><INPUT TYPE="RADIO" NAME="creditCard" VALUE="discover">
      Discover
</DL>
```

Credit Card:

    ○ Visa

    ○ Master Card

    ⊙ Java Smart Card

    ○ American Express

    ○ Discover

Figure 16–15 Radio buttons in HTML.

NAME

Unlike the NAME attribute of most input elements, this NAME is shared by multiple elements. All radio buttons associated with the same name are grouped logically so that no more than one can be selected at any given time. Note that attribute values are case sensitive, so the following would result in two radio buttons that are *not* logically connected.

```
<INPUT TYPE="RADIO" NAME="Foo" VALUE="Value1">
<INPUT TYPE="RADIO" NAME="FOO" VALUE="Value2">
```

Core Warning

Be sure the NAME of each radio button in a logical group matches exactly.

VALUE

The VALUE attribute supplies the value that gets transmitted with the NAME when the form is submitted. It doesn't affect the appearance of the radio button. Instead, normal text and HTML markup are placed around the radio button, just as with check boxes.

CHECKED

If the CHECKED attribute is supplied, then the radio button is initially checked when the associated Web page is loaded. Otherwise, it is initially unchecked.

ONCLICK, ONFOCUS, and ONBLUR

These attributes supply JavaScript code to be executed when the button is clicked, receives the input focus, and loses the focus, respectively.

16.6 Combo Boxes and List Boxes

A SELECT element presents a set of options to the user. If only a single entry can be selected and no visible size has been specified, the options are presented in a combo box (drop-down menu); list boxes are used when multiple selections are permitted or a specific visible size has been specified. The choices themselves are specified by OPTION entries embedded in the SELECT element. The typical format is as follows:

```
<SELECT NAME="Name" ...>
  <OPTION VALUE="Value1">Choice 1 Text
  <OPTION VALUE="Value2">Choice 2 Text
  ...
  <OPTION VALUE="ValueN">Choice N Text
</SELECT>
```

The HTML 4.0 specification suggests the use of OPTGROUP (with a single attribute of LABEL) to enclose OPTION elements in order to create cascading menus, but neither Netscape nor Internet Explorer supports this element.

HTML Element: `<SELECT NAME="..." ...> ... </SELECT>`

Attributes: NAME (required), SIZE, MULTIPLE, ONCLICK, ONFOCUS, ONBLUR, ONCHANGE

SELECT creates a combo box or list box for selecting among choices. You specify each choice with an OPTION element enclosed between `<SELECT ...>` and `</SELECT>`.

NAME

NAME identifies the form to the servlet or CGI program.

SIZE

SIZE gives the number of visible rows. If SIZE is used, the SELECT menu is usually represented as a list box instead of a combo box. A combo box is the normal representation when neither SIZE nor MULTIPLE is supplied.

MULTIPLE

The MULTIPLE attribute specifies that multiple entries can be selected simultaneously. If MULTIPLE is omitted, only a single selection is permitted.

ONCLICK, ONFOCUS, ONBLUR, and ONCHANGE

These nonstandard attributes are supported by browsers that understand JavaScript. They indicate code to be executed when the entry is clicked on, gains the input focus, loses the input focus, and loses the focus after having been changed, respectively.

HTML Element: `<OPTION ...>` (End Tag Optional)
Attributes: SELECTED, VALUE

Only valid inside a SELECT element, this element specifies the menu choices.

VALUE

VALUE gives the value to be transmitted with the NAME of the SELECT menu if the current option is selected. This is *not* the text that is displayed to the user; that is specified by separate text listed after the OPTION tag.

SELECTED

If present, SELECTED specifies that the particular menu item shown is selected when the page is first loaded.

The following example creates a menu of programming language choices. Because only a single selection is allowed and no visible SIZE is specified, it is displayed as a combo box. Figures 16–16 and 16–17 show the initial appearance and the appearance after the user activates the menu by clicking on it. If the entry Java is active when the form is submitted, then language=java is sent to the server-side program. Notice that it is the VALUE attribute, not the descriptive text, that is transmitted.

```
Favorite language:
<SELECT NAME="language">
  <OPTION VALUE="c">C
  <OPTION VALUE="c++">C++
  <OPTION VALUE="java" SELECTED>Java
  <OPTION VALUE="lisp">Lisp
  <OPTION VALUE="perl">Perl
  <OPTION VALUE="smalltalk">Smalltalk
</SELECT>
```

Favorite language: Java

Figure 16–16 A SELECT element displayed as a combo box (drop-down menu).

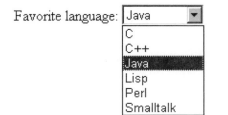

Figure 16–17 Choosing options from a SELECT menu.

The second example shows a SELECT element rendered as a list box. If more than one entry is active when the form is submitted, then more than one value is sent, listed as separate entries (repeating the NAME). For instance, in the example shown in Figure 16–18, language=java&language=perl gets added to the data being sent to the server. Multiple entries that share the same name is the reason servlet authors need be familiar with the getParameterValues method of HttpServletRequest in addition to the more common getParameter method. See Chapter 3 (Handling the Client Request: Form Data) for details.

```
Languages you know:<BR>
<SELECT NAME="language" MULTIPLE>
  <OPTION VALUE="c">C
  <OPTION VALUE="c++">C++
  <OPTION VALUE="java" SELECTED>Java
  <OPTION VALUE="lisp">Lisp
  <OPTION VALUE="perl" SELECTED>Perl
  <OPTION VALUE="smalltalk">Smalltalk
</SELECT>
```

Languages you know:

Figure 16–18 A SELECT element that specifies MULTIPLE or SIZE results in a list box.

16.7 File Upload Controls

HTML Element: `<INPUT TYPE="FILE" ...>` (No End Tag)

Attributes: NAME (required), VALUE (ignored), SIZE, MAXLENGTH, ACCEPT, ONCHANGE, ONSELECT, ONFOCUS, ONBLUR (nonstandard)

This element results in a filename textfield next to a Browse button. Users can enter a path directly in the textfield or click on the button to bring up a file selection dialog that lets them interactively choose the path to a file. When the form is submitted, the *contents* of the file are transmitted as long as an ENCTYPE of multipart/form-data was specified in the initial FORM declaration. This element provides a convenient way to make user-support pages, where the user sends a description of the problem along with any associated data or configuration files.

Core Tip

Always specify `ENCTYPE="multipart/form-data"` *in forms with file upload controls.*

NAME

The NAME attribute identifies the textfield when the form is submitted.

VALUE

For security reasons, this attribute is ignored. Only the end user can specify a filename.

SIZE and MAXLENGTH

The SIZE and MAXLENGTH attributes are used the same way as in textfields, specifying the number of visible and maximum allowable characters, respectively.

ACCEPT

The ACCEPT attribute is intended to be a comma-separated list of MIME types used to restrict the available filenames. However, very few browsers support this attribute.

ONCHANGE, ONSELECT, ONFOCUS, and ONBLUR

These attributes are used by browsers that support JavaScript to specify the action to take when the mouse leaves the textfield after a change has occurred, when the user selects text in the textfield, when the textfield gets the input focus, and when it loses the input focus, respectively.

For example, the following code creates a file upload control. Figure 16–19 shows the initial result, and Figure 16–20 shows a typical pop-up window that results when the Browse button is activated.

```
<FORM ACTION="http://localhost:8088/SomeProgram"
      ENCTYPE="multipart/form-data">
Enter data file below:<BR>
<INPUT TYPE="FILE" NAME="fileName">
</FORM>
```

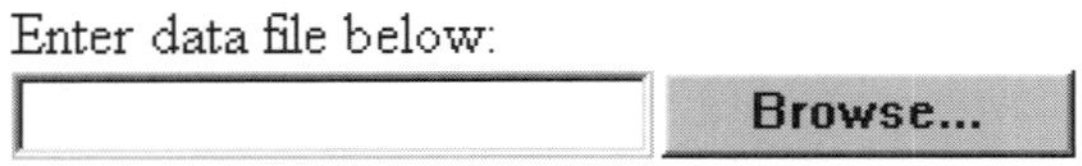

Figure 16–19 Initial look of a file upload control.

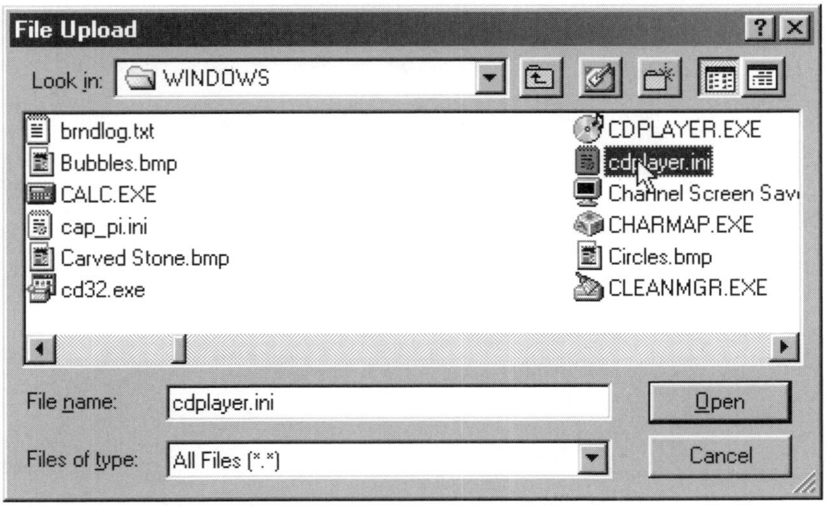

Figure 16–20 A file chooser resulting from the user clicking on Browse in a file upload control.

16.8 Server-Side Image Maps

In HTML, an element called MAP lets you associate URLs with various regions of an image; then, when the image is clicked in one of the designated regions, the browser loads the appropriate URL. This form of mapping is known as a *client-side image map*, since the determination of which URL to contact is made on the client and no server-side program is involved. HTML also supports *server-side image maps* that can be used within HTML forms. With such maps, an image is drawn, and when the user clicks on it, the coordinates of the click are sent to a server-side program.

Client-side image maps are simpler and more efficient than server-side ones and should be used when all you want to do is associate a fixed set of URLs with some predefined image regions. However, server-side image maps are appropriate if the URL needs to be computed (e.g,. for weather maps), the regions change frequently, or other form data needs to be included with the request. This section discusses two approaches to server-side image maps.

IMAGE—Standard Server-Side Image Maps

The usual way to create server-side image maps is by means of an <INPUT TYPE="IMAGE" ...> element inside a form.

HTML Element: **<INPUT TYPE="IMAGE" ...>** (No End Tag)
Attributes: NAME (required), SRC, ALIGN

This element displays an image that, when clicked, sends the form to the servlet or other server-side program specified by the enclosing form's ACTION. The name itself is not sent; instead, *name*.x=*xpos* and *name*.y=*ypos* are transmitted, where *xpos* and *ypos* are the coordinates of the mouse click relative to the upper-left corner of the image.

NAME

The NAME attribute identifies the textfield when the form is submitted.

SRC

SRC designates the URL of the associated image.

ALIGN

The ALIGN attribute has the same options (TOP, MIDDLE, BOTTOM, LEFT, RIGHT) and default (BOTTOM) as the ALIGN attribute of the IMG element and is used in the same way.

Listing 16.5 shows a simple example, where the form's ACTION specifies the EchoServer developed in Section 16.12. Figures 16–21 and 16–22 show the results before and after the image is clicked.

Listing 16.5 ImageMap.html

```
<!DOCTYPE HTML PUBLIC "-//W3C//DTD HTML 4.0 Transitional//EN">
<HTML>
<HEAD>
  <TITLE>The IMAGE Input Control</TITLE>
</HEAD>

<BODY>
<H1 ALIGN="CENTER">The IMAGE Input Control</H1>
Which island is Java? Click and see if you are correct.

<FORM ACTION="http://localhost:8088/GeographyTester">
  <INPUT TYPE="IMAGE" NAME="map" SRC="images/indonesia.gif">
</FORM>

Of course, image maps can be implemented <B>in</B>
Java as well. :-)

</BODY>
</HTML>
```

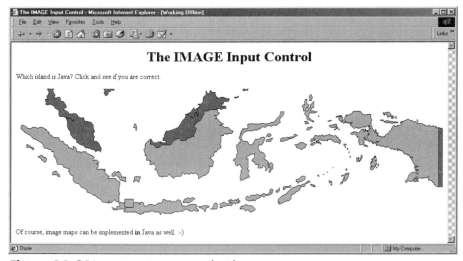

Figure 16–21 An IMAGE input control with NAME="map".

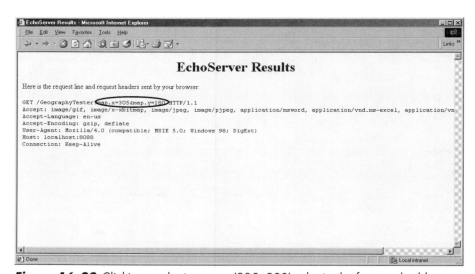

Figure 16–22 Clicking on the image at (305, 280) submits the form and adds map.x=305&map.y=280 to the form data.

ISMAP—Alternative Server-Side Image Maps

ISMAP is an optional attribute of the IMG element and can be used in a similar manner to the <INPUT TYPE="IMAGE" ...> FORM entry. ISMAP is not actually a FORM element at all, but can still be used for simple connections to servlets or CGI programs. If an image with ISMAP is inside a hypertext link, then clicking on the image results in the coordinates of the click being sent to the specified URL. Coordinates are separated by commas and are specified in pixels relative to the top-left corner of the image.

For instance, Listing 16.6 embeds an image that uses the ISMAP attribute inside a hypertext link to http://localhost:8088/ChipTester, which is answered by the mini HTTP server developed in Section 16.12. Figure 16–23 shows the initial result, which is identical to what would have been shown had the ISMAP attribute been omitted. However, when the mouse button is pressed 271 pixels to the right and 184 pixels below the top-left corner of the image, the browser requests the URL http://localhost:8088/ChipTester?271,184 (as is shown in Figure 16–24).

If a server-side image map is used simply to select among a static set of destination URLs, then a client-side MAP element is a much better option because the server doesn't have to be contacted just to decide which URL applies. If the image map is intended to be mixed with other input elements, then the IMAGE input type is preferred instead. However, for a stand-alone image map where the URL associated with a region changes frequently or requires calculation, an image with ISMAP is a reasonable choice.

Listing 16.6 `IsMap.html`

```
<!DOCTYPE HTML PUBLIC "-//W3C//DTD HTML 4.0 Transitional//EN">
<HTML>
<HEAD>
  <TITLE>The ISMAP Attribute</TITLE>
</HEAD>

<BODY>

<H1 ALIGN="CENTER">The ISMAP Attribute</H1>
<H2>Select a pin:</H2>
<A HREF="http://localhost:8088/ChipTester">
<IMG SRC="images/chip.gif" WIDTH=495 HEIGHT=200 ALT="Chip"
     BORDER=0 ISMAP></A>

</BODY>
</HTML>
```

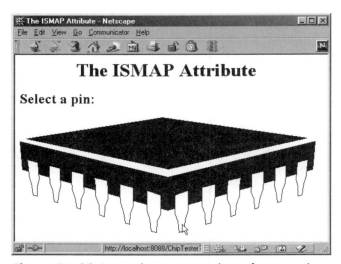

Figure 16–23 Setting the `ISMAP` attribute of an `IMG` element inside a hypertext link changes what happens when the image is selected.

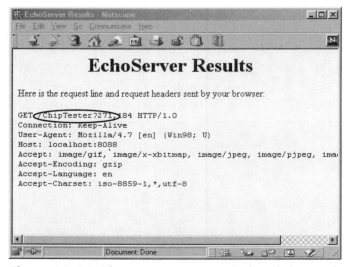

Figure 16–24 When an `ISMAP` image is selected, the coordinates of the selection are transmitted with the URL.

16.9 Hidden Fields

Hidden fields do not affect the appearance of the page that is presented to the user. Instead, they store fixed names and values that are sent unchanged to the server, regardless of user input. Hidden fields are typically used for three purposes.

First, they are one method of tracking users as they move around within a site (see Section 9.1, "The Need for Session Tracking"). Servlet authors typically rely on the servlet session tracking API (Section 9.2) rather than attempting to implement session tracking at this low level.

Second, hidden fields are used to provide predefined input to a server-side program when a variety of static HTML pages act as front ends to the same program on the server. For example, an on-line store might pay commissions to people who refer customers to their site. In this scenario, the referring page could let visitors search the store's catalog by means of a form, but embed a hidden field listing its referral ID.

Third, hidden fields are used to store contextual information in pages that are dynamically generated. For example, in the order confirmation page of the on-line store developed in Section 9.4, each row in the table corresponds to a particular item being ordered (see Figure 9–6). The user can modify the number of items ordered, but there is no visible form element that stores the item ID. So, a hidden form is used (see Listing 9.5).

HTML Element: `<INPUT TYPE="HIDDEN" NAME="..." VALUE="...">`
(No End Tag)

Attributes: NAME (required), VALUE

This element stores a name and a value, but no graphical element is created in the browser. The name/value pair is added to the form data when the form is submitted. For instance, with the following example, `itemID=hall001` will always get sent with the form data.

```
<INPUT TYPE="HIDDEN" NAME="itemID" VALUE="hall001">
```

Note that the term "hidden" does not mean that the field cannot be discovered by the user, since it is clearly visible in the HTML source. Because there is no reliable way to "hide" the HTML that generates a page, authors are cautioned not to use hidden fields to embed passwords or other sensitive information.

16.10 Grouping Controls

HTML 4.0 defines the FIELDSET element, with an associated LEGEND, that can be used to visually group controls within a form. This capability is quite useful but is supported only by Internet Explorer. Hopefully, Netscape version 5 will add support for this element. In the meantime, you should reserve use of this element to intranet applications where all your users are using Internet Explorer.

Core Warning

As of version 4.7, Netscape does not support the FIELDSET *element.*

HTML Element: <FIELDSET>

Attributes: None.

This element is used as a container to enclose controls and, optionally, a LEGEND element. It has no attributes beyond the universal ones for style sheets, language, and so forth. Listing 16.7 gives an example, with the result shown in Figure 16–25.

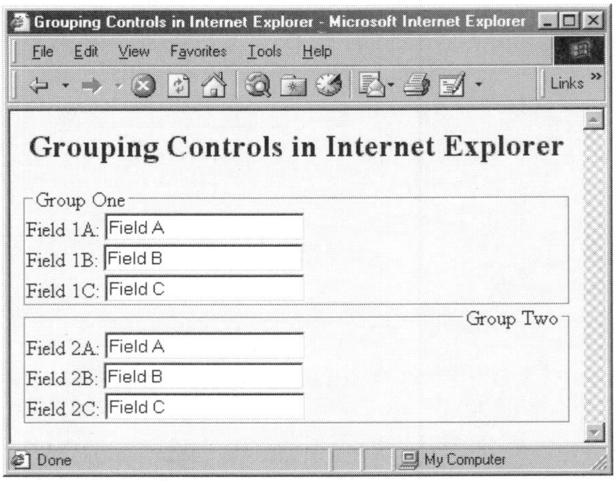

Figure 16–25 The FIELDSET element lets you visually group related controls.

Listing 16.7 `Fieldset.html`

```
<!DOCTYPE HTML PUBLIC "-//W3C//DTD HTML 4.0 Transitional//EN">
<HTML>
<HEAD>
  <TITLE>Grouping Controls in Internet Explorer</TITLE>
</HEAD>

<BODY BGCOLOR="#FDF5E6">
<H2 ALIGN="CENTER">Grouping Controls in Internet Explorer</H2>

<FORM ACTION="http://localhost:8088/SomeProgram">

<FIELDSET>
<LEGEND>Group One</LEGEND>
Field 1A: <INPUT TYPE="TEXT" NAME="field1A" VALUE="Field A"><BR>
Field 1B: <INPUT TYPE="TEXT" NAME="field1B" VALUE="Field B"><BR>
Field 1C: <INPUT TYPE="TEXT" NAME="field1C" VALUE="Field C"><BR>
</FIELDSET>

<FIELDSET>
<LEGEND ALIGN="RIGHT">Group Two</LEGEND>
Field 2A: <INPUT TYPE="TEXT" NAME="field2A" VALUE="Field A"><BR>
Field 2B: <INPUT TYPE="TEXT" NAME="field2B" VALUE="Field B"><BR>
Field 2C: <INPUT TYPE="TEXT" NAME="field2C" VALUE="Field C"><BR>
</FIELDSET>

</FORM>

</BODY>
</HTML>
```

HTML Element: `<LEGEND>`
Attributes: ALIGN

This element, legal only within an enclosing FIELDSET, places a label on the etched border that is drawn around the group of controls.

ALIGN

This attribute controls the position of the label. Legal values are TOP, BOTTOM, LEFT, and RIGHT, with TOP being the default. In Figure 16–25, the first group has the default legend alignment, and the second group stipulates ALIGN="RIGHT". In HTML, style sheets are often a better way to control element alignment, since they permit a single change to be propagated to multiple places.

16.11 Controlling Tab Order

HTML 4.0 defines a TABINDEX attribute that can be used in any of the visual HTML elements. Its value is an integer, and it controls the order in which elements receive the input focus when the TAB key is pressed. Unfortunately, however, it is supported only by Internet Explorer. Nevertheless, you can use TABINDEX even for pages that will be viewed by multiple browsers, as long as the designated tabbing order is a convenience to the user, not a necessity for proper operation of the page.

Core Warning

As of version 4.7, Netscape does not support the TABINDEX *attribute.*

Listing 16.8 `Tabindex.html`

```
<!DOCTYPE HTML PUBLIC "-//W3C//DTD HTML 4.0 Transitional//EN">
<HTML>
<HEAD>
  <TITLE>Controlling TAB Order</TITLE>
</HEAD>

<BODY BGCOLOR="#FDF5E6">
<H2 ALIGN="CENTER">Controlling TAB Order</H2>

<FORM ACTION="http://localhost:8088/SomeProgram">
Field 1 (first tab selection):
<INPUT TYPE="TEXT" NAME="field1" TABINDEX=1><BR>
Field 2 (third tab selection):
<INPUT TYPE="TEXT" NAME="field2" TABINDEX=3><BR>
Field 3 (second tab selection):
<INPUT TYPE="TEXT" NAME="field3" TABINDEX=2><BR>
</FORM>

</BODY>
</HTML>
```

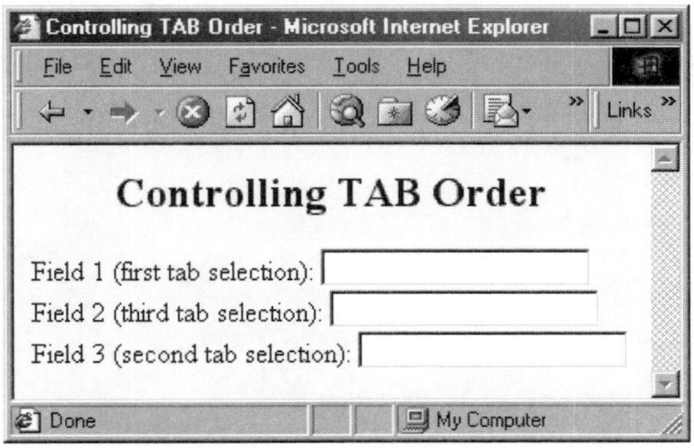

Figure 16–26 In Internet Explorer, repeatedly pressing the TAB key cycles the input focus among the first, third, and second text fields, in that order (as dictated by TABINDEX). In Netscape, the input focus would cycle among the first, second, and third fields, in that order (based on the order the elements appear on the page).

16.12 A Debugging Web Server

This section presents a mini "Web server" that is useful when you are trying to understand the behavior of HTML forms. I used it for many of the examples earlier in the chapter. It simply reads all the HTTP data sent to it by the browser, then returns a Web page with those lines embedded within a PRE element. This server is also extremely useful for debugging servlets. When something goes wrong, the first task is to determine if the problem lies in the way in which you collect data or the way in which you process it. Starting the EchoServer on, say, port 8088 of your local machine, then changing your forms to specify http://localhost:8088/ lets you see if the data being collected is in the format you expect.

EchoServer

Listing 16.9 presents the top-level server code. You typically run it from the command line, specifying a port to listen on or accepting the default of 8088. It then accepts repeated HTTP requests from clients, packaging all HTTP data sent to it inside a Web page that is returned to the client. In most cases, the server reads until it gets a blank line, indicating the end of GET, HEAD, or most other types of HTTP requests. In the case of POST, however, the server checks the Content-Length request header and reads that many bytes beyond the blank line.

Listing 16.9 `EchoServer.java`

```java
import java.net.*;
import java.io.*;
import java.util.StringTokenizer;

/** A simple HTTP server that generates a Web page
 *  showing all the data that it received from
 *  the Web client (usually a browser). To use this,
 *  start it on the system of your choice, supplying
 *  a port number if you want something other than
 *  port 8088. Call this system server.com. Next,
 *  start a Web browser on the same or a different
 *  system, and connect to http://server.com:8088/whatever.
 *  The resultant Web page will show the data that your browser
 *  sent. For debugging in servlet or CGI programming,
 *  specify http://server.com:8088/whatever as the
 *  ACTION of your HTML form. You can send GET
 *  or POST data; either way, the resultant page
 *  will show what your browser sent.
 */

public class EchoServer extends NetworkServer {
  protected int maxRequestLines = 50;
  protected String serverName = "EchoServer";

  /** Supply a port number as a command-line
   *  argument. Otherwise port 8088 will be used.
   */

  public static void main(String[] args) {
    int port = 8088;
    if (args.length > 0) {
      try {
        port = Integer.parseInt(args[0]);
      } catch(NumberFormatException nfe) {}
    }
    new EchoServer(port, 0);
  }

  public EchoServer(int port, int maxConnections) {
    super(port, maxConnections);
    listen();
  }

  /** Overrides the NetworkServer handleConnection
   *  method to read each line of data received, save it
   *  into an array of strings, then send it
   *  back embedded inside a PRE element in an
   *  HTML page.
   */
```

Listing 16.9 `EchoServer.java` (continued)

```
public void handleConnection(Socket server)
    throws IOException{
  System.out.println
      (serverName + ": got connection from " +
        server.getInetAddress().getHostName());
  BufferedReader in = SocketUtil.getReader(server);
  PrintWriter out = SocketUtil.getWriter(server);
  String[] inputLines = new String[maxRequestLines];
  int i;
  for (i=0; i<maxRequestLines; i++) {
    inputLines[i] = in.readLine();
    if (inputLines[i] == null) // Client closed connection
      break;
    if (inputLines[i].length() == 0) { // Blank line
      if (usingPost(inputLines)) {
        readPostData(inputLines, i, in);
        i = i + 2;
      }
      break;
    }
  }
  printHeader(out);
  for (int j=0; j<i; j++) {
    out.println(inputLines[j]);
  }
  printTrailer(out);
  server.close();
}

// Send standard HTTP response and top of a standard Web page.
// Use HTTP 1.0 for compatibility with all clients.

private void printHeader(PrintWriter out) {
  out.println
    ("HTTP/1.0 200 OK\r\n" +
     "Server: " + serverName + "\r\n" +
     "Content-Type: text/html\r\n" +
     "\r\n" +
     "<!DOCTYPE HTML PUBLIC " +
       "\"-//W3C//DTD HTML 4.0 Transitional//EN\">\n" +
     "<HTML>\n" +
     "<HEAD>\n" +
     "  <TITLE>" + serverName + " Results</TITLE>\n" +
     "</HEAD>\n" +
     "\n" +
     "<BODY BGCOLOR=\"#FDF5E6\">\n" +
     "<H1 ALIGN=\"CENTER\">" + serverName +
       " Results</H1>\n" +
```

Listing 16.9 `EchoServer.java` (continued)

```
            "Here is the request line and request headers\n" +
            "sent by your browser:\n" +
            "<PRE>");
    }

    // Print bottom of a standard Web page.

    private void printTrailer(PrintWriter out) {
        out.println
            ("</PRE>\n" +
             "</BODY>\n" +
             "</HTML>\n");
    }

    // Normal Web page requests use GET, so this
    // server can simply read a line at a time.
    // However, HTML forms can also use POST, in which
    // case we have to determine the number of POST bytes
    // that are sent so we know how much extra data
    // to read after the standard HTTP headers.

    private boolean usingPost(String[] inputs) {
        return(inputs[0].toUpperCase().startsWith("POST"));
    }

    private void readPostData(String[] inputs, int i,
                              BufferedReader in)
        throws IOException {
        int contentLength = contentLength(inputs);
        char[] postData = new char[contentLength];
        in.read(postData, 0, contentLength);
        inputs[++i] = new String(postData, 0, contentLength);
    }

    // Given a line that starts with Content-Length,
    // this returns the integer value specified.

    private int contentLength(String[] inputs) {
        String input;
        for (int i=0; i<inputs.length; i++) {
            if (inputs[i].length() == 0)
                break;
            input = inputs[i].toUpperCase();
            if (input.startsWith("CONTENT-LENGTH"))
                return(getLength(input));
        }
        return(0);
    }
```

Listing 16.9 `EchoServer.java` (continued)

```java
  private int getLength(String length) {
    StringTokenizer tok = new StringTokenizer(length);
    tok.nextToken();
    return(Integer.parseInt(tok.nextToken()));
  }
}
```

ThreadedEchoServer

Listing 16.10 presents a multithreaded variation of the `EchoServer`, useful when your server needs to accept multiple simultaneous client requests.

Listing 16.10 `ThreadedEchoServer.java`

```java
import java.net.*;
import java.io.*;

/** A multithreaded variation of EchoServer. */

public class ThreadedEchoServer extends EchoServer
                                implements Runnable {
  public static void main(String[] args) {
    int port = 8088;
    if (args.length > 0) {
      try {
        port = Integer.parseInt(args[0]);
      } catch(NumberFormatException nfe) {}
    }
    ThreadedEchoServer echoServer =
      new ThreadedEchoServer(port, 0);
    echoServer.serverName = "Threaded Echo Server";
  }

  public ThreadedEchoServer(int port, int connections) {
    super(port, connections);
  }

  /** The new version of handleConnection starts
   *  a thread. This new thread will call back to the
   *  <I>old</I> version of handleConnection, resulting
   *  in the same server behavior in a multithreaded
   *  version. The thread stores the Socket instance
   *  since run doesn't take any arguments, and since
   *  storing the socket in an instance variable risks
   *  having it overwritten if the next thread starts
```

Listing 16.10 `ThreadedEchoServer.java` **(continued)**

```java
   *   before the run method gets a chance to
   *   copy the socket reference.
   */

  public void handleConnection(Socket server) {
    Connection connectionThread = new Connection(this, server);
    connectionThread.start();
  }

  public void run() {
    Connection currentThread =
      (Connection)Thread.currentThread();
    try {
      super.handleConnection(currentThread.serverSocket);
    } catch(IOException ioe) {
      System.out.println("IOException: " + ioe);
      ioe.printStackTrace();
    }
  }
}

/** This is just a Thread with a field to store a
 *  Socket object. Used as a thread-safe means to pass
 *  the Socket from handleConnection to run.
 */

class Connection extends Thread {
  protected Socket serverSocket;

  public Connection(Runnable serverObject,
                    Socket serverSocket) {
    super(serverObject);
    this.serverSocket = serverSocket;
  }
}
```

NetworkServer

Listings 16.11 and 16.12 present some utilities classes that simplify networking. The `EchoServer` is built on top of them.

Listing 16.11 `NetworkServer.java`

```java
import java.net.*;
import java.io.*;

/** A starting point for network servers. You'll need to
 *  override handleConnection, but in many cases
 *  listen can remain unchanged. NetworkServer uses
 *  SocketUtil to simplify the creation of the
 *  PrintWriter and BufferedReader.
 *  @see SocketUtil
 */

public class NetworkServer {
  private int port, maxConnections;

  /** Build a server on specified port. It will continue
   *  to accept connections, passing each to
   *  handleConnection, until an explicit exit
   *  command is sent (e.g., System.exit) or the
   *  maximum number of connections is reached. Specify
   *  0 for maxConnections if you want the server
   *  to run indefinitely.
   */

  public NetworkServer(int port, int maxConnections) {
    setPort(port);
    setMaxConnections(maxConnections);
  }

  /** Monitor a port for connections. Each time one
   *  is established, pass resulting Socket to
   *  handleConnection.
   */

  public void listen() {
    int i=0;
    try {
      ServerSocket listener = new ServerSocket(port);
      Socket server;
      while((i++ < maxConnections) || (maxConnections == 0)) {
        server = listener.accept();
        handleConnection(server);
      }
    } catch (IOException ioe) {
      System.out.println("IOException: " + ioe);
      ioe.printStackTrace();
    }
  }
}
```

Listing 16.11 `NetworkServer.java` (continued)

```java
/** This is the method that provides the behavior
 *  to the server, since it determines what is
 *  done with the resulting socket. <B>Override this
 *  method in servers you write.</B>
 *  <P>
 *  This generic version simply reports the host
 *  that made the connection, shows the first line
 *  the client sent, and sends a single line
 *  in response.
 */

protected void handleConnection(Socket server)
    throws IOException{
  BufferedReader in = SocketUtil.getReader(server);
  PrintWriter out = SocketUtil.getWriter(server);
  System.out.println
    ("Generic Network Server: got connection from " +
     server.getInetAddress().getHostName() + "\n" +
     "with first line '" + in.readLine() + "'");
  out.println("Generic Network Server");
  server.close();
}

/** Gets the max connections server will handle before
 *  exiting. A value of 0 indicates that server
 *  should run until explicitly killed.
 */

public int getMaxConnections() {
  return(maxConnections);
}

/** Sets max connections. A value of 0 indicates that
 *  server should run indefinitely (until explicitly
 *  killed).
 */

public void setMaxConnections(int maxConnections) {
  this.maxConnections = maxConnections;
}

/** Gets port on which server is listening. */

public int getPort() {
  return(port);
}
```

Listing 16.11 `NetworkServer.java` (continued)

```java
  /** Sets port. <B>You can only do before "connect"
   *  is called.</B> That usually happens in the constructor.
   */

  protected void setPort(int port) {
    this.port = port;
  }
}
```

Listing 16.12 `SocketUtil.java`

```java
import java.net.*;
import java.io.*;

/** A shorthand way to create BufferedReaders and
 *  PrintWriters associated with a Socket.
 */

public class SocketUtil {
  /** Make a BufferedReader to get incoming data. */

  public static BufferedReader getReader(Socket s)
      throws IOException {
    return(new BufferedReader(
      new InputStreamReader(s.getInputStream())));
  }

  /** Make a PrintWriter to send outgoing data.
   *  This PrintWriter will automatically flush stream
   *  when println is called.
   */

  public static PrintWriter getWriter(Socket s)
      throws IOException {
    // 2nd argument of true means autoflush
    return(new PrintWriter(s.getOutputStream(), true));
  }
}
```

USING APPLETS AS SERVLET FRONT ENDS

Topics in This Chapter

- Sending GET data and having the browser display the results
- Sending GET data and processing the results within the applet (HTTP tunneling)
- Using object serialization to exchange high-level data structures between applets and servlets
- Sending POST data and processing the results within the applet
- Bypassing the HTTP server altogether

Chapter 17

HTML forms, discussed in Chapter 16, provide a simple but limited way of collecting user input and transmitting it to a servlet or CGI program. Occasionally, however, a more sophisticated user interface is required. Applets give you more control over the size, color, and font of the GUI controls; provide more built-in capability (sliders, line drawing, pop-up windows, and the like); let you track mouse and keyboard events; support the development of custom input forms (dials, thermometers, draggable icons, and so forth); and let you send a single user submission to multiple server-side programs. This extra capability comes at a cost, however, as it tends to require much more effort to design an interface in the Java programming language than it does using HTML forms, particularly if the interface contains a lot of formatted text. So, the choice between HTML forms and applets will depend upon the application.

With HTML forms, GET and POST requests are handled almost exactly the same way. All the input elements are identical; only the METHOD attribute of the FORM element needs to change. With applets, however, there are three distinct approaches. In the first approach, covered in Section 17.1, the applet imitates a GET-based HTML form, with GET data being transmitted and the resultant page being displayed by the browser. Section 17.2 (A Multisystem Search Engine Front End) gives an example. In the second approach, covered in Section 17.3, the applet sends GET data to a servlet and then processes the results itself. Section 17.4 (A Query Viewer

That Uses Object Serialization and HTTP Tunneling) gives an example. In the third approach, covered in Section 17.6, the applet sends POST data to a servlet and then processes the results itself. Section 17.6 (An Applet That Sends POST Data) gives an example. Finally, Section 17.7 serves as a reminder that an applet can bypass the HTTP server altogether and talk directly to a custom server program running on the applet's home machine.

This chapter assumes that you already have some familiarity with basic applets and focuses on the techniques to allow them to communicate with server-side programs. Readers who are unfamiliar with applets should consult a general introduction to the Java programming language. *Core Web Programming* or *Core Java* (both from Prentice Hall) are two good choices.

17.1 Sending Data with GET and Displaying the Resultant Page

The showDocument method instructs the browser to display a particular URL. Recall that you can transmit GET data to a servlet or CGI program by appending it to the program's URL after a question mark (?). Thus, to send GET data from an applet, you simply need to append the data to the string from which the URL is built, then create the URL object and call showDocument in the normal manner. A basic template for doing this in applets follows, assuming that baseURL is a string representing the URL of the server-side program and that someData is the information to be sent with the request.

```
try {
  URL programURL = new URL(baseURL + "?" + someData);
  getAppletContext().showDocument(programURL);
} catch(MalformedURLException mue) { ... }
```

However, when data is sent by a browser, it is *URL encoded*, which means that spaces are converted to plus signs (+) and nonalphanumeric characters into a percent sign (%) followed by the two hex digits representing that character, as discussed in Section 16.2 (The FORM Element). The preceding example assumes that someData has already been encoded properly and fails if it has not been. JDK 1.1 has a URLEncoder class with a static encode method that can perform this encoding. So, if an applet is contacting a server-side program that normally receives GET data from HTML forms, the applet needs to encode the value of each entry, but not the equal sign (=) between each entry name and its value or the ampersand (&) between each name/value pair. So, you cannot necessarily simply call URLEncoder.encode(someData) but instead need to selectively encode the value parts of each name/value pair. This could be accomplished as follows:

```
String someData =
  name1 + "=" + URLEncoder.encode(val1) + "&" +
  name2 + "=" + URLEncoder.encode(val2) + "&" +
  ...
  nameN + "=" + URLEncoder.encode(valN);
try {
  URL programURL = new URL(baseURL + "?" + someData);
  getAppletContext().showDocument(programURL);
} catch(MalformedURLException mue) { ... }
```

The following section gives a full-fledged example.

17.2 A Multisystem Search Engine Front End

In Section 6.3 (A Front End to Various Search Engines), the SearchSpec class (Listing 6.2) was used by a servlet to generate the specific URLs needed to redirect requests to various different search engines. The SearchSpec class can be used by applets as well. Listing 17.1 shows an applet that creates a textfield to gather user input. When the user submits the data, the applet URL-encodes the textfield value and generates three distinct URLs with embedded GET data: one each for the Google, Infoseek, and Lycos search engines. The applet then uses showDocument to instruct the browser to display the results of those URLs in three different frame cells. The results are shown in Figures 17–1 and 17–2. HTML forms cannot be used for this application since a form can submit its data to only a single URL.

Listing 17.2 shows the top-level HTML document used and Listing 17.3 shows the HTML used for the frame cell actually containing the applet. Please refer to this book's Web site (http://www.coreservlets.com/) for the three tiny HTML files used for the initial contents of the bottom three frame cells shown in Figure 17–1.

Listing 17.1 `SearchApplet.java`

```java
import java.applet.Applet;
import java.awt.*;
import java.awt.event.*;
import java.net.*;
import coreservlets.SearchSpec;

/** An applet that reads a value from a TextField,
 *  then uses it to build three distinct URLs with embedded
 *  GET data: one each for Google, Infoseek, and Lycos.
 *  The browser is directed to retrieve each of these
 *  URLs, displaying them in side-by-side frame cells.
 *  Note that standard HTML forms cannot automatically
 *  perform multiple submissions in this manner.
 */

public class SearchApplet extends Applet
                          implements ActionListener {
  private TextField queryField;
  private Button submitButton;

  public void init() {
    setFont(new Font("Serif", Font.BOLD, 18));
    add(new Label("Search String:"));
    queryField = new TextField(40);
    queryField.addActionListener(this);
    add(queryField);
    submitButton = new Button("Send to Search Engines");
    submitButton.addActionListener(this);
    add(submitButton);
  }

  /** Submit data when button is pressed <B>or</B>
   *  user presses Return in the TextField.
   */

  public void actionPerformed(ActionEvent event) {
    String query = URLEncoder.encode(queryField.getText());
    SearchSpec[] commonSpecs = SearchSpec.getCommonSpecs();
    // Omitting HotBot (last entry), as they use JavaScript to
    // pop result to top-level frame. Thus the length-1 below.
    for(int i=0; i<commonSpecs.length-1; i++) {
      try {
        SearchSpec spec = commonSpecs[i];
        // The SearchSpec class builds URLs of the
        // form needed by some common search engines.
        URL searchURL = new URL(spec.makeURL(query, "10"));
        String frameName = "results" + i;
        getAppletContext().showDocument(searchURL, frameName);
      } catch(MalformedURLException mue) {}
    }
  }
}
```

Figure 17-1 `SearchApplet` allows the user to enter a search string.

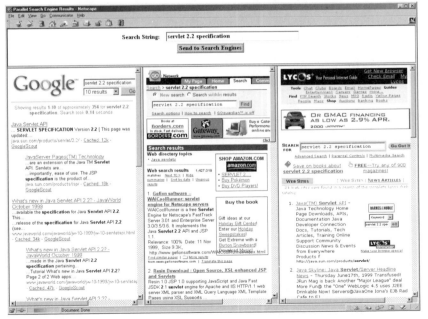

Figure 17-2 Submitting the query yields side-by-side results from three different search engines.

Listing 17.2 `ParallelSearches.html`

```
<!DOCTYPE HTML PUBLIC "-//W3C//DTD HTML 4.0 Frameset//EN">
<HTML>
<HEAD>
  <TITLE>Parallel Search Engine Results</TITLE>
</HEAD>

<FRAMESET ROWS="120,*">
  <FRAME SRC="SearchAppletFrame.html" SCROLLING="NO">
  <FRAMESET COLS="*,*,*">
    <FRAME SRC="GoogleResultsFrame.html" NAME="results0">
    <FRAME SRC="InfoseekResultsFrame.html" NAME="results1">
    <FRAME SRC="LycosResultsFrame.html" NAME="results2">
  </FRAMESET>
</FRAMESET>
```

Listing 17.3 `SearchAppletFrame.html`

```
<!DOCTYPE HTML PUBLIC "-//W3C//DTD HTML 4.0 Transitional//EN">
<HTML>
<HEAD>
  <TITLE>Search Applet Frame</TITLE>
</HEAD>

<BODY BGCOLOR="WHITE">
<CENTER>
<APPLET CODE="SearchApplet.class" WIDTH=600 HEIGHT=100>
  <B>This example requires a Java-enabled browser.</B>
</APPLET>
</CENTER>
</BODY>
</HTML>
```

17.3 Sending Data with GET and Processing the Results Directly (HTTP Tunneling)

In the previous example, an applet instructs the browser to display the output of a server-side program in a particular frame. Using the browser to display results is a reasonable approach when working with existing services, since most CGI programs are already set up to return HTML documents. However, if you are developing *both* the client and the server sides of the process, it seems a bit wasteful to always send back an entire HTML document; in some cases, it would be nice to simply return data to an applet that is already running. The applet could then present the data in a graph or some other custom display. This approach is sometimes known as *HTTP tunneling* since a custom communication protocol is embedded within HTTP: proxies, encryption, server redirection, connections through firewalls, and all.

There are two main variations to this approach. Both make use of the URL-Connection class to open an input stream from a URL. The difference lies in the type of stream they use. The first option is to use a BufferedInputStream or some other low-level stream that lets you read binary or ASCII data from an arbitrary server-side program. That approach is covered in the first subsection. The second option is to use an ObjectInputStream to directly read high-level data structures. That approach, covered in the second subsection, is available only when the server-side program is also written in the Java programming language.

Reading Binary or ASCII Data

An applet can read the content sent by the server by first creating a URLConnection derived from the URL of the server-side program and then attaching a BufferedInputStream to it. Seven main steps are required to implement this approach on the client, as described below. I'm omitting the server-side code since the client code described here works with arbitrary server-side programs or static Web pages.

Note that many of the stream operations throw an IOException, so the following statements need to be enclosed in a try/catch block.

1. **Create a URL object referring to applet's home host.** You can pass an absolute URL string to the URL constructor (e.g., "http://host/path"), but since browser security restrictions prohibit connections from applets to machines other than the home server, it makes more sense to build a URL based upon the hostname from which the applet was loaded.

   ```
   URL currentPage = getCodeBase();
   String protocol = currentPage.getProtocol();
   String host = currentPage.getHost();
   int port = currentPage.getPort();
   String urlSuffix = "/servlet/SomeServlet";
   URL dataURL = new URL(protocol, host, port, urlSuffix);
   ```

2. **Create a URLConnection object.** The openConnection method of URL returns a URLConnection object. This object will be used to obtain streams with which to communicate.

   ```
   URLConnection connection = dataURL.openConnection();
   ```

3. **Instruct the browser not to cache the URL data.** The first thing you do with the URLConnection object is to specify that the browser not cache it. This guarantees that you get a fresh result each time.

   ```
   connection.setUseCaches(false);
   ```

4. **Set any desired HTTP headers.** If you want to set HTTP request headers (see Chapter 4), you can use setRequest-Property to do so.

   ```
   connection.setRequestProperty("header", "value");
   ```

5. **Create an input stream.** There are a variety of appropriate streams, but a common one is BufferedReader. It is at the point where you create the input stream that the connection to the Web server is actually established behind the scenes.

   ```
   BufferedReader in =
     new BufferedReader(new InputStreamReader(
                             connection.getInputStream()));
   ```

6. **Read each line of the document.** The HTTP specification stipulates that the server closes the connection when it is done. When the connection is closed, readLine returns null. So, simply read until you get null.

   ```
   String line;
   while ((line = in.readLine()) != null) {
     doSomethingWith(line);
   }
   ```

7. **Close the input stream.**

   ```
   in.close();
   ```

Reading Serialized Data Structures

The approach shown in the previous subsection makes good sense when your applet is talking to an arbitrary server-side program or reading the content of static Web pages. However, when an applet talks to a servlet, you can do even better. Rather than sending binary or ASCII data, the servlet can transmit arbitrary data structures by using the Java serialization mechanism. The applet can read this data in a single step by using `readObject`; no long and tedious parsing is required. The steps required to implement HTTP tunneling are summarized below. Again, note that the statements need to be enclosed within a `try/catch` block in your actual applet.

The Client Side

An applet needs to perform the following seven steps to read serialized data structures sent by a servlet. Only Steps 5 and 6 differ from what is required to read ASCII data. These steps are slightly simplified by the omission of the `try/catch` blocks.

1. **Create a `URL` object referring to the applet's home host.** As before, since the URL must refer to the host from which the applet was loaded, it makes the most sense to specify a URL suffix and construct the rest of the URL automatically.

   ```
   URL currentPage = getCodeBase();
   String protocol = currentPage.getProtocol();
   String host = currentPage.getHost();
   int port = currentPage.getPort();
   String urlSuffix = "/servlet/SomeServlet";
   URL dataURL = new URL(protocol, host, port, urlSuffix);
   ```

2. **Create a `URLConnection` object.** The `openConnection` method of `URL` returns a `URLConnection` object. This object will be used to obtain streams with which to communicate.

   ```
   URLConnection connection = dataURL.openConnection();
   ```

3. **Instruct the browser not to cache the URL data.** The first thing you do with the `URLConnection` object is to specify that the browser not cache it. This guarantees that you get a fresh result each time.

   ```
   connection.setUseCaches(false);
   ```

4. **Set any desired HTTP headers.** If you want to set HTTP request headers (see Chapter 4), you can use `setRequest-Property` to do so.

    ```
    connection.setRequestProperty("header", "value");
    ```

5. **Create an `ObjectInputStream`.** The constructor for this class simply takes the raw input stream from the `URLConnection`. It is at the point where you create the input stream that the connection to the Web server is actually established.

    ```
    ObjectInputStream in =
      new ObjectInputStream(connection.getInputStream());
    ```

6. **Read the data structure with `readObject`.** The return type of `readObject` is `Object`, so you need to make a typecast to whatever more specific type the server actually sent.

    ```
    SomeClass value = (SomeClass)in.readObject();
    doSomethingWith(value);
    ```

7. **Close the input stream.**

    ```
    in.close();
    ```

The Server Side

A servlet needs to perform the following four steps to send serialized data structures to an applet. Assume that `request` and `response` are the `Http-ServletRequest` and `HttpServletResponse` objects supplied to the `doGet` and `doPost` methods. Again, these steps are simplified slightly by the omission of the required `try/catch` blocks.

1. **Specify that binary content is being sent.** This task is accomplished by designating

    ```
    application/x-java-serialized-object
    ```

    as the MIME type of the response. This is the standard MIME type for objects encoded with an `ObjectOutputStream`, although in practice, since the applet (not the browser) is reading the result, the MIME type is not very important. See the discussion of `Content-Type` in Section 7.2 (HTTP 1.1 Response Headers and Their Meaning) for more information on MIME types.

    ```
    String contentType =
      "application/x-java-serialized-object";
    response.setContentType(contentType);
    ```

2. **Create an `ObjectOutputStream`.**

   ```
   ObjectOutputStream out =
       new ObjectOutputStream(response.getOutputStream());
   ```

3. **Write the data structure by using `writeObject`.** Most built-in data structures can be sent this way. Classes *you* write, however, must implement the `Serializable` interface. This is a simple requirement, however, since `Serializable` defines no methods. Simply declare that your class implements it.

   ```
   SomeClass value = new SomeClass(...);
   out.writeObject(value);
   ```

4. **Flush the stream to be sure all content has been sent to the client.**

   ```
   out.flush();
   ```

The following section gives an example of this approach.

17.4 A Query Viewer That Uses Object Serialization and HTTP Tunneling

Many people are curious about what types of queries are sent to the major search engines. This is partly idle curiosity ("Is it really true that 64 percent of the queries at AltaVista are from employers looking for programmers that know Java technology?") and partly so that HTML authors can arrange their page content to fit the types of queries normally submitted, hoping to improve their site's ranking with the search engines.

This section presents an applet/servlet combination that displays the fictitious `super-search-engine.com` "live," continually updating sample queries to visitors that load their query viewer page. Listing 17.4 shows the main applet, which makes use of an auxiliary class (Listing 17.5) to retrieve the queries in a background thread. Once the user initiates the process, the applet places a sample query in a scrolling text area every half-second, as shown in Figure 17–3. Finally, Listing 17.6 shows the servlet that generates the queries on the server. It generates a random sampling of actual recent user queries and sends 50 of them to the client for each request.

If you download the applet and servlet source code from `http://www.coreservlets.com/` and try this application yourself, be aware that it will only work when you load the top-level HTML page by using

HTTP (i.e., by using a URL of the form `http://...` to request the page from a Web server). Loading it directly off your disk through a `file:` URL fails since the applet connects back to its home site to contact the servlet. Besides, `URLConnection` fails for non-HTTP applets in general.

Listing 17.4 `ShowQueries.java`

```java
import java.applet.Applet;
import java.awt.*;
import java.awt.event.*;
import java.net.*;

/** Applet reads arrays of strings packaged inside
 *   a QueryCollection and places them in a scrolling
 *   TextArea. The QueryCollection obtains the strings
 *   by means of a serialized object input stream
 *   connected to the QueryGenerator servlet.
 */

public class ShowQueries extends Applet
                         implements ActionListener, Runnable {
  private TextArea queryArea;
  private Button startButton, stopButton, clearButton;
  private QueryCollection currentQueries;
  private QueryCollection nextQueries;
  private boolean isRunning = false;
  private String address =
    "/servlet/coreservlets.QueryGenerator";
  private URL currentPage;

  public void init() {
    setBackground(Color.white);
    setLayout(new BorderLayout());
    queryArea = new TextArea();
    queryArea.setFont(new Font("Serif", Font.PLAIN, 14));
    add(queryArea, BorderLayout.CENTER);
    Panel buttonPanel = new Panel();
    Font buttonFont = new Font("SansSerif", Font.BOLD, 16);
    startButton = new Button("Start");
    startButton.setFont(buttonFont);
    startButton.addActionListener(this);
    buttonPanel.add(startButton);
    stopButton = new Button("Stop");
    stopButton.setFont(buttonFont);
    stopButton.addActionListener(this);
    buttonPanel.add(stopButton);
    clearButton = new Button("Clear TextArea");
```

Listing 17.4 ShowQueries.java **(continued)**

```java
    clearButton.setFont(buttonFont);
    clearButton.addActionListener(this);
    buttonPanel.add(clearButton);
    add(buttonPanel, BorderLayout.SOUTH);
    currentPage = getCodeBase();
    // Request a set of sample queries. They
    // are loaded in a background thread, and
    // the applet checks to see if they have finished
    // loading before trying to extract the strings.
    currentQueries = new QueryCollection(address, currentPage);
    nextQueries = new QueryCollection(address, currentPage);
  }

  /** If you press the "Start" button, the system
   *  starts a background thread that displays
   *  the queries in the TextArea. Pressing "Stop"
   *  halts the process, and "Clear" empties the
   *  TextArea.
   */

  public void actionPerformed(ActionEvent event) {
    if (event.getSource() == startButton) {
      if (!isRunning) {
        Thread queryDisplayer = new Thread(this);
        isRunning = true;
        queryArea.setText("");
        queryDisplayer.start();
        showStatus("Started display thread...");
      } else {
        showStatus("Display thread already running...");
      }
    } else if (event.getSource() == stopButton) {
      isRunning = false;
      showStatus("Stopped display thread...");
    } else if (event.getSource() == clearButton) {
      queryArea.setText("");
    }
  }

  /** The background thread takes the currentQueries
   *  object and every half-second places one of the queries
   *  the object holds into the bottom of the TextArea. When
   *  all of the queries have been shown, the thread copies
   *  the value of the nextQueries object into
   *  currentQueries, sends a new request to the server
   *  in order to repopulate nextQueries, and repeats
   *  the process.
   */
```

Listing 17.4 ShowQueries.java **(continued)**

```java
public void run() {
  while(isRunning) {
    showQueries(currentQueries);
    currentQueries = nextQueries;
    nextQueries = new QueryCollection(address, currentPage);
  }
}

private void showQueries(QueryCollection queryEntry) {
  // If request has been sent to server but the result
  // isn't back yet, poll every second. This should
  // happen rarely but is possible with a slow network
  // connection or an overloaded server.
  while(!queryEntry.isDone()) {
    showStatus("Waiting for data from server...");
    pause(1);
  }
  showStatus("Received data from server...");
  String[] queries = queryEntry.getQueries();
  String linefeed = "\n";
  // Put a string into TextArea every half-second.
  for(int i=0; i<queries.length; i++) {
    if (!isRunning) {
      return;
    }
    queryArea.append(queries[i]);
    queryArea.append(linefeed);
    pause(0.5);
  }
}

public void pause(double seconds) {
  try {
    Thread.sleep((long)(seconds*1000));
  } catch(InterruptedException ie) {}
}
}
```

Listing 17.5 QueryCollection.java

```java
import java.net.*;
import java.io.*;

/** When this class is built, it returns a value
 *  immediately, but this value returns false for isDone
 *  and null for getQueries. Meanwhile, it starts a Thread
 *  to request an array of query strings from the server,
 *  reading them in one fell swoop by means of an
 *  ObjectInputStream. Once they've all arrived, they
 *  are placed in the location getQueries returns,
 *  and the isDone flag is switched to true.
 *  Used by the ShowQueries applet.
 */

public class QueryCollection implements Runnable {
  private String[] queries;
  private String[] tempQueries;
  private boolean isDone = false;
  private URL dataURL;

  public QueryCollection(String urlSuffix, URL currentPage) {
    try {
      // Only the URL suffix need be supplied, since
      // the rest of the URL is derived from the current page.
      String protocol = currentPage.getProtocol();
      String host = currentPage.getHost();
      int port = currentPage.getPort();
      dataURL = new URL(protocol, host, port, urlSuffix);
      Thread queryRetriever = new Thread(this);
      queryRetriever.start();
    } catch(MalformedURLException mfe) {
      isDone = true;
    }
  }

  public void run() {
    try {
      tempQueries = retrieveQueries();
      queries = tempQueries;
    } catch(IOException ioe) {
      tempQueries = null;
      queries = null;
    }
    isDone = true;
  }

  public String[] getQueries() {
    return(queries);
  }

  public boolean isDone() {
    return(isDone);
  }
```

Listing 17.5 `QueryCollection.java` (continued)

```java
private String[] retrieveQueries() throws IOException {
  URLConnection connection = dataURL.openConnection();
  // Make sure browser doesn't cache this URL, since
  // I want different queries for each request.
  connection.setUseCaches(false);
  // Use ObjectInputStream so I can read a String[]
  // all at once.
  ObjectInputStream in =
    new ObjectInputStream(connection.getInputStream());
  try {
    // The return type of readObject is Object, so
    // I need a typecast to the actual type.
    String[] queryStrings = (String[])in.readObject();
    return(queryStrings);
  } catch(ClassNotFoundException cnfe) {
    return(null);
  }
}
}
```

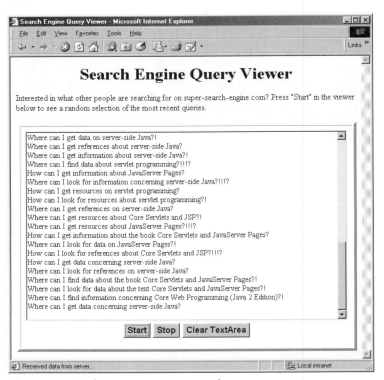

Figure 17–3 The `ShowQueries` applet in action.

Listing 17.6 `QueryGenerator.java`

```java
package coreservlets;

import java.io.*;
import javax.servlet.*;
import javax.servlet.http.*;

/** Servlet that generates an array of strings and
 *  sends them via an ObjectOutputStream to applet
 *  or other Java client.
 */

public class QueryGenerator extends HttpServlet {
  public void doGet(HttpServletRequest request,
                    HttpServletResponse response)
      throws ServletException, IOException {
    boolean useNumbering = true;
    String useNumberingFlag =
      request.getParameter("useNumbering");
    if ((useNumberingFlag == null) ||
        useNumberingFlag.equals("false")) {
      useNumbering = false;
    }
    String contentType =
      "application/x-java-serialized-object";
    response.setContentType(contentType);
    ObjectOutputStream out =
      new ObjectOutputStream(response.getOutputStream());
    String[] queries = getQueries(useNumbering);
    // If you send a nonstandard data structure, be
    // sure it is defined with "implements Serializable".
    out.writeObject(queries);
    out.flush();
  }

  public void doPost(HttpServletRequest request,
                     HttpServletResponse response)
      throws ServletException, IOException {
    doGet(request, response);
  }

  private String[] getQueries(boolean useNumbering) {
    String[] queries = new String[50];
    for(int i=0; i<queries.length; i++) {
      queries[i] = randomQuery();
      if (useNumbering) {
        queries[i] = "" + (i+1) + ": " + queries[i];
      }
    }
    return(queries);
  }
```

Listing 17.6 `QueryGenerator.java` **(continued)**

```java
// The real, honest-to-goodness queries people have sent :-)

private String randomQuery() {
  String[] locations = { "Where ", "How " };
  String[] actions =
    { "can I look for ", "can I find ", "can I get " };
  String[] sources =
    { "information ", "resources ", "data ", "references " };
  String[] prepositions = { "on ", "about ", "concerning " };
  String[] subjects =
    { "the book Core Servlets and JavaServer Pages",
      "the text Core Servlets and JavaServer Pages",
      "Core Servlets and JavaServer Pages",
      "Core Servlets and JSP",
      "the book Core Web Programming (Java 2 Edition)",
      "Core Web Programming (Java 2 Edition)",
      "servlet programming", "JavaServer Pages", "JSP",
      "Java alternatives to CGI", "server-side Java" };
  String[] endings = { "?", "?", "?", "?!", "?!!!?" };
  String[][] sentenceTemplates =
    { locations, actions, sources,
      prepositions, subjects, endings };
  String query = "";
  for(int i=0; i<sentenceTemplates.length; i++) {
    query = query + randomEntry(sentenceTemplates[i]);
  }
  return(query);
}

private String randomEntry(String[] strings) {
  int index = (int)(Math.random()*strings.length);
  return(strings[index]);
}
}
```

17.5 Sending Data by POST and Processing the Results Directly (HTTP Tunneling)

With GET data, an applet has two options for the results of a submission: tell the browser to display the results (construct a URL object and call `getApplet-Context().showDocument`) or process the results itself (construct a URL object, get a URLConnection, open an input stream, and read the results).

These two options are discussed in Sections 17.1 and 17.3, respectively. With POST data, however, only the second option is available since the URL constructor has no method to let you associate POST data with it. Sending POST data has some of the same advantages and disadvantages as when applets send GET data. The two main disadvantages are that the server-side program must be on the host from which the applet was loaded, and that the applet is required to display all the results itself: it cannot pass HTML to the browser in a portable manner. On the plus side, the server-side program can be simpler (not needing to wrap the results in HTML) and the applet can update its display without requiring the page to be reloaded. Furthermore, applets that communicate using POST can use serialized data streams to send data *to* a servlet, in addition to reading serialized data *from* servlets. This is quite an advantage, since serialized data simplifies communication and HTTP tunneling lets you piggyback on existing connections through firewalls even when direct socket connections are prohibited. Applets using GET can read serialized data (see Section 17.4) but are unable to send it since it is not legal to append arbitrary binary data to URLs.

Thirteen steps are required for the applet to send POST data to the server and read the results, as shown below. Although there are many required steps, each step is relatively simple. The code is slightly simplified by the omission of `try/catch` blocks around the statements.

1. **Create a URL object referring to the applet's home host.**
   As before, since the URL must refer to the host the applet came from, it makes the most sense to specify a URL suffix and construct the rest of the URL automatically.

   ```
   URL currentPage = getCodeBase();
   String protocol = currentPage.getProtocol();
   String host = currentPage.getHost();
   int port = currentPage.getPort();
   String urlSuffix = "/servlet/SomeServlet";
   URL dataURL =
       new URL(protocol, host, port, urlSuffix);
   ```

2. **Create a URLConnection object.** This object will be used to obtain input and output streams that connect to the server.

   ```
   URLConnection connection = dataURL.openConnection();
   ```

3. **Instruct the browser not to cache the results.**

   ```
   connection.setUseCaches(false);
   ```

4. **Tell the system to permit you to send data, not just read it.**

   ```
   connection.setDoOutput(true);
   ```

5. **Create a `ByteArrayOutputStream` to buffer the data that will be sent to the server.** The purpose of the `ByteArrayOutputStream` here is the same as it is with the persistent (keep-alive) HTTP connections shown in Section 7.4 — to determine the size of the output so that the `Content-Length` header can be set. The `ByteArrayOutputStream` constructor specifies an initial buffer size, but this value is not critical since the buffer will grow automatically if necessary.

```
ByteArrayOutputStream byteStream =
  new ByteArrayOutputStream(512);
```

6. **Attach an output stream to the `ByteArrayOutputStream`.** Use a `PrintWriter` to send normal form data. To send serialized data structures, use an `ObjectOutputStream` instead.

```
PrintWriter out = new PrintWriter(byteStream, true);
```

7. **Put the data into the buffer.** For form data, use `print`. For high-level serialized objects, use `writeObject`.

```
String val1 = URLEncoder.encode(someVal1);
String val2 = URLEncoder.encode(someVal2);
String data = "param1=" + val1 +
              "&param2=" + val2; // Note '&'
out.print(data);  // Note print, not println
out.flush(); // Necessary since no println used
```

8. **Set the `Content-Length` header.** This header is required for POST data, even though it is unused with GET requests.

```
connection.setRequestProperty
  ("Content-Length", String.valueOf(byteStream.size()));
```

9. **Set the `Content-Type` header.** Netscape uses `multipart/form-data` by default, but regular form data requires a setting of `application/x-www-form-urlencoded`, which is the default with Internet Explorer. So, for portability you should set this value explicitly when sending regular form data. The value is irrelevant when sending serialized data.

```
connection.setRequestProperty
  ("Content-Type", "application/x-www-form-urlencoded");
```

10. **Send the real data.**

```
byteStream.writeTo(connection.getOutputStream());
```

11. **Open an input stream.** You typically use a `BufferedReader` for ASCII or binary data and an `ObjectInputStream` for serialized Java objects.

```
BufferedReader in =
    new BufferedReader(new InputStreamReader
                        (connection.getInputStream()));
```

12. **Read the result.**
    The specific details will depend on what type of data the server sends. Here is an example that does something with each line sent by the server:

```
String line;
while((line = in.readLine()) != null) {
  doSomethingWith(line);
}
```

13. **Pat yourself on the back.** Yes, the procedure for handling POST is long and tedious. Fortunately, it is a relatively rote process. Besides, you can always download an example from www.coreservlets.com and use it as a starting point.

The next section gives an example of an applet that performs these steps.

17.6 An Applet That Sends POST Data

Listing 17.7 presents an applet that follows the approach outlined in the previous section. The applet uses a `URLConnection` and an attached `ByteArrayOutputStream` to send POST data to a URL the user specifies. The applet also makes use of the `LabeledTextField` class, shown previously in Listing 2.2 and available for download from http://www.coreserv-lets.com/.

Figures 17–4 and 17–5 show the results of submitting the data to the `ShowParameters` servlet and `EchoServer` HTTP server, respectively.

Listing 17.7 `SendPost.java`

```java
import java.applet.Applet;
import java.awt.*;
import java.awt.event.*;
import java.net.*;
import java.io.*;

/** Applet that reads firstName, lastName, and
 *  emailAddress parameters and sends them via
 *  POST to the host, port, and URI specified.
 */

public class SendPost extends Applet
                      implements ActionListener {
  private LabeledTextField firstNameField, lastNameField,
                           emailAddressField, hostField,
                           portField, uriField;
  private Button sendButton;
  private TextArea resultsArea;
  URL currentPage;

  public void init() {
    setBackground(Color.white);
    setLayout(new BorderLayout());
    Panel inputPanel = new Panel();
    inputPanel.setLayout(new GridLayout(9, 1));
    inputPanel.setFont(new Font("Serif", Font.BOLD, 14));
    firstNameField =
      new LabeledTextField("First Name:", 15);
    inputPanel.add(firstNameField);
    lastNameField =
      new LabeledTextField("Last Name:", 15);
    inputPanel.add(lastNameField);
    emailAddressField =
      new LabeledTextField("Email Address:", 25);
    inputPanel.add(emailAddressField);
    Canvas separator1 = new Canvas();
    inputPanel.add(separator1);
    hostField =
      new LabeledTextField("Host:", 15);

    // Applets loaded over the network can only connect
    // to the server from which they were loaded.
    hostField.getTextField().setEditable(false);

    currentPage = getCodeBase();
    // getHost returns empty string for applets from local disk.
    String host = currentPage.getHost();
    String resultsMessage = "Results will be shown here...";
    if (host.length() == 0) {
      resultsMessage = "Error: you must load this applet\n" +
```

Listing 17.7　`SendPost.java` (continued)

```
                        "from a real Web server via HTTP,\n" +
                        "not from the local disk using\n" +
                        "a 'file:' URL. It is fine,\n" +
                        "however, if the Web server is\n" +
                        "running on your local system.";
      setEnabled(false);
    }
    hostField.getTextField().setText(host);
    inputPanel.add(hostField);
    portField =
      new LabeledTextField("Port (-1 means default):", 4);
    String portString = String.valueOf(currentPage.getPort());
    portField.getTextField().setText(portString);
    inputPanel.add(portField);
    uriField =
      new LabeledTextField("URI:", 40);
    String defaultURI = "/servlet/coreservlets.ShowParameters";
    uriField.getTextField().setText(defaultURI);
    inputPanel.add(uriField);
    Canvas separator2 = new Canvas();
    inputPanel.add(separator2);
    sendButton = new Button("Submit Data");
    sendButton.addActionListener(this);
    Panel buttonPanel = new Panel();
    buttonPanel.add(sendButton);
    inputPanel.add(buttonPanel);
    add(inputPanel, BorderLayout.NORTH);
    resultsArea = new TextArea();
    resultsArea.setFont(new Font("Monospaced", Font.PLAIN, 14));
    resultsArea.setText(resultsMessage);
    add(resultsArea, BorderLayout.CENTER);
  }

  public void actionPerformed(ActionEvent event) {
    try {
      String protocol = currentPage.getProtocol();
      String host = hostField.getTextField().getText();
      String portString = portField.getTextField().getText();
      int port;
      try {
        port = Integer.parseInt(portString);
      } catch(NumberFormatException nfe) {
        port = -1; // I.e., default port of 80
      }
      String uri = uriField.getTextField().getText();
      URL dataURL = new URL(protocol, host, port, uri);
      URLConnection connection = dataURL.openConnection();

      // Make sure browser doesn't cache this URL.
      connection.setUseCaches(false);
```

Listing 17.7 `SendPost.java` **(continued)**

```java
    // Tell browser to allow me to send data to server.
    connection.setDoOutput(true);

    ByteArrayOutputStream byteStream =
      new ByteArrayOutputStream(512); // Grows if necessary
    // Stream that writes into buffer
    PrintWriter out = new PrintWriter(byteStream, true);
    String postData =
      "firstName=" + encodedValue(firstNameField) +
      "&lastName=" + encodedValue(lastNameField) +
      "&emailAddress=" + encodedValue(emailAddressField);

    // Write POST data into local buffer
    out.print(postData);
    out.flush(); // Flush since above used print, not println

    // POST requests are required to have Content-Length
    String lengthString =
      String.valueOf(byteStream.size());
    connection.setRequestProperty
      ("Content-Length", lengthString);

    // Netscape sets the Content-Type to multipart/form-data
    // by default. So, if you want to send regular form data,
    // you need to set it to
    // application/x-www-form-urlencoded, which is the
    // default for Internet Explorer. If you send
    // serialized POST data with an ObjectOutputStream,
    // the Content-Type is irrelevant, so you could
    // omit this step.
    connection.setRequestProperty
      ("Content-Type", "application/x-www-form-urlencoded");

    // Write POST data to real output stream
    byteStream.writeTo(connection.getOutputStream());

    BufferedReader in =
      new BufferedReader(new InputStreamReader
                          (connection.getInputStream()));
    String line;
    String linefeed = "\n";
    resultsArea.setText("");
    while((line = in.readLine()) != null) {
      resultsArea.append(line);
      resultsArea.append(linefeed);
    }
  } catch(IOException ioe) {
    // Print debug info in Java Console
    System.out.println("IOException: " + ioe);
  }
}
```

Listing 17.7 `SendPost.java` **(continued)**

```
    // LabeledTextField is really a Panel with a Label and
    // TextField inside it. This extracts the TextField part,
    // gets the text inside it, URL-encodes it, and
    // returns the result.

    private String encodedValue(LabeledTextField field) {
      String rawValue = field.getTextField().getText();
      return(URLEncoder.encode(rawValue));
    }
}
```

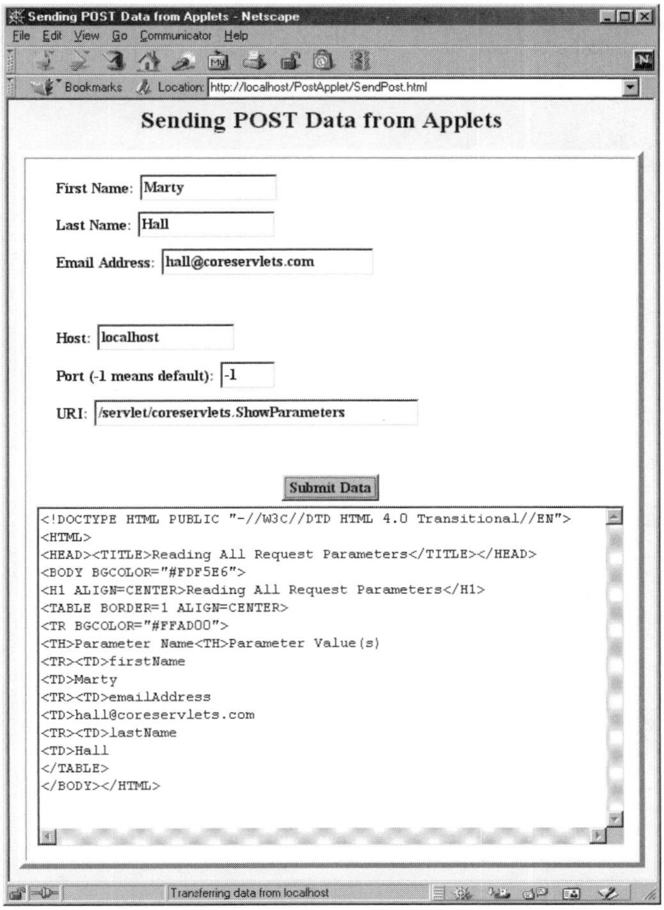

Figure 17–4 Result of using `SendPost` to send POST data to the `ShowParameters` servlet, which is presented in Section 3.4 (Example: Reading All Parameters).

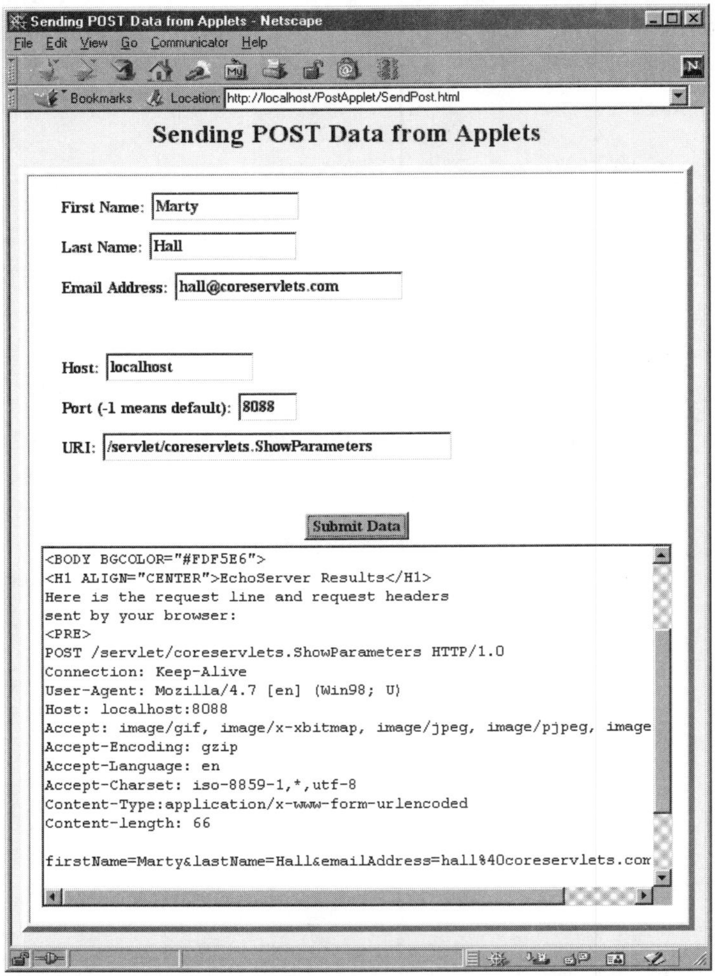

Figure 17–5 Result of using `SendPost` to send `POST` data to the `EchoServer` HTTP server, which is presented in Section 16.12 (A Debugging Web Server).

17.7 Bypassing the HTTP Server

Although applets can only open network connections to the same machine they were loaded from, they need not necessarily connect on the same *port* (e.g., 80, the HTTP port). So, applets are permitted to use raw sockets, JDBC, or RMI to communicate with custom clients running on the server host.

Applets do these operations in exactly the same manner as do normal Java programs, so you can use whatever approaches to socket, JDBC, and RMI programming that you are already familiar with, provided that the network server is on the same host as the Web server that delivered the applet.

JDBC AND
DATABASE
CONNECTION
POOLING

Topics in This Chapter

- The seven basic steps in connecting to databases
- Simple database retrieval example
- Some utilities that simplify JDBC usage
- Formatting a database result as plain text or HTML
- An interactive graphical query viewer
- Precompiled queries
- A connection pool library
- A comparison of servlet performance with and without connection pooling
- Sharing connection pools

Chapter 18

J DBC provides a standard library for accessing relational databases. Using the JDBC API, you can access a wide variety of different SQL databases with exactly the same Java syntax. It is important to note that although JDBC standardizes the mechanism for connecting to databases, the syntax for sending queries and committing transactions, and the data structure representing the result, it does *not* attempt to standardize the SQL syntax. So, you can use any SQL extensions your database vendor supports. However, since most queries follow standard SQL syntax, using JDBC lets you change database hosts, ports, and even database vendors with minimal changes in your code.

DILBERT reprinted by permission of United Syndicate, Inc.

Officially, JDBC is not an acronym and thus does not stand for anything. Unofficially, "Java Database Connectivity" is commonly used as the long form of the name.

> **Core Note**
>
> *JDBC is not an acronym.*

Although a complete tutorial on database programming is beyond the scope of this chapter, I'll cover the basics of using JDBC here, assuming you are already familiar with SQL. For more details on JDBC, see `http://java.sun.com/products/jdbc/`, the on-line API for `java.sql`, or the JDBC tutorial at `http://java.sun.com/docs/books/tutorial/jdbc/`. If you don't already have access to a database, you might find mySQL a good choice for practice. It is free for non-Microsoft operating systems as well as for educational or research use on Windows. For details, see `http://www.mysql.com/`.

18.1 Basic Steps in Using JDBC

There are seven standard steps in querying databases:

1. Load the JDBC driver.
2. Define the connection URL.
3. Establish the connection.
4. Create a statement object.
5. Execute a query or update.
6. Process the results.
7. Close the connection.

Here are some details of the process.

Load the Driver

The driver is the piece of software that knows how to talk to the actual database server. To load the driver, all you need to do is to load the appropriate class; a `static` block in the class itself automatically makes a driver instance and registers it with the JDBC driver manager. To make your code as flexible as possible, it is best to avoid hard-coding the reference to the class name.

These requirements bring up two interesting questions. First, how do you load a class without making an instance of it? Second, how can you refer to a class whose name isn't known when the code is compiled? The answer to both questions is: use `Class.forName`. This method takes a string representing a fully qualified class name (i.e., one that includes package names) and loads the corresponding class. This call could throw a `ClassNotFound-Exception`, so should be inside a `try/catch` block. Here is an example:

```
try {
  Class.forName("connect.microsoft.MicrosoftDriver");
  Class.forName("oracle.jdbc.driver.OracleDriver");
  Class.forName("com.sybase.jdbc.SybDriver");
} catch(ClassNotFoundException cnfe) {
  System.err.println("Error loading driver: " + cnfe);
}
```

One of the beauties of the JDBC approach is that the database server requires no changes whatsoever. Instead, the JDBC driver (which is on the client) translates calls written in the Java programming language into the specific format required by the server. This approach means that you have to obtain a JDBC driver specific to the database you are using; you will need to check its documentation for the fully qualified class name to use. Most database vendors supply free JDBC drivers for their databases, but there are many third-party vendors of drivers for older databases. For an up-to-date list, see `http://java.sun.com/products/jdbc/drivers.html`. Many of these driver vendors supply free trial versions (usually with an expiration date or with some limitations on the number of simultaneous connections), so it is easy to learn JDBC without paying for a driver.

In principle, you can use `Class.forName` for any class in your `CLASSPATH`. In practice, however, most JDBC driver vendors distribute their drivers inside JAR files. So, be sure to include the path to the JAR file in your `CLASSPATH` setting.

Define the Connection URL

Once you have loaded the JDBC driver, you need to specify the location of the database server. URLs referring to databases use the `jdbc:` protocol and have the server host, port, and database name (or reference) embedded within the URL. The exact format will be defined in the documentation that comes with the particular driver, but here are two representative examples:

```
String host = "dbhost.yourcompany.com";
String dbName = "someName";
int port = 1234;
String oracleURL = "jdbc:oracle:thin:@" + host +
                   ":" + port + ":" + dbName;
String sybaseURL = "jdbc:sybase:Tds:" + host +
                   ":" + port + ":" + "?SERVICENAME=" + dbName;
```

JDBC is most often used from servlets or regular desktop applications but is also sometimes employed from applets. If you use JDBC from an applet, remember that, to prevent hostile applets from browsing behind corporate firewalls, browsers prevent applets from making network connections anywhere except to the server from which they were loaded. Consequently, to use JDBC from applets, either the database server needs to reside on the same machine as the HTTP server or you need to use a proxy server that reroutes database requests to the actual server.

Establish the Connection

To make the actual network connection, pass the URL, the database username, and the password to the getConnection method of the Driver-Manager class, as illustrated in the following example. Note that getConnection throws an SQLException, so you need to use a try/catch block. I'm omitting this block from the following example since the methods in the following steps throw the same exception, and thus you typically use a single try/catch block for all of them.

```
String username = "jay_debesee";
String password = "secret";
Connection connection =
  DriverManager.getConnection(oracleURL, username, password);
```

An optional part of this step is to look up information about the database by using the getMetaData method of Connection. This method returns a DatabaseMetaData object which has methods to let you discover the name and version of the database itself (getDatabaseProductName, getDatabaseProductVersion) or of the JDBC driver (getDriverName, getDriverVersion). Here is an example:

```
DatabaseMetaData dbMetaData = connection.getMetaData();
String productName =
  dbMetaData.getDatabaseProductName();
System.out.println("Database: " + productName);
String productVersion =
  dbMetaData.getDatabaseProductVersion();
System.out.println("Version: " + productVersion);
```

Other useful methods in the Connection class include prepareStatement (create a PreparedStatement; discussed in Section 18.6), prepareCall (create a CallableStatement), rollback (undo statements since last commit), commit (finalize operations since last commit), close (terminate connection), and isClosed (has the connection either timed out or been explicitly closed?).

Create a Statement

A `Statement` object is used to send queries and commands to the database and is created from the `Connection` as follows:

```
Statement statement = connection.createStatement();
```

Execute a Query

Once you have a `Statement` object, you can use it to send SQL queries by using the `executeQuery` method, which returns an object of type `Result-Set`. Here is an example:

```
String query = "SELECT col1, col2, col3 FROM sometable";
ResultSet resultSet = statement.executeQuery(query);
```

To modify the database, use `executeUpdate` instead of `executeQuery`, and supply a string that uses `UPDATE`, `INSERT`, or `DELETE`. Other useful methods in the `Statement` class include `execute` (execute an arbitrary command) and `setQueryTimeout` (set a maximum delay to wait for results). You can also create parameterized queries where values are supplied to a precompiled fixed-format query. See Section 18.6 for details.

Process the Results

The simplest way to handle the results is to process them one row at a time, using the `ResultSet`'s `next` method to move through the table a row at a time. Within a row, `ResultSet` provides various get*Xxx* methods that take a column index or column name as an argument and return the result as a variety of different Java types. For instance, use `getInt` if the value should be an integer, `getString` for a `String`, and so on for most other data types. If you just want to display the results, you can use `getString` regardless of the actual column type. However, if you use the version that takes a column index, note that columns are indexed starting at 1 (following the SQL convention), not at 0 as with arrays, vectors, and most other data structures in the Java programming language.

Core Warning

The first column in a `ResultSet` *row has index 1, not 0.*

Here is an example that prints the values of the first three columns in all rows of a `ResultSet`.

```
while(resultSet.next()) {
  System.out.println(results.getString(1) + " " +
                     results.getString(2) + " " +
                     results.getString(3));
}
```

In addition to the get*Xxx* and next methods, other useful methods in the ResultSet class include findColumn (get the index of the named column), wasNull (was the last get*Xxx* result SQL NULL? Alternatively, for strings you can simply compare the return value to null), and getMetaData (retrieve information about the ResultSet in a ResultSetMetaData object).

The getMetaData method is particularly useful. Given only a ResultSet, you have to know about the name, number, and type of the columns to be able to process the table properly. For most fixed-format queries, this is a reasonable expectation. For ad hoc queries, however, it is useful to be able to dynamically discover high-level information about the result. That is the role of the ResultSetMetaData class: it lets you determine the number, names, and types of the columns in the ResultSet. Useful ResultSetMetaData methods include getColumnCount (the number of columns), getColumn-Name(colNumber) (a column name, indexed starting at 1), getColumnType (an int to compare against entries in java.sql.Types), isReadOnly (is entry a read-only value?), isSearchable (can it be used in a WHERE clause?), isNullable (is a null value permitted?), and several others that give details on the type and precision of the column. ResultSetMetaData does *not* include the number of rows, however; the only way to determine that is to repeatedly call next on the ResultSet until it returns false.

Close the Connection

To close the connection explicitly, you would do:

```
connection.close();
```

You should postpone this step if you expect to perform additional database operations, since the overhead of opening a connection is usually large. In fact, reusing existing connections is such an important optimization that Section 18.7 develops a library just for that purpose and Section 18.8 shows some typical timing results.

18.2 Basic JDBC Example

Listing 18.3 presents a simple class called `FruitTest` that follows the seven steps outlined in the previous section to show a simple table called `fruits`. It uses the command-line arguments to determine the host, port, database name, and driver type to use, as shown in Listings 18.1 and 18.2. Rather than putting the driver name and the logic for generating an appropriately formatted database URL directly in this class, these two tasks are spun off to a separate class called `DriverUtilities`, shown in Listing 18.4. This separation minimizes the places that changes have to be made when different drivers are used.

This example does not depend on the way in which the database table was actually created, only on its resultant format. So, for example, an interactive database tool could have been used. In fact, however, JDBC was also used to create the tables, as shown in Listing 18.5. For now, just skim quickly over this listing, as it makes use of utilities not discussed until the next section.

Also, a quick reminder to those who are not familiar with packages. Since `FruitTest` is in the `coreservlets` package, it resides in a subdirectory called `coreservlets`. Before compiling the file, I set my CLASSPATH to include the directory *containing* the `coreservlets` directory (the JAR file containing the JDBC drivers should be in the CLASSPATH also, of course). With this setup, I compile simply by doing "`javac FruitTest.java`" from within the `coreservlets` subdirectory. But to run `FruitTest`, I need to refer to the full package name with "`java coreservlets.FruitTest ...`".

Listing 18.1 `FruitTest` **result (connecting to Oracle on Solaris)**

```
Prompt> java coreservlets.FruitTest dbhost1.apl.jhu.edu PTE
        hall xxxx oracle
Database: Oracle
Version: Oracle7 Server Release 7.2.3.0.0 - Production Release
PL/SQL Release 2.2.3.0.0 - Production

Comparing Apples and Oranges
============================
QUARTER   APPLES   APPLESALES   ORANGES   ORANGESALES   TOPSELLER
   1      32248    $3547.28     18459     $3138.03      Maria
   2      35009    $3850.99     18722     $3182.74      Bob
   3      39393    $4333.23     18999     $3229.83      Joe
   4      42001    $4620.11     19333     $3286.61      Maria
```

Listing 18.2   `FruitTest` result (connecting to Sybase on NT)

```
Prompt> java coreservlets.FruitTest dbhost2.apl.jhu.edu 605741
        hall xxxx sybase
Database: Adaptive Server Anywhere
Version: 6.0.2.2188


Comparing Apples and Oranges
==============================
quarter   apples   applesales   oranges   orangesales   topseller
      1    32248     $3547.28     18459      $3138.03    Maria
      2    35009     $3850.99     18722      $3182.74    Bob
      3    39393     $4333.23     18999      $3229.83    Joe
      4    42001     $4620.11     19333      $3286.61    Maria
```

Listing 18.3   `FruitTest.java`

```java
package coreservlets;

import java.sql.*;

/** A JDBC example that connects to either an Oracle or
 *  a Sybase database and prints out the values of
 *  predetermined columns in the "fruits" table.
 */

public class FruitTest {

  /** Reads the hostname, database name, username, password,
   *  and vendor identifier from the command line. It
   *  uses the vendor identifier to determine which
   *  driver to load and how to format the URL. The
   *  driver, URL, username, host, and password are then
   *  passed to the showFruitTable method.
   */

  public static void main(String[] args) {
    if (args.length < 5) {
      printUsage();
      return;
    }
    String vendorName = args[4];
    int vendor = DriverUtilities.getVendor(vendorName);
    if (vendor == DriverUtilities.UNKNOWN) {
      printUsage();
      return;
    }
```

Listing 18.3 `FruitTest.java` (continued)

```java
    String driver = DriverUtilities.getDriver(vendor);
    String host = args[0];
    String dbName = args[1];
    String url = DriverUtilities.makeURL(host, dbName, vendor);
    String username = args[2];
    String password = args[3];
    showFruitTable(driver, url, username, password);
  }

  /** Get the table and print all the values. */

  public static void showFruitTable(String driver,
                                    String url,
                                    String username,
                                    String password) {
    try {
      // Load database driver if not already loaded.
      Class.forName(driver);
      // Establish network connection to database.
      Connection connection =
        DriverManager.getConnection(url, username, password);
      // Look up info about the database as a whole.
      DatabaseMetaData dbMetaData = connection.getMetaData();
      String productName =
        dbMetaData.getDatabaseProductName();
      System.out.println("Database: " + productName);
      String productVersion =
        dbMetaData.getDatabaseProductVersion();
      System.out.println("Version: " + productVersion + "\n");
      System.out.println("Comparing Apples and Oranges\n" +
                         "============================");
      Statement statement = connection.createStatement();
      String query = "SELECT * FROM fruits";
      // Send query to database and store results.
      ResultSet resultSet = statement.executeQuery(query);
      // Look up information about a particular table.
      ResultSetMetaData resultsMetaData =
        resultSet.getMetaData();
      int columnCount = resultsMetaData.getColumnCount();
      // Column index starts at 1 (a la SQL) not 0 (a la Java).
      for(int i=1; i<columnCount+1; i++) {
        System.out.print(resultsMetaData.getColumnName(i) +
                         "   ");
      }
      System.out.println();
      // Print results.
      while(resultSet.next()) {
```

Listing 18.3 `FruitTest.java` (continued)

```java
        // Quarter
        System.out.print("     " + resultSet.getInt(1));
        // Number of Apples
        System.out.print("      " + resultSet.getInt(2));
        // Apple Sales
        System.out.print("    $" + resultSet.getFloat(3));
        // Number of Oranges
        System.out.print("      " + resultSet.getInt(4));
        // Orange Sales
        System.out.print("    $" + resultSet.getFloat(5));
        // Top Salesman
        System.out.println("       " + resultSet.getString(6));
      }
    } catch(ClassNotFoundException cnfe) {
      System.err.println("Error loading driver: " + cnfe);
    } catch(SQLException sqle) {
      System.err.println("Error connecting: " + sqle);
    }
  }

  private static void printUsage() {
    System.out.println("Usage: FruitTest host dbName " +
                       "username password oracle|sybase.");
  }
}
```

Listing 18.4 `DriverUtilities.java`

```java
package coreservlets;

/** Some simple utilities for building Oracle and Sybase
 *  JDBC connections. This is <I>not</I> general-purpose
 *  code -- it is specific to my local setup.
 */

public class DriverUtilities {
  public static final int ORACLE = 1;
  public static final int SYBASE = 2;
  public static final int UNKNOWN = -1;
```

Listing 18.4 `DriverUtilities.java` (continued)

```java
/** Build a URL in the format needed by the
 *  Oracle and Sybase drivers I am using.
 */

public static String makeURL(String host, String dbName,
                             int vendor) {
  if (vendor == ORACLE) {
    return("jdbc:oracle:thin:@" + host + ":1521:" + dbName);
  } else if (vendor == SYBASE) {
    return("jdbc:sybase:Tds:" + host  + ":1521" +
           "?SERVICENAME=" + dbName);
  } else {
    return(null);
  }
}

/** Get the fully qualified name of a driver. */

public static String getDriver(int vendor) {
  if (vendor == ORACLE) {
    return("oracle.jdbc.driver.OracleDriver");
  } else if (vendor == SYBASE) {
    return("com.sybase.jdbc.SybDriver");
  } else {
    return(null);
  }
}

/** Map name to int value. */

public static int getVendor(String vendorName) {
  if (vendorName.equalsIgnoreCase("oracle")) {
    return(ORACLE);
  } else if (vendorName.equalsIgnoreCase("sybase")) {
    return(SYBASE);
  } else {
    return(UNKNOWN);
  }
}
}
```

Listing 18.5 `FruitCreation.java`

```java
package coreservlets;

import java.sql.*;

/** Creates a simple table named "fruits" in either
 *  an Oracle or a Sybase database.
 */

public class FruitCreation {
  public static void main(String[] args) {
    if (args.length < 5) {
      printUsage();
      return;
    }
    String vendorName = args[4];
    int vendor = DriverUtilities.getVendor(vendorName);
    if (vendor == DriverUtilities.UNKNOWN) {
      printUsage();
      return;
    }
    String driver = DriverUtilities.getDriver(vendor);
    String host = args[0];
    String dbName = args[1];
    String url =
      DriverUtilities.makeURL(host, dbName, vendor);
    String username = args[2];
    String password = args[3];
    String format =
      "(quarter int, " +
      "apples int, applesales float, " +
      "oranges int, orangesales float, " +
      "topseller varchar(16))";
    String[] rows =
    { "(1, 32248, 3547.28, 18459, 3138.03, 'Maria')",
      "(2, 35009, 3850.99, 18722, 3182.74, 'Bob')",
      "(3, 39393, 4333.23, 18999, 3229.83, 'Joe')",
      "(4, 42001, 4620.11, 19333, 3286.61, 'Maria')" };
    Connection connection =
      DatabaseUtilities.createTable(driver, url,
                                    username, password,
                                    "fruits", format, rows,
                                    false);
    // Test to verify table was created properly. Reuse
    // old connection for efficiency.
    DatabaseUtilities.printTable(connection, "fruits",
                                 11, true);
  }

  private static void printUsage() {
    System.out.println("Usage: FruitCreation host dbName " +
                       "username password oracle|sybase.");
  }
}
```

18.3 Some JDBC Utilities

In many applications, you don't need to process query results a row at a time. For example, in servlets and JSP pages, it is common to simply format the database results (treating all values as strings) and present them to the user in an HTML table (see Sections 18.4 and 18.8), in an Excel spreadsheet (see Section 11.2), or distributed throughout the page. In such a case, it simplifies processing to have methods that retrieve and store an entire `ResultSet` for later display.

This section presents two classes that provide this basic functionality along with a few formatting, display, and table creation utilities. The core class is `DatabaseUtilities`, which implements static methods for four common tasks:

1. **`getQueryResults`**
   This method connects to a database, executes a query, retrieves all the rows as arrays of strings, and puts them inside a `DBResults` object (see Listing 18.7). This method also places the database product name, database version, the names of all the columns and the `Connection` object into the `DBResults` object. There are two versions of `getQueryResults`: one that makes a new connection and another that uses an existing connection.

2. **`createTable`**
   Given a table name, a string denoting the column formats, and an array of strings denoting the row values, this method connects to a database, removes any existing versions of the designated table, issues a `CREATE TABLE` command with the designated format, then sends a series of `INSERT INTO` commands for each of the rows. Again, there are two versions: one that makes a new connection and another that uses an existing connection.

3. **`printTable`**
   Given a table name, this method connects to the specified database, retrieves all the rows, and prints them on the standard output. It retrieves the results by turning the table name into a query of the form "`SELECT * FROM tableName`" and passing it to `getQueryResults`.

4. **printTableData**

   Given a DBResults object from a previous query, this method prints it on the standard output. This is the underlying method used by printTable, but it is also useful for debugging arbitrary database results.

Listing 18.6 gives the main code, and Listing 18.7 presents the auxiliary DBResults class that stores the accumulated results and returns them as arrays of strings (getRow) or wrapped up inside an HTML table (toHTML-Table). For example, the following two statements perform a database query, retrieve the results, and format them inside an HTML table that uses the column names as headings with a cyan background color.

```
DBResults results =
  DatabaseUtilities.getQueryResults(driver, url,
                                    username, password,
                                    query, true);
out.println(results.toHTMLTable("CYAN"));
```

Since an HTML table can do double duty as an Excel spreadsheet (see Section 11.2), the toHTMLTable method provides an extremely simple method for building tables or spreadsheets from database results.

Remember that the source code for DatabaseUtilities and DBResults, like all the source code in the book, can be downloaded from www.core-servlets.com and used or adapted without restriction.

Listing 18.6 DatabaseUtilities.java

```java
package coreservlets;

import java.sql.*;

public class DatabaseUtilities {

  /** Connect to database, execute specified query,
   *  and accumulate results into DBRresults object.
   *  If the database connection is left open (use the
   *  close argument to specify), you can retrieve the
   *  connection with DBResults.getConnection.
   */

  public static DBResults getQueryResults(String driver,
                                          String url,
                                          String username,
                                          String password,
                                          String query,
                                          boolean close) {
```

Listing 18.6 `DatabaseUtilities.java` (continued)

```java
    try {
      Class.forName(driver);
      Connection connection =
        DriverManager.getConnection(url, username, password);
      return(getQueryResults(connection, query, close));
    } catch(ClassNotFoundException cnfe) {
      System.err.println("Error loading driver: " + cnfe);
      return(null);
    } catch(SQLException sqle) {
      System.err.println("Error connecting: " + sqle);
      return(null);
    }
  }

  /** Retrieves results as in previous method but uses
   *  an existing connection instead of opening a new one.
   */

  public static DBResults getQueryResults(Connection connection,
                                          String query,
                                          boolean close) {
    try {
      DatabaseMetaData dbMetaData = connection.getMetaData();
      String productName =
        dbMetaData.getDatabaseProductName();
      String productVersion =
        dbMetaData.getDatabaseProductVersion();
      Statement statement = connection.createStatement();
      ResultSet resultSet = statement.executeQuery(query);
      ResultSetMetaData resultsMetaData =
        resultSet.getMetaData();
      int columnCount = resultsMetaData.getColumnCount();
      String[] columnNames = new String[columnCount];
      // Column index starts at 1 (a la SQL) not 0 (a la Java).
      for(int i=1; i<columnCount+1; i++) {
        columnNames[i-1] =
          resultsMetaData.getColumnName(i).trim();
      }
      DBResults dbResults =
        new DBResults(connection, productName, productVersion,
                      columnCount, columnNames);
      while(resultSet.next()) {
        String[] row = new String[columnCount];
        // Again, ResultSet index starts at 1, not 0.
        for(int i=1; i<columnCount+1; i++) {
          String entry = resultSet.getString(i);
          if (entry != null) {
            entry = entry.trim();
          }
```

Listing 18.6 `DatabaseUtilities.java` **(continued)**

```
      row[i-1] = entry;
    }
    dbResults.addRow(row);
  }
  if (close) {
    connection.close();
  }
  return(dbResults);
} catch(SQLException sqle) {
  System.err.println("Error connecting: " + sqle);
  return(null);
}
}

/** Build a table with the specified format and rows. */

public static Connection createTable(String driver,
                                     String url,
                                     String username,
                                     String password,
                                     String tableName,
                                     String tableFormat,
                                     String[] tableRows,
                                     boolean close) {
  try {
    Class.forName(driver);
    Connection connection =
      DriverManager.getConnection(url, username, password);
    return(createTable(connection, username, password,
                       tableName, tableFormat,
                       tableRows, close));
  } catch(ClassNotFoundException cnfe) {
    System.err.println("Error loading driver: " + cnfe);
    return(null);
  } catch(SQLException sqle) {
    System.err.println("Error connecting: " + sqle);
    return(null);
  }
}

/** Like the previous method, but uses existing connection. */

public static Connection createTable(Connection connection,
                                     String username,
                                     String password,
                                     String tableName,
                                     String tableFormat,
                                     String[] tableRows,
                                     boolean close) {
```

Listing 18.6 `DatabaseUtilities.java` **(continued)**

```java
    try {

      Statement statement = connection.createStatement();
      // Drop previous table if it exists, but don't get
      // error if it doesn't. Thus the separate try/catch here.
      try {
        statement.execute("DROP TABLE " + tableName);
      } catch(SQLException sqle) {}
      String createCommand =
        "CREATE TABLE " + tableName + " " + tableFormat;
      statement.execute(createCommand);
      String insertPrefix =
        "INSERT INTO " + tableName + " VALUES";
      for(int i=0; i<tableRows.length; i++) {
        statement.execute(insertPrefix + tableRows[i]);
      }
      if (close) {
        connection.close();
        return(null);
      } else {
        return(connection);
      }
    } catch(SQLException sqle) {
      System.err.println("Error creating table: " + sqle);
      return(null);
    }
  }

  public static void printTable(String driver,
                                String url,
                                String username,
                                String password,
                                String tableName,
                                int entryWidth,
                                boolean close) {
    String query = "SELECT * FROM " + tableName;
    DBResults results =
      getQueryResults(driver, url, username,
                      password, query, close);
    printTableData(tableName, results, entryWidth, true);
  }

  /** Prints out all entries in a table. Each entry will
   *  be printed in a column that is entryWidth characters
   *  wide, so be sure to provide a value at least as big
   *  as the widest result.
   */
```

Listing 18.6 `DatabaseUtilities.java` **(continued)**

```
public static void printTable(Connection connection,
                              String tableName,
                              int entryWidth,
                              boolean close) {
  String query = "SELECT * FROM " + tableName;
  DBResults results =
    getQueryResults(connection, query, close);
  printTableData(tableName, results, entryWidth, true);
}

public static void printTableData(String tableName,
                                  DBResults results,
                                  int entryWidth,
                                  boolean printMetaData) {
  if (results == null) {
    return;
  }
  if (printMetaData) {
    System.out.println("Database: " +
                       results.getProductName());
    System.out.println("Version: " +
                       results.getProductVersion());
    System.out.println();
  }
  System.out.println(tableName + ":");
  String underline =
    padString("", tableName.length()+1, "=");
  System.out.println(underline);
  int columnCount = results.getColumnCount();
  String separator =
    makeSeparator(entryWidth, columnCount);
  System.out.println(separator);
  String row = makeRow(results.getColumnNames(), entryWidth);
  System.out.println(row);
  System.out.println(separator);
  int rowCount = results.getRowCount();
  for(int i=0; i<rowCount; i++) {
    row = makeRow(results.getRow(i), entryWidth);
    System.out.println(row);
  }
  System.out.println(separator);
}
```

Listing 18.6 `DatabaseUtilities.java` **(continued)**

```java
// A String of the form "|  xxx  |  xxx  |  xxx  |"

private static String makeRow(String[] entries,
                              int entryWidth) {

  String row = "|";
  for(int i=0; i<entries.length; i++) {
    row = row + padString(entries[i], entryWidth, " ");
    row = row + " |";
  }
  return(row);
}

// A String of the form "+------+------+------+"

private static String makeSeparator(int entryWidth,
                                    int columnCount) {
  String entry = padString("", entryWidth+1, "-");
  String separator = "+";
  for(int i=0; i<columnCount; i++) {
    separator = separator + entry + "+";
  }
  return(separator);
}

private static String padString(String orig, int size,
                                String padChar) {
  if (orig == null) {
    orig = "<null>";
  }
  // Use StringBuffer, not just repeated String concatenation
  // to avoid creating too many temporary Strings.
  StringBuffer buffer = new StringBuffer("");
  int extraChars = size - orig.length();
  for(int i=0; i<extraChars; i++) {
    buffer.append(padChar);
  }
  buffer.append(orig);
  return(buffer.toString());
}
}
```

Listing 18.7 `DBResults.java`

```java
package coreservlets;

import java.sql.*;
import java.util.*;

/** Class to store completed results of a JDBC Query.
 *  Differs from a ResultSet in several ways:
 *  <UL>
 *    <LI>ResultSet doesn't necessarily have all the data;
 *        reconnection to database occurs as you ask for
 *        later rows.
 *    <LI>This class stores results as strings, in arrays.
 *    <LI>This class includes DatabaseMetaData (database product
 *        name and version) and ResultSetMetaData
 *        (the column names).
 *    <LI>This class has a toHTMLTable method that turns
 *        the results into a long string corresponding to
 *        an HTML table.
 *  </UL>
 */

public class DBResults {
  private Connection connection;
  private String productName;
  private String productVersion;
  private int columnCount;
  private String[] columnNames;
  private Vector queryResults;
  String[] rowData;

  public DBResults(Connection connection,
                   String productName,
                   String productVersion,
                   int columnCount,
                   String[] columnNames) {
    this.connection = connection;
    this.productName = productName;
    this.productVersion = productVersion;
    this.columnCount = columnCount;
    this.columnNames = columnNames;
    rowData = new String[columnCount];
    queryResults = new Vector();
  }

  public Connection getConnection() {
    return(connection);
  }
```

Listing 18.7 `DBResults.java` **(continued)**

```java
public String getProductName() {
  return(productName);
}

public String getProductVersion() {
  return(productVersion);
}

public int getColumnCount() {
  return(columnCount);
}

public String[] getColumnNames() {
  return(columnNames);
}

public int getRowCount() {
  return(queryResults.size());
}

public String[] getRow(int index) {
  return((String[])queryResults.elementAt(index));
}

public void addRow(String[] row) {
  queryResults.addElement(row);
}

/** Output the results as an HTML table, with
 *  the column names as headings and the rest of
 *  the results filling regular data cells.
 */

public String toHTMLTable(String headingColor) {
  StringBuffer buffer =
    new StringBuffer("<TABLE BORDER=1>\n");
  if (headingColor != null) {
    buffer.append("  <TR BGCOLOR=\"" + headingColor +
                  "\">\n    ");
  } else {
    buffer.append("  <TR>\n    ");
  }
  for(int col=0; col<getColumnCount(); col++) {
    buffer.append("<TH>" + columnNames[col]);
```

Listing 18.7 `DBResults.java` (continued)

```
    }
    for(int row=0; row<getRowCount(); row++) {
      buffer.append("\n  <TR>\n     ");
      String[] rowData = getRow(row);
      for(int col=0; col<getColumnCount(); col++) {
        buffer.append("<TD>" + rowData[col]);
      }
    }
    buffer.append("\n</TABLE>");
    return(buffer.toString());
  }
}
```

18.4 Applying the Database Utilities

Now, let's see how the database utilities of Section 18.3 can simplify the retrieval and display of database results. Listing 18.8 presents a class that connects to the database specified on the command line and prints out all entries in the `employees` table. Listings 18.9 and 18.10 show the results when connecting to Oracle and Sybase databases, respectively. Listing 18.11 shows a similar class that performs the same database lookup but formats the results in an HTML table. Listing 18.12 shows the raw HTML result. I'll put an HTML table like this in a real Web page in Section 18.8 (Connection Pooling: A Case Study).

Listing 18.13 shows the JDBC code used to create the `employees` table.

Listing 18.8 `EmployeeTest.java`

```java
package coreservlets;

import java.sql.*;

/** Connect to Oracle or Sybase and print "employees" table. */

public class EmployeeTest {
  public static void main(String[] args) {
    if (args.length < 5) {
      printUsage();
      return;
    }
    String vendorName = args[4];
    int vendor = DriverUtilities.getVendor(vendorName);
    if (vendor == DriverUtilities.UNKNOWN) {
      printUsage();
      return;
    }
    String driver = DriverUtilities.getDriver(vendor);
    String host = args[0];
    String dbName = args[1];
    String url =
      DriverUtilities.makeURL(host, dbName, vendor);
    String username = args[2];
    String password = args[3];
    DatabaseUtilities.printTable(driver, url,
                                 username, password,
                                 "employees", 12, true);

  }

  private static void printUsage() {
    System.out.println("Usage: EmployeeTest host dbName " +
                       "username password oracle|sybase.");
  }
}
```

Listing 18.9 `EmployeeTest` result (connecting to Oracle on Solaris)

```
Prompt> java coreservlets.EmployeeTest dbhost1.apl.jhu.edu PTE
        hall xxxx oracle
Database: Oracle
Version: Oracle7 Server Release 7.2.3.0.0 - Production Release
PL/SQL Release 2.2.3.0.0 - Production

employees:
==========
+-------------+-------------+-------------+-------------+-------------+
|          ID | FIRSTNAME   |   LASTNAME  |   LANGUAGE  |      SALARY |
+-------------+-------------+-------------+-------------+-------------+
|           1 |         Wye |       Tukay |       COBOL |       42500 |
|           2 |       Britt |        Tell |         C++ |       62000 |
|           3 |         Max |     Manager |        none |       15500 |
|           4 |       Polly |     Morphic |   Smalltalk |       51500 |
|           5 |       Frank |    Function | Common Lisp |       51500 |
|           6 |      Justin |Timecompiler |        Java |       98000 |
|           7 |         Sir |        Vlet |        Java |      114750 |
|           8 |         Jay |        Espy |        Java |      128500 |
+-------------+-------------+-------------+-------------+-------------+
```

Listing 18.10 `EmployeeTest` result (connecting to Sybase on NT)

```
Prompt> java coreservlets.EmployeeTest dbhost2.apl.jhu.edu 605741
        hall xxxx sybase
Database: Adaptive Server Anywhere
Version: 6.0.2.2188

employees:
==========
+-------------+-------------+-------------+-------------+-------------+
|          id | firstname   |   lastname  |   language  |      salary |
+-------------+-------------+-------------+-------------+-------------+
|           1 |         Wye |       Tukay |       COBOL |     42500.0 |
|           2 |       Britt |        Tell |         C++ |     62000.0 |
|           3 |         Max |     Manager |        none |     15500.0 |
|           4 |       Polly |     Morphic |   Smalltalk |     51500.0 |
|           5 |       Frank |    Function | Common Lisp |     51500.0 |
|           6 |      Justin |Timecompiler |        Java |     98000.0 |
|           7 |         Sir |        Vlet |        Java |    114750.0 |
|           8 |         Jay |        Espy |        Java |    128500.0 |
+-------------+-------------+-------------+-------------+-------------+
```

Listing 18.11 EmployeeTest2.java

```
package coreservlets;

import java.sql.*;

/** Connect to Oracle or Sybase and print "employees" table
 *  as an HTML table.
 */

public class EmployeeTest2 {
  public static void main(String[] args) {
    if (args.length < 5) {
      printUsage();
      return;
    }
    String vendorName = args[4];
    int vendor = DriverUtilities.getVendor(vendorName);
    if (vendor == DriverUtilities.UNKNOWN) {
      printUsage();
      return;
    }
    String driver = DriverUtilities.getDriver(vendor);
    String host = args[0];
    String dbName = args[1];
    String url =
      DriverUtilities.makeURL(host, dbName, vendor);
    String username = args[2];
    String password = args[3];
    String query = "SELECT * FROM employees";
    DBResults results =
      DatabaseUtilities.getQueryResults(driver, url,
                                        username, password,
                                        query, true);
    System.out.println(results.toHTMLTable("CYAN"));
  }

  private static void printUsage() {
    System.out.println("Usage: EmployeeTest2 host dbName " +
                       "username password oracle|sybase.");
  }
}
```

Listing 18.12 `EmployeeTest2` result (connecting to Sybase on NT)

```
Prompt> java coreservlets.EmployeeTest2 dbhost2 605741
        hall xxxx sybase
<TABLE BORDER=1>
  <TR BGCOLOR="CYAN">
    <TH>id<TH>firstname<TH>lastname<TH>language<TH>salary
  <TR>
    <TD>1<TD>Wye<TD>Tukay<TD>COBOL<TD>42500.0
  <TR>
    <TD>2<TD>Britt<TD>Tell<TD>C++<TD>62000.0
  <TR>
    <TD>3<TD>Max<TD>Manager<TD>none<TD>15500.0
  <TR>
    <TD>4<TD>Polly<TD>Morphic<TD>Smalltalk<TD>51500.0
  <TR>
    <TD>5<TD>Frank<TD>Function<TD>Common Lisp<TD>51500.0
  <TR>
    <TD>6<TD>Justin<TD>Timecompiler<TD>Java<TD>98000.0
  <TR>
    <TD>7<TD>Sir<TD>Vlet<TD>Java<TD>114750.0
  <TR>
    <TD>8<TD>Jay<TD>Espy<TD>Java<TD>128500.0
</TABLE>
```

Listing 18.13 `EmployeeCreation.java`

```java
package coreservlets;

import java.sql.*;

/** Make a simple "employees" table using DatabaseUtilities. */

public class EmployeeCreation {
  public static Connection createEmployees(String driver,
                                           String url,
                                           String username,
                                           String password,
                                           boolean close) {

    String format =
      "(id int, firstname varchar(32), lastname varchar(32), " +
      "language varchar(16), salary float)";
    String[] employees =
      {"(1, 'Wye', 'Tukay', 'COBOL', 42500)",
       "(2, 'Britt', 'Tell',   'C++',   62000)",
       "(3, 'Max',   'Manager', 'none',  15500)",
       "(4, 'Polly', 'Morphic', 'Smalltalk', 51500)",
```

Listing 18.13 EmployeeCreation.java (continued)

```java
             "(5, 'Frank', 'Function', 'Common Lisp', 51500)",
             "(6, 'Justin', 'Timecompiler', 'Java', 98000)",
             "(7, 'Sir', 'Vlet', 'Java', 114750)",
             "(8, 'Jay', 'Espy', 'Java', 128500)" };
    return(DatabaseUtilities.createTable(driver, url,
                                         username, password,
                                         "employees",
                                         format, employees,
                                         close));
  }

  public static void main(String[] args) {
    if (args.length < 5) {
      printUsage();
      return;
    }
    String vendorName = args[4];
    int vendor = DriverUtilities.getVendor(vendorName);
    if (vendor == DriverUtilities.UNKNOWN) {
      printUsage();
      return;
    }
    String driver = DriverUtilities.getDriver(vendor);
    String host = args[0];
    String dbName = args[1];
    String url =
      DriverUtilities.makeURL(host, dbName, vendor);
    String username = args[2];
    String password = args[3];
    createEmployees(driver, url, username, password, true);
  }

  private static void printUsage() {
    System.out.println("Usage: EmployeeCreation host dbName " +
                       "username password oracle|sybase.");
  }
}
```

18.5 An Interactive Query Viewer

Up to this point, all the database results have been based upon queries that were known at the time the program was written. In many real applications, however, queries are derived from user input that is not known until runtime.

Sometimes the queries follow a fixed format even though certain values change. You should make use of prepared statements in such a case; see Section 18.6 for details. Other times, however, even the query format is variable. Fortunately, this situation presents no problem, since `ResultSetMetaData` can be used to determine the number, names, and types of columns in a `ResultSet`, as was discussed in Section 18.1 (Basic Steps in Using JDBC). In fact, the database utilities of Listing 18.6 store that metadata in the `DBResults` object that is returned from the `showQueryData` method. Access to this metadata makes it straightforward to implement an interactive graphical query viewer as shown in Figures 18–1 through 18–5. The code to accomplish this result is presented in the following subsection.

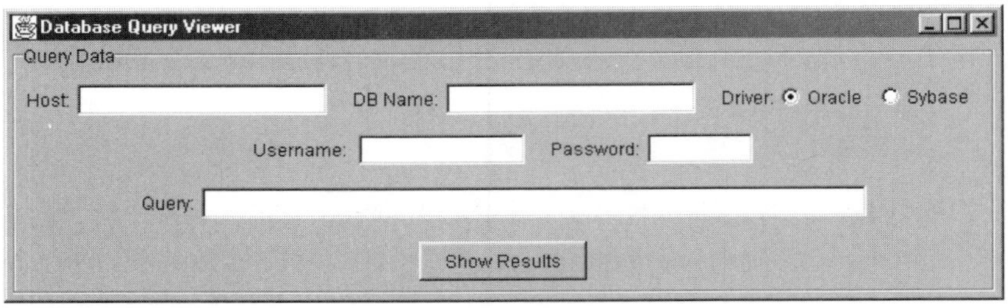

Figure 18–1 Initial appearance of the query viewer.

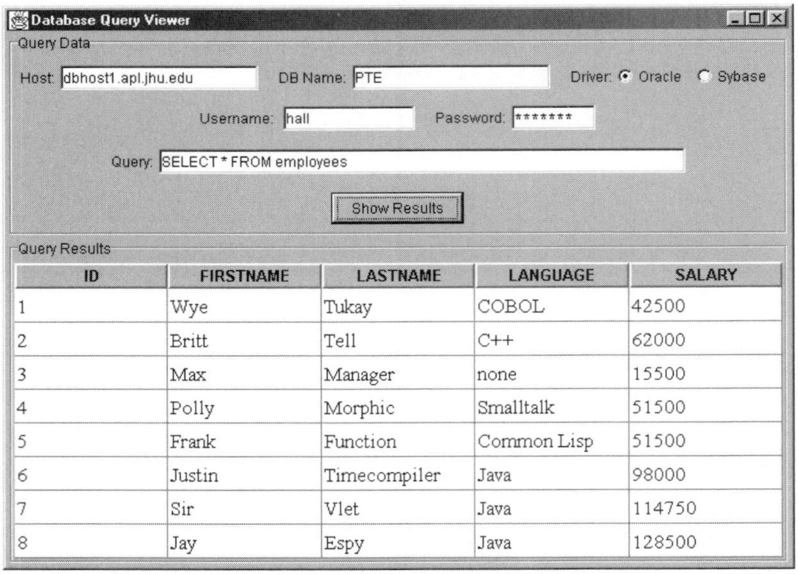

Figure 18–2 Query viewer after a request for the complete `employees` table from an Oracle database.

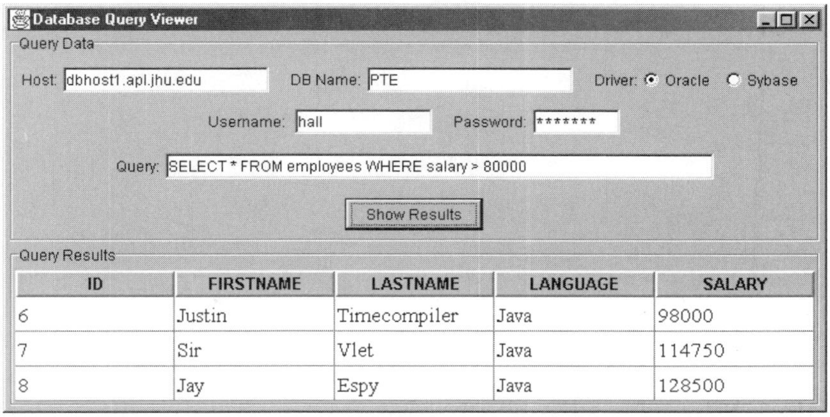

Figure 18–3 Query viewer after a request for part of the `employees` table from an Oracle database.

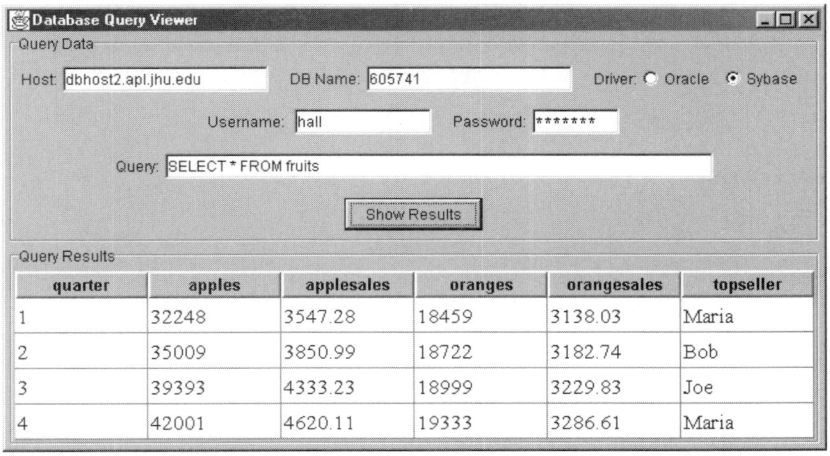

Figure 18–4 Query viewer after a request for the complete `fruits` table from a Sybase database.

Query Viewer Code

Building the display shown in Figures 18–1 through 18–5 is relatively straightforward. In fact, given the database utilities shown earlier, it takes substantially more code to build the user interface than it does to communicate with the database. The full code is shown in Listing 18.14, but I'll give a

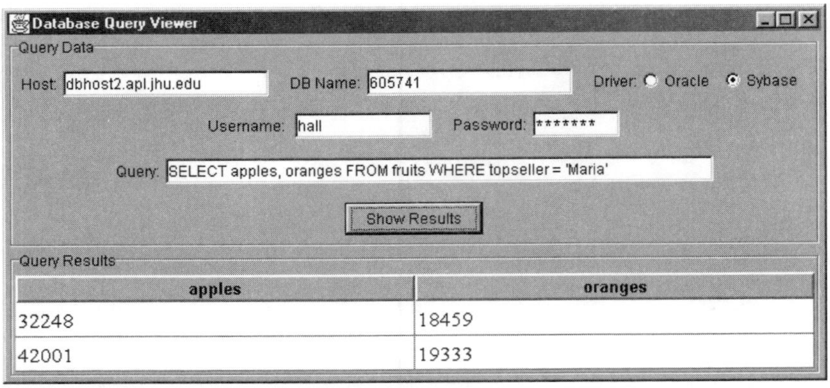

Figure 18–5 Query viewer after a request for part of the `fruits` table from a Sybase database.

quick summary of the process that takes place when the user presses the "Show Results" button.

First, the system reads the host, port, database name, username, password, and driver type from the user interface elements shown. Next, it submits the query and stores the result, as below:

```
DBResults results =
   DatabaseUtilities.getQueryResults(driver, url,
                                     username, password,
                                     query, true);
```

Next, the system passes these results to a custom table model (see Listing 18.15). If you are not familiar with the Swing GUI library, a table model acts as the glue between a `JTable` and the actual data.

```
DBResultsTableModel model = new DBResultsTableModel(results);
JTable table = new JTable(model);
```

Finally, the system places this `JTable` in the bottom region of the `JFrame` and calls `pack` to tell the `JFrame` to resize itself to fit the table.

Listing 18.14 QueryViewer.java

```java
package coreservlets;

import java.awt.*;
import java.awt.event.*;
import javax.swing.*;
import javax.swing.table.*;

/** An interactive database query viewer. Connects to
 *  the specified Oracle or Sybase database, executes a query,
 *  and presents the results in a JTable.
 */

public class QueryViewer extends JFrame
                         implements ActionListener{
  public static void main(String[] args) {
    new QueryViewer();
  }

  private JTextField hostField, dbNameField,
                     queryField, usernameField;
  private JRadioButton oracleButton, sybaseButton;
  private JPasswordField passwordField;
  private JButton showResultsButton;
  private Container contentPane;
  private JPanel tablePanel;

  public QueryViewer () {
    super("Database Query Viewer");
    WindowUtilities.setNativeLookAndFeel();
    addWindowListener(new ExitListener());
    contentPane = getContentPane();
    contentPane.add(makeControlPanel(), BorderLayout.NORTH);
    pack();
    setVisible(true);
  }

  /** When the "Show Results" button is pressed or
   *  RETURN is hit while the query textfield has the
   *  keyboard focus, a database lookup is performed,
   *  the results are placed in a JTable, and the window
   *  is resized to accommodate the table.
   */

  public void actionPerformed(ActionEvent event) {
    String host = hostField.getText();
    String dbName = dbNameField.getText();
    String username = usernameField.getText();
```

Listing 18.14 QueryViewer.java (continued)

```
String password =
  String.valueOf(passwordField.getPassword());
String query = queryField.getText();
int vendor;
if (oracleButton.isSelected()) {
  vendor = DriverUtilities.ORACLE;
} else {
  vendor = DriverUtilities.SYBASE;
}
if (tablePanel != null) {
  contentPane.remove(tablePanel);
}
tablePanel = makeTablePanel(host, dbName, vendor,
                            username, password,
                            query);
contentPane.add(tablePanel, BorderLayout.CENTER);
pack();
}

// Executes a query and places the result in a
// JTable that is, in turn, inside a JPanel.

private JPanel makeTablePanel(String host,
                              String dbName,
                              int vendor,
                              String username,
                              String password,
                              String query) {
  String driver = DriverUtilities.getDriver(vendor);
  String url = DriverUtilities.makeURL(host, dbName, vendor);
  DBResults results =
    DatabaseUtilities.getQueryResults(driver, url,
                                      username, password,
                                      query, true);
  JPanel panel = new JPanel(new BorderLayout());
  if (results == null) {
    panel.add(makeErrorLabel());
    return(panel);
  }
  DBResultsTableModel model =
    new DBResultsTableModel(results);
  JTable table = new JTable(model);
  table.setFont(new Font("Serif", Font.PLAIN, 17));
  table.setRowHeight(28);
  JTableHeader header = table.getTableHeader();
  header.setFont(new Font("SansSerif", Font.BOLD, 13));
  panel.add(table, BorderLayout.CENTER);
  panel.add(header, BorderLayout.NORTH);
```

Listing 18.14 QueryViewer.java (continued)

```
    panel.setBorder
      (BorderFactory.createTitledBorder("Query Results"));
    return(panel);
  }

  // The panel that contains the textfields, check boxes,
  // and button.

  private JPanel makeControlPanel() {
    JPanel panel = new JPanel(new GridLayout(0, 1));
    panel.add(makeHostPanel());
    panel.add(makeUsernamePanel());
    panel.add(makeQueryPanel());
    panel.add(makeButtonPanel());
    panel.setBorder
      (BorderFactory.createTitledBorder("Query Data"));
    return(panel);
  }

  // The panel that has the host and db name textfield and
  // the driver radio buttons. Placed in control panel.

  private JPanel makeHostPanel() {
    JPanel panel = new JPanel();
    panel.add(new JLabel("Host:"));
    hostField = new JTextField(15);
    panel.add(hostField);
    panel.add(new JLabel("    DB Name:"));
    dbNameField = new JTextField(15);
    panel.add(dbNameField);
    panel.add(new JLabel("    Driver:"));
    ButtonGroup vendorGroup = new ButtonGroup();
    oracleButton = new JRadioButton("Oracle", true);
    vendorGroup.add(oracleButton);
    panel.add(oracleButton);
    sybaseButton = new JRadioButton("Sybase");
    vendorGroup.add(sybaseButton);
    panel.add(sybaseButton);
    return(panel);
  }

  // The panel that has the username and password textfields.
  // Placed in control panel.

  private JPanel makeUsernamePanel() {
    JPanel panel = new JPanel();
    usernameField = new JTextField(10);
```

Listing 18.14 `QueryViewer.java` (continued)

```java
      passwordField = new JPasswordField(10);
      panel.add(new JLabel("Username: "));
      panel.add(usernameField);
      panel.add(new JLabel("    Password:"));
      panel.add(passwordField);
      return(panel);
    }

    // The panel that has textfield for entering queries.
    // Placed in control panel.

    private JPanel makeQueryPanel() {
      JPanel panel = new JPanel();
      queryField = new JTextField(40);
      queryField.addActionListener(this);
      panel.add(new JLabel("Query:"));
      panel.add(queryField);
      return(panel);
    }

    // The panel that has the "Show Results" button.
    // Placed in control panel.

    private JPanel makeButtonPanel() {
      JPanel panel = new JPanel();
      showResultsButton = new JButton("Show Results");
      showResultsButton.addActionListener(this);
      panel.add(showResultsButton);
      return(panel);
    }

    // Shows warning when bad query sent.

    private JLabel makeErrorLabel() {
      JLabel label = new JLabel("No Results", JLabel.CENTER);
      label.setFont(new Font("Serif", Font.BOLD, 36));
      return(label);
    }
  }
```

Listing 18.15 DBResultsTableModel.java

```java
package coreservlets;

import javax.swing.table.*;

/** Simple class that tells a JTable how to extract
 *  relevant data from a DBResults object (which is
 *  used to store the results from a database query).
 */

public class DBResultsTableModel extends AbstractTableModel {
  private DBResults results;

  public DBResultsTableModel(DBResults results) {
    this.results = results;
  }

  public int getRowCount() {
    return(results.getRowCount());
  }

  public int getColumnCount() {
    return(results.getColumnCount());
  }

  public String getColumnName(int column) {
    return(results.getColumnNames()[column]);
  }

  public Object getValueAt(int row, int column) {
    return(results.getRow(row)[column]);
  }
}
```

Listing 18.16 `WindowUtilities.java`

```java
package coreservlets;

import javax.swing.*;
import java.awt.*;

/** A few utilities that simplify using windows in Swing. */

public class WindowUtilities {

  /** Tell system to use native look and feel, as in previous
   *  releases. Metal (Java) LAF is the default otherwise.
   */

  public static void setNativeLookAndFeel() {
    try {
      UIManager.setLookAndFeel
        (UIManager.getSystemLookAndFeelClassName());
    } catch(Exception e) {
      System.out.println("Error setting native LAF: " + e);
    }
  }

  public static void setJavaLookAndFeel() {
    try {
      UIManager.setLookAndFeel
        (UIManager.getCrossPlatformLookAndFeelClassName());
    } catch(Exception e) {
      System.out.println("Error setting Java LAF: " + e);
    }
  }

  public static void setMotifLookAndFeel() {
    try {
      UIManager.setLookAndFeel
        ("com.sun.java.swing.plaf.motif.MotifLookAndFeel");
    } catch(Exception e) {
      System.out.println("Error setting Motif LAF: " + e);
    }
  }
}
```

Listing 18.17 `ExitListener.java`

```java
package coreservlets;

import java.awt.*;
import java.awt.event.*;

/** A listener that you attach to the top-level Frame
 *  or JFrame of your application, so quitting the
 *  frame exits the application.
 */

public class ExitListener extends WindowAdapter {
  public void windowClosing(WindowEvent event) {
    System.exit(0);
  }
}
```

18.6 Prepared Statements (Precompiled Queries)

If you are going to execute similar SQL statements multiple times, using "prepared" statements can be more efficient than executing a raw query each time. The idea is to create a parameterized statement in a standard form that is sent to the database for compilation before actually being used. You use a question mark to indicate the places where a value will be substituted into the statement. Each time you use the prepared statement, you simply replace some of the marked parameters, using a set*Xxx* call corresponding to the entry you want to set (using 1-based indexing) and the type of the parameter (e.g., `setInt`, `setString`, and so forth). You then use `executeQuery` (if you want a `ResultSet` back) or `execute`/`executeUpdate` (for side effects) as with normal statements. For instance, if you were going to give raises to all the personnel in the `employees` database, you might do something like the following:

```java
Connection connection =
  DriverManager.getConnection(url, user, password);
String template =
  "UPDATE employees SET salary = ? WHERE id = ?";
PreparedStatement statement =
  connection.prepareStatement(template);
float[] newSalaries = getNewSalaries();
```

```
int[] employeeIDs = getIDs();
for(int i=0; i<employeeIDs.length; i++) {
  statement.setFloat(1, newSalaries[i]);
  statement.setInt(2, employeeIDs[i]);
  statement.execute();
}
```

The performance advantages of prepared statements can vary significantly, depending on how well the server supports precompiled queries and how efficiently the driver handles raw queries. For example, Listing 18.18 presents a class that sends 40 different queries to a database using prepared statements, then repeats the same 40 queries using regular statements. With a PC and a 28.8K modem connection to the Internet to talk to an Oracle database, prepared statements took only *half* the time of raw queries, averaging 17.5 seconds for the 40 queries as compared with an average of 35 seconds for the raw queries. Using a fast LAN connection to the same Oracle database, prepared statements took only about 70 percent of the time required by raw queries, averaging 0.22 seconds for the 40 queries as compared with an average of 0.31 seconds for the regular statements. With Sybase, prepared statement times were virtually identical to times for raw queries both with the modem connection and with the fast LAN connection. To get performance numbers for your setup, download `DriverUtilities.java` from `http://www.coreservlets.com/`, add information about your drivers to it, then run the `PreparedStatements` program yourself.

Listing 18.18 `PreparedStatements.java`

```
package coreservlets;

import java.sql.*;

/** An example to test the timing differences resulting
 *  from repeated raw queries vs. repeated calls to
 *  prepared statements. These results will vary dramatically
 *  among database servers and drivers.
 */

public class PreparedStatements {
  public static void main(String[] args) {
    if (args.length < 5) {
      printUsage();
      return;
    }
    String vendorName = args[4];
    int vendor = DriverUtilities.getVendor(vendorName);
```

Listing 18.18 PreparedStatements.java **(continued)**

```java
    if (vendor == DriverUtilities.UNKNOWN) {
      printUsage();
      return;
    }
    String driver = DriverUtilities.getDriver(vendor);
    String host = args[0];
    String dbName = args[1];
    String url =
      DriverUtilities.makeURL(host, dbName, vendor);
    String username = args[2];
    String password = args[3];
    // Use "print" only to confirm it works properly,
    // not when getting timing results.
    boolean print = false;
    if ((args.length > 5) && (args[5].equals("print"))) {
      print = true;
    }
    Connection connection =
      getConnection(driver, url, username, password);
    if (connection != null) {
      doPreparedStatements(connection, print);
      doRawQueries(connection, print);
    }
  }

  private static void doPreparedStatements(Connection conn,
                                           boolean print) {
    try {
      String queryFormat =
        "SELECT lastname FROM employees WHERE salary > ?";
      PreparedStatement statement =
        conn.prepareStatement(queryFormat);
      long startTime = System.currentTimeMillis();
      for(int i=0; i<40; i++) {
        statement.setFloat(1, i*5000);
        ResultSet results = statement.executeQuery();
        if (print) {
          showResults(results);
        }
      }
      long stopTime = System.currentTimeMillis();
      double elapsedTime = (stopTime - startTime)/1000.0;
      System.out.println("Executing prepared statement " +
                         "40 times took " +
                         elapsedTime + " seconds.");
    } catch(SQLException sqle) {
      System.out.println("Error executing statement: " + sqle);
    }
  }
```

Listing 18.18 `PreparedStatements.java` (continued)

```
public static void doRawQueries(Connection conn,
                                boolean print) {
  try {
    String queryFormat =
      "SELECT lastname FROM employees WHERE salary > ";
    Statement statement = conn.createStatement();
    long startTime = System.currentTimeMillis();
    for(int i=0; i<40; i++) {
      ResultSet results =
        statement.executeQuery(queryFormat + (i*5000));
      if (print) {
        showResults(results);
      }
    }
    long stopTime = System.currentTimeMillis();
    double elapsedTime = (stopTime - startTime)/1000.0;
    System.out.println("Executing raw query " +
                       "40 times took " +
                       elapsedTime + " seconds.");
  } catch(SQLException sqle) {
    System.out.println("Error executing query: " + sqle);
  }
}

private static void showResults(ResultSet results)
    throws SQLException {
  while(results.next()) {
    System.out.print(results.getString(1) + " ");
  }
  System.out.println();
}

private static Connection getConnection(String driver,
                                        String url,
                                        String username,
                                        String password) {
  try {
    Class.forName(driver);
    Connection connection =
      DriverManager.getConnection(url, username, password);
    return(connection);
  } catch(ClassNotFoundException cnfe) {
    System.err.println("Error loading driver: " + cnfe);
    return(null);
  } catch(SQLException sqle) {
    System.err.println("Error connecting: " + sqle);
    return(null);
  }
}
```

Listing 18.18 `PreparedStatements.java` **(continued)**

```
    private static void printUsage() {
        System.out.println("Usage: PreparedStatements host " +
                           "dbName username password " +
                           "oracle|sybase [print].");
    }
}
```

18.7 Connection Pooling

Opening a connection to a database is a time-consuming process. For short queries, it can take much longer to open the connection than to perform the actual database retrieval. Consequently, it makes sense to reuse `Connection` objects in applications that connect repeatedly to the same database. This section presents a class for *connection pooling*: preallocating database connections and recycling them as clients connect. Servlets and JSP pages can benefit significantly from this class since the database to which any given servlet or JSP page connects is typically known in advance (e.g., specified in the `init` method). For example, the servlet shown in Section 18.8 shows a sevenfold performance gain by making use of this connection pool class.

A connection pool class should be able to perform the following tasks:

1. Preallocate the connections.
2. Manage available connections.
3. Allocate new connections.
4. Wait for a connection to become available.
5. Close connections when required.

I'll sketch out the approach to each of these steps here. The full code for the `ConnectionPool` class is shown in Listing 18.19. As with all classes in the book, you can download the source code from `http://www.coreserv-lets.com/`.

1. **Preallocate the connections.**
    Perform this task in the class constructor. Allocating more connections in advance speeds things up if there will be many concurrent requests later but causes an initial delay. As a result, a servlet that preallocates very many connections should build the

connection pool from its `init` method, and you should be sure that the servlet is initialized prior to a "real" client request. The following code uses vectors to store available idle connections and unavailable, busy connections. Assume that `makeNew-Connection` uses a URL, username, and password stored previously, then simply calls the `getConnection` method of `DriverManager`.

```
availableConnections = new Vector(initialConnections);
busyConnections = new Vector();
for(int i=0; i<initialConnections; i++) {
  availableConnections.addElement(makeNewConnection());
}
```

2. **Manage available connections.**
   If a connection is required and an idle connection is available, put it in the list of busy connections and then return it. The busy list is used to check limits on the total number of connections as well as when the pool is instructed to explicitly close all connections. One caveat: connections can time out, so before returning the connection, confirm that it is still open. If not, discard the connection and repeat the process. Discarding a connection opens up a slot that can be used by processes that needed a connection when the connection limit had been reached, so use `notifyAll` to tell all waiting threads to wake up and see if they can proceed (e.g., by allocating a new connection).

```
public synchronized Connection getConnection()
    throws SQLException {
  if (!availableConnections.isEmpty()) {
    Connection existingConnection =
      (Connection)availableConnections.lastElement();
    int lastIndex = availableConnections.size() - 1;
    availableConnections.removeElementAt(lastIndex);
    if (existingConnection.isClosed()) {
      notifyAll(); // Freed up a spot for anybody waiting.
      return(getConnection()); // Repeat process.
    } else {
      busyConnections.addElement(existingConnection);
      return(existingConnection);
    }
  }
}
```

3. **Allocate new connections.**
   If a connection is required, there is no idle connection available, and the connection limit has not been reached, then start a background thread to allocate a new connection. Then, wait for the first available connection, whether or not it is the newly allocated one.

```
if ((totalConnections() < maxConnections) &&
    !connectionPending) { // Pending = connecting in bg
  makeBackgroundConnection();
}
  try {
    wait(); // Give up lock and suspend self.
  } catch(InterruptedException ie) {}
  return(getConnection()); // Try again.
```

4. **Wait for a connection to become available.**
   This situation occurs when there is no idle connection and you've reached the limit on the number of connections. This waiting should be accomplished without continual polling. The natural approach is to use the `wait` method, which gives up the thread synchronization lock and suspends the thread until `notify` or `notifyAll` is called. Since `notifyAll` could stem from several possible sources, threads that wake up still need to test to see if they can proceed. In this case, the simplest way to accomplish this task is to recursively repeat the process of trying to obtain a connection.

```
try {
  wait();
} catch(InterruptedException ie) {}
return(getConnection());
```

It may be that you don't want to let clients wait and would rather throw an exception when no connections are available and the connection limit has been reached. In such a case, do the following instead:

```
throw new SQLException("Connection limit reached");
```

5. **Close connections when required.**
   Note that connections are closed when they are garbage collected, so you don't always have to close them explicitly. But, you sometimes want more explicit control over the process.

```
    public synchronized void closeAllConnections() {
      // The closeConnections method loops down Vector, calling
      // close and ignoring any exceptions thrown.
      closeConnections(availableConnections);
      availableConnections = new Vector();
      closeConnections(busyConnections);
      busyConnections = new Vector();
    }
```

The full class follows.

Listing 18.19 `ConnectionPool.java`

```java
package coreservlets;

import java.sql.*;
import java.util.*;

/** A class for preallocating, recycling, and managing
 *  JDBC connections.
 */

public class ConnectionPool implements Runnable {
  private String driver, url, username, password;
  private int maxConnections;
  private boolean waitIfBusy;
  private Vector availableConnections, busyConnections;
  private boolean connectionPending = false;

  public ConnectionPool(String driver, String url,
                        String username, String password,
                        int initialConnections,
                        int maxConnections,
                        boolean waitIfBusy)
      throws SQLException {
    this.driver = driver;
    this.url = url;
    this.username = username;
    this.password = password;
    this.maxConnections = maxConnections;
    this.waitIfBusy = waitIfBusy;
    if (initialConnections > maxConnections) {
      initialConnections = maxConnections;
    }
    availableConnections = new Vector(initialConnections);
    busyConnections = new Vector();
    for(int i=0; i<initialConnections; i++) {
      availableConnections.addElement(makeNewConnection());
    }
  }
```

Listing 18.19 `ConnectionPool.java` **(continued)**

```java
public synchronized Connection getConnection()
    throws SQLException {
  if (!availableConnections.isEmpty()) {
    Connection existingConnection =
      (Connection)availableConnections.lastElement();
    int lastIndex = availableConnections.size() - 1;
    availableConnections.removeElementAt(lastIndex);
    // If connection on available list is closed (e.g.,
    // it timed out), then remove it from available list
    // and repeat the process of obtaining a connection.
    // Also wake up threads that were waiting for a
    // connection because maxConnection limit was reached.
    if (existingConnection.isClosed()) {
      notifyAll(); // Freed up a spot for anybody waiting
      return(getConnection());
    } else {
      busyConnections.addElement(existingConnection);
      return(existingConnection);
    }
  } else {

    // Three possible cases:
    // 1) You haven't reached maxConnections limit. So
    //    establish one in the background if there isn't
    //    already one pending, then wait for
    //    the next available connection (whether or not
    //    it was the newly established one).
    // 2) You reached maxConnections limit and waitIfBusy
    //    flag is false. Throw SQLException in such a case.
    // 3) You reached maxConnections limit and waitIfBusy
    //    flag is true. Then do the same thing as in second
    //    part of step 1: wait for next available connection.

    if ((totalConnections() < maxConnections) &&
        !connectionPending) {
      makeBackgroundConnection();
    } else if (!waitIfBusy) {
      throw new SQLException("Connection limit reached");
    }
    // Wait for either a new connection to be established
    // (if you called makeBackgroundConnection) or for
    // an existing connection to be freed up.
    try {
      wait();
    } catch(InterruptedException ie) {}
    // Someone freed up a connection, so try again.
    return(getConnection());
  }
}
```

Listing 18.19 `ConnectionPool.java` (continued)

```java
// You can't just make a new connection in the foreground
// when none are available, since this can take several
// seconds with a slow network connection. Instead,
// start a thread that establishes a new connection,
// then wait. You get woken up either when the new connection
// is established or if someone finishes with an existing
// connection.

private void makeBackgroundConnection() {
  connectionPending = true;
  try {
    Thread connectThread = new Thread(this);
    connectThread.start();
  } catch(OutOfMemoryError oome) {
    // Give up on new connection
  }
}

public void run() {
  try {
    Connection connection = makeNewConnection();
    synchronized(this) {
      availableConnections.addElement(connection);
      connectionPending = false;
      notifyAll();
    }
  } catch(Exception e) { // SQLException or OutOfMemory
    // Give up on new connection and wait for existing one
    // to free up.
  }
}

// This explicitly makes a new connection. Called in
// the foreground when initializing the ConnectionPool,
// and called in the background when running.

private Connection makeNewConnection()
    throws SQLException {
  try {
    // Load database driver if not already loaded
    Class.forName(driver);
    // Establish network connection to database
    Connection connection =
      DriverManager.getConnection(url, username, password);
    return(connection);
  } catch(ClassNotFoundException cnfe) {
    // Simplify try/catch blocks of people using this by
    // throwing only one exception type.
    throw new SQLException("Can't find class for driver: " +
                           driver);
  }
}
```

Listing 18.19 `ConnectionPool.java` **(continued)**

```java
public synchronized void free(Connection connection) {
  busyConnections.removeElement(connection);
  availableConnections.addElement(connection);
  // Wake up threads that are waiting for a connection
  notifyAll();
}

public synchronized int totalConnections() {
  return(availableConnections.size() +
         busyConnections.size());
}

/** Close all the connections. Use with caution:
 *  be sure no connections are in use before
 *  calling. Note that you are not <I>required</I> to
 *  call this when done with a ConnectionPool, since
 *  connections are guaranteed to be closed when
 *  garbage collected. But this method gives more control
 *  regarding when the connections are closed.
 */

public synchronized void closeAllConnections() {
  closeConnections(availableConnections);
  availableConnections = new Vector();
  closeConnections(busyConnections);
  busyConnections = new Vector();
}

private void closeConnections(Vector connections) {
  try {
    for(int i=0; i<connections.size(); i++) {
      Connection connection =
        (Connection)connections.elementAt(i);
      if (!connection.isClosed()) {
        connection.close();
      }
    }
  } catch(SQLException sqle) {
    // Ignore errors; garbage collect anyhow
  }
}

public synchronized String toString() {
  String info =
    "ConnectionPool(" + url + "," + username + ")" +
    ", available=" + availableConnections.size() +
    ", busy=" + busyConnections.size() +
    ", max=" + maxConnections;
  return(info);
}
}
```

18.8 Connection Pooling: A Case Study

OK, so we have a `ConnectionPool` class: what good does it do us? Let's find out. Listing 18.20 presents a simple servlet that allocates a `ConnectionPool` in its `init` method, then, for each request, performs a simple database lookup and places the results in an HTML table. Listing 18.21 and Figure 18–6 show an HTML document that places a copy of this servlet in each of 25 frame cells. Since the servlet stipulates that it not be cached by the browser, this document results in 25 near simultaneous HTTP requests and thus 25 near simultaneous database lookups using connection pooling. This request pattern is similar to what would occur on high-traffic sites even when only a single servlet is used for each page.

Listing 18.22 shows a variation of the servlet that uses a "pool" of only a single connection, and Listing 18.23 shows a third variation that doesn't use connection pooling at all. Each of these two servlets is also placed in a framed document nearly identical to that of Listing 18.21. Timing results are shown in Table 18.1.

One small reminder: since these servlets load a JDBC driver, the driver needs to be made accessible to the Web server. With most servers, you can make the driver accessible by placing the JAR file containing the driver into the server's `lib` directory or by unpacking the JAR file in the `classes` directory. See your server's documentation for definitive instructions.

Table 18.1 Connection pool timing results	
Condition	*Average Time*
Slow modem connection to database, 10 initial connections, 50 max connections (`ConnectionPoolServlet`)	11 seconds
Slow modem connection to database, recycling a single connection (`ConnectionPoolServlet2`)	22 seconds
Slow modem connection to database, no connection pooling (`ConnectionPoolServlet3`)	82 seconds

Table 18.1   Connection pool timing results

Condition	Average Time
Fast LAN connection to database, 10 initial connections, 50 max connections (`ConnectionPoolServlet`)	1.8 seconds
Fast LAN connection to database, recycling a single connection (`ConnectionPoolServlet2`)	2.0 seconds
Fast LAN connection to database, no connection pooling (`ConnectionPoolServlet3`)	2.8 seconds

Listing 18.20 `ConnectionPoolServlet.java`

```java
package coreservlets;

import java.io.*;
import javax.servlet.*;
import javax.servlet.http.*;
import java.sql.*;

/** A servlet that reads information from a database and
 *  presents it in an HTML table. It uses connection
 *  pooling to optimize the database retrieval. A good
 *  test case is ConnectionPool.html, which loads many
 *  copies of this servlet into different frame cells.
 */

public class ConnectionPoolServlet extends HttpServlet {
  private ConnectionPool connectionPool;

  public void doGet(HttpServletRequest request,
                    HttpServletResponse response)
      throws ServletException, IOException {
    String table;
    try {
      String query =
        "SELECT firstname, lastname " +
        " FROM employees WHERE salary > 70000";
      Connection connection = connectionPool.getConnection();
      DBResults results =
          DatabaseUtilities.getQueryResults(connection,
                                            query, false);
      connectionPool.free(connection);
```

Listing 18.20 `ConnectionPoolServlet.java` (continued)

```
      table = results.toHTMLTable("#FFAD00");
    } catch(Exception e) {
      table = "Error: " + e;
    }
    response.setContentType("text/html");
    // Prevent the browser from caching the response. See
    // Section 7.2 of Core Servlets and JSP for details.
    response.setHeader("Pragma", "no-cache"); // HTTP 1.0
    response.setHeader("Cache-Control", "no-cache"); // HTTP 1.1
    PrintWriter out = response.getWriter();
    String title = "Connection Pool Test";
    out.println(ServletUtilities.headWithTitle(title) +
                "<BODY BGCOLOR=\"#FDF5E6\">\n" +
                "<CENTER>\n" +
                table + "\n" +
                "</CENTER>\n</BODY></HTML>");
  }

  /** Initialize the connection pool when servlet is
   *  initialized. To avoid a delay on first access, load
   *  the servlet ahead of time yourself or have the
   *  server automatically load it after reboot.
   */

  public void init() {
    int vendor = DriverUtilities.SYBASE;
    String driver = DriverUtilities.getDriver(vendor);
    String host = "dbhost2.apl.jhu.edu";
    String dbName = "605741";
    String url = DriverUtilities.makeURL(host, dbName, vendor);
    String username = "hall";
    String password = "xxxx"; // Changed :-)
    try {
      connectionPool =
        new ConnectionPool(driver, url, username, password,
                           initialConnections(),
                           maxConnections(),
                           true);
    } catch(SQLException sqle) {
      System.err.println("Error making pool: " + sqle);
      getServletContext().log("Error making pool: " + sqle);
      connectionPool = null;
    }
  }

  public void destroy() {
    connectionPool.closeAllConnections();
  }
```

Listing 18.20 `ConnectionPoolServlet.java` **(continued)**

```java
  /** Override this in subclass to change number of initial
   *  connections.
   */

  protected int initialConnections() {
    return(10);
  }

  /** Override this in subclass to change maximum number of
   *  connections.
   */

  protected int maxConnections() {
    return(50);
  }
}
```

Listing 18.21 `ConnectionPool.html`

```html
<!DOCTYPE HTML PUBLIC "-//W3C//DTD HTML 4.0 Frameset//EN">
<HTML>
<HEAD><TITLE>Servlet Connection Pooling: A Test</TITLE></HEAD>

<!-- Causes 25 near simultaneous requests for same servlet. -->

<FRAMESET ROWS="*,*,*,*,*" BORDER=0 FRAMEBORDER=0 FRAMESPACING=0>
  <FRAMESET COLS="*,*,*,*,*">
    <FRAME SRC="/servlet/coreservlets.ConnectionPoolServlet">
    <FRAME SRC="/servlet/coreservlets.ConnectionPoolServlet">
    <FRAME SRC="/servlet/coreservlets.ConnectionPoolServlet">
    <FRAME SRC="/servlet/coreservlets.ConnectionPoolServlet">
    <FRAME SRC="/servlet/coreservlets.ConnectionPoolServlet">
  </FRAMESET>
  <FRAMESET COLS="*,*,*,*,*">
    <FRAME SRC="/servlet/coreservlets.ConnectionPoolServlet">
    <FRAME SRC="/servlet/coreservlets.ConnectionPoolServlet">
    <FRAME SRC="/servlet/coreservlets.ConnectionPoolServlet">
    <FRAME SRC="/servlet/coreservlets.ConnectionPoolServlet">
    <FRAME SRC="/servlet/coreservlets.ConnectionPoolServlet">
  </FRAMESET>
  <FRAMESET COLS="*,*,*,*,*">
    <FRAME SRC="/servlet/coreservlets.ConnectionPoolServlet">
    <FRAME SRC="/servlet/coreservlets.ConnectionPoolServlet">
    <FRAME SRC="/servlet/coreservlets.ConnectionPoolServlet">
    <FRAME SRC="/servlet/coreservlets.ConnectionPoolServlet">
```

Listing 18.21 `ConnectionPool.html` (continued)

```
      <FRAME SRC="/servlet/coreservlets.ConnectionPoolServlet">
   </FRAMESET>
   <FRAMESET COLS="*,*,*,*,*">
      <FRAME SRC="/servlet/coreservlets.ConnectionPoolServlet">
      <FRAME SRC="/servlet/coreservlets.ConnectionPoolServlet">
      <FRAME SRC="/servlet/coreservlets.ConnectionPoolServlet">
      <FRAME SRC="/servlet/coreservlets.ConnectionPoolServlet">
      <FRAME SRC="/servlet/coreservlets.ConnectionPoolServlet">
   </FRAMESET>
   <FRAMESET COLS="*,*,*,*,*">
      <FRAME SRC="/servlet/coreservlets.ConnectionPoolServlet">
      <FRAME SRC="/servlet/coreservlets.ConnectionPoolServlet">
      <FRAME SRC="/servlet/coreservlets.ConnectionPoolServlet">
      <FRAME SRC="/servlet/coreservlets.ConnectionPoolServlet">
      <FRAME SRC="/servlet/coreservlets.ConnectionPoolServlet">
   </FRAMESET>
</FRAMESET>

</HTML>
```

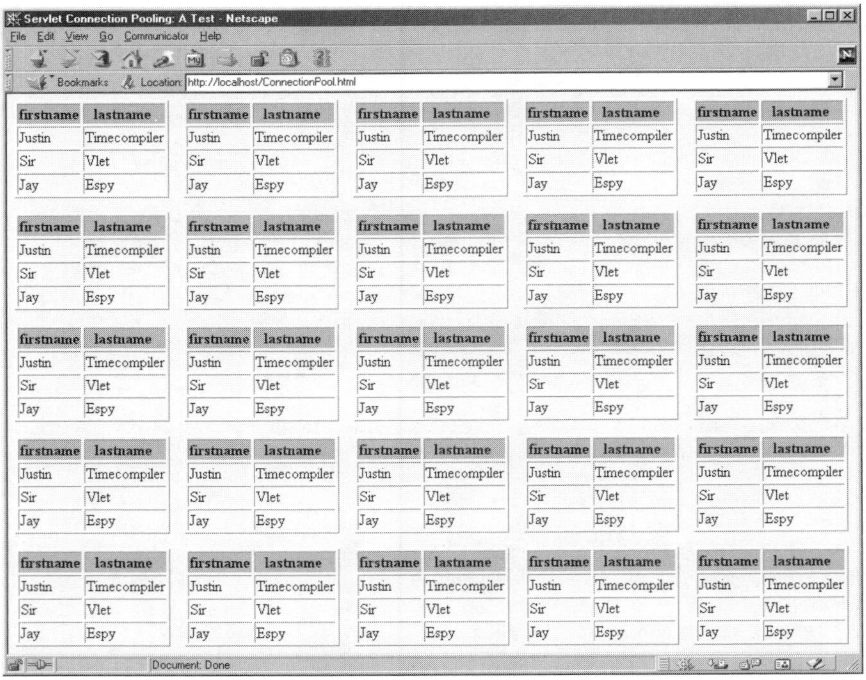

Figure 18–6 A framed document that forces 25 nearly simultaneous requests for the same servlet.

Listing 18.22 ConnectionPoolServlet2.java

```java
package coreservlets;

/** A variation of ConnectionPoolServlet that uses only
 *  a single connection, queueing up all requests to it.
 *  Used to compare timing results.
 */

public class ConnectionPoolServlet2
       extends ConnectionPoolServlet {

  protected int initialConnections() {
    return(1);
  }

  protected int maxConnections() {
    return(1);
  }
}
```

Listing 18.23 ConnectionPoolServlet3.java

```java
package coreservlets;

import java.io.*;
import javax.servlet.*;
import javax.servlet.http.*;
import java.sql.*;

/** A variation of ConnectionPoolServlet that does NOT
 *  use connection pooling. Used to compare timing
 *  benefits of connection pooling.
 */

public class ConnectionPoolServlet3 extends HttpServlet {
  private String url, username, password;

  public void doGet(HttpServletRequest request,
                    HttpServletResponse response)
      throws ServletException, IOException {
    String table;
    String query =
      "SELECT firstname, lastname " +
      " FROM employees WHERE salary > 70000";
    try {
      Connection connection =
        DriverManager.getConnection(url, username, password);
```

Listing 18.23 ConnectionPoolServlet3.java (continued)

```java
      DBResults results =
        DatabaseUtilities.getQueryResults(connection,
                                          query, true);
      table = results.toHTMLTable("#FFAD00");
    } catch(Exception e) {
      table = "Exception: " + e;
    }
    response.setContentType("text/html");
    // Prevent the browser from caching the response. See
    // Section 7.2 of Core Servlets and JSP for details.
    response.setHeader("Pragma", "no-cache"); // HTTP 1.0
    response.setHeader("Cache-Control", "no-cache"); // HTTP 1.1
    PrintWriter out = response.getWriter();
    String title = "Connection Pool Test (*No* Pooling)";
    out.println(ServletUtilities.headWithTitle(title) +
                "<BODY BGCOLOR=\"#FDF5E6\">\n" +
                "<CENTER>\n" +
                table + "\n" +
                "</CENTER>\n</BODY></HTML>");
  }

  public void init() {
    try {
      int vendor = DriverUtilities.SYBASE;
      String driver = DriverUtilities.getDriver(vendor);
      Class.forName(driver);
      String host = "dbhost2.apl.jhu.edu";
      String dbName = "605741";
      url = DriverUtilities.makeURL(host, dbName, vendor);
      username = "hall";
      password = "xxxx"; // Changed :-)
    } catch(ClassNotFoundException e) {
      System.err.println("Error initializing: " + e);
      getServletContext().log("Error initializing: " + e);
    }
  }
}
```

18.9 Sharing Connection Pools

In the previous example, each servlet had its own connection pool. This approach makes sense when different servlets perform substantially different tasks and thus talk to different databases. However, it is also quite common for some or all of the servlets on a server to talk to the same database and thus to share a connection pool. There are two main approaches to sharing pools: using the servlet context (a servlet-specific technique) and using static methods or singleton classes (a general Java technique).

Using the Servlet Context to Share Connection Pools

You can call the servlet `getServletContext` method to get an object of type `ServletContext` that is shared by all servlets on the server (or within a Web application if your server supports Web applications). This `ServletContext` object has a `setAttribute` method that takes a `String` and an `Object` and stores the `Object` in a table with the `String` as a key. You can obtain the `Object` at a later time by calling `getAttribute` with the `String` (this method returns `null` if there is no value associated with the key).

So, for example, a group of servlets that all use the books database could share pools by having each servlet perform the following steps:

```
ServletContext context = getServletContext();
ConnectionPool bookPool =
  (ConnectionPool)context.getAttribute("book-pool");
if (bookPool == null) {
  bookPool = new ConnectionPool(...);
  context.setAttribute("book-pool", bookPool);
}
```

Using Singleton Classes to Share Connection Pools

Rather than using the `ServletContext` to share connection pools, you can use normal static methods. For example, you could write a `BookPool` class with static `getPool` and `setPool` methods and have each servlet check `BookPool.getPool` to see if the value is non-null, instantiating a new `ConnectionPool` if necessary. However, each servlet has to repeat similar code, and a servlet could accidentally overwrite the shared pool that `BookPool.getPool` returns.

A better approach is to use a *singleton class* to encapsulate the desired behavior. A singleton class is simply a class for which only a single instance can be created, enforced through use of a private constructor. The instance is retrieved through a static method that checks if there is already an object allocated, returning it if so and allocating and returning a new one if not. For example, here is the outline of a singleton `BookPool` class. Each servlet that used it would obtain the connection pool by simply calling `BookPool.getInstance()`.

```java
public class BookPool extends ConnectionPool {
  private BookPool pool = null;

  private BookPool(...) {
    super(...); // Call parent constructor
    ...
  }

  public static synchronized BookPool getInstance() {
    if (pool == null) {
      pool = new BookPool(...);
    }
    return(pool);
  }
}
```

SERVLET AND JSP
QUICK
REFERENCE

Appendix A

A.1 Overview of Servlets and JavaServer Pages

Advantages of Servlets

- **Efficient**: threads instead of OS processes, one servlet copy, persistence
- **Convenient**: lots of high-level utilities
- **Powerful**: talking to server, sharing data, pooling, persistence
- **Portable**: run on virtually all operating systems and servers
- **Secure**: no shell escapes, no buffer overflows
- **Inexpensive**: inexpensive plug-ins if servlet support not bundled

Advantages of JSP

- **Versus ASP**: better language for dynamic part, portable
- **Versus PHP**: better language for dynamic part
- **Versus pure servlets**: more convenient to create HTML
- **Versus SSI**: much more flexible and powerful
- **Versus JavaScript**: server-side, richer language
- **Versus static HTML**: dynamic features

Free Servlet and JSP Software

- **Tomcat**: http://jakarta.apache.org/

- **JSWDK**: http://java.sun.com/products/servlet/download.html
- **JRun**: http://www.allaire.com/products/jrun/
- **ServletExec**: http://newatlanta.com/
- **LiteWebServer**: http://www.gefionsoftware.com/
- **Java Web Server**: http://www.sun.com/software/jwebserver/try/

Documentation

- http://java.sun.com/products/jsp/download.html
- http://java.sun.com/products/servlet/2.2/javadoc/
- http://www.java.sun.com/j2ee/j2sdkee/techdocs/api/

Servlet Compilation: CLASSPATH Entries

- The servlet classes (usually in install_dir/lib/servlet.jar)
- The JSP classes (usually in install_dir/lib/jsp.jar, ...jspengine.jar, or ...jasper.jar)
- The top-level directory of servlet installation directory (e.g., install_dir/webpages/WEB-INF/classes)

Tomcat 3.0 Standard Directories

- **install_dir/webpages/WEB-INF/classes**
  Standard location for servlet classes.
- **install_dir/classes**
  Alternate location for servlet classes.
- **install_dir/lib**
  Location for JAR files containing classes.

Tomcat 3.1 Standard Directories

- **install_dir/webapps/ROOT/WEB-INF/classes**
  Standard location for servlet classes.
- **install_dir/classes**
  Alternate location for servlet classes.
- **install_dir/lib**
  Location for JAR files containing classes.

JSWDK 1.0.1 Standard Directories

- **install_dir/webpages/WEB-INF/servlet**s
  Standard location for servlet classes.
- **install_dir/classes**
  Alternate location for servlet classes.
- **install_dir/lib**
  Location for JAR files containing classes.

Java Web Server 2.0 Standard Directories

- **install_dir/servlets**
  Location for frequently changing servlet classes. Auto-reloading.
- **install_dir/classes**
  Location for infrequently changing servlet classes.
- **install_dir/lib**
  Location for JAR files containing classes.

A.2 First Servlets

Simple Servlet

```
HelloWWW.java
```

```java
import java.io.*;
import javax.servlet.*;
import javax.servlet.http.*;

public class HelloWWW extends HttpServlet {
  public void doGet(HttpServletRequest request,
                    HttpServletResponse response)
      throws ServletException, IOException {
    response.setContentType("text/html");
    PrintWriter out = response.getWriter();
    String docType =
      "<!DOCTYPE HTML PUBLIC \"-//W3C//DTD HTML 4.0 " +
      "Transitional//EN\">\n";
    out.println(docType +
                "<HTML>\n" +
                "<HEAD><TITLE>Hello WWW</TITLE></HEAD>\n" +
                "<BODY>\n" +
                "<H1>Hello WWW</H1>\n" +
                "</BODY></HTML>");
  }
}
```

Installing Servlets

- Put in servlet directories shown in Section A.1.
- Put in subdirectories corresponding to their package.

Invoking Servlets

- http://host/servlet/ServletName
- http://host/servlet/package.ServletName
- Arbitrary location defined by server-specific customization.

Servlet Life Cycle

- **public void init() throws ServletException,
  public void init(ServletConfig config) throws ServletException**
  Executed once when the servlet is first loaded. *Not* called for each request. Use `getInitParameter` to read initialization parameters.
- **public void service(HttpServletRequest request,
  HttpServletResponse response)
  throws ServletException, IOException**
  Called in a new thread by server for each request. Dispatches to `doGet`, `doPost`, etc. Do not override this method!
- **public void doGet(HttpServletRequest request,
  HttpServletResponse response)
  throws ServletException, IOException**
  Handles GET requests. Override to provide your behavior.
- **public void doPost(HttpServletRequest request,
  HttpServletResponse response)
  throws ServletException, IOException**
  Handles POST requests. Override to provide your behavior. If you want GET and POST to act identically, call `doGet` here.
- **doPut**, **doTrace**, **doDelete**, etc.
  Handles the uncommon HTTP requests of PUT, TRACE, etc.
- **public void destroy()**
  Called when server deletes servlet instance. *Not* called after each request.
- **public long getLastModified(HttpServletRequest request)**
  Called by server when client sends conditional GET due to cached copy. See Section 2.8.
- **SingleThreadModel**
  If this interface implemented, causes server to avoid concurrent invocations.

A.3 Handling the Client Request: Form Data

Reading Parameters

- **request.getParameter**: returns first value
- **request.getParameterValues**: returns array of all values

Example Servlet

`ThreeParams.java`

```
package coreservlets;

import java.io.*;
import javax.servlet.*;
import javax.servlet.http.*;

public class ThreeParams extends HttpServlet {
  public void doGet(HttpServletRequest request,
                    HttpServletResponse response)
      throws ServletException, IOException {
    response.setContentType("text/html");
    PrintWriter out = response.getWriter();
    String title = "Reading Three Request Parameters";
    out.println(ServletUtilities.headWithTitle(title) +
                "<BODY BGCOLOR=\"#FDF5E6\">\n" +
                "<H1 ALIGN=CENTER>" + title + "</H1>\n" +
                "<UL>\n" +
                "  <LI><B>param1</B>: "
                + request.getParameter("param1") + "\n" +
                "  <LI><B>param2</B>: "
                + request.getParameter("param2") + "\n" +
                "  <LI><B>param3</B>: "
                + request.getParameter("param3") + "\n" +
                "</UL>\n" +
                "</BODY></HTML>");
  }
}
```

Example Form

`ThreeParamsForm.html`

```
<!DOCTYPE HTML PUBLIC "-//W3C//DTD HTML 4.0 Transitional//EN">
<HTML>
<HEAD>
  <TITLE>Collecting Three Parameters</TITLE>
</HEAD>
<BODY BGCOLOR="#FDF5E6">
<H1 ALIGN="CENTER">Collecting Three Parameters</H1>

<FORM ACTION="/servlet/coreservlets.ThreeParams">
  First Parameter:   <INPUT TYPE="TEXT" NAME="param1"><BR>
  Second Parameter:  <INPUT TYPE="TEXT" NAME="param2"><BR>
  Third Parameter:   <INPUT TYPE="TEXT" NAME="param3"><BR>
  <CENTER>
    <INPUT TYPE="SUBMIT">
  </CENTER>
</FORM>

</BODY>
</HTML>
```

Filtering HTML-Specific Characters

- Must replace <, >, ", & with <, >, ", and &. Use `ServletUtilities.filter(htmlString)` for this substitution. See Section 3.6.

A.4 Handling the Client Request: HTTP Request Headers

Methods That Read Request Headers

These are all methods in `HttpServletRequest`.

- **public String getHeader(String headerName)**
  Returns value of an arbitrary header. Returns `null` if header not in request.
- **public Enumeration getHeaders(String headerName)**
  Returns values of all occurrences of header in request. 2.2 only.
- **public Enumeration getHeaderNames()**
  Returns names of all headers in current request.
- **public long getDateHeader(String headerName)**
  Reads header that represents a date and converts it to Java date format (milliseconds since 1970).

- **public int getIntHeader(String headerName)**
  Reads header that represents an integer and converts it to an `int`.
  Returns -1 if header not in request. Throws `NumberFormatException`
  for non-ints.
- **public Cookie[] getCookies()**
  Returns array of `Cookie` objects. Array is zero-length if no cookies. See
  Chapter 8.
- **public int getContentLength()**
  Returns value of `Content-Length` header as `int`. Returns -1 if
  unknown.
- **public String getContentType()**
  Returns value of `Content-Type` header if it exists in request (i.e., for
  attached files) or `null` if not.
- **public String getAuthType()**
  Returns `"BASIC"`, `"DIGEST"`, `"SSL"`, or `null`.
- **public String getRemoteUser()**
  Returns username if authentication used; `null` otherwise.

Other Request Information

- **public String getMethod()**
  Returns HTTP request method (`"GET"`, `"POST"`, `"HEAD"`, etc.)
- **public String getRequestURI()**
  Returns part of the URL that came after host and port.
- **public String getProtocol()**
  Returns HTTP version (`"HTTP/1.0"` or `"HTTP/1.1"`, usually).

Common HTTP 1.1 Request Headers

See RFC 2616. Get RFCs on-line starting at http://www.rfc-editor.org/.
- **Accept**: MIME types browser can handle.
- **Accept-Encoding**: encodings (e.g., gzip or compress) browser can
  handle. See compression example in Section 4.4.
- **Authorization**: user identification for password-protected pages. See
  example in Section 4.5. Normal approach is to not use HTTP
  authorization but instead use HTML forms to send username/password
  and then for servlet to store info in session object.
- **Connection**: In HTTP 1.0, `keep-alive` means browser can handle
  persistent connection. In HTTP 1.1, persistent connection is default.
  Servlets should set `Content-Length` with `setContentLength` (using
  `ByteArrayOutputStream` to determine length of output) to support
  persistent connections. See example in Section 7.4.

- **Cookie**: cookies sent to client by server sometime earlier. Use `getCookies`, not `getHeader`. See Chapter 8.
- **Host**: host given in original URL. This is a required header in HTTP 1.1.
- **If-Modified-Since**: indicates client wants page only if it has been changed after specified date. Don't handle this situation directly; implement `getLastModified` instead. See example in Section 2.8.
- **Referer**: URL of referring Web page.
- **User-Agent**: string identifying the browser making the request.

A.5 Accessing the Standard CGI Variables

You should usually think in terms of request info, response info, and server info, not CGI variables.

Capabilities Not Discussed Elsewhere
- **getServletContext().getRealPath("uri")**: maps URI to real path
- **request.getRemoteHost()**: name of host making request
- **request.getRemoteAddress()**: IP address of host making request

Servlet Equivalent of CGI Variables
- AUTH_TYPE: `request.getAuthType()`
- CONTENT_LENGTH: `request.getContentLength()`
- CONTENT_TYPE: `request.getContentType()`
- DOCUMENT_ROOT: `getServletContext().getRealPath("/")`
- HTTP_XXX_YYY: `request.getHeader("Xxx-Yyy")`
- PATH_INFO: `request.getPathInfo()`
- PATH_TRANSLATED: `request.getPathTranslated()`
- QUERY_STRING: `request.getQueryString()`
- REMOTE_ADDR: `request.getRemoteAddr()`
- REMOTE_HOST: `request.getRemoteHost()`
- REMOTE_USER: `request.getRemoteUser()`
- REQUEST_METHOD: `request.getMethod()`
- SCRIPT_NAME: `request.getServletPath()`
- SERVER_NAME: `request.getServerName()`
- SERVER_PORT: `request.getServerPort()`
- SERVER_PROTOCOL: `request.getProtocol()`
- SERVER_SOFTWARE: `getServletContext().getServerInfo()`

A.6 Generating the Server Response: HTTP Status Codes

Format of an HTTP Response

Status line (HTTP version, status code, message), response headers, blank line, document, in that order. For example:

```
HTTP/1.1 200 OK
Content-Type: text/plain

Hello World
```

Methods That Set Status Codes

These are methods in `HttpServletResponse`. Set status codes before you send any document content to browser.

- **public void setStatus(int statusCode)**
  Use a constant for the code, not an explicit `int`.
- **public void sendError(int code, String message)**
  Wraps message inside small HTML document.
- **public void sendRedirect(String url)**
  Relative URLs permitted in 2.2.

Status Code Categories

- **100-199**: informational; client should respond with some other action.
- **200-299**: request was successful.
- **300-399**: file has moved. Usually includes a Location header indicating new address.
- **400-499**: error by client.
- **500-599**: error by server.

Common HTTP 1.1 Status Codes

- **200 (OK)**: Everything is fine; document follows. Default for servlets.
- **204 (No Content)**: Browser should keep displaying previous document.
- **301 (Moved Permanently)**: Requested document permanently moved elsewhere (indicated in `Location` header). Browsers go to new location automatically.
- **302 (Found)**: Requested document temporarily moved elsewhere (indicated in Location header). Browsers go to new location automatically. Servlets should use `sendRedirect`, not `setStatus`, when setting this header. See example in Section 6.3.

- **401 (Unauthorized)**: Browser tried to access password-protected page without proper `Authorization` header. See example in Section 4.5.
- **404 (Not Found)**: No such page. Servlets should use `sendError` to set this header. See example in Section 6.3.

A.7 Generating the Server Response: HTTP Response Headers

Setting Arbitrary Headers

These are methods in `HttpServletResponse`. Set response headers before you send any document content to browser.

- **public void setHeader(String headerName, String headerValue)**
  Sets an arbitrary header.
- **public void setDateHeader(String headerName,**
  **   long milliseconds)**
  Converts milliseconds since 1970 to a date string in GMT format.
- **public void setIntHeader(String headerName, int headerValue)**
  Prevents need to convert `int` to `String` before calling `setHeader`.
- **addHeader**, **addDateHeader**, **addIntHeader**
  Adds new occurrence of header instead of replacing. 2.2 only.

Setting Common Headers

- **setContentType**: Sets the `Content-Type` header. Servlets almost always use this. See Table 7.1 for the most common MIME types.
- **setContentLength**: Sets the `Content-Length` header. Used for persistent HTTP connections. Use `ByteArrayOutputStream` to buffer document before sending it, to determine size. See Section 7.4 for an example.
- **addCookie**: Adds a value to the `Set-Cookie` header. See Chapter 8.
- **sendRedirect**: Sets the `Location` header (plus changes status code). See example in Section 6.3.

Common HTTP 1.1 Response Headers

- **Allow**: the request methods server supports. Automatically set by the default `service` method when servlet receives `OPTIONS` requests.
- **Cache-Control**: A `no-cache` value prevents browsers from caching results. Send `Pragma` header with same value in case browser only understands HTTP 1.0.
- **Content-Encoding**: the way document is encoded. Browser reverses this encoding before handling document. Servlets must confirm that

browser supports a given encoding (by checking the `Accept-Encoding` request header) before using it. See compression example in Section 4.4.

- **Content-Length**: the number of bytes in the response. See `setContentLength` above.

- **Content-Type**: the MIME type of the document being returned. See `setContentType` above.

- **Expires**: the time at which document should be considered out-of-date and thus should no longer be cached. Use `setDateHeader` to set this header.

- **Last-Modified**: the time document was last changed. Don't set this header explicitly; provide a `getLastModified` method instead. See example in Section 2.8.

- **Location**: the URL to which browser should reconnect. Use `sendRedirect` instead of setting this header directly. For an example, see Section 6.3.

- **Pragma**: a value of `no-cache` instructs HTTP 1.0 clients not to cache document. See the `Cache-Control` response header (Section 7.2).

- **Refresh**: the number of seconds until browser should reload page. Can also include URL to connect to. For an example, see Section 7.3.

- **Set-Cookie**: the cookies that browser should remember. Don't set this header directly; use `addCookie` instead. See Chapter 8 for details.

- **WWW-Authenticate**: the authorization type and realm client should supply in its `Authorization` header in the next request. For an example, see Section 4.5.

Generating GIF Images from Servlets

- **Create an Image.**
  Use the `createImage` method of `Component`.

- **Draw into the Image.**
  Call `getGraphics` on the `Image`, then do normal drawing operations.

- **Set the Content-Type response header.**
  Use `response.setContentType("image/gif")`.

- **Get an output stream.**
  Use `response.getOutputStream()`.

- **Send the Image down output stream in GIF format.**
  Use Jef Poskanzer's `GifEncoder`. See http://www.acme.com/java/.

A.8 Handling Cookies

Typical Uses of Cookies

- Identifying a user during an e-commerce session
- Avoiding username and password
- Customizing a site
- Focusing advertising

Problems with Cookies

- It's a privacy problem, not a security problem.
- Privacy problems include: servers can remember what you did in previous sessions; if you give out personal information, servers can link that information to your previous actions; servers can share cookie information through use of a cooperating third party like doubleclick.net (by each loading image off the third-party site); poorly designed sites could store sensitive information like credit card numbers directly in the cookie.

General Usage

- **Sending cookie to browser (standard approach):**
  ```
  Cookie c = new Cookie("name", "value");
  c.setMaxAge(...);
  // Set other attributes.
  response.addCookie(c);
  ```
- **Sending cookie to browser (simplified approach):**
  Use `LongLivedCookie` class (Section 8.5).
- **Reading cookies from browser (standard approach):**
  ```
  Cookie[] cookies = response.getCookies();
  for(int i=0; i<cookies.length; i++) {
    Cookie c = cookies[i];
    if (c.getName().equals("someName")) {
      doSomethingWith(c);
      break;
    }
  }
  ```
- **Reading cookies from browser (simplified approach):**
  Extract cookie or cookie value from cookie array by using `ServletUtilities.getCookie` or `ServletUtilities.getCookieValue`.

Cookie Methods

- **getComment/setComment**: gets/sets comment. Not supported in version 0 cookies (which is what most browsers now support).

- **getDomain/setDomain**: lets you specify domain to which cookie applies. Current host must be part of domain specified.
- **getMaxAge/setMaxAge**: gets/sets the cookie expiration time (in seconds). If you fail to set this, cookie applies to current browsing session only. See `LongLivedCookie` helper class (Section 8.5).
- **getName/setName**: gets/sets the cookie name. For new cookies, you supply name to constructor, not to `setName`. For incoming cookie array, you use `getName` to find the cookie of interest.
- **getPath/setPath**: gets/sets the path to which cookie applies. If unspecified, cookie applies to URLs that are within or below directory containing current page.
- **getSecure/setSecure**: gets/sets flag indicating whether cookie should apply only to SSL connections or to all connections.
- **getValue/setValue**: gets/sets value associated with cookie. For new cookies, you supply value to constructor, not to `setValue`. For incoming cookie array, you use `getName` to find the cookie of interest, then call `getValue` on the result.
- **getVersion/setVersion**: gets/sets the cookie protocol version. Version 0 is the default; stick with that until browsers start supporting version 1.

A.9 Session Tracking

Looking Up Session Information: getValue

```
HttpSession session = request.getSession(true);
ShoppingCart cart =
  (ShoppingCart)session.getValue("shoppingCart");
if (cart == null) { // No cart already in session
  cart = new ShoppingCart();
  session.putValue("shoppingCart", cart);
}
doSomethingWith(cart);
```

Associating Information with a Session: putValue

```
HttpSession session = request.getSession(true);
session.putValue("referringPage", request.getHeader("Referer"));
ShoppingCart cart =
  (ShoppingCart)session.getValue("previousItems");
if (cart == null) { // No cart already in session
  cart = new ShoppingCart();
  session.putValue("previousItems", cart);
}
String itemID = request.getParameter("itemID");
if (itemID != null) {
  cart.addItem(Catalog.getItem(itemID));
}
```

HttpSession Methods

- **public Object getValue(String name) [2.1]**
  public Object getAttribute(String name) [2.2]
  Extracts a previously stored value from a session object. Returns `null` if no value is associated with given name.

- **public void putValue(String name, Object value) [2.1]**
  public void setAttribute(String name, Object value) [2.2]
  Associates a value with a name. If value implements `HttpSessionBindingListener`, its `valueBound` method is called. If previous value implements `HttpSessionBindingListener`, its `valueUnbound` method is called.

- **public void removeValue(String name) [2.1]**
  public void removeAttribute(String name) [2.2]
  Removes any values associated with designated name. If value being removed implements `HttpSessionBindingListener`, its `valueUnbound` method is called.

- **public String[] getValueNames() [2.1]**
  public Enumeration getAttributeNames() [2.2]
  Returns the names of all attributes in the session.

- **public String getId()**
  Returns the unique identifier generated for each session.

- **public boolean isNew()**
  Returns `true` if the client (browser) has never seen the session; `false` otherwise.

- **public long getCreationTime()**
  Returns time at which session was first created (in milliseconds since 1970). To get a value useful for printing, pass value to `Date` constructor or the `setTimeInMillis` method of `GregorianCalendar`.

- **public long getLastAccessedTime()**
  Returns time at which the session was last sent from the client.

- **public int getMaxInactiveInterval()**
  public void setMaxInactiveInterval(int seconds)
  Gets or sets the amount of time, in seconds, that a session should go without access before being automatically invalidated. A negative value indicates that session should never time out. *Not* the same as cookie expiration date.

- **public void invalidate()**
  Invalidates the session and unbinds all objects associated with it.

Encoding URLs

In case servlet is using URL rewriting to implement session tracking, you should give the system a chance to encode the URLs.

- **Regular URLs**
  ```
  String originalURL = someRelativeOrAbsoluteURL;
  String encodedURL = response.encodeURL(originalURL);
  out.println("<A HREF=\"" + encodedURL + "\">...</A>");
  ```
- **Redirect URLs**
  ```
  String originalURL = someURL; // Relative URL OK in 2.2
  String encodedURL = response.encodeRedirectURL(originalURL);
  response.sendRedirect(encodedURL);
  ```

A.10 JSP Scripting Elements

Types of Scripting Elements

- **Expressions: <%= expression %>**
  Evaluated and inserted into servlet's output. You can also use
  ```
  <jsp:expression>
  expression
  </jsp:expression>
  ```
- **Scriptlets: <% code %>**
  Inserted into servlet's _jspService method (called by service). You can also use
  ```
  <jsp:scriptlet>
  code
  </jsp:scriptlet>
  ```
- **Declarations: <%! code %>**
  Inserted into body of servlet class, outside of any existing methods. You can also use
  ```
  <jsp:declaration>
  code
  </jsp:declaration>
  ```

Template Text

- Use <\% to get <% in output.
- <%-- JSP Comment --%>
- <!-- HTML Comment -->
- All other non-JSP-specific text passed through to output page.

Predefined Variables

Implicit objects automatically available in expressions and scriptlets (not declarations).

- **request**: the HttpServletRequest associated with request.

- **response**: the HttpServletResponse associated with response to client.
- **out**: the JspWriter (PrintWriter subclass) used to send output to the client.
- **session**: the HttpSession object associated with request. See Chapter 9.
- **application**: the ServletContext as obtained by getServletConfig().getContext(). Shared by all servlets and JSP pages on server or in Web application. See Section 15.1.
- **config**: the ServletConfig object for this page.
- **pageContext**: the PageContext object associated with current page. See Section 13.4 for a discussion of its use.
- **page**: synonym for this (current servlet instance); not very useful now. Placeholder for future.

A.11 The JSP page Directive: Structuring Generated Servlets

The import Attribute

- <%@ page import="package.class" %>
- <%@ page import="package.class1,...,package.classN" %>

The contentType Attribute

- <%@ page contentType="MIME-Type" %>
- <%@ page contentType="MIME-Type; charset=Character-Set" %>
- Cannot be invoked conditionally. Use
  <% response.setContentType("..."); %> for that.

Example of Using contentType

Excel.jsp

```
<%@ page contentType="application/vnd.ms-excel" %>
<%-- Note that there are tabs, not spaces, between columns. --%>
1997    1998    1999    2000    2001 (Anticipated)
12.3    13.4    14.5    15.6    16.7
```

Example of Using setContentType

```
ApplesAndOranges.jsp
```

```html
<!DOCTYPE HTML PUBLIC "-//W3C//DTD HTML 4.0 Transitional//EN">
<!-- HEAD part removed. -->
<BODY><CENTER><H2>Comparing Apples and Oranges</H2>

<%
String format = request.getParameter("format");
if ((format != null) && (format.equals("excel"))) {
  response.setContentType("application/vnd.ms-excel");
}
%>
<TABLE BORDER=1>
  <TR><TH></TH><TH>Apples<TH>Oranges
  <TR><TH>First Quarter<TD>2307<TD>4706
  <TR><TH>Second Quarter<TD>2982<TD>5104
  <TR><TH>Third Quarter<TD>3011<TD>5220
  <TR><TH>Fourth Quarter<TD>3055<TD>5287
</TABLE>

</CENTER></BODY></HTML>
```

The isThreadSafe Attribute

- `<%@ page isThreadSafe="true" %> <%!-- Default --%>`
- `<%@ page isThreadSafe="false" %>`
- A value of `true` means that *you* have made your code threadsafe and that the system can send multiple concurrent requests. A value of `false` means that the servlet resulting from JSP document will implement `SingleThreadModel` (see Section 2.6).
- Non-threadsafe code:
  ```
  <%! private int idNum = 0; %>
  <% String userID = "userID" + idNum;
     out.println("Your ID is " + userID + ".");
     idNum = idNum + 1; %>
  ```
- Threadsafe code:
  ```
  <%! private int idNum = 0; %>
  <% synchronized(this) {
       String userID = "userID" + idNum;
       out.println("Your ID is " + userID + ".");
       idNum = idNum + 1;
     } %>
  ```

The session Attribute

- `<%@ page session="true" %> <%!-- Default --%>`
- `<%@ page session="false" %>`

The buffer Attribute

- `<%@ page buffer="sizekb" %>`
- `<%@ page buffer="none" %>`
- Servers can use a larger buffer than you specify, but not a smaller one. For example, `<%@ page buffer="32kb" %>` means the document content should be buffered and not sent to the client until at least 32 kilobytes have been accumulated or the page is completed.

The autoflush Attribute

- `<%@ page autoflush="true" %> <%!-- Default --%>`
- `<%@ page autoflush="false" %>`
- A value of `false` is illegal when `buffer="none"` is also used.

The extends Attribute

- `<%@ page extends="package.class" %>`

The info Attribute

- `<%@ page info="Some Message" %>`

The errorPage Attribute

- `<%@ page errorPage="Relative URL" %>`
- The exception thrown will be automatically available to the designated error page by means of the `exception` variable. See Listings 11.5 and 11.6 for examples.

The isErrorPage Attribute

- `<%@ page isErrorPage="true" %>`
- `<%@ page isErrorPage="false" %> <%!-- Default --%>`
- See Listings 11.5 and 11.6 for examples.

The language Attribute

- `<%@ page language="cobol" %>`
- For now, don't bother with this attribute since `java` is both the default and the only legal choice.

XML Syntax

- **Usual syntax:**
  ```
  <%@ page attribute="value" %>
  <%@ page import="java.util.*" %>
  ```
- **XML equivalent:**
  ```
  <jsp:directive.page attribute="value" />
  <jsp:directive.page import="java.util.*" />
  ```

A.12 Including Files and Applets in JSP Documents

Including Files at Page Translation Time

- ```
  <%@ include file="Relative URL" %>
  ```
- Changing included file does not necessarily cause retranslation of JSP document. You have to manually change JSP document or update its modification date. Convenient way:
  ```
  <%-- Navbar.jsp modified 3/1/00 --%>
  <%@ include file="Navbar.jsp" %>
  ```

Including Files at Request Time

- ```
  <jsp:include page="Relative URL" flush="true" />
  ```
- Servlets can use `include` method of `RequestDispatcher` to accomplish similar result. See Section 15.3.
- Because of a bug, you must use .html or .htm extensions for included files used with the Java Web Server.

Applets for the Java Plug-In: Simple Case

- **Regular form:**
  ```
  <APPLET CODE="MyApplet.class"
          WIDTH=475 HEIGHT=350>
  </APPLET>
  ```
- **JSP form for Java Plug-in:**
  ```
  <jsp:plugin type="applet"
              code="MyApplet.class"
              width="475" height="350">
  </jsp:plugin>
  ```

Attributes of jsp:plugin

All attribute names are case sensitive; all attribute values require single or double quotes.

- **type**: for applets, this attribute should have a value of `applet`.

- **code**: used identically to the CODE attribute of APPLET.
- **width**: used identically to the WIDTH attribute of APPLET.
- **height**: used identically to the HEIGHT attribute of APPLET.
- **codebase**: used identically to the CODEBASE attribute of APPLET.
- **align**: used identically to the ALIGN attribute of APPLET and IMG.
- **hspace**: used identically to the HSPACE attribute of APPLET.
- **vspace**: used identically to the VSPACE attribute of APPLET.
- **archive**: used identically to the ARCHIVE attribute of APPLET.
- **name**: used identically to the NAME attribute of APPLET.
- **title**: used identically to the rare TITLE attribute of APPLET (and virtually all other HTML elements in HTML 4.0), specifying a title that could be used for a tool-tip or for indexing.
- **jreversion**: identifies the version of the Java Runtime Environment (JRE) that is required. The default is 1.1.
- **iepluginurl**: designates a URL from which the plug-in for Internet Explorer can be downloaded.
- **nspluginurl**: designates a URL from which the plug-in for Netscape can be downloaded.

Parameters in HTML: jsp:param

- **Regular form:**

```
<APPLET CODE="MyApplet.class"
        WIDTH=475 HEIGHT=350>
  <PARAM NAME="PARAM1" VALUE="VALUE1">
  <PARAM NAME="PARAM2" VALUE="VALUE2">
</APPLET>
```

- **JSP form for Java Plug-In:**

```
<jsp:plugin type="applet"
            code="MyApplet.class"
            width="475" height="350">
  <jsp:params>
    <jsp:param name="PARAM1" value="VALUE1" />
    <jsp:param name="PARAM2" value="VALUE2" />
  </jsp:params>
</jsp:plugin>
```

Alternative Text

- **Regular form:**

```
<APPLET CODE="MyApplet.class"
        WIDTH=475 HEIGHT=350>
  <B>Error: this example requires Java.</B>
</APPLET>
```

- **JSP form for Java Plug-In:**

```
<jsp:plugin type="applet"
```

```
            code="MyApplet.class"
            width="475" height="350">
  <jsp:fallback>
    <B>Error: this example requires Java.</B>
  </jsp:fallback>
</jsp:plugin>
```
- The Java Web Server does not properly handle `jsp:fallback`.

A.13 Using JavaBeans with JSP

Basic Requirements for Class to be a Bean

1. Have a zero-argument (empty) constructor.
2. Have no public instance variables (fields).
3. Access persistent values through methods called get*Xxx* (or is*Xxx*) and set*Xxx*.

Basic Bean Use

- `<jsp:useBean id="name" class="package.Class" />`
- `<jsp:getProperty name="name" property="property" />`
- `<jsp:setProperty name="name" property="property"`
                    `value="value" />`

  The `value` attribute can take a JSP expression.

Associating Properties with Request Parameters

- **Individual properties:**
  ```
  <jsp:setProperty
      name="entry"
      property="numItems"
      param="numItems" />
  ```
- **Automatic type conversion:** for primitive types, performed according to `valueOf` method of wrapper class.
- **All properties:**
  ```
  <jsp:setProperty name="entry" property="*" />
  ```

Sharing Beans: The scope Attribute of jsp:useBean

Examples of sharing beans given in Chapter 15.

- **page**
  Default value. Indicates that, in addition to being bound to a local variable, bean object should be placed in `PageContext` object for duration of current request.

- **application**
  Means that, in addition to being bound to a local variable, bean will be stored in shared `ServletContext` available through predefined `application` variable or by a call to `getServletContext()`.
- **session**
  Means that, in addition to being bound to a local variable, bean will be stored in `HttpSession` object associated with current request, where it can be retrieved with `getValue`.
- **request**
  Signifies that, in addition to being bound to a local variable, bean object should be placed in `ServletRequest` object for duration of current request, where it is available by means of the `getAttribute` method.

Conditional Bean Creation

- A `jsp:useBean` element results in a new bean being instantiated only if no bean with the same `id` and `scope` can be found. If a bean with the same `id` and `scope` *is* found, the preexisting bean is simply bound to the variable referenced by `id`.
- You can make `jsp:setProperty` statements conditional on new bean creation:

```
<jsp:useBean ...>
  statements
</jsp:useBean>
```

A.14 Creating Custom JSP Tag Libraries

The Tag Handler Class

- Implement `Tag` interface by extending `TagSupport` (no tag body or tag body included verbatim) or `BodyTagSupport` (tag body is manipulated).
- `doStartTag`: code to run at beginning of tag
- `doEndTag`: code to run at end of tag
- `doAfterBody`: code to process tag body

The Tag Library Descriptor File

- Within `taglib` element, contains `tag` element for each tag handler. E.g.:

```
<tag>
  <name>prime</name>
  <tagclass>coreservlets.tags.PrimeTag</tagclass>
  <info>Outputs a random N-digit prime.</info>
  <bodycontent>EMPTY</bodycontent>
  <attribute>
    <name>length</name>
    <required>false</required>
  </attribute>
</tag>
```

The JSP File

- `<%@ taglib uri="some-taglib.tld" prefix="prefix" %>`
- `<prefix:tagname />`
- `<prefix:tagname>body</prefix:tagname>`

Assigning Attributes to Tags

- **Tag handler**:
  Implements `setXxx` for each attribute xxx.
- **Tag Library Descriptor:**

```
<tag>
  ...
  <attribute>
    <name>length</name>
    <required>false</required>
    <rtexprvalue>true</rtexprvalue> <%-- sometimes --%>
  </attribute>
</tag>
```

Including the Tag Body

- **Tag handler**:
  You should return `EVAL_BODY_INCLUDE` instead of `SKIP_BODY` from `doStartTag`.
- **Tag Library Descriptor:**

```
<tag>
  ...
  <bodycontent>JSP</bodycontent>
</tag>
```

Optionally Including the Tag Body

- **Tag handler**:
  Return EVAL_BODY_INCLUDE or SKIP_BODY at different times, depending on value of request time parameter.

Manipulating the Tag Body

- **Tag handler**:
  You should extend BodyTagSupport, implement doAfterBody. Call getBodyContent to get BodyContent object describing tag body. BodyContent has three key methods: getEnclosingWriter, getReader, and getString. Return SKIP_BODY from doAfterBody.

Including or Manipulating the Tag Body Multiple Times

- **Tag handler**:
  To process body again, return EVAL_BODY_TAG from doAfterBody. To finish, return SKIP_BODY.

Using Nested Tags

- **Tag handler**:
  Nested tags can use findAncestorWithClass to find the tag in which they are nested. Place data in field of enclosing tag.

- **Tag Library Descriptor:**
  Declare all tags separately, regardless of nesting structure in real page.

A.15 Integrating Servlets and JSP

Big Picture

- Servlet handles initial request, reads parameters, cookies, session information, etc.

- Servlet then does whatever computations and database lookups are needed.

- Servlet then stores data in beans.

- Servlet forwards request to one of many possible JSP pages to present final result.

- JSP page extracts needed values from beans.

Request Forwarding Syntax

```
String url = "/path/presentation1.jsp";
RequestDispatcher dispatcher =
  getServletContext().getRequestDispatcher(url);
dispatcher.forward();
```

Forwarding to Regular HTML Pages

- If initial servlet handles GET requests only, no change is necessary.
- If initial servlet handles POST, then change destination page from SomePage.html to SomePage.jsp so that it, too, can handle POST.

Setting Up Globally Shared Beans

- **Initial servlet:**
  ```
  Type1 value1 = computeValueFromRequest(request);
  getServletContext().setAttribute("key1", value1);
  ```
- **Final JSP document:**
  ```
  <jsp:useBean id="key1" class="Type1" scope="application" />
  ```

Setting Up Session Beans

- **Initial servlet:**
  ```
  Type1 value1 = computeValueFromRequest(request);
  HttpSession session = request.getSession(true);
  session.putValue("key1", value1);
  ```
- **Final JSP document:**
  ```
  <jsp:useBean id="key1" class="Type1" scope="session" />
  ```

Interpreting Relative URLs in the Destination Page

- URL of original servlet is used for forwarded requests. Browser does not know real URL, so it will resolve relative URLs with respect to original servlet's URL.

Getting a RequestDispatcher by Alternative Means (2.2 Only)

- **By name:** use getNamedDispatcher method of ServletContext.
- **By path relative to initial servlet's location:** use the getRequestDispatcher method of HttpServletRequest rather than the one from ServletContext.

Including Static or Dynamic Content

- **Basic usage:**
  ```
  response.setContentType("text/html");
  PrintWriter out = response.getWriter();
  out.println("...");
  RequestDispatcher dispatcher =
    getServletContext().getRequestDispatcher("/path/resource");
  dispatcher.include(request, response);
  out.println("...");
  ```
- JSP equivalent is `jsp:include`, not the JSP `include` directive.

Forwarding Requests from JSP Pages

- `<jsp:forward page="Relative URL" />`

A.16 Using HTML Forms

The FORM Element

- **Usual form:**
  ```
  <FORM ACTION="URL" ...> ... </FORM>
  ```
- **Attributes:** ACTION (required), METHOD, ENCTYPE, TARGET, ONSUBMIT, ONRESET, ACCEPT, ACCEPT-CHARSET

Textfields

- **Usual form:**
  ```
  <INPUT TYPE="TEXT" NAME="..." ...> (no end tag)
  ```
- **Attributes:** NAME (required), VALUE, SIZE, MAXLENGTH, ONCHANGE, ONSELECT, ONFOCUS, ONBLUR, ONKEYDOWN, ONKEYPRESS, ONKEYUP
- Different browsers have different rules regarding the situations where pressing Enter in a textfield submits the form. So, include a button or image map that submits the form explicitly.

Password Fields

- **Usual form:**
  ```
  <INPUT TYPE="PASSWORD" NAME="..." ...> (no end tag)
  ```
- **Attributes:** NAME (required), VALUE, SIZE, MAXLENGTH, ONCHANGE, ONSELECT, ONFOCUS, ONBLUR, ONKEYDOWN, ONKEYPRESS, ONKEYUP
- Always use POST with forms that contain password fields.

Text Areas

- **Usual form:**
  ```
  <TEXTAREA NAME="..." ROWS=xxx COLS=yyy> ...
     Some text
  </TEXTAREA>
  ```
- **Attributes:** NAME (required), ROWS (required), COLS (required), WRAP (nonstandard), ONCHANGE, ONSELECT, ONFOCUS, ONBLUR, ONKEYDOWN, ONKEYPRESS, ONKEYUP
- White space in initial text is maintained and HTML markup between start and end tags is taken literally, except for character entities such as <, ©, and so forth.

Submit Buttons

- **Usual form:**
  ```
  <INPUT TYPE="SUBMIT" ...> (no end tag)
  ```
- **Attributes:** NAME, VALUE, ONCLICK, ONDBLCLICK, ONFOCUS, ONBLUR
- When a submit button is clicked, the form is sent to the servlet or other server-side program designated by the ACTION parameter of the FORM.

Alternative Push Buttons

- **Usual form:**
  ```
  <BUTTON TYPE="SUBMIT" ...>
     HTML Markup
  </BUTTON>
  ```
- **Attributes:** NAME, VALUE, ONCLICK, ONDBLCLICK, ONFOCUS, ONBLUR
- Internet Explorer only.

Reset Buttons

- **Usual form:**
  ```
  <INPUT TYPE="RESET" ...> (no end tag)
  ```
- **Attributes:** VALUE, NAME, ONCLICK, ONDBLCLICK, ONFOCUS, ONBLUR
  Except for VALUE, attributes are only for use with JavaScript.

Alternative Reset Buttons

- **Usual form:**
  ```
  <BUTTON TYPE="RESET" ...>
     HTML Markup
  </BUTTON>
  ```
- **Attributes:** VALUE, NAME, ONCLICK, ONDBLCLICK, ONFOCUS, ONBLUR
- Internet Explorer only.

JavaScript Buttons

- **Usual form:**
  ```
  <INPUT TYPE="BUTTON" ...> (no end tag)
  ```
- **Attributes:** NAME, VALUE, ONCLICK, ONDBLCLICK, ONFOCUS, ONBLUR

Alternative JavaScript Buttons

- **Usual form:**
  ```
  <BUTTON TYPE="BUTTON" ...>
    HTML Markup
  </BUTTON>
  ```
- **Attributes:** NAME, VALUE, ONCLICK, ONDBLCLICK, ONFOCUS, ONBLUR
- Internet Explorer only.

Check Boxes

- **Usual form:**
  ```
  <INPUT TYPE="CHECKBOX" NAME="..." ...> (no end tag)
  ```
- **Attributes:** NAME (required), VALUE, CHECKED, ONCLICK, ONFOCUS, ONBLUR
- Name/value transmitted only if check box is checked.

Radio Buttons

- **Usual form:**
  ```
  <INPUT TYPE="RADIO" NAME="..." VALUE="..." ...>
  ```
  (no end tag)
- **Attributes:** NAME (required), VALUE (required), CHECKED, ONCLICK, ONFOCUS, ONBLUR
- You indicate a group of radio buttons by providing all of them with the same NAME.

Combo Boxes

- **Usual form:**
  ```
  <SELECT NAME="Name" ...>
    <OPTION VALUE="Value1">Choice 1 Text
    <OPTION VALUE="Value2">Choice 2 Text
    ...
    <OPTION VALUE="ValueN">Choice N Text
  </SELECT>
  ```
- **SELECT Attributes:** NAME (required), SIZE, MULTIPLE, ONCLICK, ONFOCUS, ONBLUR, ONCHANGE
- **OPTION Attributes:** SELECTED, VALUE

File Upload Controls

- **Usual form:**
  `<INPUT TYPE="FILE" ...>` (no end tag)
- **Attributes:** NAME (required), VALUE (ignored), SIZE, MAXLENGTH, ACCEPT, ONCHANGE, ONSELECT, ONFOCUS, ONBLUR (nonstandard)
- Use an ENCTYPE of `multipart/form-data` in the FORM declaration.

Server-Side Image Maps

- **Usual form:**
  `<INPUT TYPE="IMAGE" ...>` (no end tag)
- **Attributes:** NAME (required), SRC, ALIGN
- You can also provide an ISMAP attribute to a standard IMG element that is inside an `<A HREF...>` element.

Hidden Fields

- **Usual form:**
  `<INPUT TYPE="HIDDEN" NAME="..." VALUE="...">` (no end tag)
- **Attributes:** NAME (required), VALUE

Internet Explorer Features

- **FIELDSET (with LEGEND):** groups controls
- **TABINDEX:** controls tabbing order
- Both capabilities are part of HTML 4.0 spec; neither is supported by Netscape 4.

A.17 Using Applets As Servlet Front Ends

Sending Data with GET and Displaying the Resultant Page

```
String someData =
  name1 + "=" + URLEncoder.encode(val1) + "&" +
  name2 + "=" + URLEncoder.encode(val2) + "&" +
  ...
  nameN + "=" + URLEncoder.encode(valN);
try {
  URL programURL = new URL(baseURL + "?" + someData);
  getAppletContext().showDocument(programURL);
} catch(MalformedURLException mue) { ... }
```

Sending Data with GET and Processing the Results Directly (HTTP Tunneling)

1. **Create a URL object referring to applet's home host.** You usually build a URL based upon the hostname from which the applet was loaded.

   ```
   URL currentPage = getCodeBase();
   String protocol = currentPage.getProtocol();
   String host = currentPage.getHost();
   int port = currentPage.getPort();
   String urlSuffix = "/servlet/SomeServlet";
   URL dataURL = new URL(protocol, host, port, urlSuffix);
   ```

2. **Create a URLConnection object.** The openConnection method of URL returns a URLConnection object. This object will be used to obtain streams with which to communicate.

   ```
   URLConnection connection = dataURL.openConnection();
   ```

3. **Instruct the browser not to cache the URL data.**

   ```
   connection.setUseCaches(false);
   ```

4. **Set any desired HTTP headers.** If you want to set HTTP request headers (see Chapter 4), you can use setRequest-Property to do so.

   ```
   connection.setRequestProperty("header", "value");
   ```

5. **Create an input stream.** There are several appropriate streams, but a common one is BufferedReader. It is at the point where you create the input stream that the connection to the Web server is actually established behind the scenes.

   ```
   BufferedReader in =
     new BufferedReader(new InputStreamReader(
                           connection.getInputStream()));
   ```

6. **Read each line of the document.** Simply read until you get null.

   ```
   String line;
   while ((line = in.readLine()) != null) {
     doSomethingWith(line);
   }
   ```

7. **Close the input stream.**

   ```
   in.close();
   ```

Sending Serialized Data: The Applet Code

1. **Create a URL object referring to the applet's home host.** It is best to specify a URL suffix and construct the rest of the URL automatically.
   ```
   URL currentPage = getCodeBase();
   String protocol = currentPage.getProtocol();
   String host = currentPage.getHost();
   int port = currentPage.getPort();
   String urlSuffix = "/servlet/SomeServlet";
   URL dataURL = new URL(protocol, host, port, urlSuffix);
   ```
2. **Create a URLConnection object.** The openConnection method of URL returns a URLConnection object. This object will be used to obtain streams with which to communicate.
   ```
   URLConnection connection = dataURL.openConnection();
   ```
3. **Instruct the browser not to cache the URL data.**
   ```
   connection.setUseCaches(false);
   ```
4. **Set any desired HTTP headers.**
   ```
   connection.setRequestProperty("header", "value");
   ```
5. **Create an ObjectInputStream.** The constructor for this class simply takes the raw input stream from the URLConnection.
   ```
   ObjectInputStream in =
     new ObjectInputStream(connection.getInputStream());
   ```
6. **Read the data structure with readObject.** The return type of readObject is Object, so you need to make a typecast to whatever more specific type the server actually sent.
   ```
   SomeClass value = (SomeClass)in.readObject();
   doSomethingWith(value);
   ```
7. **Close the input stream.**
   ```
   in.close();
   ```

Sending Serialized Data: The Servlet Code

1. **Specify that binary content is being sent.** To do so, designate
   `application/x-java-serialized-object`
   as the MIME type of the response. This is the standard MIME type for objects encoded with an ObjectOutputStream, although in practice, since the applet (not the browser) is reading the result, the MIME type is not very important. See the discussion of Content-Type in Section 7.2 for more information on MIME types.
   ```
   String contentType =
     "application/x-java-serialized-object";
   response.setContentType(contentType);
   ```

2. **Create an ObjectOutputStream.**
```
ObjectOutputStream out =
    new ObjectOutputStream(response.getOutputStream());
```
3. **Write the data structure by using `writeObject`.** Most built-in data structures can be sent this way. Classes *you* write, however, must implement the `Serializable` interface.
```
SomeClass value = new SomeClass(...);
out.writeObject(value);
```
4. **Flush the stream to be sure all content has been sent to the client.**
```
out.flush();
```

Sending Data by POST and Processing the Results Directly (HTTP Tunneling)

1. **Create a URL object referring to the applet's home host.** It is best to specify a URL suffix and construct the rest of the URL automatically.
```
URL currentPage = getCodeBase();
String protocol = currentPage.getProtocol();
String host = currentPage.getHost();
int port = currentPage.getPort();
String urlSuffix = "/servlet/SomeServlet";
URL dataURL =
    new URL(protocol, host, port, urlSuffix);
```
2. **Create a `URLConnection` object.**
```
URLConnection connection = dataURL.openConnection();
```
3. **Instruct the browser not to cache the results.**
```
connection.setUseCaches(false);
```
4. **Tell the system to permit you to send data, not just read it.**
```
connection.setDoOutput(true);
```
5. **Create a `ByteArrayOutputStream` to buffer the data that will be sent to the server.** The purpose of the `ByteArray-OutputStream` here is the same as it is with the persistent (keep-alive) HTTP connections shown in Section 7.4 — to determine the size of the output so that the `Content-Length` header can be set.
```
ByteArrayOutputStream byteStream =
    new ByteArrayOutputStream(512);
```
6. **Attach an output stream to the `ByteArrayOutputStream`.** Use a `PrintWriter` to send normal form data. To send serialized data structures, use an `ObjectOutputStream` instead.
```
PrintWriter out = new PrintWriter(byteStream, true);
```

7. **Put the data into the buffer.** For form data, use `print`. For high-level serialized objects, use `writeObject`.
```
String val1 = URLEncoder.encode(someVal1);
String val2 = URLEncoder.encode(someVal2);
String data = "param1=" + val1 +
              "&param2=" + val2; // Note '&'
out.print(data);   // Note print, not println
out.flush(); // Necessary since no println used
```
8. **Set the `Content-Length` header.** This header is required for POST data, even though it is unused with GET requests.
```
connection.setRequestProperty
    ("Content-Length", String.valueOf(byteStream.size()));
```
9. **Set the `Content-Type` header.** Netscape uses `multi-part/form-data` by default, but regular form data requires a setting of `application/x-www-form-urlencoded`, which is the default with Internet Explorer. So, for portability you should set this value explicitly when sending regular form data. The value is irrelevant when you are sending serialized data.
```
connection.setRequestProperty
    ("Content-Type", "application/x-www-form-urlencoded");
```
10. **Send the real data.**
```
byteStream.writeTo(connection.getOutputStream());
```
11. **Open an input stream.** You typically use a `BufferedReader` for ASCII or binary data and an `ObjectInputStream` for serialized Java objects.
```
BufferedReader in =
  new BufferedReader(new InputStreamReader
                    (connection.getInputStream()));
```
12. **Read the result.**
The specific details will depend on what type of data the server sends. Here is an example that does something with each line sent by the server:
```
String line;
while((line = in.readLine()) != null) {
  doSomethingWith(line);
}
```

Bypassing the HTTP Server

Applets can talk directly to servers on their home host, using any of:
- Raw sockets
- Sockets with object streams
- JDBC
- RMI
- Other network protocols

A.18 JDBC and Database Connection Pooling

Basic Steps in Using JDBC

1. **Load the JDBC driver.** See http://java.sun.com/prod-ucts/jdbc/drivers.html for available drivers. Example:

```
Class.forName("package.DriverClass");
Class.forName("oracle.jdbc.driver.OracleDriver");
```

2. **Define the connection URL.** The exact format will be defined in the documentation that comes with the particular driver.

```
String host = "dbhost.yourcompany.com";
String dbName = "someName";
int port = 1234;
String oracleURL = "jdbc:oracle:thin:@" + host +
                   ":" + port + ":" + dbName;
String sybaseURL = "jdbc:sybase:Tds:" + host   +
                   ":" + port + ":" + "?SERVICENAME=" +
                   dbName;
```

3. **Establish the connection.**

```
String username = "jay_debesee";
String password = "secret";
Connection connection =
  DriverManager.getConnection(oracleURL, username, password)
```

An optional part of this step is to look up information about the database by using the `getMetaData` method of `Connection`. This method returns a `DatabaseMetaData` object which has methods to let you discover the name and version of the database itself (`getDatabaseProductName`, `getDatabaseProductVersion`) or of the JDBC driver (`getDriverName`, `getDriverVersion`).

4. **Create a statement object.**

```
Statement statement = connection.createStatement();
```

5. **Execute a query or update.**

```
String query = "SELECT col1, col2, col3 FROM sometable";
ResultSet resultSet = statement.executeQuery(query);
```

6. **Process the results.** Use `next` to get a new row. Use `getXxx(index)` or `getXxx(columnName)` to extract values from a row. First column has index 1, not 0.

```
while(resultSet.next()) {
  System.out.println(results.getString(1) + " " +
                     results.getString(2) + " " +
                     results.getString(3));
}
```

7. **Close the connection.**

```
connection.close();
```

Database Utilities

These are static methods in the DatabaseUtilities class (Listing 18.6).

- **getQueryResults**

  Connects to a database, executes a query, retrieves all the rows as arrays of strings, and puts them inside a DBResults object (see Listing 18.7). Also places the database product name, database version, the names of all the columns and the Connection object into the DBResults object. There are two versions of getQueryResults: one makes a new connection, the other uses an existing connection. DBResults has a simple toHTMLTable method that outputs result in HTML, which can be used as either a real HTML table or as an Excel spreadsheet (see Section 11.2).

- **createTable**

  Given a table name, a string denoting the column formats, and an array of strings denoting the row values, this method connects to a database, removes any existing versions of the designated table, issues a CREATE TABLE command with the designated format, then sends a series of INSERT INTO commands for each of the rows. Again, there are two versions: one makes a new connection, and the other uses an existing connection.

- **printTable**

  Given a table name, this method connects to the specified database, retrieves all the rows, and prints them on the standard output. It retrieves the results by turning the table name into a query of the form "SELECT * FROM tableName" and passing it to getQueryResults.

- **printTableData**

  Given a DBResults object from a previous query, this method prints it on the standard output. This is the underlying method used by printTable, but it is also useful for debugging arbitrary database results.

Prepared Statements (Precompiled Queries)

- **Use `connection.prepareStatement` to make precompiled form. Mark parameters with question marks.**

  ```
  String template =
    "UPDATE employees SET salary = ? WHERE id = ?";
  PreparedStatement statement =
    connection.prepareStatement(template);
  ```

- **Use `statement.setXxx` to specify parameters to query.**

  ```
  statement.setFloat(1, 1.234);
  statement.setInt(2, 5);
  ```

- Use **execute** to perform operation.

```
statement.execute();
```

Steps in Implementing Connection Pooling

If you don't care about implementation details, just use the `ConnectionPool` class developed in Chapter 18. Otherwise, follow these steps.

1. **Preallocate the connections.**

   Perform this task in the class constructor. Call the constructor from servlet's `init` method. The following code uses vectors to store available idle connections and unavailable, busy connections.

```
availableConnections = new Vector(initialConnections);
busyConnections = new Vector();
for(int i=0; i<initialConnections; i++) {
  availableConnections.addElement(makeNewConnection());
}
```

2. **Manage available connections.**

   If a connection is required and an idle connection is available, put it in the list of busy connections and then return it. The busy list is used to check limits on the total number of connections as well as when the pool is instructed to explicitly close all connections. Discarding a connection opens up a slot that can be used by processes that needed a connection when the connection limit had been reached, so use `notifyAll` to tell all waiting threads to wake up and see if they can proceed.

```
public synchronized Connection getConnection()
    throws SQLException {
  if (!availableConnections.isEmpty()) {
    Connection existingConnection =
      (Connection)availableConnections.lastElement();
    int lastIndex = availableConnections.size() - 1;
    availableConnections.removeElementAt(lastIndex);
    if (existingConnection.isClosed()) {
      notifyAll(); // Freed up a spot for anybody waiting.
      return(getConnection()); // Repeat process.
    } else {
      busyConnections.addElement(existingConnection);
      return(existingConnection);
    }
  }
}
```

3. **Allocate new connections.**

   If a connection is required, there is no idle connection available, and the connection limit has not been reached, then start a background thread to allocate a new connection. Then, wait for the first available connection, whether or not it is the newly allocated one.

```
if ((totalConnections() < maxConnections) &&
    !connectionPending) { // Pending = connecting in bg
  makeBackgroundConnection();
  try {
    wait(); // Give up lock and suspend self.
  } catch(InterruptedException ie) {}
  return(getConnection()); // Try again.
```

4. **Wait for a connection to become available.**

    This situation occurs when there is no idle connection and you've reached the limit on the number of connections. This waiting should be accomplished without continual polling. It is best to use the `wait` method, which gives up the thread synchronization lock and suspends the thread until `notify` or `notifyAll` is called.

```
try {
  wait();
} catch(InterruptedException ie) {}
return(getConnection());
```

5. **Close connections when required.**

    Note that connections are closed when they are garbage collected, so you don't always have to close them explicitly. But, you sometimes want more explicit control over the process.

```
public synchronized void closeAllConnections() {
  // The closeConnections method loops down Vector, calling
  // close and ignoring any exceptions thrown.
  closeConnections(availableConnections);
  availableConnections = new Vector();
  closeConnections(busyConnections);
  busyConnections = new Vector();
}
```

Connection pool timing results	
Condition	*Average Time*
Slow modem connection to database, 10 initial connections, 50 max connections (`ConnectionPoolServlet`)	11 seconds
Slow modem connection to database, recycling a single connection (`ConnectionPoolServlet2`)	22 seconds

Connection pool timing results	
Condition	*Average Time*
Slow modem connection to database, no connection pooling (`ConnectionPoolServlet3`)	82 seconds
Fast LAN connection to database, 10 initial connections, 50 max connections (`ConnectionPoolServlet`)	1.8 seconds
Fast LAN connection to database, recycling a single connection (`ConnectionPoolServlet2`)	2.0 seconds
Fast LAN connection to database, no connection pooling (`ConnectionPoolServlet3`)	2.8 seconds

Index